SENIOR
Australian
AGRICULTURE

4th Edition

Anne Clark

PASCAL
PRESS

© 2003 Anne Clark and Pascal Press

First published in 2003
Reprinted 2004, 2009
4th Edition for HSC syllabus changes 2013
Reprinted 2016, 2020

Pascal Press
PO Box 250
Glebe NSW 2037
(02) 8585 4044
www.pascalpress.com.au

National Library of Australia
Catalogue-in-Publication data

Clark, A (Anne), 1963–
Senior Australian agriculture.

4th ed.
ISBN 978 1 74125 459 4

1. Agriculture – Australia. I. Title

630.994

Publisher: Penelope Naidoo
Project Management: Publishing Options Pty Ltd, Melbourne
Edited by David Morrison
4th Edition project editor: Mark Dixon
4th Edition HSC syllabus updates edited by Ian Rohr
Cover and text design by Gail McManus Graphics
Page design by Crackerjack Desktop Services
4th Edition typeset by Grizzly Graphics (Leanne Richters)
Printed by Vivar Printing/Green Giant Press

Disclaimer
Every effort has been made to trace and acknowledge copyright. However, should any infringement have occurred, the publishers would be pleased to be contacted by the copyright owners.

Contents

List of practicals

Preface

The fourth edition of Senior Australian Agriculture provides students at Years 11 and 12 with a comprehensive textbook that lays a sound foundation in understanding and appreciating the essential aspects of agriculture and its dynamic nature. It has been written specifically for the Stage 6 syllabus in New South Wales, and also suits senior courses in all other states.

The book encourages students to take an enquiry-based approach to their learning. Activities, practicals, Internet sites, research and extension activities are integrated with the theoretical text. A large range of diagrams and photos, together with a user-friendly design, further enhance the learning experience.

Special emphasis is given to the application of technology to agricultural activities both on the farm and in the business world. The broad ethical, legal and sustainability issues affecting today's agriculturalists are also covered.

Students are provided with templates for completing a farm survey and a range of electives. A concluding section on study skills will help them approach their final examination with confidence.

Acknowledgements

The author and publisher gratefully acknowledge the various sources of diagrams and data that have been used in compiling this text.

Overview of Australian Agriculture

chapter 1

In this chapter you will learn about:

- the importance of agriculture
- the key events in the history of Australian agriculture
- some problems facing agriculture
- the requirements for sustainable agriculture
- different types of agricultural production
- the major production areas in Australia.

The importance of agriculture

The word 'agriculture' is derived from the Latin word 'Ager' meaning a field. Agriculture is the science of cultivating the ground and raising plants and animals. It has been an important activity throughout human history [1.1].

1.1 Importance of agriculture

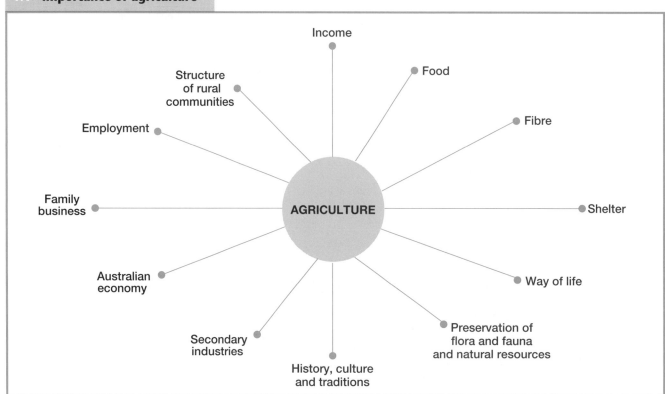

Food, fibre, shelter

Agriculture provides humans with their most basic needs of food, fibre and shelter.

Activity 1.1

Complete the following table listing examples of food, fibre and shelter.

	Food	Fibre	Shelter
Plant origin			
Animal origin			

Food production

Activity 1.2

1 Graph [1.2] shows how wheat and sheep production has changed over time. What factors affect production?
2 Table [1.4] shows the level of consumption of meat, calculated as carcase equivalent weight, over time.
   a Plot total meat consumption over time.
   b What trends are apparent?
   c How does consumer demand affect agricultural production?

carcase equivalent weight
weight of an animal after slaughter and dressing

consumer demand
quantity of goods buyers will buy at a particular price

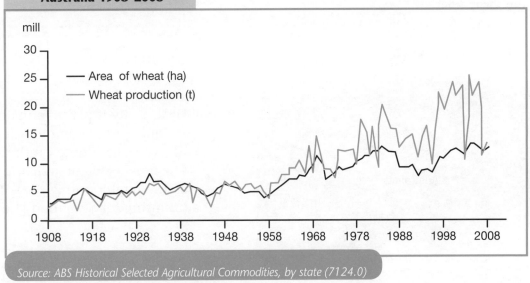

1.2 Wheat production in Australia 1908–2008

Source: ABS Historical Selected Agricultural Commodities, by state (7124.0)

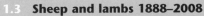

1.3 Sheep and lambs 1888–2008

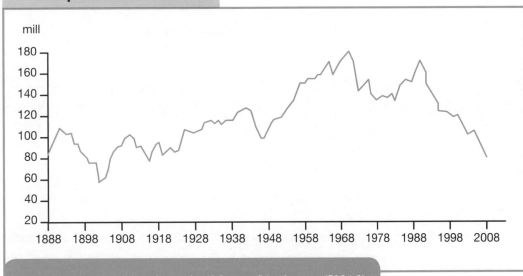

Source: ABS Historical Selected Agricultural Commodities, by state (7124.0)

Table 1.4 shows the level of consumption of lamb and poultry from 1970–2010 per capita.

1.4	Poultry and lamb consumption per capita 1970–2010
Poultry kg	**Lamb and mutton kg**
10.4	36.4
20.1	19.8
24.6	21.3
32.9	18.3
41.7	10.1

Source: ABARE Agricultural statistics report 2010

1.5 **Australia traditionally rode on the sheep's back**

Economic income

Agriculture is a primary industry providing farmers and Australia with saleable products and income.

Historically it played a major role in developing rural communities and the economy with Australia 'riding on the sheep's back' [1.5].

The gross value of agricultural commodities was $33.6 billion in 2001, with exports accounting for $8 billion [1.6].

primary industry
the sector of the economy related to farming, fishing, forestry and mining activities

gross value
total worth of products

1.6 **Net and gross value of farm production**

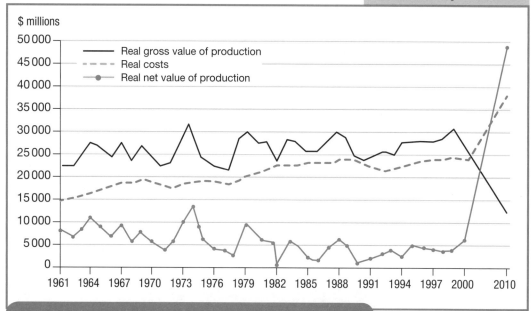

Source: Australian Bureau of Agricultural and Resources Economics, 2011

Activity 1.3

net value
monetary value of production after costs have been deducted

1 Graph [1.6] shows the gross value and the net value of farm production over time.
  a What factors affect income levels?
  b What methods could be used to stop fluctuations in returns?

2 With reference to the Australian Bureau of Statistics' website **www.abs.gov.au** answer the following questions.
  a What is the current value of agricultural production?
  b What are the most profitable enterprises?
  c What are our major exports?
  d What is the debt level of agriculture?

1.7 Gross value of agricultural commodities produced

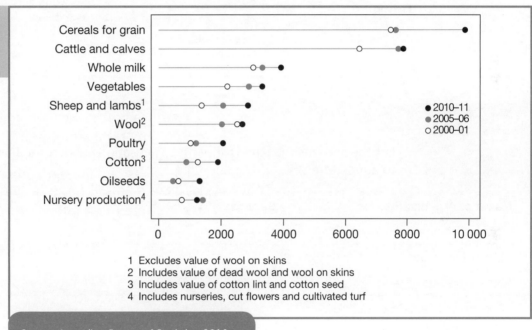

Cereals for grain
Cattle and calves
Whole milk
Vegetables
Sheep and lambs[1]
Wool[2]
Poultry
Cotton[3]
Oilseeds
Nursery production[4]

● 2010–11
● 2005–06
○ 2000–01

0   2000   4000   6000   8000   10 000

1 Excludes value of wool on skins
2 Includes value of dead wool and wool on skins
3 Includes value of cotton lint and cotton seed
4 Includes nurseries, cut flowers and cultivated turf

Source: Australian Bureau of Statistics, 2010

secondary industries
those that make up the manufacturing sector

Employment

Ninety-five percent of farms are family owned and operated. Agriculture also provides employment for rural communities and secondary industries that supply agriculture with its needs or use its raw materials for production.

1.8 Employment in agriculture

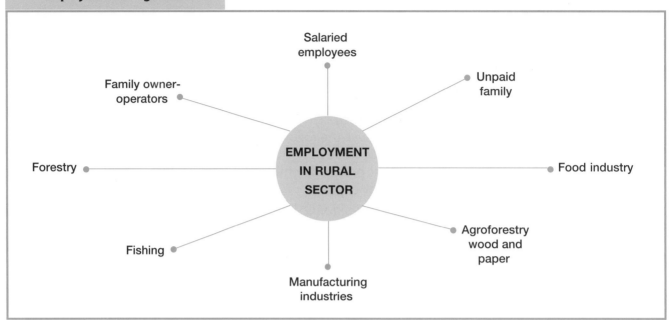

Activity 1.4

List the services that the following organisations and companies provide to agriculture:

Name of organisation	Services
Chemical companies	
Machinery dealers	
Stock and station agents	
Government agents, for example NSW Agriculture	
Veterinarians	
Banks and lending authorities	
Accountants	
Insurance brokers	
Contractors, for example shearers	
Shops and retail stores	
Fuel distributors	
Fertiliser companies	
Marketing services	
Casual labour, for example fruit pickers	

2   Why is agriculture important to the rural community?

3 Graph [1.9] shows employment over time. What trends are apparent?

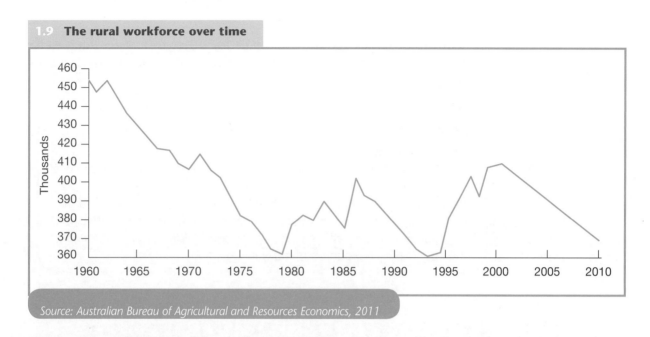

1.9 The rural workforce over time

Source: Australian Bureau of Agricultural and Resources Economics, 2011

1.10 Shearing 1930s – agriculture employed many people

4 Look at photos [1.10]–[1.12].
   a Why have employment levels declined?
   b Knowing that technology refers to new inventions such as machinery, computers, chemicals and fertilisers and that innovation refers to new ideas or practices such as direct drilling, minimum tillage and stubble mulching, what effect have innovations and technology had on rural communities?

1.11 Mechanisation replaced many jobs

1.12 Reduced employment led to a decline in rural towns

Agriculture and secondary industries

Agriculture provides the raw materials for other industries such as food manufacture and textile industries. Agriculture is a business and also a way of life.

AG FACT

New technology

An example of new technology developing for sheep farmers is the use of radio ear tags. Linked with race-side diagnostics and a central flock database the farmer can record simple measures such as bodyweight to sophisticated on-the-spot fleece tests and parasite counts. The new technology gives the ability to record detailed information about stock, their genetic background and individual histories.

History of agriculture

Early humans were nomads and hunters who were forced to move from place to place in search of food and shelter. When humans learnt to domesticate animals and cultivate crops in 10 000–15 000 BCE, they were able to establish themselves in one region. This marked the beginning of early civilisations [1.13].

Present-day plants and animals were derived from wild forms selectively bred to meet people's requirements [1.14] and [1.15].

1.13 Timeline of domestication

Time	Event
10 000 BCE	Dog domesticated
9000 BCE	Goat domesticated
8000–7000 BCE	Sheep domesticated
8000–7000 BCE	Wheat cultivated
6000 BCE	Cattle domesticated
3000 BCE	Plough invented
2000 BCE	Poultry domesticated
2000–1000 BCE	Horse domesticated
AD	Beginning of Christian era

Activity 1.5

1.14 Origins of some common plants

Plant	Probable origin
Wheat	Asia
Barley	Asia and Ethiopia
Rye	Asia
Oats	Europe
Rice	Southern India to China
Millets	Southern Asia, China
Lupins	North America
Sunflower	South America
Corn	South America
Sugar cane	Asia and Melanesian islands
Sorghum	Tropical Africa
Soybeans	Asia
Cow pea	Central Africa
Chickpea	Europe
Peanut	South America
White clover	North America
Paspalum	South America
Ryegrass	Europe and Asia
Lucerne	South West Asia
Spinach	Asia
Potatoes	Peru

Trace map [1.16] below into your workbook.

a Using tables [1.14] and [1.15] as a guide, mark the origins of the plants and animals on the map.

b Why is it important to know their origins to maximise production?

1.15 Origins of some common animals

Animal	Probable origin
Cattle	Bos taurus – Europe and Bos indicus – India
Pigs	Northern Europe, China, India and Indonesia
Poultry	Red jungle fowl of India
Sheep	Mountainous regions of Asia
Goats	Western Asia, South Africa

1.16 Origins of plants and animals

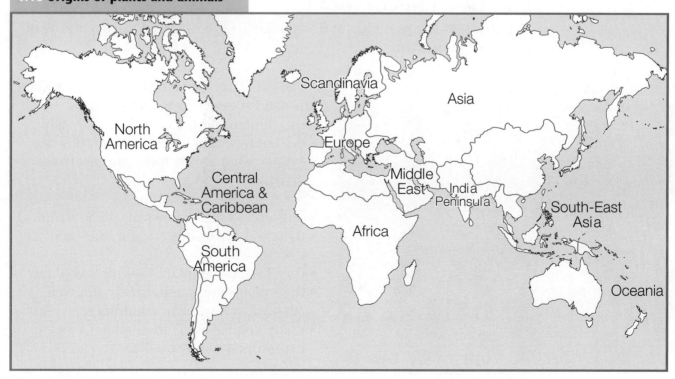

History of agriculture in Australia

It is important to gain an understanding of the history of Australian agriculture through the significant changes from Aboriginal agriculture to early European settlement and the developments that have led to today's practices.

The knowledge of what has happened in the past allows the development of greater insight and understanding that assists in creating better practices for the future.

Aboriginal peoples

European settlement caused profound environmental degradation in less than 200 years. In contrast Aboriginal peoples lived in harmony with the environment for thousands of years.

Although Aboriginal practices varied considerably in different communities around the continent, they were many features that were widespread.

The reasons Aboriginal people had minimal impact on the environment include:

- they had a deep religious respect for the land
- they understood the limitations of the land and its resources
- they were hunter gatherers and moved from region to region
- population size was based on food supply
- they were driven by survival rather than by greed
- they never depleted an area, for example replanted roots and shoots and left sufficient animals to reproduce
- they burned to promote new growth
- they used primitive irrigation and agricultural systems
- they did not introduce weeds, pests and diseases, unlike European settlers.

degradation
deterioration in the quality of the environment such as air, water and soil pollution, deforestation and extinction of flora and fauna

European settlement

The arrival of the First Fleet at Botany Bay in 1788 marked the beginning of European settlement.

1.17 One of the first areas settled by Europeans was The Rocks, Sydney

The first farm was established at Farm Cove but had little success because:

- the climate was harsh and unpredictable
- the land was uncleared and the soils near Sydney were sandy, rocky and relatively infertile
- water supplies were limited
- settlers had little knowledge of agriculture
- there was little skilled labour, only convict labour
- they had few animals, tools or machinery
- their plants and animals were not well adapted to Australian conditions
- many English agricultural practices were inappropriate in Australia.

1.18 Rabbits and foxes were introduced for hunting

Developing agriculture

James Ruse established the first experimental farms at Parramatta, Hawkesbury, Bankstown and Macquarie Fields and had greater success in these regions.

In 1813, Blaxland, Wentworth and Lawson crossed the Great Dividing Range and found well-grassed, lightly timbered lands that were ideal for grazing and cultivation.

John Macarthur introduced merinos from the Cape of Good Hope and established overseas markets for their wool. The Peppin brothers selectively bred a larger-framed, coarser-woolled sheep for the western regions. Their breeding programs increased average fleece weights from 1.4 kg in 1860 to 2.7 kg in 1890.

By 1894, huge grazing properties had been established. There were 100 million sheep and 12 million cattle in New South Wales alone.

William Farrer developed Federation wheat that was early maturing, resistant to rust and tolerant of dry conditions.

In 1876 the Smith brothers developed the stump-jump plough and this allowed better soil preparation.

John Ridley developed the stripper that removed the grain and HV McKay later modified it to sieve and bag wheat. These developments marked the beginnings of the Sunshine harvester and more efficient harvesting practices.

Improved communication and transportation systems promoted wheat storage and haulage in New South Wales.

Settlers found that soils were deficient in water and nutrients and used fallowing techniques and superphosphate to significantly increase yields.

During this period the grazing industry also underwent marked improvements. Grasses (such as oats and ryegrass) and legumes (such as lucerne, medics and clovers) were introduced and significantly increased stocking rates and soil fertility levels.

Mechanisation, refrigeration and the introduction of new breeds of animals (such as Brahman cattle) also increased productivity.

Other industries such as dairying and horticulture were established in Australia and underwent many periods of expansion.

rust
fungal disease of plants where leaves and stems become spotted and turn reddish brown in colour

fallowing
ploughing, then leaving land bare to reduce weed competition and conserve water

legumes
plants of the leguminosae family, often used for feed, food or as a soil improving crop

Extension Activity

1 Discuss the similarities and differences in land practices between Aboriginal peoples and early Europeans.

2 Describe the features of a sustainable agricultural system.

1.19 Wool production 1908–2008

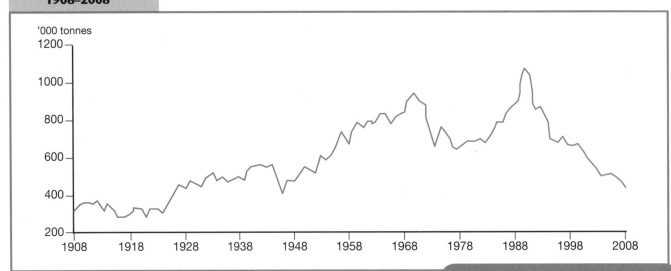

'000 tonnes

Source: Australian Bureau of Statistics, 2010

1.20 Beef and dairy cattle numbers 1861–1999

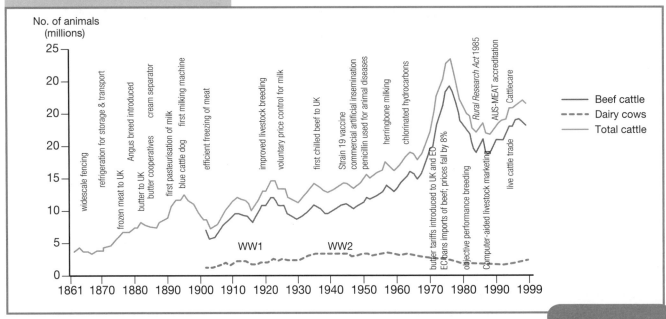

No. of animals (millions)

Legend:
- Beef cattle
- Dairy cows
- Total cattle

Timeline labels: widescale fencing; refrigeration for storage & transport; frozen meat to UK; Angus breed introduced; butter to UK; cream separator; butter cooperatives; first pasteurisation of milk; blue cattle dog; first milking machine; efficient freezing of meat; improved livestock breeding; voluntary price control for milk; first chilled beef to UK; Strain 19 vaccine; commercial artificial insemination; penicillin used for animal diseases; herringbone milking; chlorinated hydrocarbons; butter tariffs introduced to UK and EC; EC bans imports of beef; prices fall by 8%; objective performance breeding; computer-aided livestock marketing; *Rural Research Act* 1985; AUS-MEAT accreditation; live cattle trade; Cattlecare

WW1   WW2

Source: ANRA, 2011

1.21 Early tractor used in Australia

1.22 Carting hay 1940s

Problems in agriculture

Through Australian agricultural history there have been many times of great prosperity often followed by times of little income or severe losses. There are many pressures that have led to dramatic changes to current agricultural practice [1.23].

Boom and bust

All agricultural production has undergone periods of prosperity and depression due to many factors including:

- Australia is the driest continent in the world and has an unreliable climate
- only 25 per cent of Australia has a growing season of more than five months
- plants and animals were poorly adapted to Australian conditions
- Australia has a small local population and there is a heavy dependence on overseas markets
- long-term dependence on a limited range of products, for example wheat, sheep and cattle
- poor, infertile soils
- low-quality pastures
- competition from weeds, pests and diseases
- inadequate tools and machinery
- high input and labour costs
- high risk
- lack of information, communication and transport
- production lag hindered decision-making
- fluctuating supply and demand
- uncertain income
- large distances to markets
- highly protected and competitive global market including heavily subsidised markets such as the European Union (EU) and the USA
- need for economic efficiency to compete on world market.

protected
the buying and selling of goods is restricted to benefit some industries in a country

1.23 Factors affecting agriculture

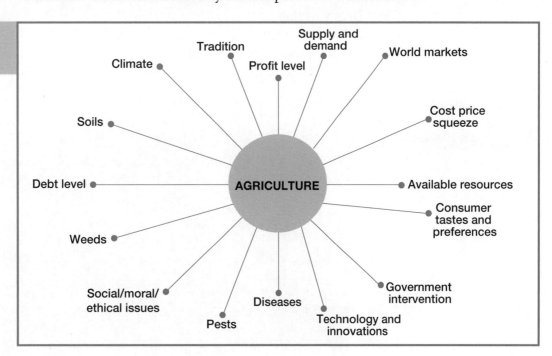

Climate · Tradition · Supply and demand · World markets · Profit level · Cost price squeeze · Soils · Debt level · AGRICULTURE · Available resources · Consumer tastes and preferences · Weeds · Social/moral/ethical issues · Pests · Diseases · Technology and innovations · Government intervention

Changes in agriculture

Over the decades there have been many changes including:

- less people working on the land
- fewer properties [1.25]
- bigger farms as the average farm has doubled in size due to technological and economic reasons
- lower incomes due to cost price squeeze; for example in the last 40 years, input costs have increased by 1200 per cent and prices by only 230 per cent [1.26]
- increase in the average age of farmers
- innovations and technological changes; for example machinery such as tractors (16.5 million worldwide), fertilisers, vaccines and herbicides
- new breeding systems and genetic engineering (such as broiler chickens that grow twice as fast with half the feed of earlier strains)
- increased rural indebtedness
- drift of people from rural areas to the city
- reduced importance of agriculture to the gross domestic product and export market
- change from traditional European and USA markets to Asian markets
- massive clearing, for example two thirds of Australia's forests (40 million hectares) and one third of all scrub woodland (63 million hectares) have been cleared
- major land degradation; for example more than half of all cropping and pastoral land is affected by erosion, salinity, acidity, structural and soil fertility problems
- highest extinction rate of mammals in the world with 15 per cent or 46 mammal species now extinct
- introduction of more than 500 species including weeds, pests and diseases
- waterways contaminated by soil runoff, algal blooms, fertilisers, pesticides and heavy metals
- greater social awareness; for example moral and ethical issues such as animal welfare and genetic engineering
- consumer demand for clean food not contaminated with chemical residues.

genetic engineering
the alteration of the chromosome structure of cells to control the characteristics of offspring

runoff
removal of soil by running water

1.24 **Loss of valuable trees increased erosion and salinity problems**

1.25 Number of farms

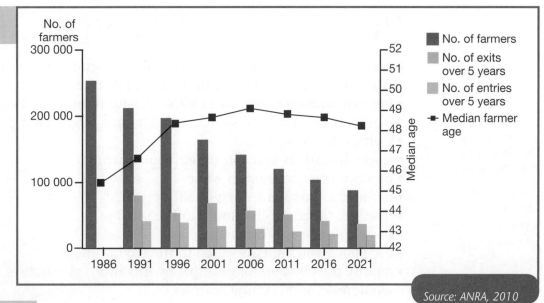

Source: ANRA, 2010

1.26 Farm income and profit levels

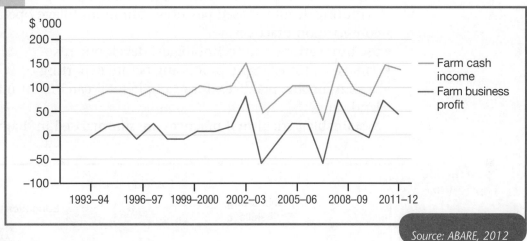

Source: ABARE, 2012

Activity 1.6

1. Table 1.27 shows the area of land affected now and in the future by rising salt.
   a. Graph the figures.
   b. What trends are apparent?
2. Dryland salinity was observed and explained in terms of extensive clearing of native woodlands in Western Australia in the mid 1920s. Why was mass clearing still conducted until late last century?

1.27 Areas at risk of rising salinity

Asset	Units	2000	2020	2050
Agricultural land	hectares	4 650 000	6 371 000	13 660 000
Remnant and perennial vegetation	hectares	631 000	777 000	2 020 000
Important wetlands	number	80	81	130

Source: NLWRA 2001

Sustainable agriculture

Farmers have maximised efficiency and production at the expense of the environment. To be sustainable agriculturalists must:

- improve management; for example greater training and education
- maintain or improve resources; for example whole farm planning
- plan for the long term
- research markets and consumer requirements
- produce what consumers want
- produce a consistent, high-quality product
- diversify to reduce risk and stabilise income
- have up-to-date information
- use plants and animals suited to the environment
- modify the climate; for example by irrigation, glasshouses, mulches, windbreaks and housing animals
- use land only to its capabilities
- improve resources; for example use fertilisers, crop rotation, green manuring, legume-based pastures, minimum tillage operations and soil conservation practices
- use innovations and technological developments
- value add; for example processing before exporting
- use sustainable practices; for example total catchment management and land care.

Sustainable agricultural practices are summarised in diagram [1.28] below.

diversify
have a variety of enterprises to stabilise income

value add
modifying a product to increase its value

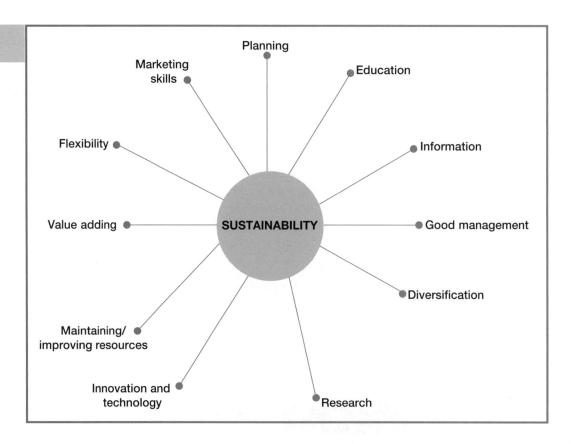

1.28 Sustainable agriculture

Extension Activity

1 Discuss the effect of physical, biological, social, historical and economic factors on sustainable production.

2 Evaluate the impact of innovation, ethics and current issues on agricultural systems.

Intensive and extensive agriculture

Agricultural production can be divided into the two categories: intensive production and extensive production.

Both types of production are important but vary in many features including:

- location
- types of plants and animals grown
- feed conversion efficiency of animals
- stocking rates
- potential for breeding programs
- capital invested
- amount of land used
- digestive systems of animals
- type of feedstuffs used
- incidence of diseases
- labour requirements
- marketing options.

1.29 Characteristics of intensive and extensive agriculture

Characteristics	Intensive	Extensive
Location	Near towns and cities, so perishable products are close to markets	No set area, but generally away from main centres where land is expensive
Land size	Small, for example 3–30 hectares	Much larger scale, for example more than 200 hectares
Plants and animals	Pigs, poultry, goats, fish, lot-feeding and horticultural products	Sheep, cattle, goats, deer and large-scale cropping such as wheat
Digestive systems	Mainly monogastrics, for example pigs and poultry	Mainly ruminants, for example sheep, cattle, deer and goats
Food conversion efficiency	Highly efficient, diets are strictly regulated and animals are confined so that they do not waste energy grazing or keeping warm	Less efficient. Feed quality varies with pasture type and seasons. Animals also waste energy grazing and keeping warm
Feed	Cereals, concentrates and additives. All feed is purchased and carefully regulated	Pastures, for example grasses and legumes, hays, cereals and silage
Stocking rates	Very intensive, animals confined to small cages or yards and no grazing or activity is allowed	Depends on quality of pastures and climate. Animals are allowed to graze freely
Incidence of disease	Animals are drenched and vaccinated and hygiene is a major concern, however, once disease is established it rapidly affects all animals	Animals are drenched and vaccinated but disease is less of a problem because of the low stocking rates

▶

Characteristics	Intensive	Extensive
Breeding programs	Effective, as animals have short life-cycles and are easily accessible for mating and artificial insemination (AI)	Less effective, as animals have longer life-cycles and are less accessible
Labour	High labour, machinery and technology requirements	Seasonal labour demand, for example for shearing and harvesting
Capital invested	Huge cost of land, machinery, equipment, labour and feed	Land, labour and feed costs are less expensive, however, initial outlay is approximately the same because more land is required
Markets	Mainly domestic for perishable products but some export markets	Domestic and export

Activity 1.7

1.30 Intensive plant production in Australia

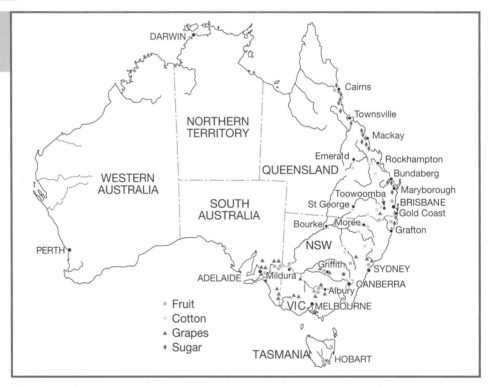

Map [1.30] shows the location of intensive crops in Australia
  a List reasons for their location.
  b What are the disadvantages of intensive production?

Extension Activity

1 Discuss the moral, ethical and social issues regarding intensive production and animal welfare.

2 Discuss the economic, social and environmental factors that affect the type and location of intensive animal production systems.

Production areas in Australia

1.31 Agricultural production in Australia

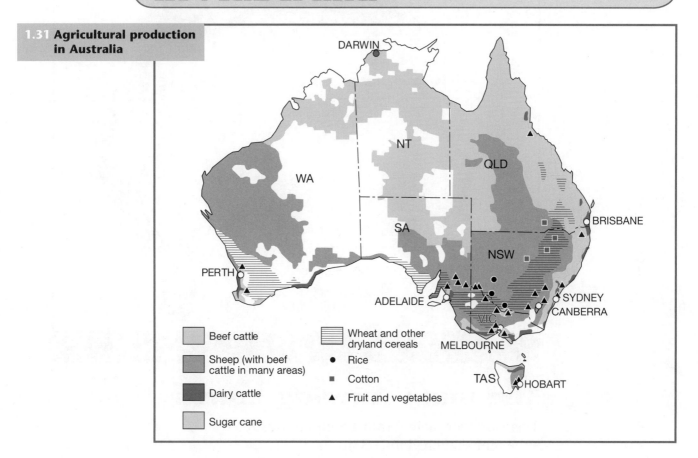

Legend:
- Beef cattle
- Sheep (with beef cattle in many areas)
- Dairy cattle
- Sugar cane
- Wheat and other dryland cereals
- ● Rice
- ■ Cotton
- ▲ Fruit and vegetables

Climate is one of the major factors affecting agricultural production. The continent of Australia is relatively dry and 50 per cent of the land surface receives less than 300 mm of rainfall per year. Agricultural production is directly affected by the amount of rain a region receives and its seasonality and reliability. Map [1.32] on the next page shows Australia's rainfall regions.

Coastal regions receive the highest rainfall, and amount and reliability decreases with distance from the coast. Northern regions receive the bulk of their rainfall during the summer, whereas southern regions have predominantly winter rainfall.

The growing season

effective rainfall
where rainfall exceeds one-third of the evaporative demand

The growing season is the number of consecutive months of effective rainfall. Seventy five percent of Australia has a growing season of less than five months and these regions only support grazing systems based on drought-resistant native pastures, trees and shrubs. Most cropping areas have a growing season of 5–9 months and intensive agricultural production occurs in regions with a growing season of 9–12 months.

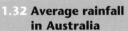

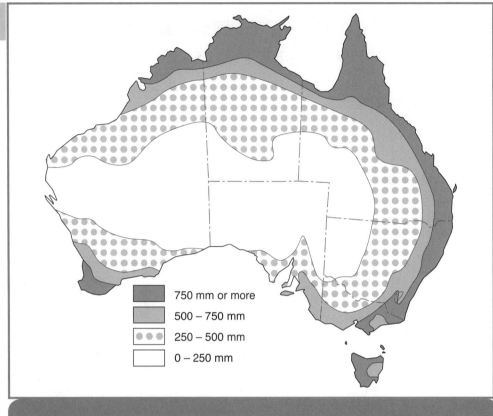

1.32 Average rainfall in Australia

Legend:
- 750 mm or more
- 500 – 750 mm
- 250 – 500 mm
- 0 – 250 mm

Source: Based on Bailey J, Climate and the Farmer, Curriculum Development Centre, Canberra, 1979

The main farming zones

There are four main farming zones in Australia:
- the temperate region [1.33]
- the subtropical region, [1.38] on page 22
- the tropical region, [1.42] on page 24
- the arid and semi-arid region, [1.46] on page 25.

These areas have a diverse array of climates, soil types and agricultural production as indicated in the following sections.

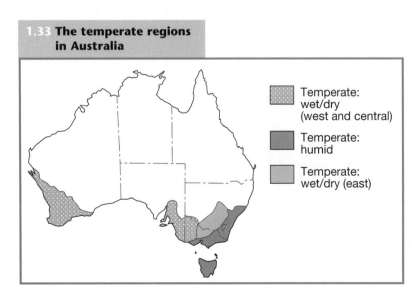

1.33 The temperate regions in Australia

Legend:
- Temperate: wet/dry (west and central)
- Temperate: humid
- Temperate: wet/dry (east)

The temperate region

The temperate region contains some of the most productive land in Australia and consists of a wide range of farming activities including wheat, sheep, cattle, dairying, viticulture, fruit and vegetable production.

evaporation
the loss of water vapour from soil or water surfaces through heat and wind

1.34 Comparison of the four main temperate zones

Characteristic	Wet/dry west	Wet/dry central	Wet/dry east	Humid zone
Location	Triangle in south-eastern Western Australia	Southern Australia and part of north-western Victoria. 150 000 sq. km in size	Western slopes and plains of NSW	Whole of Tasmania and a belt from south-eastern part of South Australia through southern Victoria to central coast of NSW
Temperature	Mild	Cool wet winters and hot dry summers	High temperatures and evaporation rates in summer	Cool winters and warm to hot summers
Rainfall	Reliable. 1500 mm in the south-west to 300 mm on the north-eastern side, mostly in the winter from May to October	250–1000 mm, mostly in winter	350–700 mm, any month	Throughout the year but predominantly in winter
Soil types	Sandy textured on the coast, clayey inland. Soils commonly deficient in phosphorus	Sandy earths and red brown earths	Red earths and grey and brown soils. Low in organic matter	Sandy, heavy clays and loams; low in nitrogen and organic matter. Generally acidic
Enterprises	Wool, lamb, beef, dairying, pigs, poultry; cereal crops such as wheat	Sheep, beef, dairying, pigs, poultry, irrigated tree crops, cereal grains, grapes, apples and pears	Wool, prime lambs, beef, dairying, cereal crops, for example wheat, barley, lupins triticale, rice, sunflowers, fruits and vegetables	Sheep, beef, dairying, pigs and poultry; wheat, oats, fruit and vegetables

1.35 Viticulture production

1.36 Beef production

1.37 Fruit production

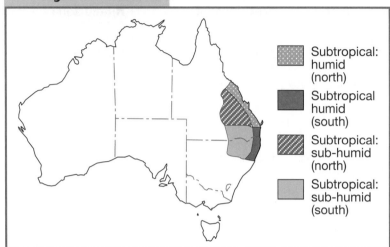

1.38 The subtropical regions in Australia

Subtropical: humid (north)

Subtropical humid (south)

Subtropical: sub-humid (north)

Subtropical: sub-humid (south)

The subtropical region

The subtropical region consists of four major zones. Enterprises include sugar cane, beef, dairying, banana, mango, avocado, macadamia, and tomato and pineapple production.

1.39 Characteristics of the subtropical regions

Characteristic	Sub-humid north zone	Sub-humid south zone	Humid north zone	Humid south zone
Location	Central Queensland, around the Burdekin, Fitzroy and Burnett rivers	Northern NSW and southern Queensland, around the Darling Downs	Strip on central coast of Queensland	Narrow strip of northern NSW and Queensland coast south of Brisbane
Rainfall	Summer monsoons. Southern part has winter westerlies. Average rainfall 550–1000 mm, 60–70% falls in the summer	640–1000 mm; 65% falls in the summer	Dry period from April to October. Wet season Dec to March. Rainfall varies from 1672 mm in Mackay to 944 mm in Rockhampton. Cyclones sometimes occur	Rainfall 900–2000 mm and occurs throughout the year
Temperatures	Summer 17–32°C, winter 7.5–25°C. Frost-free period of 250–320 days	Darling Downs, 3°C minimum in July to maximum of 30°C in January. Whole area frost-free period of 100 days	Maximum summer temperatures up to 31°C in January and December. Frosts occur in winter	Warm to hot summers and mild winters. Maximum temperatures rarely exceed 30°C. Frosts can occur
Soil types	Three main types: (a) soils of uniform texture, for example grey and brown clays (b) soils with increasing clay content (with depth), for example red and yellow earths (c) soils with marked change in texture Most are deficient in nitrogen and phosphorus	Diverse, eg black clays, red clays, granitic soils, red-brown earths and podzolics	Red and yellow earths and deep alluvial soils	Alluvial soils, light sandstone or shale and volcanic loams

▶

Characteristic	Sub-humid north zone	Sub-humid south zone	Humid north zone	Humid south zone
Enterprise	Crops: sorghum, wheat, oats, sunflower and cotton. Beef cattle such as Bos indicus bloodlines. Limited sheep and dairying	Wheat, barley, oats, safflower, sunflower and cotton. Sheep, beef, dairying, pigs and poultry. Fruit trees, vegetables and pastures	Beef and dairying. Sugar cane, sorghum and maize. Horticultural crops. Pineapples, pawpaws, mangoes, avocados and macadamia nuts	Beef, dairying and pigs. Sugar cane, soybeans and maize. Horticultural crops, bananas, avocados, nuts, pawpaws, passionfruit and watermelons
Pasture species	Rhodes grass, *stylosanthes* spp, legumes	Lucerne, phalaris, cocksfoot, fescue and white clover	Paspalum, Seteria, kikuyu, molasses and guinea grasses, white and red clover. Siratro, Stylos and lucerne	Paspalum, kikuyu, couch, red and white clover

1.40 Bos indicus cattle

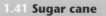

1.41 Sugar cane

AG FACT

Why Bos indicus?

Over 80% of cattle in Northern Australia possess some Bos indicus bloodlines. Bos indicus cattle are well adapted to a diet of low quality forage and cope with high levels of external and internal parasites. Their popularity in Northern Australia is because they achieve strong growth rates in harsh climatic conditions.

1.42 **The tropical regions in Australia**

Wet/dry tropics

Humid tropics

The tropical region

The tropical region has two main zones. Enterprises include sugar cane, sunflowers, rice, tobacco, soybeans, cassava, peanuts and grain sorghum.

1.43 **Characteristics of the tropical region**

Characteristics	Wet dry tropical zone	Humid tropical zone
Location	Kimberleys of Western Australia and top of Northern Territory and Cape York Peninsula	Small strip along the coast of northern Queensland
Rainfall	Has a wet and dry season	Highest rainfall in Australia. Cyclones are common
Soil types	Very infertile. Deficient in nitrogen, phosphorus and trace elements. Deltas are reasonably fertile	Fertile, alluvial lowlands. Red soils and basaltic mountain tops
Enterprises	Beef, sugar cane, sunflower, cassava and peanuts	Beef, sugar cane, peanuts, bananas and tea

1.44 **Banana production**

1.45 **Tea plantation**

1.46 The arid and semi-arid regions in Australia

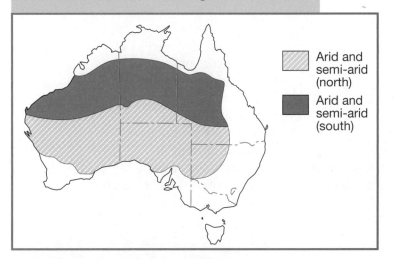

Arid and semi-arid (north)

Arid and semi-arid (south)

The arid region

This region makes up approximately 70 per cent of Australia and has a harsh environment with hot days, cold nights and low and erratic rainfall. The area contains huge grazing properties (or stations) which run sheep and cattle on native pastures.

1.47 Characteristics of the arid and semi-arid regions

Characteristics	North zone	South zone
Location	Large belt between latitudes 15° S and 33° S and longitudes 114° E and 147° E	
Rainfall	Low and unreliable. 357 mm at Winton to 310 mm at Marble Bar, mainly in the summer	Low and unreliable. 264 mm at Thargomindah to 204 mm at Wiluna, more in winter than summer
Water supplies	Mainly artesian wells	
Soil types	Infertile. Siliceous sands to hard setting clays. Soils in both areas are deficient in nitrogen, phosphorous and trace elements	
Vegetation	Sparse scrubland, eg saltbush and xerophytic midgrass	
Enterprises	Sheep and cattle	

1.48 Beef and cattle in an arid region

1 Define the following terms:
   - agriculture
   - export market
   - secondary industries
   - mechanisation
   - land degradation
   - extensive production
   - domestic market
   - consumer demand
   - technology
   - sustainable
   - intensive production
   - growing season.

2 Draw a map of Australia showing the main climatic zones.
   a Shade in the regions where the following enterprises are found:
   - wheat
   - sheep
   - bananas
   - sugar cane
   - rice
   - cotton
   - market gardens.
   b What factors determine the distribution of an enterprise?
   c Why are many intensive industries located close to cities and major markets?

3 Answer true or false to the following statements:
   a Agriculture provides us with food, fibre, shelter and income.
   b Consumer demand determines the price of a product.
   c Seventy per cent of farms are family owned.
   d The rural workforce has increased over time.
   e Plants and animals grown in Australia mainly originated from Australia.
   f Aboriginal peoples used agricultural practices.
   g Farms have increased in size over time.
   h Agricultural production is currently sustainable.
   i Innovation is the development of new ideas and practices.
   j Technology has increased the efficiency of agricultural production.

Systems

chapter

2

Introduction to systems

2.1   The farm system

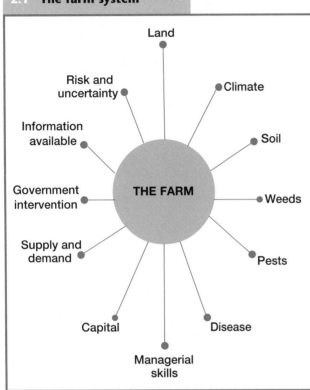

Land
Climate
Risk and uncertainty
Soil
Information available
THE FARM
Government intervention
Weeds
Supply and demand
Pests
Capital
Disease
Managerial skills

A system is a set of interacting units that react with themselves and the non-living environment.

A farm is a system and consists of many interacting units such as plants, animals, climate, soil, weeds, pests and diseases [2.1].

Systems are made up of subsystems and have inputs, processes, outputs and boundaries.

2.2   The environment

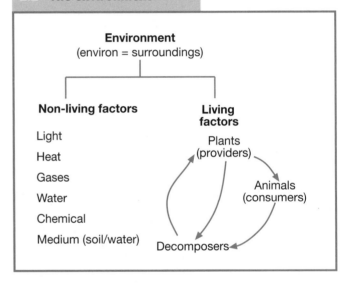

Environment
(environ = surroundings)

Non-living factors

Light
Heat
Gases
Water
Chemical
Medium (soil/water)

Living factors

Plants (providers)
Animals (consumers)
Decomposers

subsystems
smaller individual units which make up the whole system eg animal subsystem and soil subsystem

The farm system

A farm consists of many subsystems such as cropping and animal enterprises and requires many inputs or raw materials to make a product [2.6].

2.4   Water resources

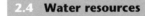

2.3   Soil resources

2.5   Animal subsystem

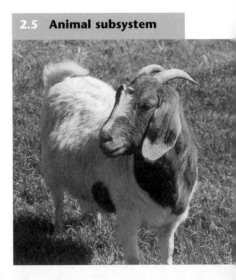

2.6 The farm system interactions and external forces

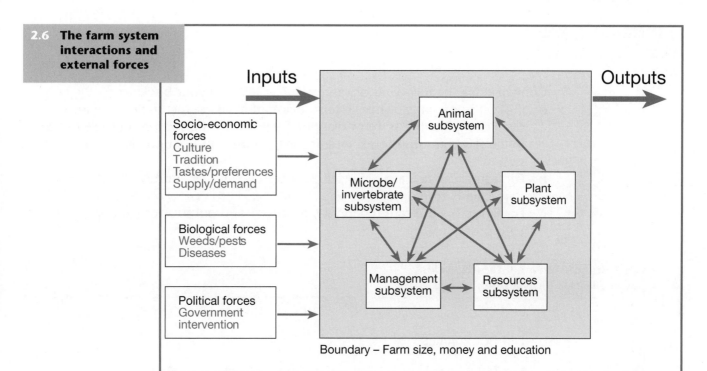

Inputs

Inputs are the raw materials (such as seed, fertiliser, fuel, labour and management) used to make a product.

Processes

Processes such as buying, shearing and drenching are the stages and alterations that the raw materials must undergo to convert them into the desired product.

Outputs

Outputs such as wool, meat, milk and fruit are the final products of the farm.

Boundaries

Boundaries are the limitations of the system and include:
- amount of land available
- climate
- topography
- fertility level of the soil
- money
- machinery
- technology
- managerial skills.

topography
refers to the slope, terrain or undulations of the land

Activity 2.1

Copy or trace the following diagrams [2.7]–[2.9] into your book.

a In [2.7] some parts of this systems diagram have been completed in lower case. Complete the systems diagram by labelling the sections in UPPER CASE to identify the subsystems, interactions, outputs and boundaries of the farm system.

b For figure 2.8 indicate the inputs, processes, outputs and boundaries for a prime lamb enterprise.

c For figure 2.9 indicate the inputs, processes and outputs for a cropping enterprise.

2.7 Label the subsystems, interactions and outputs in this farm system

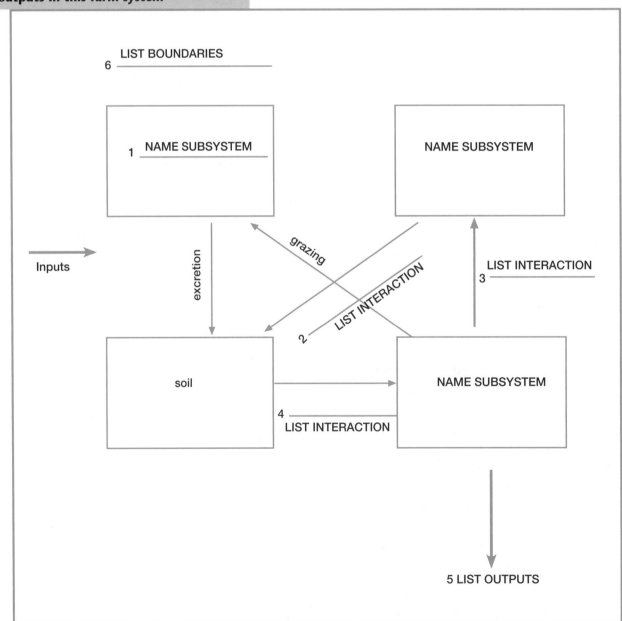

2.8　Show the inputs, processes, outputs and boundaries for a prime lamb enterprise

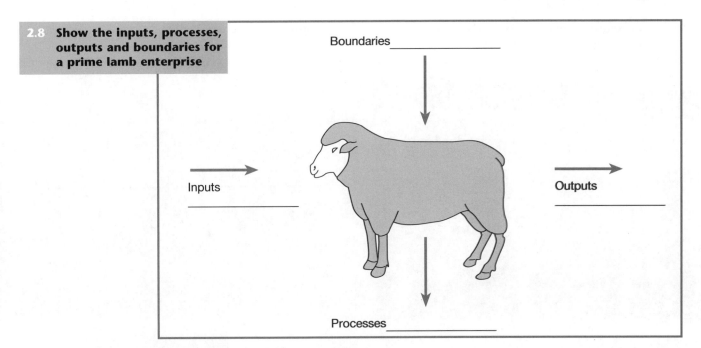

Boundaries _____

Inputs _____

Outputs _____

Processes _____

2.9　Show the inputs, processes, outputs and boundaries for a crop enterprise

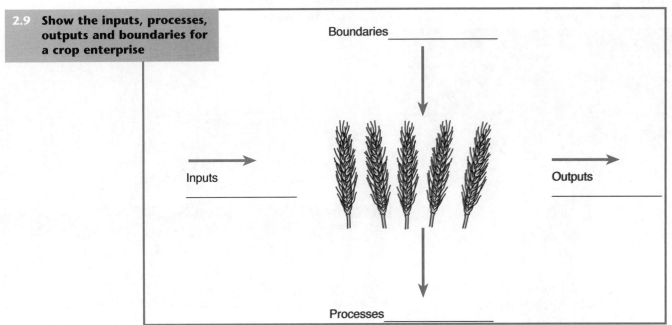

Boundaries _____

Inputs _____

Outputs _____

Processes _____

Activity 2.2

1　Study the images shown in [2.10]–[2.14] on the next page. Explain how each of the factors of flooding, limited technology, pests, weeds and topography limit production.

2　Draw an animal system and explain how the following factors affect the system.

　a　social factors such as tradition, culture, consumer demand and tastes and preferences

　b　political factors such as taxes, subsidies, interest rates and rate of exchange

　c　biological factors, for example weeds, pests and diseases

　d　physical factors such as topography, climate and soil types.

2.10 Flooding inundates roads and land

2.11 Limited technology – milk deliveries in the 1890s

2.12 Feral pigs are one type of pest

2.13 Topography – the lie of the land

2.14 Weeds such as the introduced species Paterson's curse

Models

Models are commonly used to represent a farm. The three most common types are the:
• black box model
• static model
• dynamic model.

2.15 Black box model for an oats enterprise

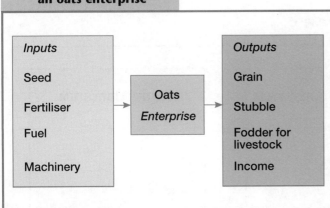

Black box model

A black box model shows the inputs and outputs of an enterprise, but does not describe the processes involved in making the final product.

Static and dynamic models

Static and dynamic models are more informative than black box models. A static model shows the basic processes that occur within a subsystem. A dynamic model shows the interactions between subsystems.

2.16 Static model of a farm

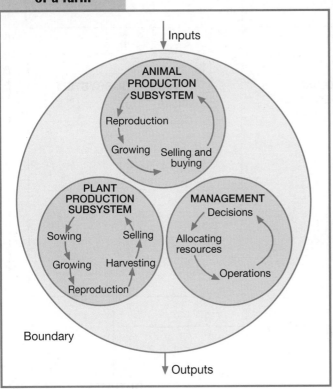

2.17 Dynamic model of a farm

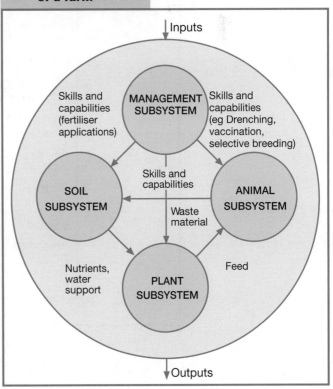

Activity 2.3

1 Explain how crop rotations benefit a farm system.
2 List two benefits and two disadvantages of leaving crop residues after harvesting.
3 The systems diagram [2.18] shows a wheat, sheep and cattle property. Explain how microbes affect the system. Consider disease, the ruminant digestive system, nitrogen fixation, decomposition of organic matter, silage and food production as some of the effects.

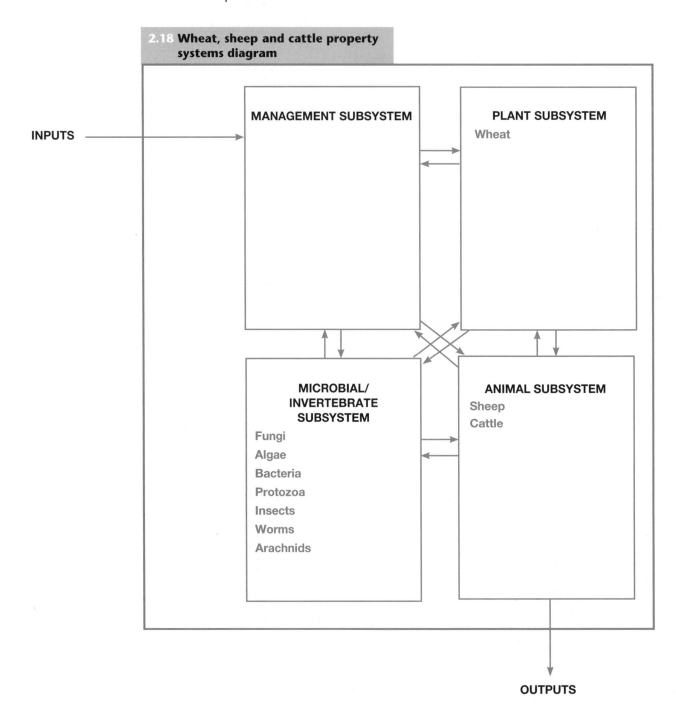

2.18 Wheat, sheep and cattle property systems diagram

INPUTS

MANAGEMENT SUBSYSTEM

PLANT SUBSYSTEM
Wheat

MICROBIAL/ INVERTEBRATE SUBSYSTEM
Fungi
Algae
Bacteria
Protozoa
Insects
Worms
Arachnids

ANIMAL SUBSYSTEM
Sheep
Cattle

OUTPUTS

Flows and cycles in natural systems

Some of the important flows and cycles in natural systems are:
- energy flow
- carbon cycling
- oxygen cycling.
- nitrogen cycling
- water cycling

Flow of energy in systems

The sun provides most systems with their source of energy.

Plants convert light energy into chemical energy during photosynthesis when carbon dioxide and water are converted into energy-rich glucose. Energy derived from the sun is converted into different forms along the food chain. At each stage of conversion, energy is lost to the system and is not recycled. Diagrams [2.19] and [2.20] show the flow of energy in an ecosystem and in an agricultural system.

Nutrients, in natural systems are recycled whereas in agricultural systems they are removed by the harvesting and sale of the produce.

In agricultural systems there is a huge loss of energy and nutrients because produce is removed and sold. Farmers have to use artificial sources of nutrients such as fertilisers to combat this loss.

photosynthesis
the conversion by plants of carbon dioxide and water into oxygen and energy-rich glucose that provides the plant with its energy needs

2.20 Flow of energy in an agricultural system

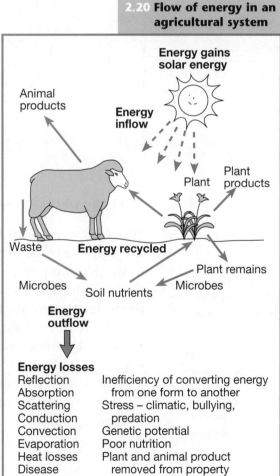

2.19 Flow of energy in an ecosystem

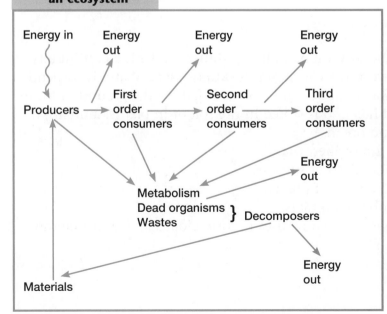

Energy losses
Reflection
Absorption
Scattering
Conduction
Convection
Evaporation
Heat losses
Disease

Inefficiency of converting energy from one form to another
Stress – climatic, bullying, predation
Genetic potential
Poor nutrition
Plant and animal product removed from property

Mineral cycling in systems

Elements such as carbon, nitrogen and oxygen are constantly recycled between the living and non-living parts of the environment. Elements are neither created nor destroyed, but converted into different forms.

2.21 An ecosystem model showing the flow of energy and nutrients in a system

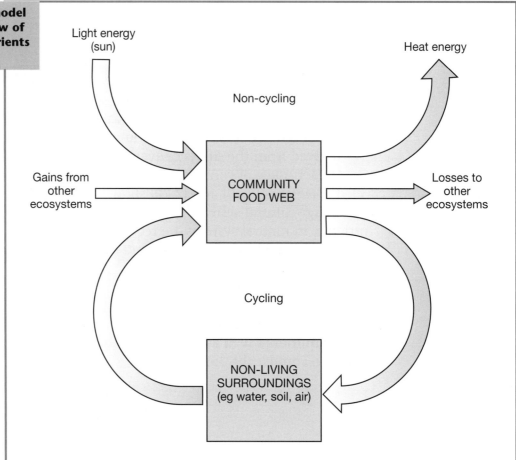

The water cycle

Water is essential for the survival of all living things. There is a continuous exchange of water between the earth and the atmosphere. Water is suspended in the atmosphere as water vapour and clouds. It falls to the ground in forms such as rain, snow and hail and is stored in the soil or in plants, animals, rivers, lakes, streams and oceans.

Water returns to the atmosphere via:
- evaporation from soil and water surfaces
- transpiration and respiration of plants
- sweating and respiration of animals.

This water vapour rises, then condenses to form clouds and continue the water cycle [2.22].

transpiration
the loss of water vapour from the surface of a plant

respiration
metabolic process of living organisms in which organic compounds are broken down to release energy as ATP

Activity 2.4

2.22 The water cycle

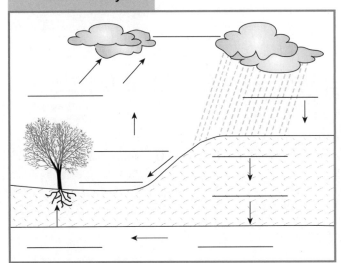

Diagram [2.22] is of the water cycle. Copy or trace the diagram into your workbook and label the diagram using the following words:
- absorption and storage
- condensation
- drainage
- evaporation
- infiltration
- precipitation
- runoff
- transpiration
- water uptake.

Practical 1

Measuring water quality

Aim

To measure the quality of water in a creek or dam

Equipment
- thermometer
- stop watch
- methylene blue
- salt meter or silver nitrate
- ascorbic acid
- string
- test tubes
- universal indicator
- sodium molybdate
- dip net

Method

1 Draw a map of the creek, river or dam.

Temperature

2 Using a thermometer measure the temperature of the water at the surface and at a depth of 10 centimetres.

(Note that the higher the temperature, the lower the amount of oxygen that is available for living organisms.)

Depth

3 Use a weight and string to measure the depth of the water.

Water flow

4 Find two points on the stream bank.
5 Measure the distance between the two points.
6 Throw a piece of wood into the creek and using a stop watch, record the time it takes for it to travel between the two points.
   Calculate the speed of the movement of the water using the formula Speed = distance divided by time.

Clarity of water

7 Collect a sample of water with a glass tube.

8 Record the clarity of the water.

Change of flow

9 Record any signs of change in the flow, for example flooding or weirs.

Smell

10 Smell a sample of water and rank on a scale of 1–10 where 0 = terrible; 5 = some smell; 7 = slight smell; 10 = no smell.

Floating or sunken objects

11 Record the presence of obstructions such as metal drums, tyres, bottles and rank the creek on a scale of 1–10 where 0 = many objects; 10 = zero objects.

Oxygen

12 Place a sample of water in a test tube.

13 Add three drops of methylene blue.

14 Note for fading of the blue colour.

15 At zero oxygen levels, methylene blue is colourless.

16 Rank the water on a scale of 1–10 where 0 = water is clear; 5 = some fading; 10 = blue.

Acidity

17 Add three drops of universal indicator to a sample of water.

18 Note the colour changes.

Colour	pH	Ranking
Red	acid 1-3	0
Green	neutral 6-7	10
Blue	alkali 11-14	0

Reading	Meaning	Score
00–05	Good	10
05–10	Fair	7
10–15	Average	5
15–25	Poor	3
More than 25	Very poor	0

The acidity level of water is influenced by rotting plants and animals and fertiliser runoff.

Salt level

19 Test a sample of water with the salt meter.

20 Rank the water accordingly.

If a salt meter is not available use the following method:

21 Half fill a test tube with water.

22 Add six drops of silver nitrate and record the cloudiness level.

23 Rank the water on a scale of 1–10 accordingly:
very cloudy=0; some cloudiness=5; clear=10.

Hardness

24 Half fill a test tube with water.

25 Add 3 drops of detergent and shake.

26 Rank the suds level on a scale of 1–10:few suds=0; slight suds=5; foam=10.

Phosphates

27 Place 2ml of water in a test tube.

28 Add 1ml of sodium molybdate solution and 0.5ml of ascorbic acid.

29 Blue colouration indicates the presence of phosphorus.

30 Rank on a scale of 1–10 where bright blue=0; pale blue=5; clear=10.

Animal life

31 Use a dip net to collect any organisms present.

32 Rank accordingly on a scale of 1–10 where no life=0; some life=5; many=10.

Human use

Monitor human use of the creek, for example for fishing and dumping waste.

Health of the creek

33 Calculate the health of the creek by calculating the total score and comparing it to the ratings of 80=excellent; 60=good; 40=fair; 20=poor; 0=terrible

Carbon and oxygen cycle

Carbon and oxygen are essential for life and photosynthesis. Respiration by plants and animals form the basis of the carbon–oxygen cycle.

During photosynthesis plants convert carbon dioxide and water into energy-rich compounds such as glucose.

Carbon dioxide is circulated by:

• plants releasing carbon dioxide during respiration
• animals eating the plants and releasing carbon dioxide during respiration
• microbes breaking down dead plants and animal remains
• the combustion of fuels for energy.

The cycle continues when plants use this carbon dioxide for photosynthesis.

2.23 The carbon cycle

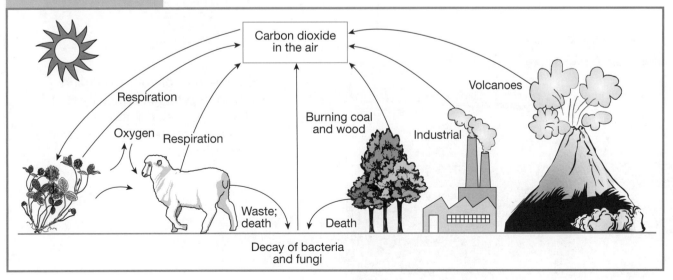

Nitrogen cycle

Nitrogen is essential for life and is a major constituent of all proteins. The atmosphere contains 78 per cent nitrogen but it is not available to plants and animals in this form.

Plants use soluble nitrate ions (NO_3) dissolved in soil moisture. These nitrate ions are derived from many sources including:

- lightning converting nitrogen and oxygen into dilute nitric acid that releases nitrate ions in the soil when it breaks down
- leguminous plants with nitrogen-fixing bacteria that convert atmospheric nitrogen into nitrates
- decomposition of plant and animal remains by soil bacteria
- free-living nitrogen-fixing bacteria in the soil converting atmospheric nitrogen into nitrates.

Other denitrifying bacteria return the nitrogen to the atmosphere and the cycle continues.

nitrate ions
chemical consisting of nitrogen and oxygen; salts or esters of nitric acid; used in explosives and fertilisers

leguminous
plants of the leguminosae family such as clover, peas and beans; root nodules contain rhizobium bacteria that can fix nitrogen

denitrifying
organisms such as bacteria that reduce nitrates to nitrites , nitrous oxide or nitrogen under anaerobic conditions to provide energy

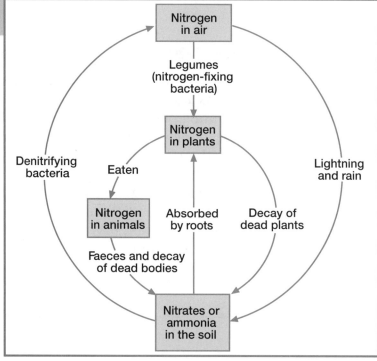

2.24 The nitrogen cycle

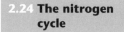

Activity 2.5

1. Outline the role of carbon and nitrogen cycles in agriculture.
2. How does the addition of superphosphate fertiliser affect the carbon cycle?

2.25 Fertiliser spreader

Natural and agricultural systems

An understanding of the similarities and differences between natural systems and agricultural systems is important in developing productive, sustainable agricultural practices.

Ecosystems

An ecosystem is a natural ecological unit and consists of living organisms that interact with themselves and the non-living environment.

An ecosystem consists of:

- producers
- consumers
- decomposers
- the non-living environment.

Natural systems are very complex, but are stable and self-regulating [2.26].

producers
organisms that make their own energy supplies; plants during photosynthesis make complex organic molecules from simple compounds

consumers
organisms that cannot create their own energy supplies and derive it from other sources, eg sheep eat grass

decomposers
organisms such as fungi and earthworms that break down plant and animal remains to derive their energy needs

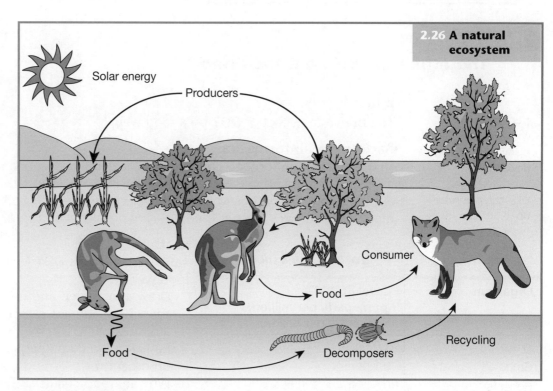

2.26 **A natural ecosystem**

AG FACT

Mammal extinction

Humans have destroyed many natural systems. They have also disrupted natural food chains and webs by introducing plants, animals, weeds, pests and diseases. Australia has one of the highest extinction rates of mammals in the world. In the last 200 years over half the mammals that have become extinct in the world have been Australian. Most of the Australian extinct and threatened mammals are medium sized and ground dwelling: the preferred diet of the introduced fox and feral cat.

2.27 A food web

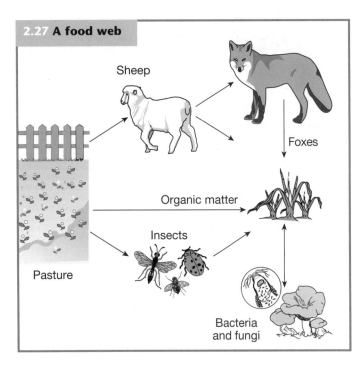

Sheep

Foxes

Organic matter

Insects

Pasture

Bacteria and fungi

Food chains and webs

Food chains show the movement of nutrients and energy within a community. All chains start with a plant and rarely have more than four links because of the loss of energy within the chain.

Food webs show how food chains interact and the relationships of the different organisms. Food webs help provide natural systems with their stability and balance.

Practical 2

The effect of DDT on a food web

persistent
chemical that takes many years to break down in the environment, eg DDT can persist for up to 50 years in the soil

Aim
To observe the effect of DDT on a food web.

Background information
DDT is a persistent organo-chloride insecticide. It is now banned because it was not biodegradable and accumulated in many food chains. DDT was absorbed into the body and because every member of a food chain ate many times its own mass in food, toxicity problems occurred.

Method
Table [2.28] shows DDT levels in a food web.

1 Draw a food web and use the data to show how humans can accumulate large amounts of DDT in their body.
2 Research the damaging effects of DDT on organisms.
3 Why are food chains and webs of importance to farmers?
4 How can farm chemicals disrupt food webs and create secondary pests?

2.28 DDT levels in a food web

Organism	Level of DDT (ppm=parts per million; ppb=parts per billion)
In soil	1.0 ppm
Crops	0.1 ppm
Rodents	0.5 ppm
Birds	1.0 ppm
Rodent predators	2.0 ppm
Cattle	1.0 ppm
River water	0.001 ppb
Marine plankton	0.01 ppm
Shellfish	1.0 ppm
Fish	0.5 ppm
Humans	5.0 ppm

Feature	Natural system	Agricultural system
Type of system	Naturally produced	Artificially produced
Number and type of organisms	Large number and great variety	Limited number and many introduced species
Complexity of system	Very complex	Simple, for example monocultures consist of areas of a single crop
Balance within system	Self regulating and balanced	Not balanced. Artificial chemicals such as pesticides, herbicides, drenches and vaccines must be used to control weeds, pests and diseases
Flow of energy and nutrients	Closed system. Matter does not leave system – energy is lost	Open system – matter and energy leave system as saleable products. Land is sometimes used beyond its capabilities with subsequent degradation of soils. Reduced fertility levels, poor structure, creation of clay pans, acidity, salinity and, leaching and erosion problems can occur. Artificial fertilisers are necessary to maintain fertility levels
Incidence of weeds, pests and diseases	Sometimes occur but are regulated by natural control methods such as predators and pathogens	Major problems: forced to use control methods such as insecticides and herbicides which have contaminated the environment, killed beneficial organisms and created secondary pests
Management of system	Self–regulated and in a state of equilibrium	Unbalanced, must be continually managed

2.29 Comparison of natural and agricultural systems

Activity 2.6

Compare and contrast the movement of energy and matter in a natural and an agricultural system.

Extension Activity

'An ecosystem is a cycle of materials driven by a flow of energy.'
Discuss this statement with reference to a particular ecosystem.

The farm ecosystem

In natural systems, nutrients are recycled and the system is usually in a state of balance that has been reached over a long period.

Farm systems, in contrast, are artificially created, have limited recycling and are not in a state of balance.

On a farm, the land is cleared, soil is cultivated, new plants and animals are introduced and artificial fertilisers, chemicals and technology are used. Farms have a greater loss of energy and materials because:
• the produce is harvested and sold
• naturally occurring balances and checks are removed.

Farmers must continually stabilise the system by controlling the living and non-living part of the environment.

Activity 2.7

1 Why are weeds, pests and diseases more important in an agricultural system than a natural system?
2 Why do agricultural systems require more management than natural systems?
3 Give examples of the mismanagement of a farm system.

Extension Activity

'The widespread use of chemicals has not eradicated one weed or pest.' Explain why this is the case.

Problems in agriculture

Through bad management, ignorance or greed, some farmers have created many problems including:
• loss of natural areas and species, for example loss of farm trees and associated flora and fauna
• depletion of non-renewable resources such as topsoil
• exploitation of resources, for example using land beyond its capabilities, which causes soil degradation and subsequent problems of reduced fertility levels, poor structure, clay pans, acidity, salinity and erosion problems
• contamination of the environment with the use of artificial chemicals such as DDT
• creation of weeds, pests and diseases by the destruction of natural regulators.

These problems can be resolved by a greater understanding of the environment and how natural systems operate.

Activity 2.8

Graph [2.30] shows the growth in the size of the world's population.
a   What is the shape of the graph?
b   What pressures does population size impose on natural and agricultural systems?

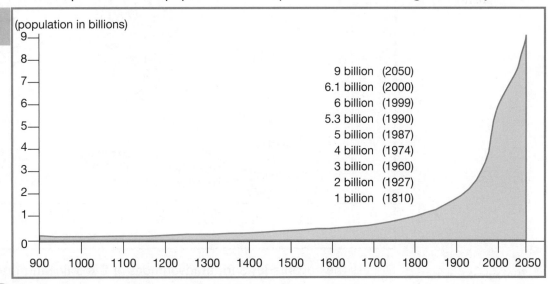

2.30 Population of the world

(population in billions)

9 billion   (2050)
6.1 billion (2000)
6 billion   (1999)
5.3 billion (1990)
5 billion   (1987)
4 billion   (1974)
3 billion   (1960)
2 billion   (1927)
1 billion   (1810)

Practical 3

Effect of agriculture on a natural system

Aim
To research the effect of agriculture on a natural system.

Method
1   Select a region and compare present conditions with those that existed before European settlement.
2   Compare similarities and differences including many criteria such as the effect on climate, topography, vegetation, resources, flora and fauna, human developments and the incidence of pollution, weeds, pests and diseases.

Results
Present your results in tabular form.

Activity 2.9

Refer to the following Internet sites for information on natural resource degradation. Summarise the information into a useful form.
www.dnr.nsw.gov.au (Department of Natural Resources)
www.mdbc.gov.au (Murray Darling Basin Commission)

Extension Activity

Discuss the impact of physical, biological, social, historical and economic factors on systems.

Research 2.10

Traditionally cotton growing included some damaging environmental practices.

2.31 Life cycle of cotton

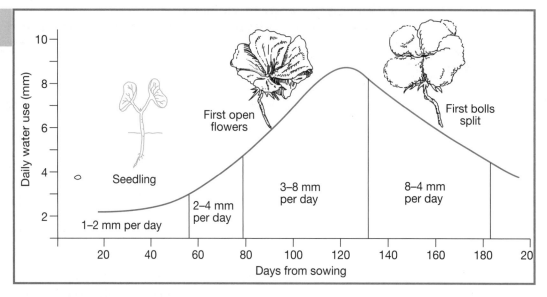

Discuss the advantages and disadvantages of the following practices:

a cultivation and minimum tillage practices
b varying irrigation techniques, for example flood irrigation and drip irrigation
c chemical usage, for example insecticides and defoliants
d problems of spray drift
e chemical residues in beef fed cotton trash
f genetically engineered plants, for example transgenic Bt cotton
g biological control methods, for example envirofeast an artificial food spray used on refuge crops such as lucerne to promote beneficial organisms.

biological control strategy for the control of pests or disease-causing organisms that uses other living organisms rather than chemical pesticides

Revision 2.11

1 Define the following words:
   - system
   - boundaries
   - the nitrogen cycle
   - food web
   - inputs
   - black box model
   - ecosystem
   - processes
   - the water cycle
   - food chain

2 Answer true or false to the following statements
   a Inputs are the raw materials used to make a product.
   b Money is a boundary.
   c Drenching and vaccinating are examples of processes.
   d Energy is not lost in natural systems.
   e All elements are recycled in a cropping system.
   f Chemicals can accumulate in food chains.
   g Water is continually being created.
   h Salinity has no effect on water quality.
   i Photosynthesis is essential for life.
   j Natural systems are stable and self regulated.

3 See page 385 for the find-a-word activity.

LOW x
[995]

996

Climate

3

chapter

In this chapter you will learn about:

- Australia's climatic elements
- the effect of radiation and temperature
- the water cycle
- how carbon dioxide and oxygen are produced
- how climate can be controlled.

The elements of climate

Climate is one of the key factors affecting agriculture. It determines what can be grown in an area and the degree of success. Climate is the general pattern of weather in a region over an extended period. It consists of many variables [3.1].

There are many climates in Australia because of:
- the tilt of the earth and the varying radiation it receives
- varying latitudes
- altitudes
- wind circulation patterns around the world
- the effect of warm and cold ocean currents
- local factors, for example mountains.

radiation
electromagnetic waves produced by the sun

latitudes
angular distance north or south (on the meridian) of a location

altitudes
height above sea level of a point or place

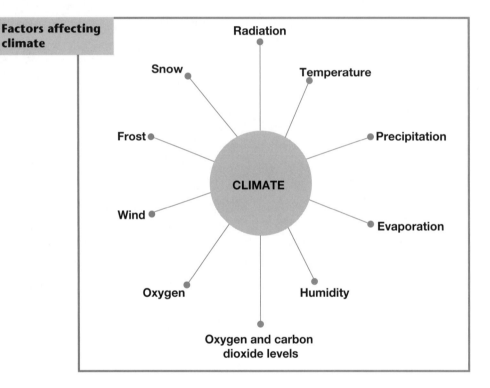

3.1 **Factors affecting climate**

Radiation
Snow
Temperature
Frost
Precipitation
CLIMATE
Wind
Evaporation
Oxygen
Humidity
Oxygen and carbon dioxide levels

Activity 3.1

1 Using map [3.2] determine the climates of the following places:
a Darwin
b Canberra
c Perth
d Alice Springs
e Brisbane
f Hobart.

2 Refer to the weather map [3.3] and state the conditions in the following areas:
a Darwin
b Canberra
c Perth
d Alice Springs
e Brisbane
f Hobart.

3 Explain why the daily weather conditions might be important to a producer who is:
a harvesting wheat
b making hay
c lambing
d sowing a crop.

4   Use the Internet to find the current weather and predicted conditions for your area.

3.2   Climatic regions of Australia

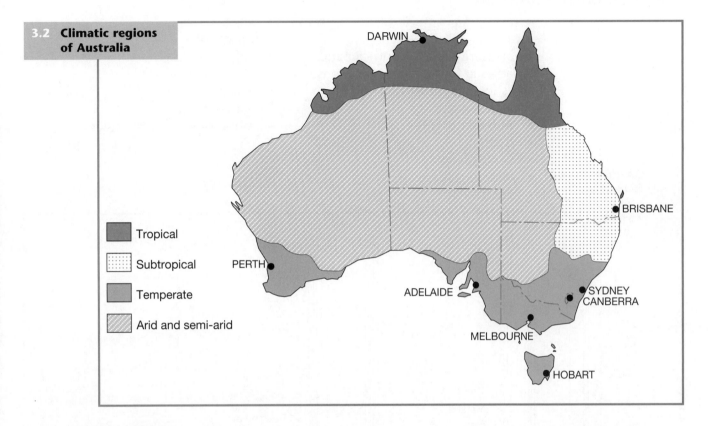

Tropical

Subtropical

Temperate

Arid and semi-arid

3.3   Weather map

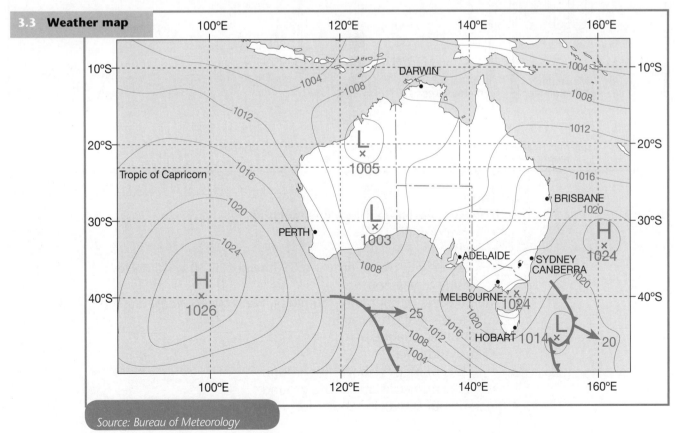

Source: Bureau of Meteorology

Practical ④

Climatic variation

Aim

To measure the following climatic variables in four different locations and show how they vary within small distances:

- temperature
- humidity
- wind speed
- wind direction
- light levels.

Equipment

- 30-centimetre ruler
- thermometer
- psychrometer
- anemometer
- photographic light meter.

3.4 Equipment used to measure climatic variables

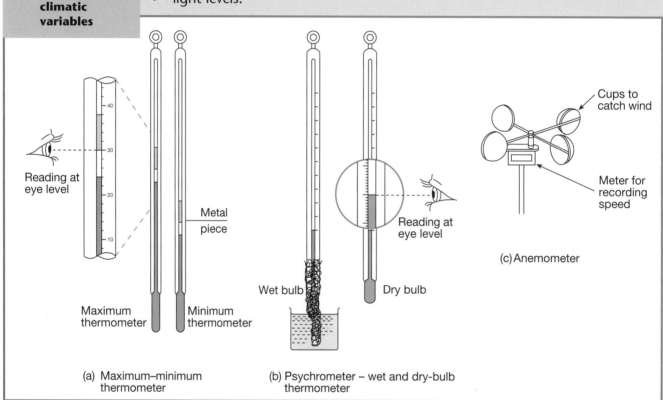

(a) Maximum–minimum thermometer

(b) Psychrometer – wet and dry-bulb thermometer

(c) Anemometer

Method

1. Choose four different localities, such as:
   - bare ground
   - a dam
   - a crop with plants growing to a height of 30 centimetres
   - inside a glasshouse.
2. Measure the temperature, humidity, wind speed, wind direction, and light levels at each location.
3. Record the variables at:
   - ground level
   - 10 centimetres above the ground
   - 30 centimetres above the ground.
4. Record your results in tabular form and state your conclusions.

Radiation

Radiation consists of electromagnetic waves produced by the sun. It includes visible sunlight, invisible heat rays and ultraviolet rays that reach the earth at a constant rate. However, different places receive different amounts of radiation because of the tilt of the earth.

3.5 The tilt of the earth and day and night

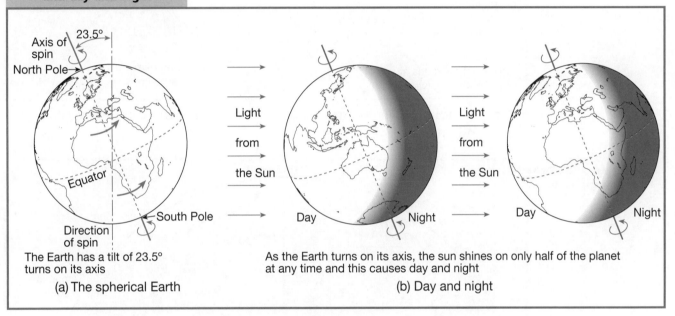

The Earth has a tilt of 23.5° turns on its axis

(a) The spherical Earth

As the Earth turns on its axis, the sun shines on only half of the planet at any time and this causes day and night

(b) Day and night

The amount of radiation reaching the earth has a major effect on the temperature of the earth, day length and seasons. It also affects:

• the climate in a particular region
• photosynthesis by plants
• plant and animal reproduction
• evaporation and transpiration
• nutrient uptake by plants
• wind production
• advection
• vitamin D production, sunburn and skin cancers.

Radiation heats the earth and prevents temperatures falling below critically low levels where life could not exist. As the earth turns on its axis, the sun only shines on half the planet at a time and this causes day and night.

The earth has a tilt of 23.5 degrees. The part of the earth tilted towards the sun receives more direct rays and has longer days and experiences summer. In the regions tilted away from the sun, the sun's energy hits the earth at an oblique angle and so they are less concentrated, resulting in winter and shorter days. In tropical regions radiation levels are similar all year so there is very little seasonal variation.

advection
the horizontal transfer of energy or heat in the atmosphere

The earth takes 365.25 days to circle the sun and this is the basis for calculating a year [3.6].

3.6 **The 24-hour day and the seasons**

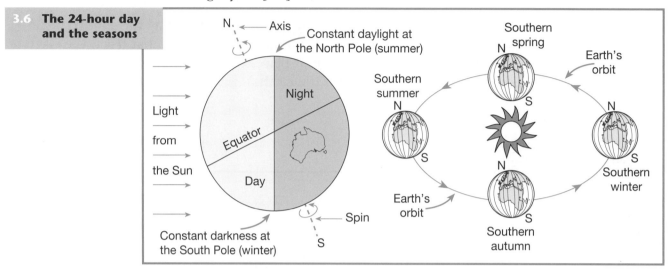

Varying radiation levels create different climates with their own specific plants and animals [3.7].

3.7 **The world's broad climatic zones**

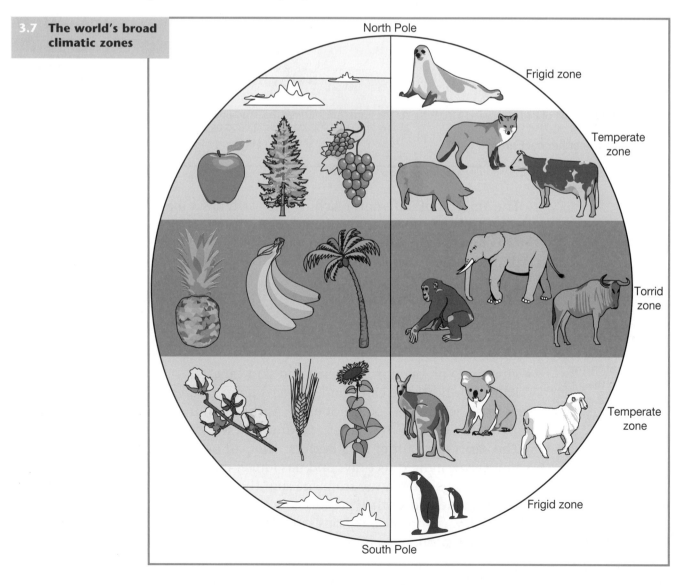

3.8 Deciduous trees, such as this oak, lose their leaves in winter so photosynthesis is limited in this season

Radiation and photosynthesis

Photosynthesis takes place in the green parts of plants such as leaves. During photosynthesis, plants convert carbon dioxide and water into energy-rich sugars such as glucose and create oxygen. Sunlight is essential for this reaction to occur. Without photosynthesis living things that depend on oxygen could not survive.

Radiation and reproduction

Day length has a major effect on plant and animal reproduction. Many plants have a light and darkness requirement to flower. There are short-day plants, long-day plants and day-neutral plants.

Short-day plants, such as daffodils and tulips, require less than 14 hours of daylight and an uninterrupted dark period to flower. Long-day plants, such as clover and radishes, require more than 14 hours of daylight and do not have a set dark requirement.

Plants such as tomatoes and carnations are not affected by light or darkness levels, and flower regardless of these.

Day length and light intensity also affect the growth and reproduction of birds and animals. Poultry lay more eggs in the spring because increasing day length promotes hormone production. Poultry are housed under increasing light conditions so that they produce eggs for the entire year.

3.10 The reproduction cycle of these geese is affected by day length

3.9 Light and dark requirements of plants		
Short day	**Long day**	**Neutral**
Strawberry	Radish	Dandelion
Cosmos	Spinach	Cucumber
Tobacco	Lettuce	Tomato

AG FACT

Geese

Artificial light is used to bring geese into production at times other than the normal production season. Benefits include earlier production and prevention of a sharp decrease in laying performance.

lux
a unit of measurement equal to one lumen per square metre

Bright light up to a maximum intensity of 50 lux also promotes egg laying whereas dim light reduces production. Dim light can be used to delay sexual maturity so that birds are bigger and produce larger eggs when they commence laying.

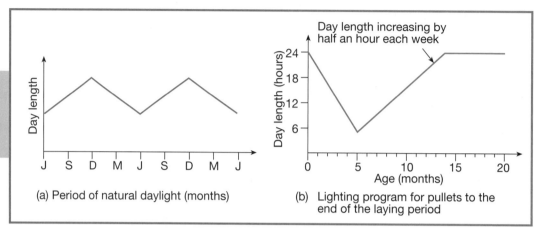

3.11 Normal day length and day length in an intensive poultry unit

(a) Period of natural daylight (months)

(b) Lighting program for pullets to the end of the laying period

3.12 These Border Leicester sheep are a British breed

Day length can also have a marked effect on the reproductive cycle of sheep. Sheep detect changing day length and this stimulates the release of hormones from the pituitary gland resulting in the initiation of the oestrous cycle. Some breeds such as the merino will mate throughout the year, whereas many British breeds conceive more readily in autumn when day length is decreasing.

oestrous
period when ova are released from the female's ovary, the animal comes on heat and mating occurs

concentration gradient
the number of molecules or ions in a given volume; results in water moving from a high concentration to a low concentration

Radiation and evaporation

Radiation increases evaporation rates reducing the amount of water available to plants.

Radiation, transpiration and nutrient uptake

Transpiration is the loss of water vapour from the surface of a plant. It keeps plants cool and increases nutrient uptake by providing a concentration gradient for water to move between the roots and leaves. However, excessive transpiration is undesirable as it can result in wilting and death.

Radiation and wind production

Wind is the horizontal movement of air across the surface of the earth. The land and sea absorb different amounts of radiant heat. As the land heats up, the air above it rises and is replaced by cooler air from the sea. This circulation generates wind including sea breezes.

Wind has many beneficial effects on agricultural production by:
- increasing pollination
- dispersing seed
- generating power, for example wind power
- pumping water
- increasing transpiration and water and nutrient uptake by plants.

However, wind also has many detrimental effects as it can:
- increase erosion
- increase evaporation and transpiration rates
- transmit diseases, such as moulds, mildews and rusts
- lodge crops
- damage sensitive flowers and reduce yields
- blow salt spray onto salt-sensitive plants
- damage produce, for example by knocking fruit off trees
- cause mass destruction by cyclones and tornadoes
- stress plants and animals, for example cold chilling winds can kill newborn lambs.

lodge
blow over

Activity 3.2

1 A study of lambing percentages on two properties in the Central Tablelands produced the results shown in [3.13].
a What was the average lambing percentage for sheltered paddocks?
b What was the average lambing percentage for open paddocks?
c Why were the survival rates higher in the sheltered paddocks?
d What other factors including those caused by poor experimental design could have affected the results?

3.13 Lambing percentages

| | Year | | | | |
Lambing percentage	1	2	3	4	5
In sheltered paddocks	100	115	110	115	118
In open paddocks	95	100	105	110	85

3.14 Windbreak design

Wind

Wind

2 Draw a plan similar to the one in [3.14] and show where trees should be planted to protect lambing ewes.

3.15 Pigs are susceptible to sunburn

Radiation and advection

Advection is the horizontal movement of energy in the atmosphere. It is undesirable in dry-land irrigation areas because it increases evaporation rates and therefore irrigation costs.

Vitamin D, sunburn and skin cancers

Vitamin D controls the absorption of calcium from the intestines and its deposition in bones. Vitamin D is produced when ultraviolet rays touch the skin. Deficiency of vitamin D can result in rickets and badly formed teeth.

Sunburn and skin cancers are caused by excessive ultraviolet light damaging skin cells. Both sunburn and skin cancers reduce productivity and are of major concern in the pig and cattle industry [3.15].

Practical 5

The relationship between light and photosynthesis

Aim
To show that light is necessary for photosynthesis to occur.

Equipment
- potted plant
- piece of cork 1 centimetre ✕ 1 centimetre
- pins
- iodine solution.

Method
1. Place the cork on one of the plant's leaves.
2. Secure the cork with pins so that no light can reach the tissue.
3. Place the plant near the window for several days.
4. Remove the leaf and cork disc.
5. Place the iodine solution on different parts of the leaf to test for starch.

Results and conclusion
Record your results and state your conclusions.

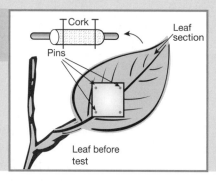

3.16 Partially cover leaf with cork

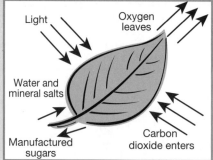

3.17 Iodine turns blue in the presence of starch

Extension Activity

'Radiation is the basis of life.' Discuss this statement.

Temperature

Temperature is a measure of a body's heat or coldness and has a major effect on:
- the type of plants and animals that can be grown in an area
- the rate of weathering and soil formation
- the rate of all biological and chemical reactions
- microbial activity.

Organisms only exist within a certain range of temperatures, called their cardinal temperature range. The maximum and minimum temperatures are the highest and lowest temperatures, respectively, that the organism can tolerate. The optimum temperature is the temperature at which the organism has greatest productivity.

microbial
at a scale that can only be seen with the aid of a microscope, for example organisms such as bacteria, fungi and protozoa

Temperature and animal production

Excessively high temperatures are undesirable and can:
- cause heat stress
- reduce appetite, shorten grazing periods and reduce food intake
- reduce productivity, for example decrease milk production
- reduce milk solids, produce inferior sperm and create thin eggshells
- cause death
- increase production costs for housing and cooling systems.

Excessively low temperatures are also detrimental and can:
- increase food consumption
- reduce respiration rates
- reduce food conversion efficiency
- increase heating costs
- cause death, for example of newborn lambs.

Activity 3.3

Table [3.18] shows the cardinal temperature range for different animals:
a   Which animal tolerates the highest and lowest temperatures?
b   Which animal has the greatest range in cardinal temperatures?
c   How can a producer make use of this information?

3.18 Critical temperatures (degrees Centigrade) for different animals

Animal	Lower critical temperature	Upper critical temperature
Broiler cockerels	16	26
Laying hens	13	23
Adult pigs	21	27
Steers	13	29

Temperature and plant production

Excessively high temperatures are undesirable in plant production and can:
- increase evaporation rates
- increase transpiration rates
- damage floral parts
- reduce yields
- cause wilting
- kill the plant.

Excessively low temperatures are also undesirable and can:
- cause dormancy, for example in grapes, peaches and plums
- reduce germination rates
- destroy flowers
- reduce yields
- cause death.

dormancy
a period of reduced metabolic activity as in seeds and dormant buds

3.19 Frost kills pumpkin flowers

Activity 3.4

3.20 Cardinal temperatures of different crops

| Plant | Cardinal temperature °C | | |
	Minimum	Optimum	Maximum
Wheat	0–5	25–31	31–37
Barley	0–5	25–31	31–37
Oats	0–5	25–31	31–37
Rye	0–5	25–31	31–37
Sunflower	4–11	31–37	36–44
Maize	4–10	36–44	43–50

Source: Bamden FW, Agricultural Studies for Secondary Schools, Longman Cheshire, Melbourne, 1985

Table [3.20] shows the cardinal temperature range for different crops:
a   Which crops withstand the lowest and highest temperatures?
b   Could maize be grown in temperate regions?
c   Why are crops classified as summer or winter growing?

Activity 3.5

The maps on the following page show average July temperatures [3.21] and number of frost-free days in Australia [3.22].
a   In what areas could low temperatures restrict agricultural production?
b   Which areas experience the greatest number of frosts?
c   How can the producer minimise the effects of frosts and low temperatures?

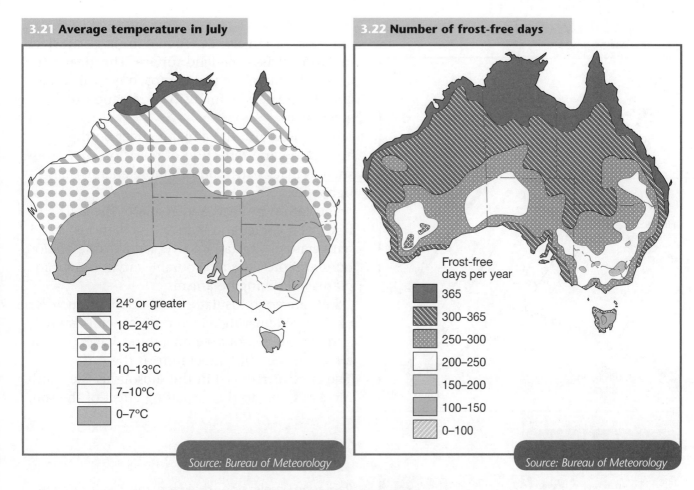

3.21 Average temperature in July

24° or greater
18–24°C
13–18°C
10–13°C
7–10°C
0–7°C

Source: Bureau of Meteorology

3.22 Number of frost-free days

Frost-free
days per year

365
300–365
250–300
200–250
150–200
100–150
0–100

Source: Bureau of Meteorology

Soil temperature

The temperature of the soil has a major effect on:
- the physical weathering of rock
- soil formation
- structure of soil aggregates
- rate of all chemical and biological reactions
- germination
- root growth
- absorption and transport of water and nutrients by plants
- plant yields
- microbial activity
- nutrient cycling.

The temperature of the soil is governed by many factors including:
- climate, for example seasonal temperatures and radiation levels
- aspect and topography
- soil colour
- amount of vegetation cover
- soil moisture content
- depth.

Soils are warmer in hotter climates, and in spring and summer because of higher temperature and radiation levels. Topography and aspect also affect soil temperature. In the southern hemisphere soils facing north are warmer

aspect
the direction in which the land faces

3.23 Aspect, slope and radiation levels

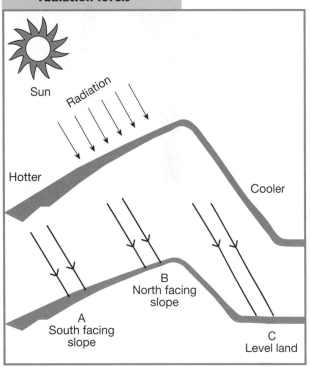

Sun

Radiation

Hotter

Cooler

A
South facing
slope

B
North facing
slope

C
Level land

because the sun's rays are concentrated in that direction. Aspect also determines the angle at which radiation strikes the land surface. The greater the angle, the more the rays approach perpendicular and the greater the intensity of radiation per given area.

Soil colour also has a major effect on the absorption and reflection of radiation. Dark soils, such as black earths absorb more energy than light soils.

Vegetation protects and insulates the soil. It keeps it cooler and reduces fluctuations in temperature. Vegetation cover reduces evaporation rates and provides a favourable environment for plants and living organisms.

Soils are good insulators and poor conductors of heat. Fluctuating day and night temperatures and varying seasonal temperatures have a major effect on the soil temperature at the surface. The effect is reduced in the subsoils as the depth increases, due to the insulating effect of the soil.

Activity 3.6

3.24 Topography, aspect and viticulture

Radiation levels, poor drainage and the incidence of frosts and mould can have a significant effect on grape production.

Explain why topography and aspect are critical in the design of vineyards.

Practical 6

The application of mulches

3.25 Mulched plants

Aim
To see the effect of mulches on the temperature and moisture content of the soil.

Equipment
- 4 bare pots of soil of about 1 square metre
- grass cuttings, plastic sheeting and bark
- thermometer
- scales
- oven.

Method

1 Leave plot 1 bare. Cover plot 2 with grass cuttings; plot 3 with plastic sheeting and plot 4 with bark.
2 At regular periods during the day:
   a Measure the temperature of the four plots.
   b Remove a sample of soil from each plot.
   c Weigh 50 grams of the soil and heat it in the oven until all water has been removed and then reweigh it.
   d Calculate the percentage moisture content in each sample using the following equation:
      Let A be the original weight of the sample
      and B be the weight of the oven dry sample.
      Percentage moisture content $= 100 \times (A - B)/A$.
   e Record the presence of any organisms in the plots
3 For each plot draw a graph of:
   a temperature versus time and
   b moisture content versus time.

Results

1 Which plot has the highest moisture content?
2 Which plot had the least fluctuations in temperature?
3 Which plot had the greatest number of organisms present?

Extension Activity

Explain the relationship between above-ground and soil temperature patterns and discuss their effect on plant growth.

Activity 3.7

3.26 Effect of sowing date on yield

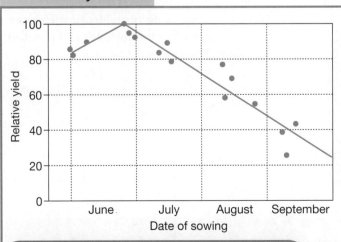

Source: Adapted from Lovett, JV et al, Plant Production Systems, *University of New England, Armidale, 1984, page 6*

1 The graph [3.26] shows the effect of the time of sowing on wheat yields.
   a What yields are obtained if wheat is planted in June or September?
   b What is the optimum planting date?
   c What climatic factors could cause the sharp decline in yields?

Vegetable	Tropical/subtropical												Warm/temperate												Cool											
	J	F	M	A	M	J	J	A	S	O	N	D	J	F	M	A	M	J	J	A	S	O	N	D	J	F	M	A	M	J	J	A	S	O	N	D
Beans	•	•	•	•	•	•	•	•	•	•	•	•	•	•					•	•	•	•			•									•	•	•
Beetroot	•	•	•	•	•	•	•	•	•	•	•		•	•		•			•	•	•	•	•		•	•								•	•	•
Carrot	•	•	•	•	•	•	•	•	•	•	•		•	•		•			•	•	•	•	•		•	•								•	•	•
Cauliflower	•	•	•	•									•	•							•													•	•	
Lettuce	•	•	•	•	•	•	•	•	•	•	•	•	•	•	•	•	•	•	•	•	•	•	•	•	•	•	•	•	•	•	•	•	•	•	•	•
Onion	•	•	•	•												•	•	•	•	•	•								•	•	•	•	•			
Peas			•	•	•	•	•	•								•	•	•	•	•	•	•									•	•	•	•	•	
Potato	•	•	•	•	•					•										•	•	•	•							•	•	•		•	•	•
Pumpkin	•	•					•	•	•	•	•									•	•	•	•											•	•	•
Sweet corn	•	•				•	•	•	•	•							•			•	•	•	•											•	•	•

Source: Adapted from Bannerman S et al, Enterprising Agriculture, Macmillan, Melbourne, 2001

3.28 The back of a seed packet

Carrot
Navarre FL

"One of the best for taste, quantity and quality – bumper crops with a delicious sweet flavour and bright colour throughout the smooth cylindrical 'Nantes type' roots."

Grows well in any open position in a light, rich soil, preferably which has not been recently manured.

GROWING FROM SEED

Seedlings emerge in 14–21 days.
Sow: In all states, all year round, direct 5mm (quarter inch) deep in rows 30cm (12in) apart. Thin seedlings to 7.5cm (3in) apart, water well to replace dislodged soil. Repeat sowings at two weekly intervals for a continuous supply.

Tip: An extra row thinned to only 3cm (1.5in) can be pulled as finger carrots when only 7–8cm long and eaten whole, raw or cooked.

Ideal for deep freezing.

Harvest: 16 to 18 weeks from sowing. Start early to spread the harvest and allow remaining roots to grow larger.

2 Table [3.27] shows a planting guide for vegetables.
  a What plants can be grown in winter in the temperate region?
  b Which vegetables grow throughout the year in the temperate zone?
  c Which vegetables have the greatest restrictions?
3 Use the information on the seed packet [3.28]:
  a What season should sowing occur in Victoria?
  b What is the growing period of the plant?
  c How should the seeds be sown?
4 Develop a vegetable growing program for your region so that vegetables are planted and eaten throughout the year.

Extension Activity

'The climate and soil provide the plant with its most basic chemical and physical resources.' Discuss this statement.

The water cycle

Water is one of the most limiting factors affecting agricultural production. Water occurs as many forms, such as:

- rain
- snow
- hail
- dew.

Water is continually recycled through natural processes [3.29].

3.29 The water cycle

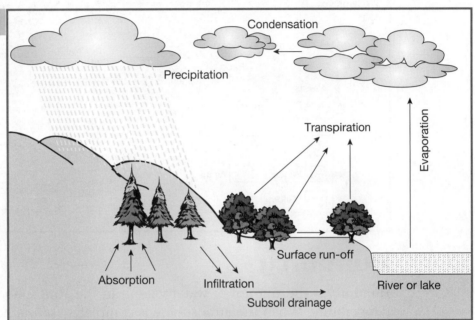

Clouds and rain

Clouds consist of suspended water droplets or ice crystals. Water evaporates from plants, rivers, lakes and oceans and is moved by air currents into the atmosphere where it cools and condenses into clouds.

Rain occurs when small water droplets attach themselves to dust, smoke and salt particles.

Dew, frosts, snow and hail

Dews occur when air cools at night and water vapour condenses into liquid.

Frosts occur when water vapour cools and forms ice on the ground when temperatures drop below freezing.

Snow is formed when water vapour condenses at temperatures below freezing point and forms ice crystals.

Activity 3.8

Study the information presented in map [3.30] over the page.
a   Which areas have predominantly summer or winter rainfall?
b   Which areas have uniform rainfall?
c   How do the different rainfall zones effect producers?

3.30 **Seasonal rainfall zones in Australia**

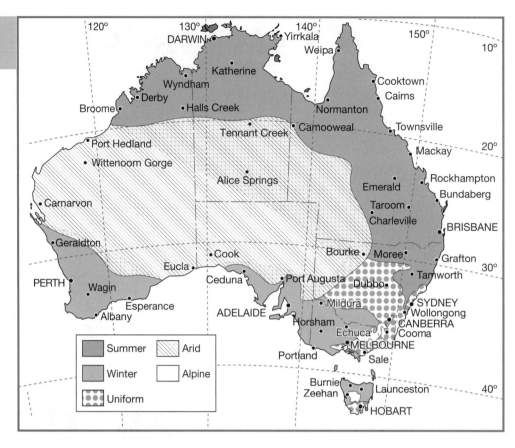

3.30 Seasonal rainfall zones in Australia

Legend:
- Summer
- Winter
- Uniform
- Arid
- Alpine

Humidity

Humidity is the amount of water vapour in the atmosphere at a particular temperature. When the atmosphere is completely saturated with water, its relative humidity is 100 per cent.

Humidity is very important and has a major effect on:
- the formation of clouds, rain, frosts, snow and hail
- evaporation and transpiration rates
- the incidence of plant diseases, such as mould and mildew
- the ability of animals to keep cool by sweating or evaporating water from their skin.

Evaporation and transpiration

Evaporation and transpiration occur because water moves from a high concentration on the plant or soil surface to a lower concentration in the atmosphere. High humidity reduces evaporation and transpiration rates, as the air is saturated with water vapour. Evaporation and transpiration are greatest when humidity is low because there is very little water in the atmosphere.

AG FACT

Rainfall reliability

The seasonality and reliability of rainfall is as important as total amount. Northern Australia has a monsoonal season and rainfall reliability declines from coastal regions to the arid centre of Australia.

Rainfall and agricultural production

Rainfall directly affects the type of agriculture that can be conducted in an area and its degree of success. Rainfall varies in total amount; seasonal distribution and reliability because of mass air circulations, ocean influences, topography and local airflows.

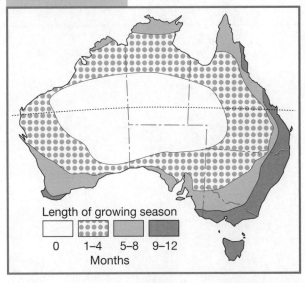

3.31 **The length of growing season in Australia**

Length of growing season

| 0 | 1–4 | 5–8 | 9–12 |

Months

Effective rainfall

Effective rainfall is rainfall that is in excess of evaporative demands. Its effectiveness depends on:
• the amount that falls
• its seasonality
• its intensity
• and how much is absorbed or lost as runoff.

   A great deal of water is not available to plants because it is lost through runoff, drainage or evaporation.

Growing season

The growing period of a plant is the time from germination to harvesting of the product. The growing season is the number of consecutive months of effective rainfall, and directly affects the type of plants that can be grown in a region. The shorter the growing season the greater are the restrictions on the type of plants that can be grown in that region.

Activity 3.9

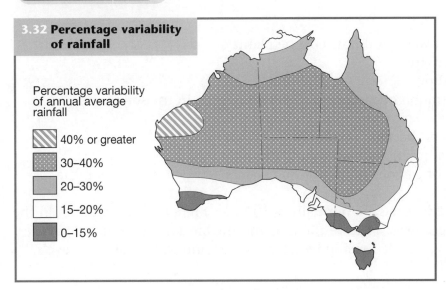

3.32 **Percentage variability of rainfall**

Percentage variability of annual average rainfall

	40% or greater
	30–40%
	20–30%
	15–20%
	0–15%

Using the information on [3.32]:
a What regions of Australia have the most reliable and unreliable rainfall?
b Why do farmers in arid regions undertake opportunity cropping?
c How does rainfall reliability influence the risk level of agriculture?

Extension Activity

'Algae is caused by climatic factors and poor management practices.'
Discuss this statement.

3.33 Water polluted with algae

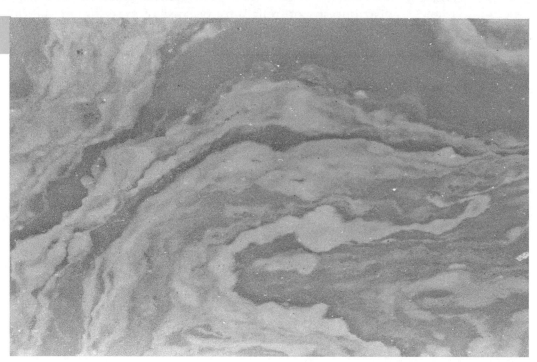

porosity
the relative percentage of air spaces in the soil; the greater the porosity the greater the aeration, water storage and drainage

gaseous exchange
the movement of gas particles such as carbon dioxide and oxygen in the soil

inverse relationship
two factors directly affecting the level of each other such as increasing oxygen levels decrease carbon dioxide levels

Carbon dioxide and oxygen

Carbon dioxide and oxygen are essential for photosynthesis and the survival of most living things, including humans.

The levels of oxygen and carbon dioxide in the soil have a major effect on:
• photosynthesis
• respiration
• root growth
• absorption of water and nutrients by plants
• microbial activity
• nutrient cycling.

The concentration of carbon dioxide and oxygen in the soil is determined by:
• the porosity of the soil
• the biological reactions that occur within the soil
• the amount of gaseous exchange that occurs between the soil and the atmosphere.

Carbon dioxide levels are normally 3–50 times higher in the soil than in the atmosphere because of plant respiration and the breakdown of organic matter. There is an inverse relationship between oxygen and carbon dioxide levels.

nitrification
the conversion of organic nitrogen compounds into nitrates by nitrifying bacteria

anaerobic
a chemical reaction that occurs in the absence of oxygen

Insufficient oxygen can result in
- poor root growth
- decreased absorption of water and nutrients by plants
- reduced plant yields
- reduced microbial activity, for example nitrogen fixation, nitrification and mineralisation
- loss of valuable nitrogen from the soil by denitrifying bacteria
- release of toxic inorganic compounds during anaerobic decomposition of organic matter.

Activity 3.10

3.34 The level of porosity in the soil and its effect on plant yields

Porosity level %	Relative yield in tonnes per hectare
2	0
5	0.2
7	0.4
10	0.6
15	0.7
20	0.7

Table [3.34] shows the results of an experiment conducted to see the effect of soil porosity levels on plant yields.
a   Graph these results.
b   What conclusions can be drawn from the results?

Controlling climate

Climate is one of the major factors affecting agricultural production. Humans have maximised production by altering the climate or modifying their operations to match their climate.

Methods commonly used include:
- using plants and animals suited to a particular climate, for example using Brahman cattle for hot tropical conditions

3.35 Hay carting in the 1930s

- selectively breeding plants and animals to suit a particular climate, for example Droughtmaster cattle for dry tropical conditions
- planning operations to match the climate, for example lambing in spring when there is plenty of feed
- irrigation, which reduces seasonal variability and provides adequate water at critical periods
- housing animals, for example pigs and poultry
- cutting hay and storing it
- planting or building windbreaks to reduce wind speed, evaporation and transpiration and to shelter animals
- mulching soils to reduce runoff, erosion and evaporation and provide a more favourable environment for plants and soil organisms

Courtesy of Doug Wythes

3.36 Glasshouses help control climate

- using conservation works to reduce runoff and erosion
- using sprinkler systems, fans and oil burners to reduce the incidence of frosts in orchards
- using hail nets and sound guns to reduce the incidence of hail damage in orchards
- growing plants in glasshouses
- building terraces on sloping country to maximise land and water use
- using refrigeration to prolong the storage life of products
- building dams for periods of water shortage
- keeping reserves for periods of drought, for example grain, hay and silage
- diversification, for example growing more than one product to stabilise income during periods of drought
- insurance against flooding, drought and bushfires
- long-term weather forecasting to allow the farmer to plan for the future.

Revision 3.11

1 Inspect the photos [3.35] – [3.38] and explain how the operations depicted assist the producer in coping with climatic extremes.
2 Answer true or false to the following statements.
   a Australia has many different climates.
   b Plant and animal reproduction is affected by day length.
   c Evaporation is the loss of water vapour from plants.
   d Transpiration assists nutrient uptake.
   e Light is essential for photosynthesis to occur.
   f High temperatures do not affect productivity as much as cold temperatures.
   g Sowing date can have a marked effect on crop yields.
   h High humidity levels promote plant growth.
   l Effective rainfall equals the annual rainfall of a region.
   j Oxygen and carbon dioxide levels cannot be regulated to increase plant growth.
3 See page 386 for the find-a-word activity.

3.37 Drilling for water

3.38 Sprinkler systems in orchards

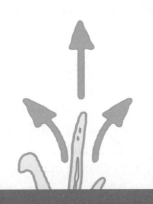

Soil and Water Resources

In this chapter you will learn about:

- constituents of soil
- formation of soils and factors affecting rate of soil formation
- human effects on soil
- soil types in Australia and the physical properties of the soil
- soil fertility and nutrient cycling
- soil degradation and management
- conservation and farming
- salinity
- water quality.

chapter

4

Constituents of soil

infiltration
downward movement of water into the soil

plasticity
ability to mould soils like plasticine – very plastic soils can compact and form clay pans if cultivated when wet

bearing strength
amount of force a soil can withstand without compaction – sandy soils have a higher bearing strength than clay-textured soils

Soils are derived from weathered rock and consist of:
• mineral matter such as sand, silt and clay
• organic matter
• water
• air
• living organisms.
The relative amounts of sand, silt and clay have a major effect on the soil's:
• fertility level
• water infiltration and drainage characteristics
• water-holding capacity
• ease of cultivation, for example plasticity and rigidity
• bearing strength
• ability to shrink and swell
• susceptibility to erosion.

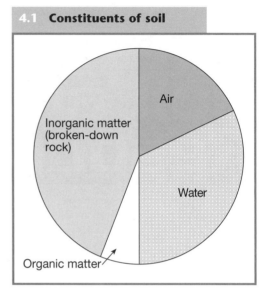

4.1 Constituents of soil

Practical 7

Constituents of soil

Aim
To identify the constituents of a soil.

Background information
Sand, silt and clay can be separated in water because they have different-sized particles. Sand has the largest-sized particles and sinks to the bottom whereas fine clay particles will float on the surface.

Equipment
• 150 grams of soil
• measuring cylinder
• water

Method
1 Weigh 150 grams of soil.
2 Place the soil in the measuring cylinder.
3 Fill the container two-thirds with water to help break down the particles.
4 Cover the end of the cylinder and shake it vigorously.
5 Place the cylinder on a bench and allow to stand for 24 hours.

Results and conclusion
1 Draw and label the layers of soil.
2 Look at the size of the different layers and calculate the relative percentage of sand, silt and clay present.
3 Identify the soil type.
4 What are the characteristics of this soil type?

Formation of soils

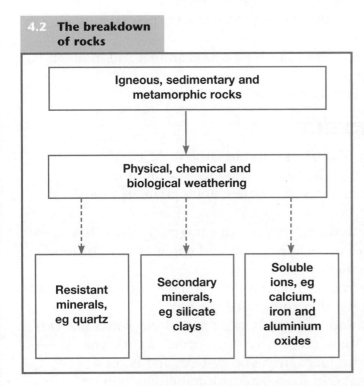

4.2 The breakdown of rocks

Igneous, sedimentary and metamorphic rocks

↓

Physical, chemical and biological weathering

| Resistant minerals, eg quartz | Secondary minerals, eg silicate clays | Soluble ions, eg calcium, iron and aluminium oxides |

Soils are formed from rocks that have been broken down by physical, chemical and biological weathering.

Physical weathering

The three main causes of physical weathering are:
• extreme temperature changes
• mechanical action, for example winds and waves
• expansion of freezing water.

Chemical weathering

Water reacts with carbon dioxide in the soil to form carbonic acid. This breaks down silicate minerals and converts feldspars into clays.

Biological weathering

Rabbits, earthworms and burrowing organisms increase the rate of chemical weathering by moving soil to the surface and exposing it to the atmosphere.

Plants push their roots through rock crevices and microbes promote soil formation by:
• decomposing organic matter
• nitrogen fixation, ammonisation and nitrification
• oxidation reactions
• mineralisation reactions
• humus formation.

ammonisation conversion of organic compounds in decaying plant material into ammonia by soil bacteria

Human effect on soils

The impact on the soil by Australia's Indigenous peoples was quite different from European impact due to different attitudes towards the land.

Indigenous impact

Indigenous peoples had minimal impact on the soil because they:
• respected the land and considered it sacred
• were hunter–gatherers who moved from one region to another, with the size of their communities being based on food availability

- did not develop cities or over-use one region
- only took what they needed
- were not profit driven
- burnt grasslands to hunt animals, but also to encourage new pasture growth and livestock to a region
- did not exploit their resources, for example allowed animal and food supplies to regenerate after use
- replanted cuttings and roots to encourage future crops.

European impact

In contrast European settlers abused the land because they:
- settled in one region and used the land beyond its capabilities
- used European farming techniques that were inappropriate in a harsh, arid climate

4.3 Governments encouraged the clearing of trees until the 1980s

- introduced new pasture and crop species that were not drought resistant and had greater nutritional demands
- introduced hard hoofed animals such as sheep and cattle that compacted the soil
- introduced weeds, pests and diseases that had no natural predators or pathogens in Australia
- introduced irrigation systems and bores that encouraged agricultural production on marginal land
- were profit driven
- did not understand ecosystems
- were not farmers, for example many were convicts or soldiers that returned from World War I and II
- were encouraged to clear and produce as much as possible, for example from 1860–1960 the government provided tax concessions for clearing trees.

4.4 Gully erosion occurs where land is used beyond its capabilities

4.5 Hard-hoofed animals compact the ground

Activity 4.1

Table [4.6] indicates the type of land use in Australia.

4.6 Land use in Australia		
Land use description	Total extent ('000 ha)	Total extent (%)
No data	187.4	0.0
Nature conservation	49 881.3	6.5
Other protected areas including Indigenous uses	102 631.2	13.4
Minimal use	120 812.3	15.7
Livestock grazing	430 100.8	56.0
Forestry	15 187.0	2.0
Dryland agriculture	40 310.8	5.2
Irrigated agriculture	2170.3	0.3
Built environment	2442.4	0.3
Waterbodies not elsewhere classified	4993.7	0.6

Source: National Land and Water Resources Audit 2001, Australian Natural Resources Atlas

a What is the total percentage of land used for agricultural production?
b Which agricultural industry uses the most land?
c What percentage of land has minimal use? What would be the reasons for it not being used?

Extension Activities

1 Discuss the detrimental effects of some agricultural practices on Australian soils.
2 What techniques can be used to maintain or improve our soils?

Factors affecting the rate of soil formation

Factors affecting the rate of soil formation include rock type or parent material, climate, topography and time.

Parent material

The parent material determines the type of soil produced and its texture, structure, mineralogy, fertility and pH.

The three most common types of rocks are:

- igneous
- sedimentary
- metamorphic.

Igneous rocks such as basalt and granite are made from magma that has cooled above or below the earth's surface.

Sedimentary rocks such as sandstone, and mudstone are made from fragments deposited in rivers, lakes or oceans and compressed to form new rock.

Metamorphic rocks such as slate, marble and gneiss are derived from pre-existing rocks that are changed by extreme temperatures and pressures under the surface of the earth.

Climate

Rainfall and temperature have a major effect on soil formation by influencing:

- mineral weathering
- speed of chemical reactions
- clay formation
- movement of clay within the soil
- leaching
- erosion.

High rainfall promotes weathering, leaching and the creation of acidic soils. In arid regions there is minimal leaching and salinity can be a problem because soluble salts accumulate in the profile. High temperatures promote organic matter breakdown and mineral weathering.

Topography

A soil can have one parent material but different characteristics depending on its slope.

Soils on upper slopes often have:

- shallow, stony profiles
- poor profile development
- low infiltration rates
- high drainage and runoff rates
- little chemical or biological activity
- fertility problems
- acidity problems due to loss of base cations.

Soils at the bottom of slopes often have a deeper profile and higher fertility levels. However they can have drainage and waterlogging problems.

Time

Soils can take thousands of years to form and must be carefully managed because they cannot be easily replaced.

mineralogy
types of naturally occurring substances of set chemical composition and physical properties such as olivine, micas and feldspars present in a rock

leaching
loss of nutrients from the soil by water moving through the soil profile

profile
vertical section of the soil showing its horizons and characteristics

cations
positive-charged ions dissolved in the soil solution

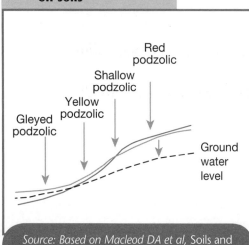

4.7 Effect of topography on soils

Red podzolic
Shallow podzolic
Yellow podzolic
Gleyed podzolic
Ground water level

Source: Based on Macleod DA et al, Soils and climate in agricultural production systems, University of New England, Armidale, 1984

Soil types in Australia

There are more than 40 different types of soils in Australia and these are classified according to:
- level of profile development
- presence or absence of calcium carbonate
- colour
- texture
- sharpness of horizons
- pH
- depth of parent material
- presence or absence of ironstone gravel.

horizons
layers of soil parallel to the surface such as topsoil and subsoil, each with its own individual characteristics

4.8 Main soil types in Australia

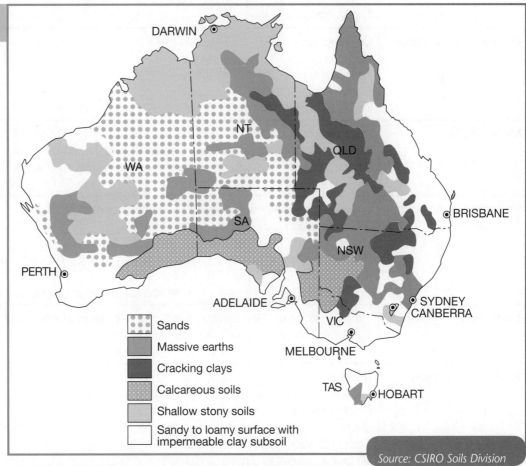

Legend:
- Sands
- Massive earths
- Cracking clays
- Calcareous soils
- Shallow stony soils
- Sandy to loamy surface with impermeable clay subsoil

Source: CSIRO Soils Division

4.9 Characteristics of some common soil types

Name	Features
Alluvium	Young immature soils transported and deposited by running water Profiles not well developed Sandy to loamy texture Very fertile Well drained Near neutral pH For example riverine, deltaic, lacustrine and alluvial fan deposits

	4.9 Characteristics of some common soil types
Name	**Features**
Black earths or chernozems	Deep black clays derived from basaltic material Found in regions with 500–1000 millimetres rainfall per year Poorly developed profiles Contain a high percentage of humus Sometimes contain calcium carbonate nodules in subsoil Fertile but crack when dry and sticky when wet For example Darling Downs
Desert soils	Reddish-brown soils In regions receiving less than 200 millimetres of rainfall per annum Poorly developed profiles Contain soluble salts on or near the surface of the soil Support little vegetation
Grey and brown soils	Greyish-brown soils Found in medium to low rainfall areas Reasonably well-developed profiles Contain sodium salts in the subsoil Found in western regions of Victoria, NSW and Queensland
Mallee soils	Reddish-brown soils Found in regions receiving 200–450 millimetres of rainfall per year A horizon has a sandy loam texture and contains sodium chloride Heavier subsoils contain calcium deposits
Podzols	In regions receiving more than 900 millimetres of rainfall per year A horizon is ash grey and has a sandy texture B horizon is red or yellow and has a heavy texture Soils are acidic and relatively infertile because clay and iron oxides are leached out of the soil and replaced by hydrogen ions Commonly found on the eastern coast and some eastern slopes of the Great Dividing Range
Podzolics	Similar to podzols but receive less rain and has less distinctive horizons A horizon is brownish-yellow and sometimes contains iron oxide Located on the eastern side of the Great Dividing Range
Red brown earths	Reddish-brown soils Found in regions receiving 380–890 millimetres of rainfall Profile fairly well-developed Subsoil is reddish-brown and contains iron oxides and clay removed from A horizon Calcium carbonate present in subsoil Surface is neutral to slightly acidic Contain little organic matter and easily eroded Found on the western slopes of eastern Australia
Red loams	Reddish-brown soils derived from basalt rock Found in moderate rainfall areas Profiles not well developed Relatively fertile Alkaline except in humid climates Found at Dorrigo, Moss Vale and Guyra

Activity 4.2

1 Draw a map of the major soil types in your region.
2 Explain how each soil was formed and discuss its physical and chemical properties.

Physical properties of soil

The physical properties of soils are described using a soil profile [4.10].

Soil profile

A soil profile is a vertical section of the soil and gives information about the soil's:

- horizons
- structure
- organic matter content
- drainage characteristics.

- parent material
- texture
- fertility level

4.10 A soil profile

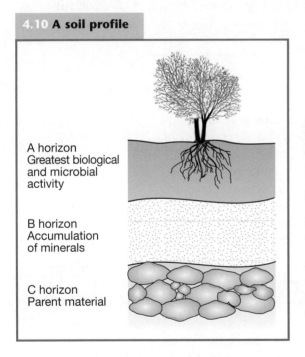

A horizon
Greatest biological and microbial activity

B horizon
Accumulation of minerals

C horizon
Parent material

4.11 A soil profile from Orange, NSW

Most soils have three horizons each with distinctive physical and chemical properties. The A horizon is the top layer and contains the topsoil, plant roots, organic matter and the greatest biological activity. The B horizon contains ions, minerals, oxides and organic matter washed down from the A horizon. The C horizon contains the parent material or bedrock from which the soil is likely to have been derived.

Practical 8

Looking at a soil profile

Aim
To investigate a soil profile.

Equipment
- shovel
- hand trowel

Method
1 Cut a trench one metre in depth.
2 Identify the main features, eg:
   - colour
   - horizons
   - amount of topsoil and organic matter
   - parent material
   - indications of poor drainage, for example bluish grey colourations
   - presence of hard layers or claypans.
3 Draw and label the soil profile.
4 Repeat the procedure in other parts of the paddock and note the differences in the profiles.

Conclusion
When analysing soil types why should many samples be taken throughout the farm?

AG FACT

Soil problems
A soil profile can give a clear indication of problems within the soil. Blue colourations can indicate water logging; salt particles – salinity; and compressed layers -clay pans. Studying the parent material also provides information about the characteristics of the soil such as fertility levels.

Mineralogy of soils

Rocks contain minerals that vary in:
- shape
- physical and chemical properties
- structure
- susceptibility to erosion.

Primary and secondary minerals

fraction
portion of the soil

The sand and silt fractions mainly contain primary minerals such as olivine, mica, quartz and feldspars. These have a tetrahedral structure with one silicon atom surrounded by four oxygen atoms [4.12].

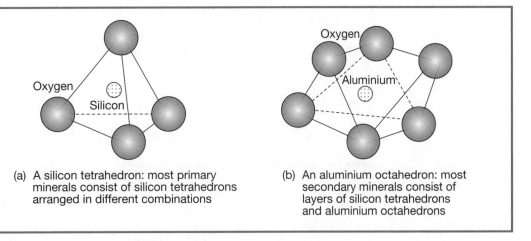

(a) A silicon tetrahedron: most primary minerals consist of silicon tetrahedrons arranged in different combinations		(b) An aluminium octahedron: most secondary minerals consist of layers of silicon tetrahedrons and aluminium octahedrons

4.12 A silicon tetrahedron and an aluminium octahedron

Secondary minerals such as kaolinite, illite and montmorillonite are found in the clay fraction. These have a platy crystalline structure consisting of silicon tetrahedral layers and aluminium octahedral layers. 1:1 minerals such as kaolinite have a silicon tetrahedral layer followed by an aluminium octahedral layer. 2:1 minerals such as montmorillonite have one aluminium octahedral layer surrounded on either side by a silicon tetrahedral layer.

Clay minerals have a negatively charged surface because cations replace one another inside the mineral. Their large surface area and negative charge greatly increase the soil's water-holding capacity and fertility level. However these minerals can shrink and swell and are easily deformed because water moves between the plates and pushes them apart. Clay soils are plastic and cohesive because of the strong attractive forces between the particles. They cannot be ploughed when too wet because they compress.

4.13 Comparison of primary and secondary minerals

Feature	Primary mineral	Secondary mineral
Source	Chemically unchanged minerals	Weathered minerals
Structure	Silicon oxygen tetrahedron	Silicon tetrahedral and aluminium octahedral layers
Location	Sand and silt fraction	Clay fraction
Surface area	Small	Large
Surface charge	Little or none	Negative
Water-holding capacity	Low	High
Potential to shrink and swell	Little	Great
Plasticity	Little	Great
Porosity	Large	Smaller
Ease of cultivation	Easily tilled	Difficult to work
Cation exchange capacity	Small	Large

4.14 Size of soil fractions

Size fraction	Diameter range (mm)
Coarse sand	2.0–0.2
Fine sand	0.20–0.02
Silt	0.02–0.002
Clay	<0.002

4.15 Characteristics of different soil particles

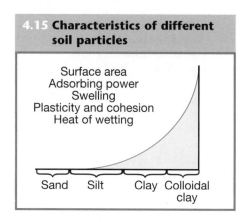

4.16 Comparison of primary and secondary minerals

Feature	Sand	Clay
Particle size	Large	Small
Minerals	Quartz	Many
Feel	Coarse	Fine
Structure	Structureless	Crumb
Infiltration and drainage	Good	Lower rates
Plasticity	Cannot be moulded	Can be shaped into a ribbon
Fertility	Low	High
Porosity	Large pores	Small pores
Water holding capacity	Low	High
Ease of cultivation	Easy	Difficult
Ability to shrink and swell	Low	High
Bearing strength	High	Low

Texture

Texture refers to the relative amounts of sand, silt and clay in a soil and has a major effect on the soil's:

- fertility level
- infiltration and drainage rates
- water-holding capacity
- bearing strength
- ease of cultivation
- shrink and swell potential
- ability to crack on drying
- susceptibility to erosion.

Sandy soils are easy to cultivate, have high bearing strengths and infiltration and drainage rates, and do not shrink or swell. However these soils cannot store a lot of water and are less fertile than clay soils.

Activity 4.3

Identify the following texture types:
- a a soil containing 33% sand, 34% silt and 33% clay
- b a soil containing 50% sand, 25% silt and 25% clay
- c a soil containing 50% clay, 20% silt and 30% sand.

4.17 The texture triangle

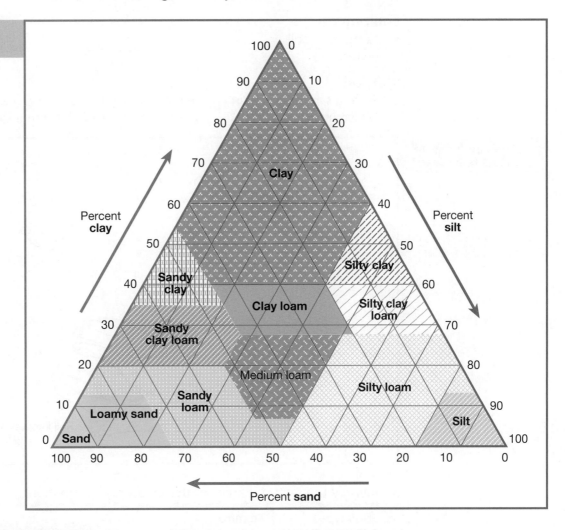

4.18 Clay soils shrink and swell and crack on drying

Practical 9

Categorising soil texture

Aim
To determine the texture of a soil by its feel and consistency.

Equipment
- samples of soil
- water

Method
1 Place a sample of soil in your hand.
2 Moisten the sample.
3 Try to roll it into a ball.
4 Try to roll it into a sausage shape.

4.19 Categorising soil texture by feel

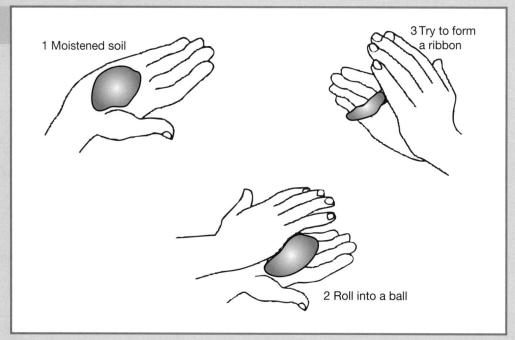

1 Moistened soil

3 Try to form a ribbon

2 Roll into a ball

5 Identify the texture based on the following information:

Soil type	Texture
Sand	Coarse, gritty and will not form a ball.
Sandy loam	Gritty, particles stick together slightly. Forms a crumbly ball.
Loam	Small amount of grit. Smoother feel. Slightly crumbly ball.
Clay loam	Sticks together well. Forms ball and crumbly sausage.
Clay	Smooth, very sticky and no grit. Forms ball and sausage

6 Repeat the procedure with other soil samples.

Results
Record your results.

Conclusion
State your conclusions from the results.

Soil structure

Structure is determined by the size, shape and arrangement of soil particles and has a major effect on:

• porosity and aeration levels
• infiltration, storage and drainage rates
• root penetration and growth
• transfer of heat within the soil
• temperature of the soil
• susceptibility of the soil to erosion.

The four most common types of structure are:

• platy
• columnar and prismatic
• blocky and sub-angular
• granular and crumby.

4.20 The structure of soils

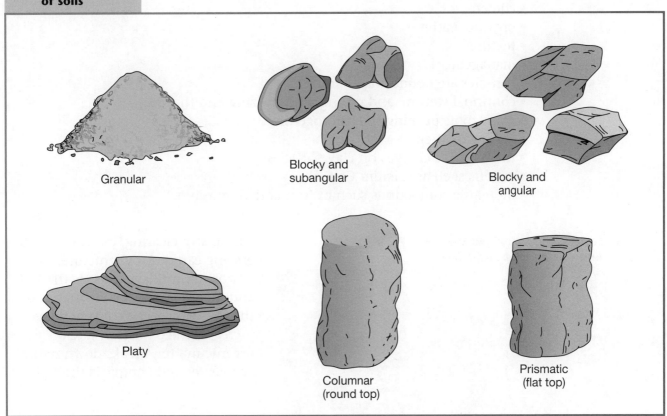

Granular

Blocky and subangular

Blocky and angular

Platy

Columnar (round top)

Prismatic (flat top)

4.21 Characteristics of each structure	
Type	**Feature**
Platy	Aggregates are arranged in thin plates or leaflets and this structure is found in any part of the profile.
Columnar and prismatic	Aggregates have vertically orientated pillars. Columnar aggregates have rounded tops and prismatic aggregates have level clean-cut tops. Common in arid and semi-arid regions.
Blocky and subangular	Aggregates are similar to six-faced blocks. Blocky aggregates have sharp rectangular faces whereas subangular particles are less distinctive. Common in subsoils of humid areas.
Spheroidal, granular and crumby	Aggregates are loosely held together and easily shaken apart.

Formation of structure

Soils have different structures because of the influence of:
• living organisms
• the type of cations present
• climate
• organic matter
• texture
• management.
  Particles are bound together by:
• continual wetting and drying, and freezing and thawing
• plant roots pushing the soil together
• organic matter
• the negative charges on clay particles
• cations such as calcium Ca^{2+}
• inorganic compounds such as iron and aluminium.

4.22 **Livestock have compacted the soil and water cannot infiltrate**

Excessive clearing, cultivation and grazing can destroy structure.

Short-term tillage loosens the soil and incorporates organic matter into the soil. However excessive tillage increases the oxidation rate of organic matter, breaks down natural aggregates and compacts the soil.

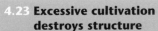
4.23 Excessive cultivation destroys structure

Poorly structured soils are undesirable because they:
• have lower porosity and infiltration rates
• are difficult to cultivate
• can set hard
• are more susceptible to erosion because the individual particles do not form aggregates and are easily moved by wind or water.

Activity 4.4

1   Scientists studied the effect of cultivation on the structure of the soil with the following results.

Number of cultivations	Structure rank (10 – good, 1 – poor)
0	10
5	5
10	3
15	1.5
20	0

2   Plot the following results with the number of cultivations on the x-axis and the ranking of structure on the y-axis.
3   State your conclusions from your analysis of the results.

Extension Activity

'A soil's texture cannot be altered but its structure can'.
Discuss this statement.

Maintaining and improving structure

Structure can be maintained or improved by:
• not over-clearing, grazing or cropping
• using land only up to its limitations
• using machinery correctly, for example cultivating at less than six kilometres per hour to reduce structural damage
• direct drilling

direct drilling
placing seed and fertiliser directly into the ground without cultivation

4.24 Deep rippers used to destroy clay pans

- using crop and pasture rotations to increase organic matter levels, bind soil particles and reduce raindrop impact and erosion
- green manuring to increase organic matter levels and bind the soil particles
- mulching and incorporating stubble into the soil
- deep ripping
- applying lime and gypsum to increase calcium levels and bind particles together.

Activity 4.5

1   This table shows the effect of cropping or pastures on soil nitrogen levels.

Time (years)	Nitrogen levels in kg/ha	
	Crops	Pastures
1	1500	1200
2	1420	1270
3	1360	1350
4	1300	1420
5	1220	1500

2   Plot nitrogen levels versus time for cropping and pastures.
3   State your conclusions from the results.

Practical 10

Gypsum and soil structure

Aim
To observe the effect of gypsum on the structure of the soil.

Equipment
- 2 large beakers
- clay samples
- water
- 1 gram of gypsum

Method
1   Fill each beaker with a mixture of clay and water and stir thoroughly.
2   Add 1 gram of gypsum to beaker 2.
3   Record what happens over a period of 24 hours.

Results
Record your results.

Conclusion
State your conclusions from the results.

Bulk density of the soil

Bulk density is the weight of a unit volume of soil and has a major effect on:
• porosity levels
• movement of gases within the soil
• water infiltration, storage and drainage
• root penetration and plant growth.

   Most soils have an average bulk density of 1.33 grams per cubic centimetre (g/cm^3). If soils are compacted there are fewer pores available for air, water and plant roots.

Porosity of the soil

The size, shape and arrangement of soil aggregates determine the amount of pore space in the soil. Porosity has a major effect on:
• water infiltration, storage and drainage
• gaseous exchange
• root growth.

   As bulk density increases, porosity levels decline and this reduces gaseous exchange and plant growth.

> ## AG FACT
>
> **Compact soil**
>
> Soil compaction has been described as the most insidious form of land degradation in agriculture. It costs money to create. It gives a high-risk of crop failure. And it costs money to mechanically remove the problem.

Practical 11

Bulk density and porosity of a soil

Aim
To measure the bulk density and porosity level of a soil.

Equipment
• 100 ml measuring cylinder
• beaker
• glass rod
• air-dried soil which has been passed through a 2 mm sieve.

Method
1 Place 50 ml of water into a beaker (V2).
2 Place 25 g (W) of soil into the dry measuring cylinder.
3 Tap the cylinder several times so that the soil is evenly packed.
4 Record the volume of the soil (V1).
5 Pour 25 ml of the water into the measuring cylinder and stir with a glass rod.
6 Wash down the sides of the cylinder and glass rod with the remaining 25 ml of water.
7 Gently agitate the measuring cylinder and record the final volume of the soil and water (V3).

Results

Calculate the bulk density and porosity of the soil using the following equations:

- Volume of soil = V1
- Volume of soil particles = V3 – V2
- Volume of the pores in the soil = V1 – (V3 – V2)
- Dry bulk density = W1 divided by V1
- Density of soil solids = W divided by V3 – V2 which equals weight of dry soil divided by volume of soil particles
- Porosity per cent = V1 – (V3 – V2) divided by V1 and multiplied by 100

Conclusions

State your conclusions from the results.

Soil colour

Colour is used to identify some soils. It gives an indication of aeration and drainage characteristics. The colour of the soil is determined by many factors including:

- parent material and mineral content
- organic matter content
- type of oxides present
- the drainage characteristics of the soil.

Black earths have a darkish colour because they contain the mineral ilmenite and a high percentage of organic matter. Iron oxides can appear yellow or blue depending on the soil's drainage characteristics.

Soil colour is sometimes used to assess the soil's fertility level. Red, dark brown and black soils are often considered more fertile than light-coloured soils. However this is not an accurate method and can be misleading.

4.25 Effect of aeration and drainage on soil colour

State of soil	Colour	Reason
Well aerated and drained	Red to brown	Iron is oxidised
↕	Yellow through to mottled yellow	Iron compounds are hydrated and oxidised
Waterlogged soils	Greyish blue	Reduced iron compounds

Soil temperature

The temperature of the soil can have a marked effect on:

- weathering and soil formation
- rate of chemical and biological reactions
- absorption of water and nutrients by plants
- root growth
- microbial activity.
- nutrient cycling
- structure of soil aggregates
- germination rates
- plant yields

The temperature of the soil is governed by many factors including:
• climate and season, for example air temperature and radiation levels
• aspect and slope and their effect on the amount of radiation hitting the surface of the soil
• soil colour, for example dark-coloured soils absorb more radiation.

Soil water

The amount of water in the soil has a major effect on:
• weathering, erosion and soil formation
• biological and chemical reactions
• nutrient uptake by plants
• photosynthesis
• transpiration
• plant yields
• microbial activity
• leaching or removal of nutrients from the soil
• nutrient cycling.

Water is stored in the pore spaces and on the surface of the soil colloids. The amount of water in the soil depends on the:
• climate
• intensity of rainfall and degree of runoff and water loss
• porosity of the soil
• infiltration and drainage rates
• soil texture
• soil structure.

Sandy soils have high infiltration rates but low water-holding capacity because of their large pores that facilitate drainage.

Clay soils have lower infiltration rates but higher water-holding capacity because of their platy structure, large surface area and negative charge.

Compacted and structureless soils have lower infiltration, storage and drainage rates because water cannot penetrate the profile.

colloids
organic and inorganic matter with small particle sizes and large surface areas

Activity 4.6

Design an experiment to determine the water-holding capacity of a soil.

Soil moisture potential

Water is held in the soil by many forces, which the plant must overcome before it can extract any water.

Water is held in the soil by:
• gravity (gravitational potential)
• adsorptive and capillary forces of the soil's pores (matric potential)
• attractive forces of ions and molecules in the soil solution (osmotic potential).

The moisture potential is the measure of the force holding the water in the soil and is calculated using these three potentials.

adsorptive
attraction of ions or compounds to the surface of a solid

capillary
movement of water through a soil due to a potential gradient and surface tension

Soil moisture characteristic

A soil moisture characteristic shows the relationship between soil water levels and moisture potential. In general, as water levels decrease more force is required to take it from the soil.

Osmosis, field capacity and permanent wilting point

Plants take up water by osmosis. This is the movement of molecules across a semi-permeable membrane from a less concentrated to a more concentrated solution.

Roots have a greater concentration of ions than the soil and this creates a potential, which moves water into the roots. Once the water enters the plant, capillarity and transpirational forces move the water up the xylem tissues.

The amount of water available to the plant equals field capacity minus permanent wilting point.

Field capacity is the amount of water the soil can hold after it is saturated and allowed to drain for 48 hours. Permanent wilting point occurs when the plant cannot extract any more water from the soil and it wilts and dies.

Activity 4.7

4.26 Soil moisture characteristics

Soil type	Field capacity	Wilting point	Available water
	(mm water per cm depth)		
Sand	0.9	0.2	0.7
Loam	3.4	1.2	2.2
Clay	3.8	2.4	1.4

Source: Lovett JV et al, Plant Production Systems, UNE, Armidale,1982

1 Table [4.26] shows the field capacity, wilting point and available moisture for three different soils.
2 Graph these figures.
3 Which soil has the greatest available water?
4 Of what relevance is this to the farmer?

Practical 12

Water storage and drainage

Aim
To compare water storage and drainage rates of three different soil types.

Equipment
• retort stand
• 3 soil samples
• funnel
• filter paper
• beaker

Method

1 Place a sample of soil into the filter.
2 Add 50 ml of water and record how long it takes for the beaker to fill with water.
3 For each soil type record how much water was collected in the beaker.

Results

1 Which soil retained the most water?
2 Could structure alter these results?
3 How could the experiment be improved?

Conclusion

State your conclusion from the results.

Extension Activity

Discuss the role of precipitation, effective rainfall, field capacity, soil moisture potential, runoff, evaporation and drainage on the amount of water available to plants.

Soil fertility

Plants require more than 16 elements to grow. Elements such as nitrogen, phosphorus and potassium are required in large amounts and are called macronutrients. Elements such as boron, cobalt and zinc are required in small amounts and are called micronutrients.

Most nutrients occur as simple ions dissolved in the soil solution. However not all nutrients are available to the plant because they are combined with minerals, organic matter or other elements.

4.27 Common form of nutrients in the soil solution

Nutrient	Common form	Nutrient	Common form
Macronutrients		**Micronutrients**	
Nitrogen – ammonium – nitrate – nitrite	NH_4^+ NO_3^- NO_2^-	Iron – ferrous – ferric	Fe^{2+} Fe^{3+}
		Copper – cuprous – cupric	Cu^+ Cu^{2+}
Phosphorus – phosphate	HPO_4^{2-} $H_2PO_4^-$	Zinc	Zn^{2+}
Potassium	K^+		
Sulfur – sulfate	SO_4^{2-}		
Calcium	Ca^{2+}		
Magnesium	Mg^{2+}		

Liebigs's law of the minimum

Liebig stated that plant growth is limited by the nutrient in the shortest supply and rises and falls according to its availability.

Cation exchange capacity

Cation exchange capacity (CEC, milliequivalents/100 g) measures the number of cation equivalents that can exchange between the soil and soil solution. In general, the higher the CEC, the greater the fertility level of the soil.

4.28 Cation exchange capacity of different soils

Material	CEC (me/100 g)
Kaolinite	3–15
Hydrous mica	20–40
Montmorillonite	80–120
Hydrous iron and aluminium oxides	3–5
Humus	150–300

Source: Macleod DA et al, Soils and climate in agricultural production systems, *University of New England, Armidale, 1984*

The cation exchange capacity is affected by many factors including:
- parent material, for example rock type, nutrient content and susceptibility to weathering
- texture
- mineralogy
- organic matter content
- form and availability of nutrients
- level of base saturation
- moisture content
- climate
- pH.

Rocks such as basalt contain a large percentage of weatherable minerals and have a high CEC. Soils containing secondary minerals, clay and organic matter also have a higher CEC.

Organic matter

Organic matter consists of dead plant and animal remains that are broken down by microbes to release nutrients and energy. Organic matter has a large surface area and negative charge that greatly increases the fertility and water holding capacity of the soil. Factors affecting organic matter levels include:
- climatic conditions
- drainage characteristics of the soil
- pH
- management.

These factors affect the amount and type of vegetation present and the level of leaching, erosion and microbial activity that occurs.

4.29 Legumes such as peas increase the fertility level of the soil

ley farming
use of pastures in production to maintain the fertility level of the soil

Over-clearing, cultivation, burning of stubble and removal of crops can significantly reduce organic matter levels.

However good management practices such as:
- minimum tillage
- crop rotations
- ley farming
- stubble mulching
- green manuring

can increase organic matter levels.

Practical 13
Organic matter in soil

Aim
To determine the organic matter content of the soil.

Background information
The organic matter content of the soil can be estimated by burning a sample of soil and measuring its change in weight.

Equipment
- crucible
- oven set at 105° celsius
- Bunsen burner
- tripod
- pipe clay triangle
- desiccator tongs
- copper wire
- soil sample

Method
Determining the weight of the crucible.
1 Place the crucible on top of the tripod and heat it for 10 minutes.
2 Place the crucible in the desiccator and weigh it when it is cool.
Determining the organic matter content of the soil.
3 Place 5 g of soil in the crucible and leave it in the oven overnight.
4 Place the crucible in the desiccator and then reweigh it when it is cool.
5 Heat the soil and crucible for 30 minutes.
6 Place it in the desiccator and weigh it again when it is cool.
7 Calculate the amount of organic matter present by measuring the percentage loss in weight of the soil.
8 Repeat the experiment with different soil samples.

Results
Record your results.

Conclusion
State your conclusions from the results.

Humus

Humus consists of organic matter that will not undergo any further decomposition. Humus is brownish-black in colour and has a large surface area and negative charge. Humus is beneficial to the soil because it binds soil particles and has a high water-holding capacity and cation exchange capacity.

Base saturation

Cation exchange capacity is not an exact measure of a soil's fertility level because it includes hydrogen and aluminium ions, which are of limited use to the plant. Base saturation measures the percentage of bases present in the soil solution and gives a better indication of fertility level.

pH

pH (or potential hydrogen) is a measure of acidity or alkalinity on a scale from 1–14. It is equal to the logarithm of one divided by hydrogen ion concentration:

$$pH = \log \left(\frac{1}{H^+} \right)$$

If pH is:
- less than 7 the soil is acidic
- greater than 7 the soil is alkaline
- equal to 7 the soil is neutral.

The measure of pH has a major effect on:
- plant growth and yields
- rate of biological and chemical reactions
- microbial activity
- nutrient availability.

pH and plants

Most plants prefer a pH of 6–7, but this can vary depending on:
- the plant type
- the plant's particular nutrient requirements
- the plant's ability to tolerate different pH levels.

4.30 Optimum pH for different plants

Plant crops	Optimum pH	Vegetables	Optimum pH	Pasture and forage crops	Optimum pH
Barley	6.5–7.5	Asparagus	6.0–7.0	Red clover	6.0–7.0
Cotton	5.5–6.5	Beans	5.5–6.5	Subterranean clover	5.0–5.5
Maize	5.5–7.0	Spinach	6.0–7.0	White clover	6.0–7.0
Oats	5.5–7.0	Cabbage	5.5–7.0	Vetches	5.5–7.0
Rice	5.5–6.5	Carrots	5.5–7.0	Lucerne	6.5–7.5
Sorghum	5.5–7.0	Cauliflower	6.0–7.0		
Soybeans	5.5–7.0	Celery	6.0–7.0		
Sunflower	5.5–6.0	Lettuce	6.0–7.0		
		Tomatoes	5.5–6.5		

4.31 Effect of pH on nutrient availability

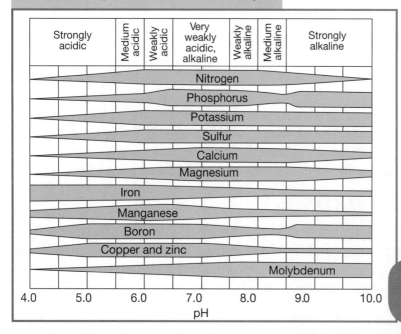

pH and nutrient availability

pH directly affects nutrient availability. Under acidic conditions, nitrogen, phosphorus, potassium, sulphur, calcium, magnesium and molybdenum are unavailable. Whereas aluminium, iron, boron, manganese, copper and zinc become more soluble and can reach toxic levels.

Adapted from Macleod DA et al, Soils and climate in agricultural production systems, University of New England, Armidale, 1984

pH and microbial activity

Most bacteria prefer a pH of 7 and acidic conditions can severely reduce the level of nitrogen fixation, nitrification and mineralisation that occurs. Microbes do however, vary in their susceptibility to pH and fungi generally tolerate more acidic conditions.

Characteristics of acidic and alkaline soils

More than 13 million hectares of New South Wales are acidic and this is undesirable because it affects:
• germination and plant yields
• microbial activity
• the fertility level of the soil
• phosphorus levels
• toxicity levels causing problems because manganese, copper, boron, zinc, iron and aluminium are released in excessive amounts.
  Acidic soils are promoted by:
• acidic parent materials
• areas of high rainfall and leaching
• the breakdown of organic matter
• some industrial wastes
• ammonium fertilisers in conjunction with shallow rooted legumes.

Acidic soils are common in high-rainfall areas because calcium ions are leached from the soil and are replaced by hydrogen ions. Carbon dioxide also reacts with rainwater to form carbonic acid and this releases hydrogen ions in the soil. Organic matter releases sulfuric and nitric acids when it is decomposed. Ammonium fertilisers also release hydrogen ions when they are broken down by microbial action. Some fossil fuels and industrial wastes release sulfur trioxide and sulfuric acid when burnt and this can also increase the soil's acidity level.

Alkaline soils are common in arid regions where there is minimal leaching, and sodium, potassium, and calcium salts accumulate in the soil. Alkaline soils are often deficient in phosphorus, copper, boron, zinc, iron, and manganese and are less productive than neutral soils.

AG FACT

Liming soil
In marginal areas liming soils (to reduce acidity levels) can cost more than the value of the land. Economic factors often make it difficult for farmers to be sustainable.

Reducing the effects of pH

A farmer can minimise the effects of pH by using tolerant plants or changing the pH of the soil.

Acidity levels can be increased by:

- increasing organic matter levels, for example by green manuring, stubble mulching and crop rotation
- using ammonia-based fertilisers such as sulphate of ammonia
- using sulfur-based compounds such as iron sulfate and elemental sulfur because they form sulfuric acid in the soil.

Acidity levels can be reduced by applying lime (calcium carbonate), which replaces hydrogen and aluminium ions with calcium ions.

Acidity levels can also be reduced by minimising leaching and the loss of cations from the soil by:

- growing perennial pastures
- using deep-rooted annuals to recover nitrogen leached from the topsoil
- sowing crops earlier in the season to reduce leaching
- incorporating stubble into the soil to provide a temporary sink for nitrate
- carefully monitoring the use of nitrogen fertilisers.

4.32 **Liming to reduce acidity levels**

Practical 14

Change pH of soil

Aim

To observe the effects of superphosphate, sulfate of ammonia and lime on the pH of a soil.

Equipment

- electronic pH tester (if available)
- universal indicator
- colour code key
- filter paper

- spatula
- tile
- samples of soil
- 1 g of sulfate of ammonia
- 1 g of superphosphate
- 1 g of lime
- 4 beakers

Measuring pH

4.33 **Measuring pH**

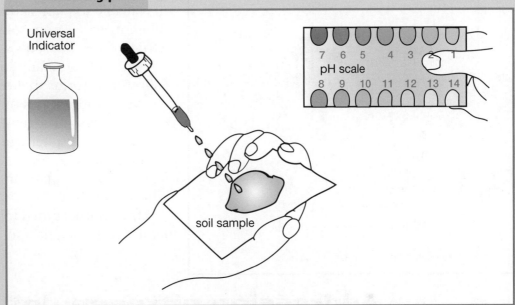

1 Place a small amount of soil onto the tile and shape it into a mound.
2 Add several drops of universal indicator and mix it with the soil until it forms a paste.
3 Place the filter paper on top of the soil and moisten the paper.
4 Look at the colour of the filter paper and compare it to the colour code.
5 Read the pH from the scale.

Setting up the experiment
1 Place 50 g of soil in 4 beakers.
2 Add the following to the appropriate beaker:
   beaker 1: 1 g of sulfate of ammonia
   beaker 2: 1 g of superphosphate
   beaker 3: 1 g of lime
   beaker 4: untreated (control)
3 Record the pH of each beaker.
(Note: 1 g of fertiliser per 50 g of soil is equivalent to 25 tonnes of fertiliser per hectare in the paddock).

Results and conclusion
1 What effect did the fertiliser have on the pH of the soil?
2 Is this experiment valid and can it be applied to field conditions?

Nutrient cycling

The basic chemical building blocks of nutrients are continually cycled. Three of the most important are nitrogen, phosphorus and potassium.

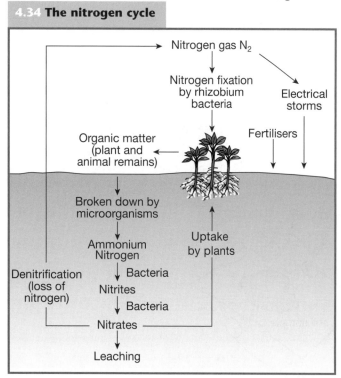

4.34 The nitrogen cycle

The nitrogen cycle

Nitrogen is a major constituent of all proteins and is essential for life. The atmosphere contains 78 per cent nitrogen but this is unavailable to plants and animals. Plants obtain nitrogen from soluble nitrate and nitrite ions in the soil's solution. These ions are derived from many sources including:

- electrical storms that combine nitrogen and oxygen and releases nitrate ions into the soil
- legumes and nitrogen-fixing bacteria that convert atmospheric nitrogen into nitrites and nitrates
- breakdown of plant and animal remains by bacteria.

Nitrogen is returned to the atmosphere by denitrifying bacteria and the cycle continues.

Addressing nitrogen deficiency

Nitrogen deficiencies are common in Australian soils because of:

- infertile parent materials
- leaching
- microbial action, for example denitrification
- erosion
- poor management.

Some rocks are resistant to weathering and release very little nitrogen. Nitrogen is also lost by leaching and by denitrifying bacteria. Poor management and excessive clearing, cultivating and grazing can also reduce nitrogen levels.

Farmers can prevent this decline by:

- conservation farming
- applying fertilisers [4.35]–[4.37]
- green manuring
- crop rotations
- stubble mulching
- ley farming.

Elements
Ca = Calcium
Cl = Chloride
K = Potassium
P = Phosphorus
S = Sulfur

4.35 Common types of fertilisers

Fertilisers	Chemical composition	Elements supplied
Phosphatic Superphosphate	$Ca(H_2PO_4)_2.CaSO_4$	P, Ca, S
Reverted superphosphate	$CaHPO_4.CaSO_4$	P, Ca, S
Rock phosphate	$Ca_3(PO_4)_2.CaF_2$	P, Ca
Potassic Sulfate of potash	K_2SO_4	K, S
Muriate of potash	KCl	K, Cl
Nitrogenous Sulfate of ammonia	$(NH_4)_2SO_4$	N, S
Nitrate of soda	$NaNO_3$	N
Urea	$CO(NH_2)_2$	N
Calcium ammonium nitrate	$Ca(NO_3)_2.NH_4NO_3$	N, Ca
Mixed Potassium nitrate	KNO_3	K,N
Blood manure	Organic mixture	N, P, K and mineral matter
Bone manure	$Ca_3(PO_4)_2$ and organic nitrogen	P, Ca, N

4.36 Principal nitrogenous fertilisers

Fertiliser	Nitrogen %
Anhydrous ammonia	82
Ammonium nitrate	33
Aqua ammonia	24
Nitrogen solution	variable
Urea	45
Urea-formaldehyde	35–40
Ammonium sulfate	20
Sodium nitrate	16
Sulfur-coated urea	39

4.37 Principal phosphatic fertilisers

Material	% available P_2O_5	% available P
Rock phosphate	25–35	11–15.4
Superphosphate	20	8.7
Triple superphosphate	46	20
Monoammonium phosphate (MAP)	48	21
Diammonium Phosphate (DAP)	53	23
Basic slag	5–20	2.2–8.8
Bone meals	17–30	7.5–13.2

AG FACT

Which fertiliser?

When buying fertiliser it is important to select the one that gives the most of the required nutrient for the least price. So, to address nitrogen deficiency, is fertiliser A containing 25% nitrogen and costing $200 per tonne better than fertiliser B containing 5% nitrogen and costing $60 per tonne? For the same amount of nitrogen, A would cost $200 and B $300.

Practical 15

Characteristics of fertilisers

Aim

To study the characteristics of different fertilisers. The characteristics should include constituents, price, form, rate of breakdown purpose, method of application and other important characteristics.

4.38 Factors affecting optimum fertiliser rate

Source: Join the Strip Club, *Department of Agriculture and Fisheries, NSW Bulletin*

Background information

Australia's soils are very old and deficient in many nutrients. Fertilisers can increase nutrient levels and combat structural and acidity problems.

Most fertilisers contain nitrogen, phosphorus, potassium or sulfur.

The type and amount of fertiliser required depends on the:

- soil type
- fertility level and moisture content
- climate, for example rainfall and temperature
- cost of fertiliser per unit of nutrient
- nutritional demand of the crop
- pH of the soil and its effect on nutrient availability
- previous cropping history of the soil
- skills and machinery required
- profitability of the operation.

Equipment

- samples of different fertilisers
- relevant information

Method

1. Look at samples of each fertiliser.
2. Find out the characteristics of each from various sources.
3. Design a table and record all relevant information.

Carbon is a major constituent of organic matter and this is important because it:
- holds nutrients, cations and trace elements
- improves the physical properties of the soil
- increases the soils cation exchange capacity
- increases the water-holding capacity of sandy soils
- binds particles into aggregates which contributes to the structural stability of clay soils
- helps prevent nutrient leaching
- buffers the soil from strong changes in pH
- is being used as a sink for greenhouses gases to stop global warming and climate change.

4.39 Soil carbon

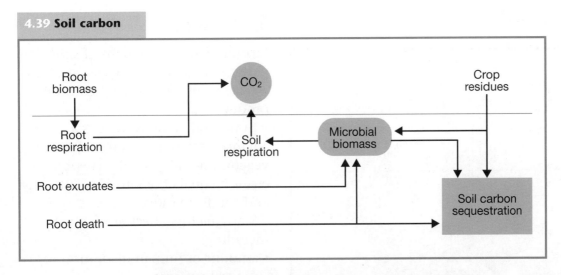

Satellites and global positioning systems

Satellites can be used to monitor many factors of agricultural interest such as vegetation, salting, erosion and water features. Global positioning systems (GPS) use satellites to determine the position of a feature on the earth's surface. They can be used during harvesting to pinpoint areas of low crop yield so that fertiliser levels can be adjusted to suit each part of a paddock.

Soil degradation and management

4.40 Drought conditions remove vegetative cover and promote erosion

Australia's soils are very old and weathered. Fifty per cent of the land needs treatment and degradation costs more than $500 million per year in lost production. Soils have been used beyond their capabilities and are eroding five hundred times faster than they can be formed. This has caused many problems including:

- increased erosion levels and loss of valuable topsoil
- reduced organic matter levels
- reduced fertility levels
- structural problems
- salinity problems
- acidity problems
- soil pollution.

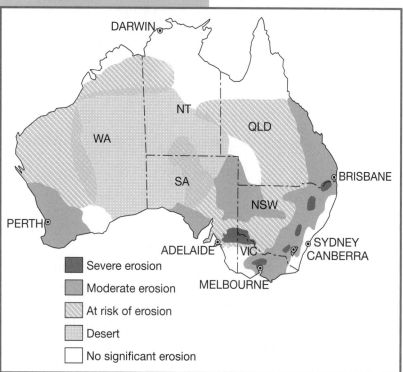

4.41 Distribution of soil erosion in Australia

DARWIN

NT

WA

QLD

SA

BRISBANE

NSW

PERTH

ADELAIDE | VIC

SYDNEY
CANBERRA

MELBOURNE

- Severe erosion
- Moderate erosion
- At risk of erosion
- Desert
- No significant erosion

Erosion

Erosion is the movement of soil particles by wind and water and has a significant effect on agricultural production.

In natural systems there is a balance between climate, soils, vegetation and animals. The rate of erosion equals the rate of weathering and soil formation.

Many factors affect erosion rate including:
- amount of human disruption to natural systems
- soil type
- structural stability of the soil
- rainfall, for example amount, intensity and duration
- wind speed
- type and extent of vegetative cover
- slope of the land.

Wind erosion

Wind removes valuable topsoil by suspension, saltation and surface creeping. Fine particles such as clay, silt and organic matter are lifted by the wind and carried away. Sand particles are bounced along the surface of the ground and heavier fragments are rolled or creep along the surface.

Wind erosion is a significant problem but can be prevented by:
- maintaining and improving the structure of the soil
- reducing cultivation
- reducing fallows
- cultivating at lower speeds
- having longer crop rotations and incorporating plant residues into the soil
- protecting the surface of the ground by not over-grazing
- building windbreaks
- cultivating at right angles to the direction of the wind
- leaving the surface rough and cloddy
- growing crops in strips with alternate rows of fallow.

Water erosion

Water also removes valuable soil material by these forms of erosion:
- gully
- sheet
- rill
- tunnel
- stream bank.

Sheet erosion removes a thin layer of topsoil from a large area of land. Rills and gullies are small depressions created on sloping land. Water can enter rabbit burrows, stump holes and tree-root cavities to create tunnels that collapse to form gullies. Streams can also undercut their banks and remove large quantities of soil.

Water erosion is a significant problem but can be prevented by:
- using land only to its capabilities
- maintaining and improving soil structure
- protecting the land surface, for example with plant material
- ploughing along the contour to increase infiltration rates and reduce runoff
- building contour banks and furrows to increase infiltration rates and divert excess water to catchment dams
- terracing land to reduce runoff and maximise land and water use.

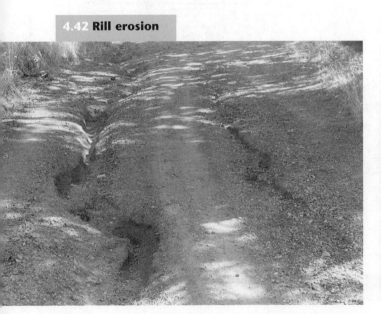

4.42 Rill erosion

4.43 Gully erosion

Conservation farming

Severe degradation occurred before settlers realised that the land was being destroyed and instigated control measures as indicated in diagram [4.44].

Conservation farming is one of the best methods of reducing erosion and maintaining soil quality.

Common techniques used include:
- using the soil only to its limits but not beyond, for example soil suitability classes
- using organic manures
- green manuring
- stubble mulching
- reducing cultivation
- using crop and pasture rotation
- planting trees.

4.44 The erosion cycle

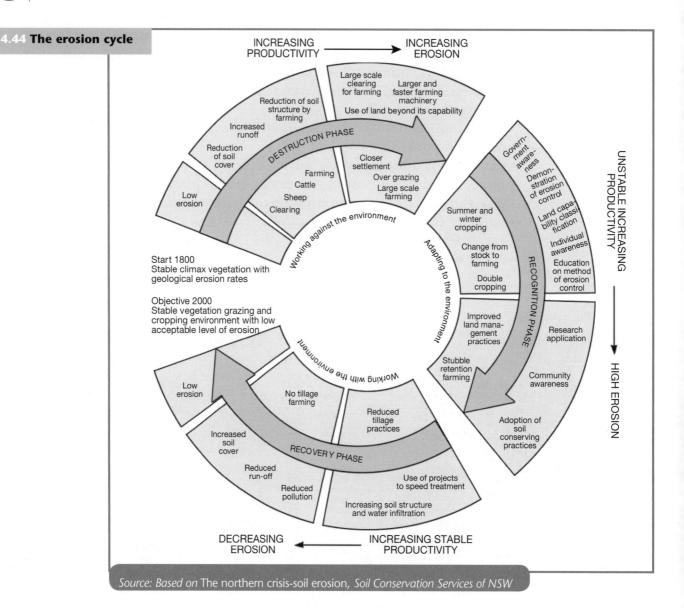

Source: Based on The northern crisis-soil erosion, *Soil Conservation Services of NSW*

Soil suitability classes

The NSW Department of Land and Water Conservation has developed a scale from 1–5 that categorises the agricultural potential of different land [4.44].

4.45 Soil suitability classes

Class	Characteristic
1	Very productive land with little or minor constraints on production. Soil can withstand regular cropping, for example cereals, oilseeds, fodder and intensive horticultural production.
2	Suitable for cropping but should have a rotation phase with improved pastures to maintain production levels.
3	Moderate level of production. Land suitable for grazing or an occasional cash or forage crop can be grown.
4	Low level of production. Land is usually only suitable for grazing because environmental constraints make arable agriculture uneconomic.
5	Very low or zero level of production. Land is only suitable for rough grazing because of severe environmental constraints.

Practical 16

Identify soil suitability classes

Aim
To identify land of different soil suitability classes.

Method
Look at the following photos [4.46]–[4.50] and classify the land using appropriate soil suitability classes.

For example 1 – excellent, all purpose agricultural land to 5 – low or zero level of production. (Note: the captions have been left blank because you have to identify each soil suitability class.)

4.46

4.47

4.48

4.49

4.50

Reduced cultivation

Traditionally soils were cultivated to control weeds, conserve moisture and provide suitable seedbeds for crops.

4.51 Minimum tillage equipment

However continual cultivation severely damaged some soils and caused:
- structural problems
- surface sealing
- clay pans and impervious layers within the soil
- lower organic matter levels
- lower infiltration rates
- greater runoff
- more erosion.

Reduced tillage systems retain crop residues, control weeds by grazing or herbicides and require fewer operations than conventional methods.

4.52 Types of reduced tillage systems	
Type	**Feature**
Reduced tillage	Crop stubble and weeds are grazed after harvest. Seedbed is prepared with fewer tillage operations and contact herbicides are used before sowing.
Minimum tillage	Stubble is retained. Weeds are controlled with herbicides during the fallow period and after the one primary cultivation.
Direct drilling	Seed is sown directly into undisturbed soil. Weeds and crop stubble are grazed during the fallow period. Fallow land is sprayed with a contact herbicide prior to sowing.
No tillage	All stubble is retained and there is no tillage during the fallow period between crops. Weeds are controlled with herbicides and the crop is sown directly into undisturbed soil.

Pasture leys

A pasture ley is an area of land used as a temporary pasture for livestock. Crops are often grown in rotation with leys to increase the fertility of the soil and to act as a disease break. They also help to diversify the enterprises and income of the property.

Nutrient budgeting

Nutrient budgeting is the balancing of the nutrients coming into the farm with those leaving. This is to:
- ensure the soil remains fertile
- prevent runoff and pollution of waterways with fertilisers
- save money by only applying the required amount of fertilisers.

Crop rotations

Farmers traditionally grew the same crop in a paddock year after year. This led to a decline in the structure and fertility levels and made the soil more susceptible to erosion. Farmers now rotate crops with leguminous crops or pastures to:

- increase organic matter levels
- increase fertility levels
- improve structure
- kill weeds
- diversify income
- reduce the incidence of erosion
- control pests and diseases that have a specific host crop.

Use of organic manures

Organic manures such as composts, sewage, and poultry litter can increase fertility levels, improve physical properties and reduce the soil's susceptibility to erosion.

Green manuring

Green manuring is the ploughing of legume crops such as cowpeas and soybeans back into the soil.

This practice improves productivity by:

- increasing organic matter levels
- reducing evaporation rates
- increasing fertility levels
- binding soil particles
- increasing moisture content
- insulating the soil's surface
- reducing the soil's susceptibility to erosion.

Stubble mulching

Stubble or crop residues were traditionally burned to remove crop residues. This practice left the ground bare and facilitated erosion.

Stubble is now left on the surface or incorporated into the soil to:

- increase organic matter levels
- reduce evaporation rates
- increase fertility levels
- bind soil particles
- protect the soil's surface
- increase the soil's moisture content
- reduce the soil's susceptibility to erosion.

Activity 4.8

1 Explain why some farmers will not use stubble mulching and minimum tillage techniques.
2 With reference to the following Internet sites determine the current level of land degradation in Australia:

www.abs.gov.au
www.daff.gov.au/abares
www.dpi.nsw.gov.au
australia.gov.au/directories/australia/
www.farmonline.com.au
www.aglinks.com.au
www.daff.qld.gov.au/home.htm
www.dpi.vic.gov.au
www.dpi.qld.gov.au
www.pir.sa.gov.au
agriculture/web-resources-list
www.dpiw.tas.gov.au

3 Draw a systems diagram to show the factors that interact on a farm to promote land degradation.

4.53 Excessive clearing promotes erosion

4.54 Grazing pressure and old age are destroying trees

Planting trees

Trees are of great benefit to all farmers because they:

- help stop erosion
- act as windbreaks and protect stock and crops
- provide shade
- reduce evaporation rates
- provide timber and other sources of income
- reduce dry land salinity by lowering water tables
- provide bees with pollen and nectar
- provide a home for many biological control agents such as birds
- increase the aesthetic appeal and value of the property.

Originally two-thirds of New South Wales was covered in forests and woodlands and these were cleared for farming, forestry, urban development and mining.

Trees are also under stress from:

- old age
- clearing
- dieback
- over-grazing
- logging
- insect attack.

Property management and catchment plans should be used to:

- identify key vegetation areas
- fence areas to exclude livestock
- preserve and extend remnant vegetation
- plant new trees
- encourage revegetation.

Combating other degradation

Some of the other factors that must be addressed with degraded soils include the loss of organic matter, reduced fertility levels and soil structure problems.

Loss of organic matter

Organic matter consists of dead plant and animal remains and improves the soils structure, fertility level and water holding capacity. Organic matter levels have declined because of continual cultivation. However this can be prevented by:
- reduced cultivation
- organic manuring
- stubble mulching.
- crop and pasture rotation
- green manuring

Reduced fertility levels

Fertility levels have declined because of excessive cropping and grazing and by the removal of saleable products. This problem can be combated by:
- using land only to its potential
- organic manuring
- stubble mulching
- crop and pasture rotation
- green manuring
- applying fertilisers.

Structural problems

Structure refers to the size, shape and arrangement of particles and has a major effect on:
- water infiltration, storage and drainage
- porosity and aeration
- germination, root penetration and plant growth
- soil temperature
- the soil's susceptibility to erosion.
  Structure can be maintained or improved by:
- only cultivating when necessary
- controlling weeds with herbicides instead of cultivation
- using crop and pasture rotations
- green manuring
- stubble mulching
- ley farming
- using gypsum.

Activity 4.9

1 Determine the constituents and cost of gypsum per tonne.
2 How does gypsum help the structure of the soil?

Salinity

Salinity is a major problem in both irrigated and dry land areas of Australia. Thirty-two million hectares of land is affected by salt and $130 million per year is lost in production.

Common table salt or sodium chloride (NaCl) is the main cause of salinity and is derived from three main sources:
• ocean salt carried inland and deposited by rainfall
• weathering of the minerals in soils and rocks
• fossils present in the soil profile.

Sodium, calcium, magnesium, and potassium chlorides occur in some rocks and when land is cleared the watertable rises and brings the salts to the surface.

Salinity can severely affect agricultural production by:
• restricting the type of plants that can be grown in a region
• reducing plant yields
• creating a blocky structure and causing surface crusting and lower infiltration and drainage rates
• contaminating livestock and domestic water
• increasing the soil's susceptibility to erosion
• causing huge reclamation costs.

Symptoms of salt-affected soils include:
• poor germination rates
• trees dying at tips
• crop leaves are smaller, darker and greenish-blue in colour
• pastures are dominated by barley grass, rushes and sedges
• salt sensitive species such as lucerne and clover disappear from pastures
• white crystals appear on the surface of the soil
• clay soils are soft and spongy when cultivated.

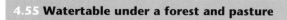

4.55 Watertable under a forest and pasture

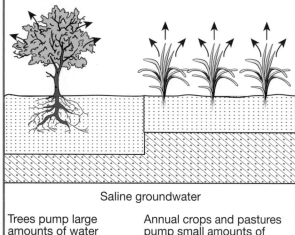

Saline groundwater

Trees pump large amounts of water out of the soil and keep the watertable below ground level

Annual crops and pastures pump small amounts of water out of the soil, which results in an increase in the height on the watertable

4.56 Movement of salt

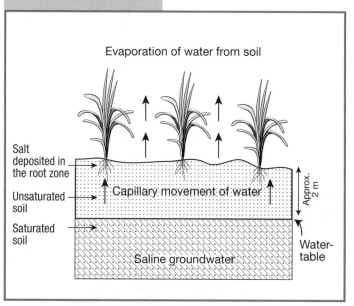

Evaporation of water from soil

Salt deposited in the root zone

Unsaturated soil

Capillary movement of water

Saturated soil

Saline groundwater

Approx. 2 m

Water-table

Salinity is common on irrigated land and is promoted by:
- irrigating soils containing soluble salts
- irrigating sandy soils with high drainage rates and rising water tables
- irrigating soils with an uneven surface where water accumulates and raises the water table
- irrigating land with inadequate slope because the whole paddock is not evenly watered
- over-irrigating
- irrigating with salty water
- not using available water in the soil, for example growing annual crops and pastures.

Activity 4.10

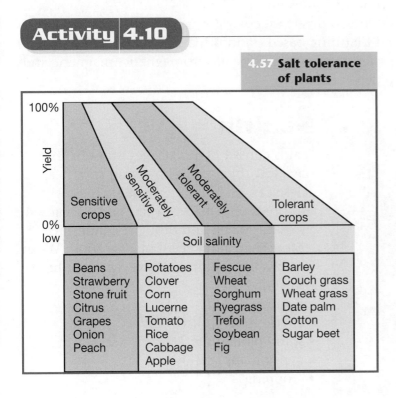

4.57 **Salt tolerance of plants**

1 Diagram [4.57] shows the tolerance level of different plants to salt. Which plants could be grown in the following soil types:
   a high salt levels?
   b medium salt levels?
   c no salt ?
2 Use the following Internet sites to research the areas of Australia affected by salinity:
   www.abs.gov.au
   www.daff.gov.au/abares
3 Draw a map of Australia showing the areas currently affected by salinity.

Controlling salinity

Salinity can be controlled by:
- carefully selecting land for irrigation
- land forming so that the ground is level
- scheduling irrigation
- using clean water
- recycling drainage water if it is clean
- improved soil, crop and water management
- revegetation of strategic sites
- pumping water from the watertable
- monitoring watertable levels and pressure with piezometers, aerial photos and conductivity meters
- district surface and sub-surface drainage to remove excess runoff.

Dryland salinity

Dryland salting occurs when vegetation is cleared and replaced with shallow-rooted plants that use less water. This results in higher infiltration rates and rising watertables.

Dryland salting can be prevented by:

- not over-clearing
- not cropping saline soils
- growing salt-tolerant trees, shrubs, and grasses such as tall wheat grass (Atropyron elongaturn) and marsh grass (Puccinellia ciliata)
- mulching
- fencing and controlling stocking rates
- deep ripping and incorporating gypsum
- putting in drainage systems to divert excess water from the area
- regional and catchment planning based on information from satellite imagery and airborne scanning devices using electromagnetic, magnetic and radiometric sensing to detect salt.

radiometric sensing
using devices which can measure acoustic or electromagnetic radiant energy

4.58 Scalding

Scalds

Scalds consist of bare clayey subsoils that have lost their topsoil by wind or water. These can be from a few square metres to hundreds of hectares in size and are caused by over-grazing and drought conditions.

More than 10 per cent of New South Wales is subject to scalding. However it can be controlled by:

- ripping
- checkerboard furrowing
- spiral ploughing
- gypsum application
- cropping.

Soil pollution

Insecticides, fungicides and heavy metals are some of the most common forms of soil pollutants. Synthetic organochlorine insecticides such as DDT, dieldrin and gamma-HCH have accumulated in the soil. Metals such as zinc, copper, nickel and chromium have accumulated from:

- the over-use of fertilisers
- chimneys
- metal refineries
- contaminated sewage sludges from industrial towns.

Greater pollution controls have been introduced and many toxic chemicals such as DDT have been banned. Maximum residue limits have been set for agricultural products and the NSW Department of Primary Industries monitors chemical residues in raw agricultural products.

specific
target and kill one
particular pest

Many new chemicals are biodegradable, specific and must pass stringent environmental requirements. Training courses such as Smartrain have also been introduced to ensure that chemicals are used properly.

Water quality

Water quality is defined by its physical, chemical, biological and aesthetic (appearance and smell) characteristics. Water quality is important for public health (drinking water), natural ecosystems, farming, fishing, mining, recreation and tourism.

Water quality is affected by:
• the surrounding environment and land use, for example industry, cities and agriculture
• dams and weirs, which modify stream flow
• droughts and floods
• groundwater contamination by urban or industrial development
• fertiliser use and runoff into waterways
• stock effluent and faecal contamination
• chemical runoff, for example herbicides
• waterways and riparian zones, which are not vegetated and exposed to runoff and erosion
• dam construction
• irrigation methods such as flood irrigation can raise water tables and salt levels.

Water resources have been abused, degraded and used beyond their capabilities. Common problems include:
• over-consumption
• contamination with industrial waste, fertilisers and pesticides
• urbanisation
• rising carp levels
• ground water contaminated by leaching from landfills and disposal areas
• river degradation
• algae contamination

4.59 Exposed roots caused by excessive water use from rivers

4.60 Water contaminated with salt

- rising watertables and salinity problems
- destruction of natural wetlands.

   Water is a valuable limited resource. The main sources of water on a farm are from:
- creeks and rivers
- lakes
- wetlands
- dams
- artificial reservoirs, for example domestic water tanks
- sub-surface water, for example bores.

   Water supplies are replenished by precipitation and lost to evaporation, discharge into oceans, sub-surface seepage and evapotranspiration.

Water pollution

Nitrates and phosphates are a major source of water pollution. High nitrate and phosphate levels promote algal growth. When algae die they release toxins that can kill fish and animals. Levels above 20 parts per million of nitrogen in water, can cause bottle-fed babies to develop the fatal disorder, methaemoglobinaemia.

   Farmers can reduce nitrate leaching by:
- growing perennial pastures that are year-round nitrogen sinks
- using deep-rooted annuals to recover nitrogen leached from the topsoil
- sowing crops earlier following rain, to maximise nutrient uptake and minimise leaching
- incorporating stubble to provide a temporary sink for nitrates
- carefully monitoring fertiliser applications.

The regulation of water availability and use

Our water resources are of major environmental, social and economic value. For more than a century our most important system of rivers and aquifers, the Murray-Darling Basin, was managed ineffectively between five states and territories. The *Water Act 2007* (Cth) was developed to meet the challenges facing water management in Australia, including:
- the over-allocation of water resources
- competing demands for water
- record low inflows (promoted by droughts)
- climate change
- maintaining and improving our resources and ecosystems.

   The Act established the Murray-Darling Basin Authority (MDBA) to develop a strategic plan for the Basin and manage it in an integrated and sustainable way. The Australian Competition and Consumer Commission (ACCC) enforced water charge and market rules in accordance with the National Water Initiative. The W*ater Amendment Act 2008* made the Murray-Darling Basin Authority a single body to oversee water resource planning. The ACCC now also controls water charges and market rules for all water service providers and transactions.

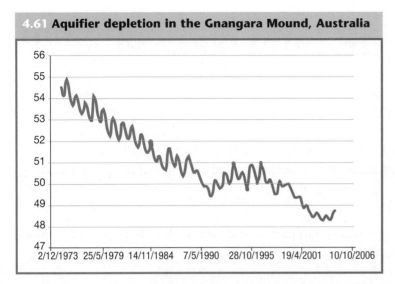

4.61 Aquifier depletion in the Gnangara Mound, Australia

The Office of Environment and Heritage (OEH):

- helps to protect NSW rivers, beaches, wetlands, groundwater systems, and estuaries and other marine environments
- purchases water for wetlands and river systems
- educates stakeholders
- manages environmental water licences
- purchases and trades water entitlements
- manages infrastructure improvement projects.

The NSW Office of Water also ensures that water is shared between the environment, cities, farmers and industry, and monitors water licensing, extraction and allocation.

Research 4.11

Select an agricultural problem and use the following Internet sites to find information on:

a   current research aimed to alleviate the problem and

b   the strategies being used to combat the problem.

www.agric.nsw.gov.au

www.infarmation.com.au

Catchment management

A catchment is a basin of land where water drains to its lowest level.
The community as a whole must be responsible for its management because problems such as salinity do not stop at boundaries.

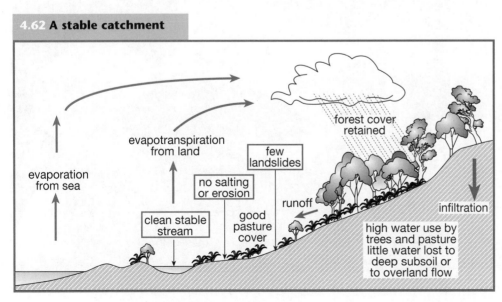

4.62 A stable catchment

Sustainable land management

To be 'sustainable' means to maintain or improve the:
• profitability of the farm
• condition and productivity of the farm's resources
• surrounding environment.

Often there is conflict between economic survival and long term sustainability. It is difficult to invest money in programs such as tree planting when farmers are not making a profit.

4.63 Landcare

Sustainable management must include all stakeholders, for example:
• the owner
• local communities
• local government
• organisations such as the National Farmers Federation
• government bodies such as the Department of Primary Industries.

Many programs have been instigated including:
• the national Landcare program [4.62]
• One Billion Trees program
• Save the Bush program
• National Soil Conservation program
• National Heritage Trust (which has supported more than 10 000 projects since 1996)
• Salt Action
• Rivercare

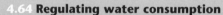

4.64 Regulating water consumption

- Farming for the Future and property management planning
- National Dryland Salinity program
- research, for example as carried out by CSIRO.
  Activities have included:
- education and community awareness programs
- funding for conservation programs
- tax concessions and interest free loans for projects
- advertising and promoting sustainable practices
- total-catchment planning and management
- whole-farm planning
- monitoring the quality of air, soil and water.
- soil-conservation works, for example contour banks and direct drill methods
- planting trees and shrubs
- incentive programs for farmers to conserve habitats of threatened species
- revegetation and biodiversity programs
- weed management
- wetland rehabilitation
- legislation such as SEPP46 (State Environmental Protection Policy) to control the clearing of native trees and pastures
- salinity control measures.

Sustainability requires the support of the whole community in order to succeed.

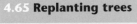
4.65 Replanting trees

AG FACT

Waterwatch

Australia is the driest inhabited continent. It has the least river water and the lowest run-off of water. Rainfall and stream-flow are the most variable in the world.

Water is a scarce resource and many of the water-based ecosystems are suffering extensive damage. Visible signs such as rising salinity and blue-green algal blooms are prevalent. To help address these problems, in 1993 the Commonwealth Government initiated Waterwatch Australia as a national community-based water monitoring program.

It encourages everyone to become active in the protection and management of our waterways. Some of the ways Waterwatch groups have improved waterways are by fencing areas of riverbanks, eradicating weeds and invasive species and reducing the use of pesticides and other pollutants. They regularly undertake biological and habitat assessments and perform physical and chemical tests to determine the health of waterways. There are now nearly 3000 groups nationally regularly monitoring about 5000 different sites. The Waterwatch network works in partnership with business and government to achieve shared and collective action for responsible natural resource management.

Revision 4.12

1 Define the following terms:
- soil
- soil profile
- texture
- porosity
- cation exchange capacity
- nitrogen cycle
- land degradation
- mulching
- Landcare
- weathering
- primary mineral
- structure
- moisture potential
- pH
- global positioning system
- soil suitability classes
- catchment management
- topography
- secondary mineral
- bulk density
- permanent wilting point
- organic matter
- erosion
- stubble
- salinity

2 Answer true or false to the following statements;
a Soil is made from weathered rock.
b Erosion is a natural process.
c Hard-hoofed animals have no effect on the soil.
d Topography is the direction the land faces.
e Texture refers to the arrangement of soil particles.
f Cation exchange capacity measures the fertility level of the soil.
g Alkaline soils are better than acidic soils.
h Lime makes soils less acidic.
i Catchment planning, whole farm planning and using soil suitability classes is an example of sustainable management.

3 With reference to figure [4.66]:
a Identify the problem areas in this diagram
b What management practices could be used to correct each of the problem areas?

4 Draw a diagram of your local catchment area indicating the main problem areas. Suggest solutions that could be used to alleviate the problems.

4.66 Sustainable land management

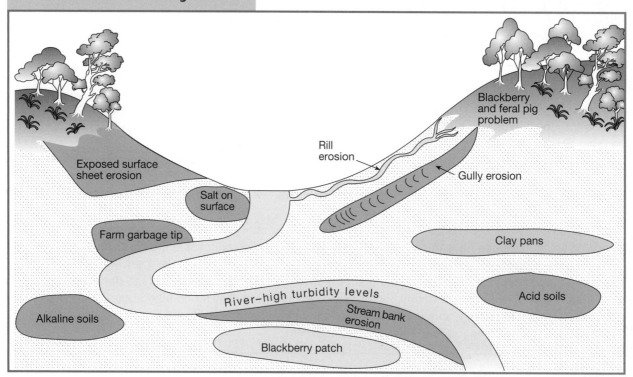

Farm Case Study

In this chapter you will learn about:

- the farm as the basic unit of production, including the physical environment and biological factors
- farm management issues
- production, including maximising profit and optimum production levels
- types of products such as competitive, complementary and supplementary
- farm records and budgets
- marketing and consumer demand
- the impact of technology
- workplace hazards and animal welfare issues.

The farm: the basic unit of production

The farm is the basic unit of agricultural production and is affected by both physical and biological factors.

5.1 Factors affecting the farm

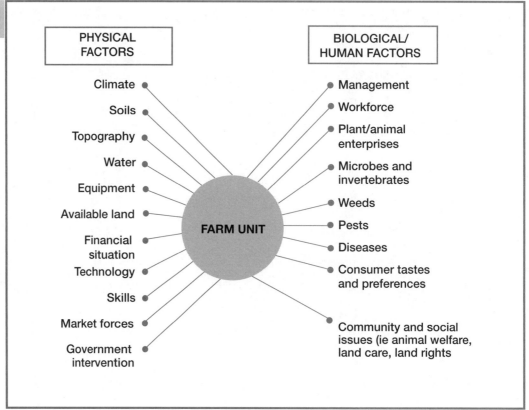

PHYSICAL FACTORS	BIOLOGICAL/ HUMAN FACTORS
Climate	Management
Soils	Workforce
Topography	Plant/animal enterprises
Water	Microbes and invertebrates
Equipment	Weeds
Available land	Pests
Financial situation	Diseases
Technology	Consumer tastes and preferences
Skills	
Market forces	Community and social issues (ie animal welfare, land care, land rights
Government intervention	

FARM UNIT

Physical environment

Physical or non-living factors that affect the farm include climate, soils, topography, water sources, equipment and level of technology, available land, the financial situation and external factors.

Climate

Important aspects of climate include:
• rainfall levels, including its seasonality and reliability
• evaporation rate
• growing season
• maximum and minimum temperatures
• frost and snow
• droughts and floods
• wind
• radiation levels.

Activity 5.1

5.2 Annual rainfall and temperature levels

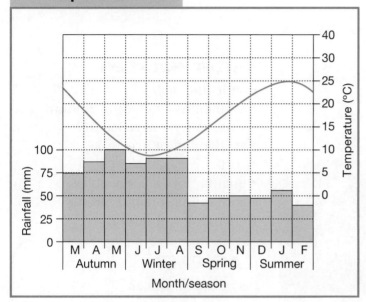

Diagram [5.2] shows rainfall and temperature levels for a property.
1 Which seasons had the highest and lowest rainfall?
2 What were the highest and lowest temperatures?
3 How could these climatic factors affect production?

Soils

The soil has a major impact on the farm unit. Major factors include:
• fertility level and cation-exchange capacity
• texture
• structure
• organic mater content
• water-holding capacity
• pH
• incidence of clay pans
• incidence of salinity
• potential to shrink and swell and crack on drying
• susceptibility to erosion.

Activity 5.2

5.3 Stubble retention

Photo [5.3] shows stubble retention in a cropping program. Give examples of management practices that are beneficial or detrimental to the soil.

Topography

Factors affecting production include:
- slope
- aspect (direction)
- rocky outcrops
- effect on drainage and fertility levels.

5.4 Pumps used to irrigate cotton

Water sources

Factors include:
- availability, including amount, seasonality and reliability
- availability of irrigation
- cost
- quality, for example algal contamination and salinity
- changing legislation.

AG FACT

Water competition
Australia is one of the most arid continents in the world. Competition for high quality water will become a huge issue for future generations.

Activity 5.3

To find the answers to these questions use the following Internet sites:

australia.gov.au/directories/australia/agriculture/web-resources-list

www.farmonline.com.au   www.aglinks.com.au
www.daff.qld.gov.au/home.htm   www.dpi.vic.gov.au
www.dpi.nsw.gov.au   www.dpi.qld.gov.au
www.pir.sa.gov.au   www.dpiw.tas.gov.au

a What is the current legislation regarding water use?
b What reforms are taking place?

Equipment and level of technology

5.5 Traditional transport

Technology that has a major effect on production includes:
- machinery
- fertilisers
- chemicals, for example drenches, vaccines and herbicides
- communication, for example the Internet and mobile phones
- transportation, for example refrigerated transport
- processing and handling facilities.

5.6 Modern harvesting equipment

5.7 Modern tomato-sowing equipment

Available land

Land is one of the most valuable resources and factors affecting its productivity include:

- amount
- soil types
- topography
- soil-suitability classes
- ownership, for example freehold, leased
- restrictions on the land, for example SEPP46
- distance to markets.

SEPP46
government legislation which restricted the clearing of land

Financial situation

Factors that can affect productivity include:

- debt level
- level of risk and uncertainty
- assets and liabilities
- stability of prices.

External factors

Outside factors that can affect the property include:

- market forces
- world supply and demand
- government intervention.

Biological factors

Some biological or human factors that affect the farm are management, workforce, plants, animals, microbes, invertebrates, weeds, pests, diseases, and consumer and societal issues.

Level of management

The decisions made by the farm manager have a huge effect on the performance of the property. Factors influencing the competency level of the manager include:

- age
- level of education

5.8 Most farms are family operated

5.9 Alpacas

- attitudes, for example conservative or a risk-taker
- skills and capabilities
- degree of flexibility.

Workforce

Factors affecting the performance of the workforce include:

- number
- availability, for example seasonal labour such as fruit-pickers
- age
- level of education
- skills and capabilities.

In a family-operated farm, the availability and the interests of family members in working the farm are important.

Animal enterprises

Animal enterprises vary in:

- type, for example alpacas, goats, sheep and dairy cattle
- number of livestock
- requirements such as labour and feed
- management
- type of production, for example intensive or extensive.

5.10 Sheep

5.11 Cattle

Plant enterprises

5.12 **Growing grapes and apples are plant enterprises**

Plant enterprises also vary in:
- type, for example cropping, orchards and viticulture
- number
- requirements
- management.

Microbes and invertebrates

Microbes and invertebrates such as bacteria, fungi, algae and protozoa can have a major effect on many processes on the property including:
- plant and animal disease
- nutrient recycling
- ruminant digestion
- nitrogen fixation
- silage production
- food production, for example cheese, wine.

protozoa
sub-kingdom of animals that are unicellular, reproduce by fission or conjunction and move by cilia or flagella

5.13 **Yeast, a form of fungi, is used in baking bread**

Activity 5.4

Table [5.14] shows the level of nitrogen fixation by different organisms.
a   How much nitrogen do legumes produce per kilogram per hectare per year?
b   How much would it cost to replace this nitrogen with artificial fertiliser?
c   What management practices encourage nitrogen fixation?
d   What other beneficial and detrimental effects do microbes and invertebrates have on agricultural production?

5.14 Microbes and nitrogen fixation

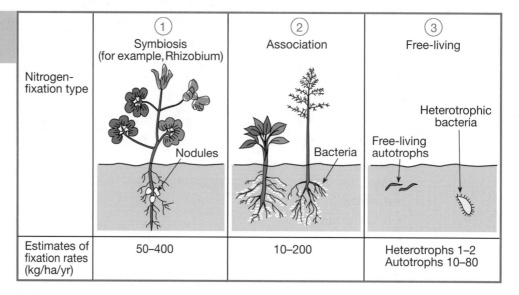

Nitrogen-fixation type	① Symbiosis (for example, Rhizobium)	② Association	③ Free-living
Estimates of fixation rates (kg/ha/yr)	50–400	10–200	Heterotrophs 1–2 Autotrophs 10–80

Weeds

Weeds have a significant effect on production by:
- competing for water, light and nutrients
- harbouring diseases
- releasing harmful chemicals, for example allelopathic reactions
- making harvesting difficult
- increasing production costs in control methods
- and contaminating the product.

allelopathic
The chemical process where some plants release toxic chemicals to inhibit the growth of other plants

AG FACT

Purple curse

Paterson's curse was introduced to Australia from Europe during the mid-nineteenth century. Since then it has spread rapidly. It is a persistent weed. The high seed production, with densities of thousands of seeds per square metre, a seed longevity of over seven years, and an ability to germinate at any time of year, given the right conditions, are some of the features which make it such a persistent weed.

Pests and diseases

Pests and diseases are undesirable because they:
- contaminate or destroy the product
- increase production costs in control methods
- reduce productivity.

Consumer tastes and preferences

Consumers demand products that are:
- fresh
- healthy
- easy to prepare
- plentiful in variety
- free of chemicals
- of the highest quality
- available throughout the year.

The level of consumer demand directly affects prices and the profitability of an enterprise.

Social issues

Moral, ethical and social issues are increasingly impacting on agricultural production. Issues include:
- genetic engineering
- animal welfare
- Indigenous land rights
- water reforms
- competition for limited physical resources such as soil and water
- environmental conservation.

Activity 5.5

1 Explain why more women are working on the land and the average age of farmers is increasing.
2 What effect does youth leaving rural areas have on agriculture and rural communities?

Farm management

Management refers to the planning, organising, running and controlling of a property and the people that work on it.

Some of the decisions a manager must make include:
- what to produce
- how much to produce
- how to produce it
- how to sell the product.

Calendar of operations

The timing of operations on a property is governed by the:
- types of enterprises on the property
- decisions made by the operator
- climate, for example length of growing season
- production length of the enterprise
- availability of labour.

Activity 5.6

5.15 Wool management calendar

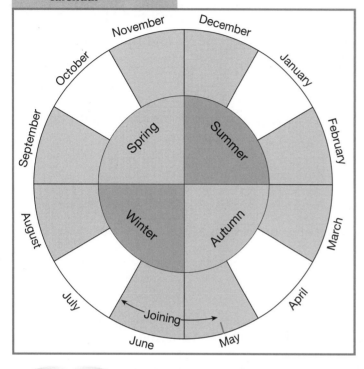

1 Complete the management calendar [5.15] for a wool enterprise:
   - The Roberts family owns a 2500-hectare property near Bathurst. They have 5000 merinos and produce fine wool.
   - Sheep are joined for six weeks from May 15 until June 30. They are pregnant for five months and lamb in November and December.
   - Lambs are marked, docked, vaccinated and ear tagged in the last week of January.
   - Lambs are weaned in March and shearing takes three weeks from September 25.
   - Sheep are dipped in October and crutched in March to avoid flystrike. They are drenched at shearing, crutching and before joining to kill internal parasites.
   - Old and inferior sheep are culled and sold in April.

docked
removal of the tail of an animal using a knife or ring – helps stop flystrike by preventing the build up of urine and faeces

crutched
removal of wool from the breech of a sheep to prevent the accumulation of urine and faeces and flystrike

2 For a plant production system outline the routine management procedures carried out in a complete cycle. Use a table similar to this to record your answer.

5.16 Management procedure cycle for a plant production system

Time scale	Management procedure

AG FACT

No plan
A study of Australian producers found that 75 % of them did not have a formal plan – a disturbing statistic for an industry as large as agriculture.

Activity 5.7

5.17 Calendar of operations on a sheep property

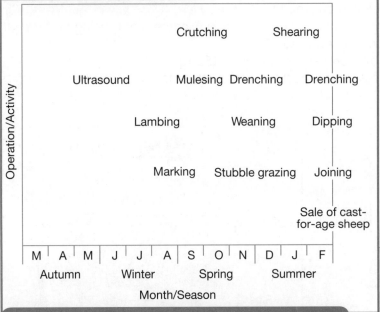

Operation/Activity

Crutching   Shearing

Ultrasound   Mulesing Drenching   Drenching

Lambing   Weaning   Dipping

Marking   Stubble grazing   Joining

Sale of cast-for-age sheep

M | A | M | J | J | A | S | O | N | D | J | F

Autumn   Winter   Spring   Summer

Month/Season

Source: Based on Brown L et al, Dynamic Agriculture, McGraw Hill

1 With reference to diagram [5.17]:
  a Why are sheep ultrasound tested?
  b What are the benefits and disadvantages of crutching and mulesing?
  c Why does lambing occur at the end of winter?
  d Why are sheep drenched, dipped, cast for age and joined at the same time?
2 State the purpose of the equipment pictured in photos and illustrations [5.18]–[5.21].

mulesing
removal of skin from the breech of a sheep that helps prevent flystrike by removing wrinkles, and preventing the accumulation of dung and urine

cast for age
checking an animal's teeth and selling the animals that are old and have broken teeth

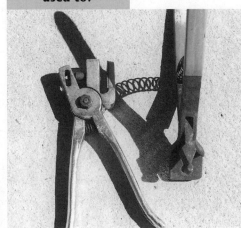

5.18 These are used to?

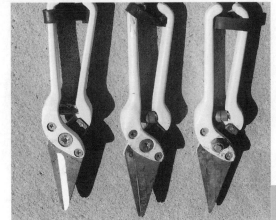

5.19 These are used to?

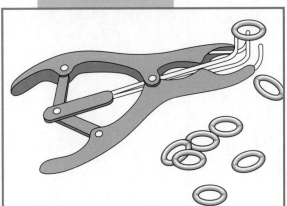

5.20 Purpose is?

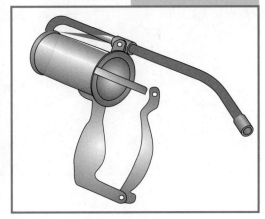

5.21 Used to?

Activity 5.8

1 Equipment and/or procedures:
   a Identify the equipment shown in [5.22] and the procedure that is being performed.
   b What procedure is being performed in [5.23]?
   c Identify the equipment shown in [5.24] and the procedure that is being performed.
   d Identify the equipment shown in [5.25]
   e Identify the product and procedure shown in [5.26].
2 Design a management calendar wheel for a beef operation in your area.

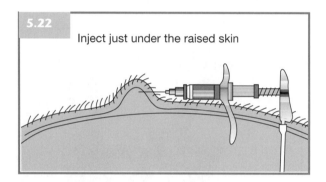

5.22 Inject just under the raised skin

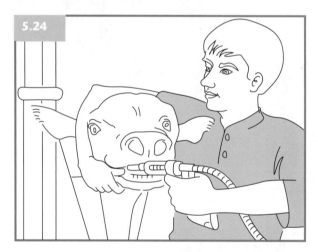

5.24

5.26

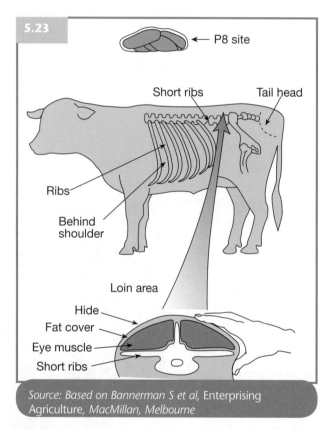

5.23

P8 site

Short ribs   Tail head

Ribs

Behind shoulder

Loin area

Hide
Fat cover
Eye muscle
Short ribs

Source: Based on Bannerman S et al, Enterprising Agriculture, *MacMillan, Melbourne*

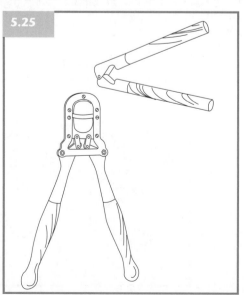

5.25

Activity 5.9

Design a management calendar wheel for cotton using the following information:

August–September
- The field is levelled to ensure efficient irrigation and mounds are built in which to sow seeds.
- The soil is irrigated if it contains insufficient moisture.

September–October
- Soil temperature is checked.
- Seed is planted.

November–February
- Pest levels are monitored.
- Pest management strategies are implemented.
- Soil moisture levels are tested and irrigated as required.
- Crop is weeded.

March–May
- Crop checked by agronomists to see if ripe and ready to pick.
- Crop sprayed with chemical defoliant to remove leaves.
- Crop harvested with cotton picker.
- Fibres packed into modules.
- Modules transported to gin where the fibre is separated from the seeds.
- Crop remains are cut and mulched back into the soil.

5.27 **Fibres harvested and packed into modules**

agronomist
consultant that specialises in plant production such as a cotton agronomist

5.28 **Machine used to mulch cotton crop**

5.29 **Cotton gin**

Management

Management refers to all the operations involved in the planning and operating of the property. The decisions made by the manager can have a huge impact on the farm's profitability and sustainability.

The decision-making process

A good decision can only be made with accurate information and planning. To make the right decision managers should take the following steps:
• realise there is a problem or that a decision must be made
• collect all relevant information
• look at the alternatives
• choose one course of action
• put the choice into action
• determine whether the results are satisfactory
• take responsibility for the decision.

Factors farmers consider when making decisions

Factors farmers consider when making a decision include:
• profitability
• supply and demand
• marketing options
• level of risk and uncertainty
• technology and infrastructure required
• effect of outside influences, for example exchange rate
• information required, for example training for a new enterprise
• government legislation
• farmers' long-term goals and ambitions
• sustainability.

Limitations on the farmer

Many factors affect a manager's decisions, including:
• goal to maximise profit
• goal to improve the property
• goal to increase annual income
• goal to improve the standard of living
• attitude to risk
• attitude to change
• degree of flexibility
• level of income and finance
• level of information
• skills and capabilities.

Many external factors also affect production, including:
• the environment
• change and uncertainty.
• lack of resources

The environment

The environment is one of the major factors affecting agricultural production. It is the surroundings in which the farm operates and consists of such variables as climate, soil, topography, weeds, pests and diseases.

Limited resources can also hinder production and include money, land, labour, technology and skills.

Activity 5.10

5.30 Effect of plant density on yield

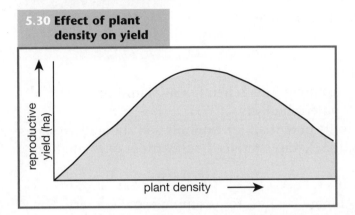

reproductive yield
yield per hectare of saleable product

Diagram [5.30] shows the effect of plant density on reproductive yield.
1   What does the graph show?
2   Of what relevance is this to the farmer?

Risk and uncertainty

Agriculture – more than any other industry – must contend with risk and uncertainty caused by:
- climate, for example droughts and floods
- weeds, pests and diseases
- varying supply and demand
- changing consumer tastes and preferences
- uncertain markets both domestic and overseas
- fluctuating income that hinders long-term planning and investment
- government intervention, for example quotas, tariffs and restrictions
- changing technology.
  Managers can reduce the level of risk and uncertainty by:
- diversification, for example conducting more than one enterprise to reduce fluctuation in income
- deriving other forms of income such as part-time jobs, share farming on other properties, or investing money in real estate or other ventures
- share farming, which reduces costs by allowing other people to farm the land in exchange for a share of the profits
- reducing fluctuations in income by obtaining future contracts for produce with a guaranteed price
- insurance, for example insuring people, livestock, buildings, machinery or crops against damage
- maintaining reserves for periods of shortage, for example storing hay, grain and silage or building more dams for greater water supply
- reducing the debt load on the property
- being flexible, for example conducting enterprises that can be changed to suit supply and demand such as wool and prime lamb production
- being well-informed, for example aware of changes in supply and demand, world markets, consumers preferences, and developments in technology
- avoiding risky enterprises.

Management practices used to address environmental sustainability

Sustainable management practices include:
- catchment planning
- whole farm planning
- whole farm systems thinking
- planning for the future, for example intergenerational planning
- budgets, for example development budgets
- use of the farm according to its potential, for example soil suitability classes
- soil conservation practices, for example reduced cultivation, crop rotation and minimum tillage
- integrated pest management
- planning for drought and climate change, for example water conservation and storage measures and drought-tolerant crop species
- water, for example build more dams
- profitability, for example increase scale of production and mechanisation to replace labour
- diversification of enterprises
- invest in areas off the farm
- improve management, for example attend college and university courses.

Activity 5.11

Month	Price/head $
January	58.50
February	53.20
March	55.90
April	53.20
May	59.50
June	58.00
July	53.00
August	57.00
September	60.00
October	65.00
November	68.00
December	63.00

The following table shows the change in price of lambs per head during a year.
a Draw a graph of prices versus time.
b If the producer had 1000 lambs and sold them in July what income would have been made?
c What income would the producer have made if the lambs had been sold in November?
d What actions can the manager take to stabilise income?

Extension Activity

'Farmers manage their resources within the limits of their abilities using imperfect information to achieve their goals by planning, organising and controlling production systems'. Discuss this statement.

Management and production

Managers must maximise efficiency, production and profitability while ensuring that the property is sustainable.

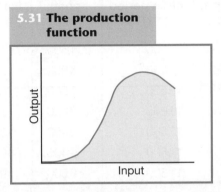

5.31 The production function

Optimum level of production

A production function is a graph showing the relationship between two or more variables such as input and output. Most production functions are S-shaped, with increasing input increasing output. However a point is reached where production reaches a maximum and then declines even if additional input is used.

marginal cost
additional expense incurred in producing one more unit of output, such as one more hectare of wheat

marginal revenue
additional income received from producing one more unit of output

For example, if the stocking rate of a paddock is continually increased, production will reach a maximum and then decline because the animals are starving. If more fertiliser is added to a crop, yields reach a maximum and then decline because of acidity problems. This phenomena is called the law of diminishing marginal returns, which states that if successive units of inputs are added a point is reached where maximum production occurs and then declines.

Maximising profit

Maximum profit occurs when marginal cost equals marginal revenue. At this point the cost of an additional unit just equals the extra revenue received from that unit.

If the farmer increased production past this point, input costs would exceed profit because of the law of diminishing marginal returns.

Practical 17

Production function and optimum level of production

Aim
To derive a production function and determine the optimum level of production.

Equipment
• calculator
• graph paper

Method
1 Draw a production function using the information in table [5.32].
2 Determine the marginal cost and revenue of each additional unit and find the optimum level of production.

5.32 Costs and returns of various levels of broiler production

Input, units of labour per production length	Broiler output per production period	Total costs	Total income
0	0	0	0
1	500	1600	1200
2	3500	5000	2700
3	8500	6500	6800
4	11000	8000	8800
5	12500	9400	10000
6	12600	9400	10000
7	11500	8500	9200

Types of products

Farmers conduct more than one enterprise to stabilise income and reduce risk and uncertainty. Types of products include:

- competitive
- complementary
- supplementary.

5.33 Types of products

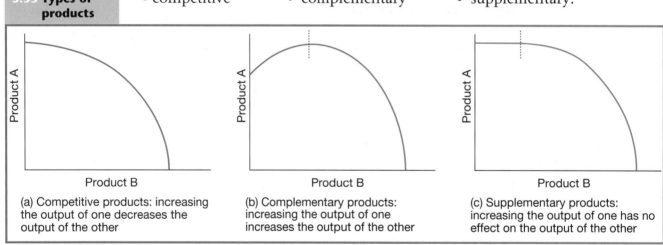

(a) Competitive products: increasing the output of one decreases the output of the other

(b) Complementary products: increasing the output of one increases the output of the other

(c) Supplementary products: increasing the output of one has no effect on the output of the other

Competitive products

Competitive products need the same resources and increasing the output of one lowers the production of the other, for example growing wheat and barley on a limited amount of land.

Complementary products

Complementary products benefit each other and increasing the output of one increases the output of the other. For example if wheat is grown in rotation with pastures the pastures increase nitrogen and organic matter levels and wheat yields. However complementary products become competitive if one enterprise expands and competes with another for the same resources.

Supplementary products

Supplementary products are not affected by one another and increasing the output of one has no effect on the output of the other. For example labour demands for wheat, sheep and cattle enterprises are seasonal and should not interfere with each other. However competition can occur if enterprises are expanded and additional labour is required.

Activity 5.12

5.34 Types of products

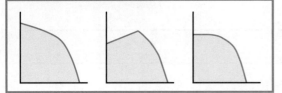

Look at the graphs in [5.34]:
1   For each graph, is the product competitive, complementary or supplementary?
2   Give one example each of a competitive, complementary and supplementary product in your region.

Farm records and budgets

The basis of farm management is keeping good records and making realistic budgets. Records must be useful, simple and concise. Records have many uses including:
- planning operations on the property
- monitoring progress of the property
- pinpointing areas of inefficiency and waste
- planning for the future
- helping with taxation returns
- preparing applications for monetary loans.

The two most common records are physical and financial records.

Physical records

Physical records commonly used by agricultural producers include:
- diaries showing daily events such as time of joining, lambing, sowing and harvesting
- rainfall records
- paddock records, for example types of crops grown and fertiliser used [5.35]
- inventories, for example of livestock, hay, grain, fertilisers and chemicals
- performance records that summarise the performance of an enterprise.

5.35 A typical paddock book

Date	Operation	Fertilisers	Sprays	Seed	Yields	Comments
2011	Sowed lupins	70kg/ha super	Nil	60kg/ha	1.2t/ha	
2012	Sowed wheat	70kg/ha of Starter 15	Nil	35kg/ha	2t/ha	
2013	Sowed forage oats	100kg/ha of Starter 15	Nil	40 kg/ha	forage	

Practical 18

Common performance indicators in your region

Complete the following table listing the performance indicators used for enterprises in your region.

Enterprise	Performance indicators
Wool	kg/head, fibre diameter, staple length, purity
Prime lambs	lambing percentage, growth rate, live weight, fat and muscle score
Wheat	yield tonnes/ha, protein content, purity

Financial records

Financial records can monitor the flow of money on the property. Some useful financial reports include:

- gross margins
- parametric budgets
- cash-flow budgets
- statement of assets
- whole-farm budgets
- statement of liabilities
- partial budgets
- equity or net worth.

5.36 Statement of assets and liabilities

Assets	Liabilities
Land	Bank loan
House	Rates (unpaid)
Livestock	Wages (unpaid)
Vehicles, for example tractor, truck, ute, motor bikes	Costs, for example fuel, fertiliser, insurance, machinery repairs and maintenance
Fodder reserves such as hay	
Grain	
Fertiliser	
Chemicals	
Fencing material	
Fuel	
Money	

Statement of assets

A statement of assets lists the farmer's possessions such as land, machinery and livestock. It includes the value of merchandise that has been purchased but not paid for.

Statement of liabilities

A statement of liabilities lists all the farmer's debts such as bank loans, mortgages and unpaid bills.

Equity

Equity is the net monetary worth of the farmer and equals all assets minus liabilities. It can be expressed in monetary terms or as a percentage of assets.

Equity is a good financial indicator of the risk level of the property. This is one analyst's view.

<40%	40%–60%	60%–90%	>90%
Critical	At risk	Fair	Strong

Cash-flow budgets

A cash-flow budget is a weekly, monthly or yearly statement showing the income and expenditure on a property.

Cash-flow budgets have many uses, including:
• monitoring the flow of income
• pinpointing areas of inefficiency and waste
• allowing the manager to plan for periods of shortage
• reminding when regular bills such as rates and electricity are due
• enabling the manager to coordinate repayments to suit debt load.

5.37 Sample cash-flow budget

Month	Jul	Aug	Sept	Oct	Nov	Dec	Jan	Feb	Mar	Apr	May	June
Income												
Wool	1000											
Ewes												
Lambs			500									
Wethers						100						
Rams												
Cattle								3000				
Total	1000		500			100		3000				
Expenditure												
Stock												
Purchases												
Rams												
Ewes			300									
Wethers				1000								
Rates												
Administration												
Repairs and maintenance					500							
Fertiliser												
AI												
Shearing and crutching												
Fuel and oil									1000			
Total			300	1000	500		500		1000			
Difference	1000		200	−1000	−500	100	−500	3000	−1000			

Gross margins

A gross margin measures the profitability of a particular enterprise and equals income minus variable costs. The gross margin includes only variable costs such as fuel, seed and fertiliser that are directly attributable to the enterprise and vary with the size of production. It does not include fixed costs such as rates and insurance because these are the same regardless of what is produced on the property.

Gross margins can be very useful because they:
- can be produced quickly
- are simple
- are easy to do and understand
- are useful for farm planning and analysis
- can compare the relative profitability of different enterprises on paper without risk or much effort
- can pinpoint areas of inefficiency and waste.

Gross margins can be calculated on a return per hectare, per dry sheep equivalent (DSE), per labour unit or per dollar invested.

Gross margins do, however, have some limitations and are not exact measures of profitability because they do not include overhead costs. They also do not allow for the farmer's own limitations such as those due to:
- climate
- soil types
- financial situation
- managerial skills and capabilities
- resources available for changing from one enterprise to another
- level of risk and uncertainty of different enterprises.

dry sheep equivalent
1 DSE equals one dry sheep or wether per hectare-it is a measure of the stocking rate of the land

5.38 Sample wheat gross margin

Income	$/ha
$/ha	$/ha
2.20 tonnes/ha @ $285.00/tonne	$627.00
A. Total income $/ha:	$627.00
Variable costs:	
Cultivation	$19.57
Sowing	$67.72
Fertiliser	$140.32
Herbicide	$62.32
Fungicide	$8.15
Contract-harvesting	$48.00
Levies	$6.40
Crop insurance	$6.43
Cartage, grading & bagging	$0.00
B. Total variable costs $/ha:	**$358.90**
C. Gross Margin (A–B) $/ha:	**$268.10**

Activity 5.13

1   Identify the following costs as fixed or variable.

Cost		Fixed/Variable	Cost		Fixed/Variable
a	accountancy fees	_____	j	permanent labour	_____
b	shearing	_____	k	fuel and oil	_____
c	drenching	_____	l	electricity	_____
d	dipping	_____	m	repairs and maintenance	_____
e	bank charges	_____	n	contract harvesting	_____
f	insurance and workers compensation	_____	o	depreciation on machinery and structures	_____
g	telephone	_____	p	cost of replacement stock, eg sheep	_____
h	stationery	_____	q	crop insurance	_____
i	vaccination	_____	r	cartage, grading and packaging	_____

2   Calculate gross margins for:
   a   breeding 1000 first cross ewe enterprise

5.39 Sample gross margin calculations

Income	Number	at	Budget
Wool (kg greasy)	4423 kg	278 c/kg	
Sales	1290 animals	$87.00 per hd	
A. Total income			
Variable costs			
Shearing	970 sheep	$242 per 100	
	19 rams	$484 per 100	
Shed labour	5 days	$180 /day	
Woolclasser	2.5 days	$216 /day	
Superannuation	9.0% wages	$350.00	
WorkCover		$155.00	
Wool packs	26 packs	$9.00 /pack	$234.00
Shed sundries	989 sheep	$0.10 /head	
Dipping		989 sheep	$0.50 /head
Crutch and wig	1009 adults	$82.00 /100	$831.00
Lamb marking	1100 lambs	$0.80 /head	
Ear tags	1100 lambs	$0.35 /head	
Animal health: drench	3140 sheep	$0.20 /head	
vaccinate	3220 sheep	$0.20 /head	
Stock purchases:			$32,417.00
freight			
livestock	189 culls	$3.00 /head	$567.00
	212 ewes	$3.00 /head	
	1100 prime lambs	$3.00 /head	
Wool	26 bales	$8.00 /bale	
Stock selling charges commission/insurance		5.5% gross	$6,212.00
yard fees	1289 head	$0.70 /head	
levy–sheep	189 head	0.80 /head	
levy–lambs	1100 head	$1.65 /head	
Wool selling charges brokerage/testing/insurance		$0.22 /kg	$973.00
Total variable costs			
Gross margin total			

b Enterprise: Young cattle 15–20 months (100 cows)

5.40 Sample gross margin calculations			
Income:	**Number**	**at**	**TOTAL**
steer yearlings 15–20 mths	30	$800.00/hd	
steer yearlings 20 mths	10	$800.00 /hd	
heifer yearlings 15–20 mths	10	$660.00 /hd	
heifer yearlings 20 mths	3	$694.00 /hd	
CFA Bull	1	$1215.00 /hd	
CFA cows	6	$663.00 /hd	
A. Total income:			
Variable costs:			
Replacements 1 Bull	1	$6000.00 /hd	
Livestock and vet costs:	$1360.00		
Ear tags		$2.00	$46.00
Pasture maintenence		$4000.00	
Livestock selling cost		$3538.00	
B. Total Variable Costs:			
Gross margin (A–B)			
Gross margin/cow			

Partial budget

5.41 Sample partial budget	
Gains	**Losses**
Money saved by not growing wheat	Cost of growing oats
Income from oats	Loss of income from wheat
Total A	**B**
	Profit = A – B

A partial budget measures the relative profitability of changing from one enterprise to another. The budget consists of two columns (gains and losses) and looks at the advantages and disadvantages of making the change. For example, a farmer wants to grow oats instead of wheat but is not sure if it would be profitable to make the change.

Partial budgets are quick and simple and compare the profitability of two enterprises. The budget does, however, have some limitations including:

- it does not include overhead costs
- it does not allow for the farmer's own limitations such as those due to climate, soils or financial situation
- it does not take account for the skills and resources available for changing from one enterprise to another.

Parametric budgeting

A parametric budget shows the effect of changing key variables such as yield or prices on the profitability of an enterprise. A revenue equation is constructed using key parameters and then analysed to see what effect the variables have on production.

Parametric budgets are useful management tools and allow the producer to quickly reassess new production possibilities if there is a change in key variables or market prices.

Activity 5.14

5.42 Effect of yield and price changes on the gross margin of wheat crops

Yield tonnes/Ha	On Farm Price ($/tonne)				
	$115/t	$135/t	$155/t	$175/t	$195/t
	Gross margin				
2.20	9	51	93	134	176
2.80	66	119	172	226	279
3.40	123	188	252	317	381
4.00	180	256	332	408	484
4.60	237	324	412	499	586
5.20	294	393	491	590	688
5.80	351	461	571	681	791

Calculate the change in gross margin per hectare that occurs in the following situations:
a yield increases from 2.2 to 5.80 tonnes/ha at $115/tonne
b prices fall from $195/tonne to $115/tonne for 2.80 tonnes/ha
c yield increases from 2.20 tonnes/ha to 4.00 tonnes/ha and price increases from $135/tonne to $175/tonne.

Development budget

A development budget shows the income and expenditure that occurs when a new enterprise is established. The budget is similar to a cash-flow budget but can extend over several years and indicate when the enterprise will become profitable.

5.43 Sample development budget

	Year				
	1	2	3	4	5
Income					
Vealer production	0	500	1000	3000	5000
Total	0	500	1000	3000	5000
Expenditure					
Clearing	1500	500			
Fertiliser	1000	500	500	500	500
Pasture establishment costs	700				
Labour costs	500	100			
Total	3700	1100	500	500	500
Net cash flow	–3700	–600	500	2500	4500

Development budgets have many advantages because they:
• are quickly produced
• are simple
• are useful for farm planning
• clearly show the main periods of debt and when cash-flow problems can occur
• are useful when applying for loans from financial institutions
• clearly show the feasibility of an idea on paper without risk.

Whole-farm budget

A whole-farm budget measures the profitability of the property and equals total income minus total costs.

A whole-farm budget has many advantages because it:
• is quickly produced
• is simple
• is useful for farm planning and analysis
• clearly show areas of inefficiency and waste
• is useful for taxation returns
• is useful when applying for loans or financial assistance.

Calculate the whole-farm budget using the following information:

Practical 19

Calculating a whole-farm budget

5.44 Sample whole-farm budget	
Enterprise	**Total gross margin**
Wheat	30 000
Prime lambs	20 000
Irrigated lucerne	15 000
Vealer production	10 000
Total income	
Operating costs	
Accounting	2 000
Bank charges	200
Insurance and workers compensation	1 800
Telephone	1 500
Stationery	200
Permanent labour	20 000
Fuel and oil	1 500
Electricity	300
Repairs	1 500
Depreciation on machinery and structures	20 000
Rates and land taxes	3 000
Total operating costs	
Net farm income = Income – Operating costs	

Assessing farm profit

Net farm income, return to total capital and return to equity are standards commonly used to determine the performance of a property. These parameters have many uses, including:

- showing the earning rate of the money invested in the property
- allowing the manager to assess the economic performance of the property relative to similar properties
- allowing the government and other major bodies to assess the performance of a large number of properties and the industry as a whole.

Net farm income

Net farm income measures the profit made by the total resources (capital, labour and management) on the farm and equals total income minus total costs.

Net farm income = Total income – Total costs

Net farm income has some limitations because it does not allow for the cost of borrowed money or the cost of the owner's labour and management.

Return to total capital

Return to capital measures how efficiently assets are allocated and used to generate profit.

Operating profit = Profit – cost of operator's labour and management.

$$\text{Percentage return to capital} = \frac{\text{Operating profit}}{\text{Total assets}} \times 100$$

If return to total capital is:

- <0% this is a poor result
- 0–5% this is a low result
- 5–10% this is a satisfactory result
- >10% this is a good result.

The formulae measure the earning rate of the farmer's resources and exclude personal factors such as taxation, living expenses and the level of equity of the operator.

Return to equity

Return to equity measures business return as a proportion of the owner's equity or capital.

$$\text{Return to equity} = \frac{\text{Business return}}{\text{Net worth}} \times 100$$

AG FACT

Returns

Return to equity and capital indicate how much the money invested in the property is returning. If the property cost $5 million and is only returning 1%, it would be worth considering if it would be more profitable to invest the money in a bank and just earn interest.

If return to equity is:

- <0% this is a poor result
- 0–5% this is a low result
- 5–10% this is a satisfactory result
- >10% this is a good result.

Consumer demand and marketing

Marketing includes all the operations in moving materials from the producer to the consumer and includes:

- buying
- transporting
- storing
- grading
- packaging
- financing
- selling and promotion.

Supply and demand

Demand

The demand curve shows the relationship between price and demand for a product.

There is an inverse relationship between the two variables so the higher the price the lower the demand.

Many factors affect demand, including the:

- price of the commodity, for example the higher the price the lower the demand
- price of similar products, for example consumers will buy cheaper alternatives if available
- tastes and preferences of the consumer
- income of the consumer and how much they have to spend
- population size and level of demand.

Fluctuations in these factors can cause the demand curve to move to the left or right.

For example, if there was a drought and a shortage of alternative products, demand would increase and the demand curve would move to the right.

Supply

The supply curve shows the relationship between price and supply of a product.

There is a direct relationship between the two variables and as price increases so does the quantity offered for sale.

Many factors affect supply, including the:

- price of product
- cost of inputs
- profitability of other enterprises
- number of farmers with enterprise
- skills of the farmer
- level of technology available
- technical efficiency of the farmer
- climatic effects, for example droughts
- effects of weeds, pests and diseases
- seasonality of production

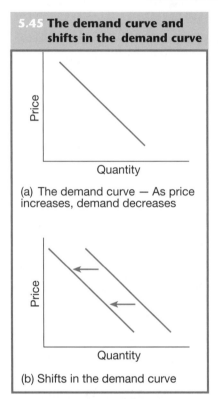

5.45 The demand curve and shifts in the demand curve

(a) The demand curve — As price increases, demand decreases

(b) Shifts in the demand curve

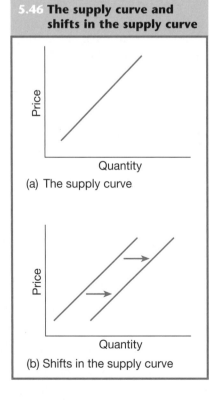

5.46 The supply curve and shifts in the supply curve

(a) The supply curve

(b) Shifts in the supply curve

5.47 Inelastic and elastic demand curves

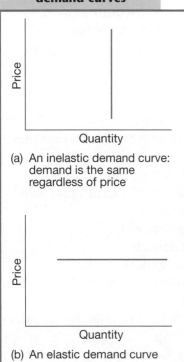

(a) An inelastic demand curve: demand is the same regardless of price

(b) An elastic demand curve

5.48 Equilibrium market price

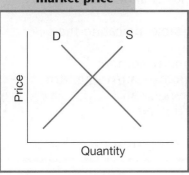

• perishability and storage life of product
• world supply and its effect on demand and price
• government restrictions or incentives such as quotas and tariffs.

Fluctuations in these factors can make the supply curve move to the left or the right.

Elasticity of supply and demand

Elasticity measures how sensitive supply and demand curves are to price changes.

$$\text{Price elasticity of supply} = \frac{\text{\% change in supply}}{\text{\% change in price}}$$

$$\text{Price elasticity of demand} = \frac{\text{\% change in quantity demanded}}{\text{\% change in price}}$$

An elastic supply curve has a small slope and is very responsive to price fluctuations. A small change in price can have a large effect on supply.

An inelastic supply curve has a steep slope and is unresponsive to price changes.

An elastic demand curve is very responsive to price changes and a perfectly elastic demand curve has a horizontal line because there is infinite demand at a particular price.

Elasticity of supply and demand is important to agricultural production because uncontrolled supply and relatively inelastic demand cause large fluctuations in the price of meat, fruit and vegetables.

Equilibrium market price

The equilibrium market price for a product occurs when supply equals demand and the supply curve intercepts the demand curve.

Equilibrium market price = the point where supply equals demand.

Activity 5.15

1   Draw a supply and demand curve for fresh fruit and vegetables.
2   How do you determine the equilibrium market price?
3   Explain the effect of the following factors on the equilibrium market price:
   a   rise in consumers' income
   b   drought
   c   introduction of greater yielding varieties
   d   increase in production costs
   e   disease outbreak.

Marketing agricultural products

Many methods are used to market agricultural products, including:
- free-market system where producers can sell to whoever they wish
- auction system where produce is sold to the highest bidder, for example live-weight selling of sheep and cattle and wool
- future contracts, for example selling produce for a set price at a set time sometime in the future
- cooperatives, such as the dairy corporations in each state
- markets, for example vegetables are sent to produce markets in major cities and then sold to retailers
- computer selling
- marketing authorities
- direct to processor, for example direct sale of tomatoes to canning factories.
  Producers use many different marketing strategies to:
- increase price
- increase profitability
- reduce risk
- increase reliability
- increase volume of sales, for example domestic and export markets
- sell to different markets and consumers, for example organic produce
- increase competition, for example auction system
- allows long-term planning, for example future markets with guaranteed prices
- minimises middle costs, for example direct marketing
- reduces handling and transport costs, for example local produce markets.

Activity 5.16

1. Why does the response of farmers to individual price changes differ in the short term from other industries?
2. Use these Internet sites to complete the following table indicating the marketing system used for each product:

   www.infarmation.com.au   www.farmonline.com.au
   www.aglinks.com.au   www.daff.qld.gov.au/home.htm
   www.dpi.vic.gov.au   www.dpi.nsw.gov.au
   www.dpi.qld.gov.au   www.pir.sa.gov.au
   www.dpiw.tas.gov.au
   australia.gov.au/directories/australia/agriculture/web-resources-list

Product	Marketing system
Wheat	Price based on protein content, hardness.
Wool	Australian Wool Corporation. Price based on fibre diameter, staple length, purity.
Cattle	Auction, live weight, paddock, direct sale to abattoirs.
Vegetables	Markets in major cities then sold to retailers for public sale. Sold direct to processors, for example canneries.
Flowers	
Cotton	
Milk	
Eggs	
Wine	
Deer	
Fruit	

Activity 5.17

Diagram [5.49] shows the wool-processing chain.

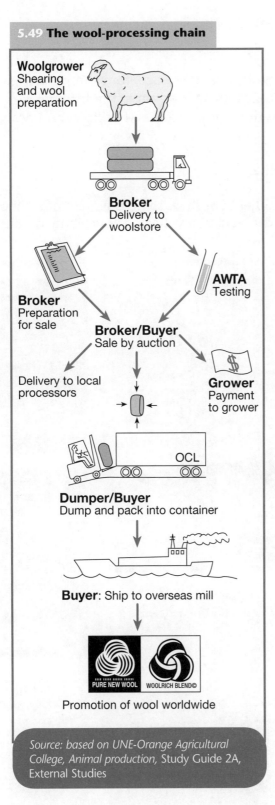

5.49 The wool-processing chain

Woolgrower
Shearing and wool preparation

Broker
Delivery to woolstore

Broker
Preparation for sale

AWTA
Testing

Broker/Buyer
Sale by auction

Delivery to local processors

Grower
Payment to grower

Dumper/Buyer
Dump and pack into container

Buyer: Ship to overseas mill

Promotion of wool worldwide

Source: based on UNE-Orange Agricultural College, Animal production, Study Guide 2A, External Studies

deregulation
free trade of produce with minimal restrictions

niche marketing
targetting a specific small sector of the total market, for example botrytis-affected wine for drinking with desserts

1 A floor price scheme was established for wool in 1974 to stabilise income and maintain wool supply. Research why the scheme was abandoned and what detrimental effects it had on production.

2 Explain why the marketing of many agricultural products including milk has been deregulated.

3 What are the advantages and disadvantages of deregulation?

4 Producers can improve the marketability of a product in many ways such as value adding or niche marketing. Explain three other ways in which producers can improve the marketability of a product.

Technology

New technology has had a profound effect on agricultural production and marketing.

Examples of changing technology include:

• mechanisation
• genetic engineering
• improved transportation and storage, for example refrigeration
• improved communication, for example the Internet
• chemicals such as drenches, vaccines, fertilisers and pesticides.

Activity 5.18

1 Photographs [5.50]–[5.56] show some examples of technology. Explain how each of these technologies has affected agricultural production.

5.50 **Computers**

5.51 **Improved communications**

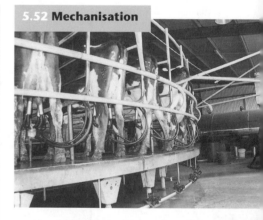

5.52 **Mechanisation**

5.53 **Chemicals**

5.54 **Satellite-positioning system**

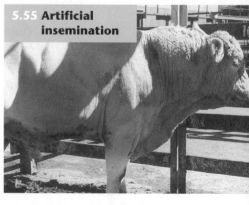

5.55 **Artificial insemination**

5.56 **Refrigeration and transportation**

2 List the technologies used in each enterprise:

Enterprise	Technology
Wheat	New seed varieties: direct drill machinery; fertiliser; herbicides; harvesting machinery; flour mills-processing and packaging.
Fruit	
Beef	
Viticulture	
Aquaculture	
Vegetables	
Rice	
Flowers	
Other	

Workplace hazards and farm injuries

Agriculture has one of the highest injury and death rates of any industry. A child is killed every 13 days on a farm in Australia.

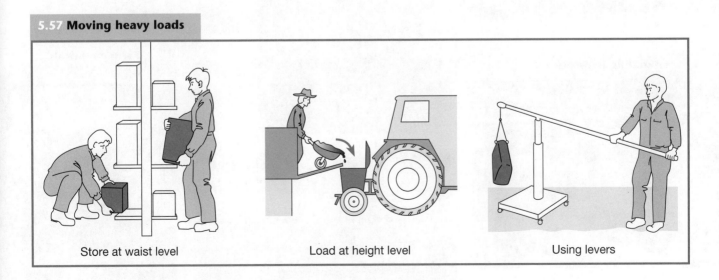

5.57 Moving heavy loads

Store at waist level   Load at height level   Using levers

Activities that can cause injury include:

- manual handling, for example lifting heavy objects
- machinery and equipment, for example motor bikes, chainsaws, power tools, rifles and silos
- tractors
- handling animals
- hazardous substances
- electricity, for example electrocution in handling irrigation pipes
- noise and hearing loss, for example shot guns
- sunburn and heat stress
- diseases such as zoonosis.

zoonosis
a disease such as rabies that is communicable to humans from animals

5.58 Correct chainsaw equipment

Safety helmet

Ear muffs or plugs

Wear close fitting clothing

High grip gloves

Safety pants or safety chaps

Approved fuel container

Safety boots with steel capped toes and non-slip soles

First-aid kit readily available

Activity 5.19

1 Identify the sources of danger in these photos.

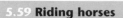

5.59 Riding horses

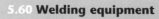

5.60 Welding equipment

5.61 Motor bikes

5.62 Handling livestock

5.63 Silos and augers

5.64 Farm chemicals

2   Identify the source of danger and preventative measures for the following situations:

Situation	Source of danger	Prevention
Shearing	spinal damage	back braces
Rifles	deafness	ear muffs
Tractor	rolling over	ROPs (Rollover protection structures)
Chemicals	poisoning	protective clothing
PTOs		
Chainsaw		
Hay bales		
Animals		
Melanomas		
Bushfires		
Zoonosis		
Electricity		
Working alone		
Lifting heavy loads		
Hand tools		

3   Place diagrams [5.65] and [5.66] in the correct sequence for handling a sheep.

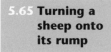

5.65 Turning a sheep onto its rump

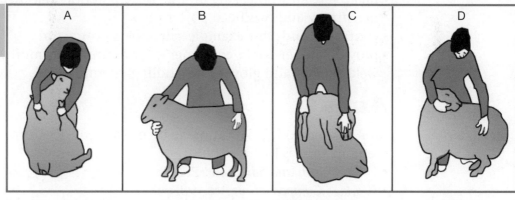

A   B   C   D

5.66 Lifting a sheep

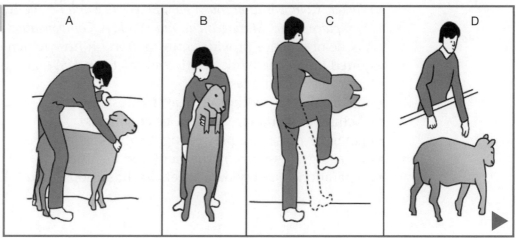

A   B   C   D

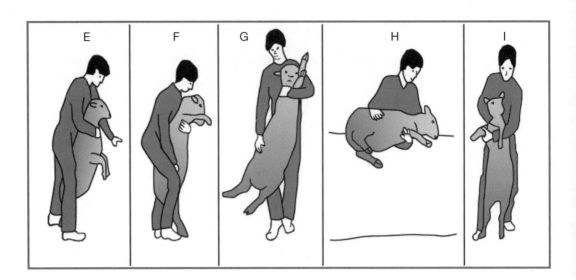

OH&S legislation

Farmers have a legal obligation to ensure the safety of their workers. They must:
- have safe work systems in place, for example provide cattle crush when dehorning cattle
- maintain working areas, for example chemicals stored in chemical cupboards
- keep equipment in a safe condition, for example chainsaws have safety guards
- make sure all workers are aware of the potential hazards, for example machinery and overhead power lines
- control hazards, for example safety bars on tractors
- provide proper safety equipment, for example ear muffs, eye protection for welding jobs and gloves for handling chemicals.

Acts

An Act refers to legislation made by parliament. Producers must abide by them. Examples include the:
- *Work Health and Safety Act 2011*
- *Workers Compensation Act 1987*
- *Workers Compensation (Bush Fire, Emergency and Rescue Services) Act 1987*
- *Workplace Injury Management and Workers Compensation Act 1998*.

A code of practice provides information on how to achieve the standards required under the work health and safety (WHS) legislation, including:
- hazardous manual tasks
- how to manage workplace health and safety risks
- labelling of workplace hazardous chemicals
- managing noise and preventing hearing loss at work
- managing the work environment and facilities
- preparation of safety data sheets for hazardous chemicals.

cloning
asexual reproduction that results in an identical individual

Animal welfare

For moral, social and ethical reasons animal cruelty is not tolerated by our society. Areas of debate include:

- scientific research on animals, for example experimentation on animals
- genetic engineering and cloning
- game hunting, for example ivory tusks from elephants
- performing animals, for example circuses, bullfighting and dancing bears
- fur hunting, for example seals
- drag-net fishing
- intensive agricultural production, for example poultry and feedlots
- operations such as mulesing
- extinction caused by mass clearing of habitats.

Extension Activity

Discuss the social, ethical and moral issues of animal welfare and agricultural production.

Revision 5.20

1 Define the following words:
- climate
- enterprises
- consumer
- risk
- liabilities
- variable cost
- demand

- management
- weeds
- farm management
- production function
- equity
- partial budget
- marketing

- technology
- microbes
- environment
- assets
- gross margin
- supply
- budget

2 Answer true or false to the following statements:
 a Gross margins show the profitability of a farm.
 b Climate refers to the daily weather conditions.
 c Demand increases with decreasing price.
 d Equity includes everything a farmer possesses.
 e Agriculture is a high-risk industry.
 f Agriculture has a high injury and death rate.
 g Marketing is the selling of a product.
 h Budgets are essential for good management.
 i Farm injuries can be prevented.
 j Animal welfare is not relevant to agriculture.

3 See page 387 for the find-a-word activity.

Farm Case Survey

This chapter provides a template of a farm survey

By completing this practical you will build on and consolidate much of what you have learnt earlier.

Property description

1 Complete the following:

Name of property_____

Owner's name _____

Location _____

Size (hectares) _____

Number of employees _____

Farm plan

| 6.1 | Aerial map of farm |

N

↑

2 Draw a map of the property and include the following information:
- location relative to major towns
- topography
- aspect
- soil types
- fences and subdivisions
- sources of water
- major roads
- problem areas, for example salinity and acidic soils.

6.2 Sources of water

6.3 Saltbush is used to control salinity

Climatic information

3   Complete the following information:

- annual rainfall _____

- seasonality, variability and effectiveness of the rainfall

  _____

- annual evaporative rate _____

- growing period of the district _____

- maximum and minimum temperatures _____

- incidence of frosts _____

- incidence of droughts or flooding _____

4   Draw a graph of yearly temperature [6.4] and rainfall levels [6.5 over].

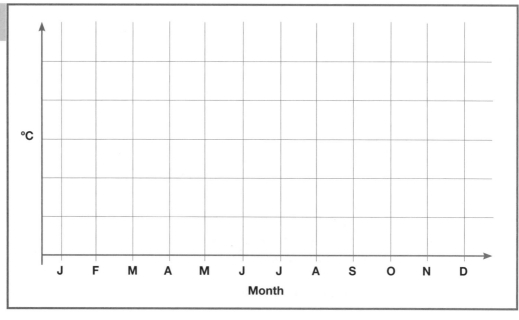

6.4 Annual average temperature

°C

J F M A M J J A S O N D

Month

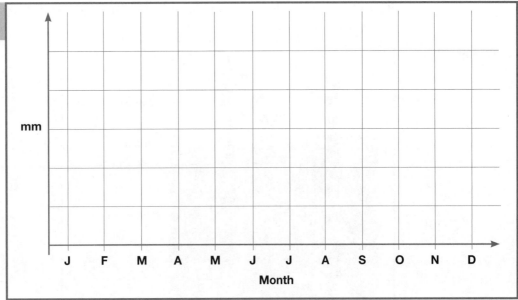

6.5 Annual average rainfall

5   In which months can summer and winter plants be grown?
_____

6   What limitations does climate impose on production?
_____

7   How has the producer minimised the effect of these limitations?
_____

Soil types

8   What are:

- the major soil types? _____
- how were they formed?_____
- their physical and chemical characteristics, including:

  – texture _____

  – structure _____

  – mineralogy _____

  – fertility level _____

  – organic matter content _____

  – water-holding capacity _____

  – pH _____

  – susceptibility to salinity problems _____

  – potential to shrink and swell _____

  – ability to compact or crack on drying _____

  – plasticity level _____

  – susceptibility to erosion _____

  – major limitations _____

9   Draw a profile for each soil type. Label their horizons and discuss their distinguishing features.

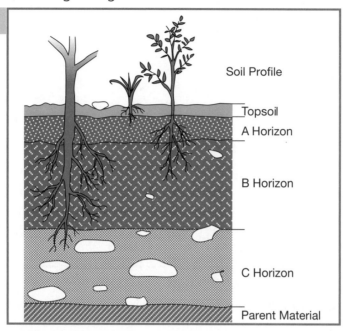

10 What management practices are used to overcome soil problems and increase soil productivity?

_____

_____

Topography

11 What is the topography of the property? _____

12 How does it affect the type of agriculture conducted on the property?

_____

_____

_____

13 How has the farmer overcome topographical problems?

_____

_____

Water sources

14 What are the main sources of water? _____

15 How has the farmer planned for periods of water shortage? _____

_____

Inventories

16 Draw up an inventory for the following:
- livestock
- machinery
- seed
- fertiliser
- chemicals, for example drenches, herbicides and insecticides
- feeds, for example hay, silage and grain.

6.7 Livestock enterprises

6.8 Machinery

6.9 Silos and grain storage

Enterprises

17 What are the main enterprises on the property?

_____

_____

_____

Animal enterprises

18 Answer the following questions for each enterprise:

- name of enterprise _____
- main products _____
- number and monetary value of livestock and products

  _____

- reproductive capacity _____
- major operations of the enterprise _____
- major inputs and costs _____
- feeding policy _____
- methods used to control pests and diseases _____
- methods used to increase quality or production levels

  _____

- marketing procedures _____

  _____

Cropping enterprises

19 For each enterprise complete the following:

- name of crop _____
- purpose or end uses _____
- amount of crop grown _____
- inputs used to grow crop, such as:

  amount of seed (kg) _____

  fertiliser (types and amount) _____

  machinery _____

  fuel _____

  labour _____

  chemicals, for example herbicides and pesticides _____

- major operations involved in producing, harvesting and marketing the crop

  _____

- methods used to control weeds, pests and diseases

  _____

  _____

- methods used to increase quality and production levels

  _____

  _____

Pasture and fodder crop production

20 Complete the following questions:

- type of pastures, for example native, natural or improved _____

_____

- purpose of pastures _____
- most important species present _____

21 Complete the following activities and questions:

a Draw and label 5 important grasses _____

b Draw and label 5 important legumes _____

c What are their distinguishing features? _____.

_____

d Which of the above plants are summer or winter growing species?

_____

e How were the pastures established? _____

_____

f How are the pastures managed? _____

_____

_____

g What are the grazing practices? _____

h How are weeds, pests and diseases controlled? _____

_____

_____

i What types and amounts of fertilisers are applied? _____

_____

22 Graph pasture dry matter production throughout the year.

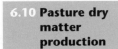

6.10 Pasture dry matter production

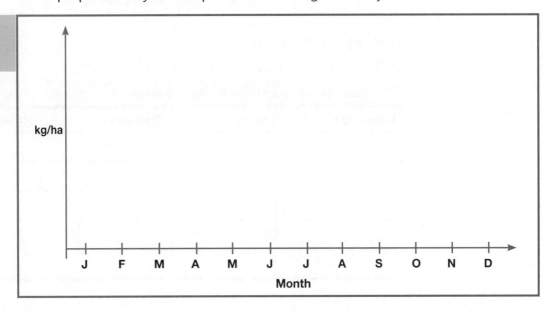

- How does the grazier compensate for periods of shortage? _____
  _____

- Estimate current and possible carrying capacity (DSE). _____
  _____

- How could productivity be improved? _____
  _____
  _____

Systems diagram

23 Draw a systems diagram of the farm and explain the interactions that occur.

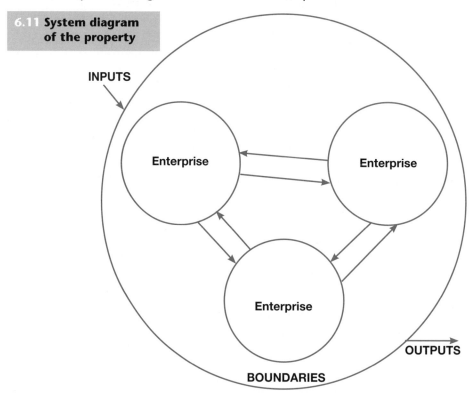

6.11 System diagram of the property

INPUTS

Enterprise

Enterprise

Enterprise

OUTPUTS

BOUNDARIES

Whole-year program

24 Draw a yearly calendar of operations for the farm.

6.12 Calendar of operations on the property

Enterprise	Month	Operation	Reason for operation

Constraints on the farmer

25 List the major constraints on the farmer such as:

- climate _____
- soil _____
- topography _____
- weeds, pests and diseases _____
- marketing _____
- financial _____
- government intervention _____
- risk management _____
- technology _____

26 How can the producer reduce the effect of these constraints?

_____

_____

_____

_____

Work safety

27 Identify the main sources of danger on the property. _____

_____

_____

_____

_____

28 How could these dangers be minimised or prevented? _____

_____

_____

_____

Sources of information

29 What are the major sources of information available to the producer? _____

_____

_____

30 Is this information useful? _____

_____

_____

6.13 Technology on the property

Technology and innovation

31 What technology and innovations are used on the property?

_____

_____

_____

_____

_____

Farm business analysis

32 Construct the following statements and budgets:
- statement of assets, liability and equity
- cash-flow budget
- gross margins for each enterprise
- whole-farm budget
- development budget for improving the property.

6.14 **Sample gross margin – yearling beef cattle enterprise**

				Amount $
Income – Cattle				
Yearling steers	_____ at $	_____	/head	_____
Yearling heifers	_____ at $	_____	/head	_____
Cast for age cows	_____ at $	_____	/head	_____
Old bulls at $ head	_____ at $	_____	/head	_____
Total income				
Variable costs				
Drench	_____ at $	_____	/head	_____
Parasite control, eg lice control	_____ at $	_____	/head	_____
Veterinary costs, eg 5-in-1 vaccine	_____ at $	_____	/calf	_____
Pregnancy test	_____ at $	_____	/head	_____
Miscellaneous, eg cost of a new bull	$ _____			_____
Total variable costs				_____
Gross margin = Income – Variable costs				_____

6.15 Sample gross margin – first cross spring lamb enterprise

	Amount $
Income – Wool	
_____ kg of wool from _____ ewes at $ _____ /kg	_____
_____ kg of wool from _____ rams at $ _____ /kg	_____
Income – Sheep	_____
_____ number of cast for age ewes at $ _____ /head	_____
_____ number of ewe lambs at $ _____ /head	_____
_____ number of wether lambs at $ _____ /head	_____
_____ number of cast for age rams at $ _____ /head	_____
Total income	_____
Variable costs	
Shearing _____ number of sheep at $ _____ /head	_____
Crutching _____ number of sheep at $ _____ /head	_____
Drenching _____ number of sheep at $ _____ /head	_____
Dipping and jetting _____ number of sheep at $ _____ /head	_____
Vaccination _____ number of sheep at $ _____ /head	_____
Miscellaneous • cost of replacement ewes _____ number at $ _____ /head	_____
• cost of replacement rams _____ number at $ _____ /head	_____
Total variable costs	_____
Gross margin = Income – Variable costs	_____

Sources of finance

33 What are the major sources of finance available to the producer?

_____

_____

Methods of improving management and production levels

34 Is the farm profitable? _____

35 What are the major causes of inefficiency and waste? _____

_____

36 How can management and productivity be improved? _____

_____

Plant Production

In this chapter you will learn about:

- the importance of plants
- Australia's plant production areas
- plant structure and reproduction
- plant requirements and activities
- factors affecting productivity
- pasture production and management
- wheat production
- the impact of technology.

Importance of plants

Plants provide us with food, fibre, shelter and oxygen to breathe. Important types of plants include:

- grain crops such as wheat, barley and rice
- grain legumes such as lupins, chickpea and peanuts
- oil crops such as canola, sunflowers, soybeans, olives, safflower, linseed, peanuts and macadamia nuts
- vegetables such as lettuce, cauliflower and pumpkin
- root crops such as turnips and carrots
- pome, citrus and stone fruit such as apples, oranges and peaches
- vine fruit such as grapes
- drug crops such as tobacco
- flowers as grown by nurseries
- pastures such as grasses and legumes
- forests such as eucalyptus or pine.

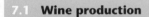
7.1 Wine production

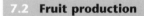
7.2 Fruit production

7.3 Canola production

7.4 Agroforestry

Activity 7.1

With reference to the table [7.5]:
a list the plant enterprises that are increasing in importance
b give reasons for these trends
c graph the value of the most popular enterprises over time.

7.5 Gross value of production by commodity, QLD, 2000–2011

Commodity	Financial year ($m)										
	2000–01	2001–02	2002–03	2003–04	2004–05	2005–06	2006–07	2007–08	2008–09	2009–10	2010–11
Crops											
Sugar cane	617.3	923.2	961.6	793.8	916.5	988.4	1,121.5	799.0	967.6	1,316.2	888.4
Cereals for grain:											
Barley	19.6	33.1	42.1	44.0	27.3	26.3	19.2	44.0	43.3	24.1	26.9
Grain sorghum	168.6	221.8	191.1	209.0	164.8	167.3	189.2	637.2	355.7	171.9	251.7
Maize	29.5	41.8	28.0	49.9	35.3	25.0	22.0	n.a.	n.a.	n.a.	40
Rice	n.a.	n.a.	n.a.	n.a.	n.a.	n.a.	0.0	0.0	0.0	0.9	0.6
Wheat	268.1	227.3	171.5	234.1	231.7	250.6	187.5	353.4	535.6	301.1	378.4
Other	15.1	12.8	24.8	20.4	16.2	15.8	11.2	5.0	80.8	1.4	12.5
Total cereals for grain	500.9	536.8	457.5	557.4	475.3	485.0	429.1	1039.6	1015.4	499.4	710.1
Fruit and nuts (d):											
Bananas	345.0	359.6	285.1	256.2	291.0	357.0	761.9	354.4	390.2	448.3	283.1
Citrus	75.7	90.6	111.8	126.6	95.2	98.2	131.6	94.1	68.1	80.5	133.2
Pineapples	44.0	40.1	32.5	37.1	33.4	88.4	91.3	n.a.	n.a.	n.a.	50.2
Other	267.9	296.0	260.6	267.7	330.8	338.3	474.5	644.5	512.9	516.6	395.1
Total fruit and nuts	732.6	786.3	689.9	687.6	750.4	881.9	1459.3	1093.0	971.2	1045.4	861.6
Vegetables:											
Potatoes	46.8	48.2	66.0	61.9	48.4	48.7	55.2	58.4	54.1	57.1	51.5
Tomatoes	135.4	140.4	123.2	165.9	90.6	158.6	169.1	209.6	187.9	144.9	229.8
Other	456.3	488.8	485.0	606.6	545.4	759.1	778.0	727.1	709.6	666.8	796.1
Total vegetables	638.5	677.4	674.2	834.4	684.4	966.4	1002.3	995.1	951.6	868.8	1077.4
Other:											
Cotton (e)	414.1	396.5	187.6	346.4	418.9	377.1	121.3	79.2	325.2	301.1	776.1
Crops for hay	22.3	22.1	50.7	40.1	41.0	112.5	194.4	201.4	136.9	136.4	111
Legumes for grain	44.4	59.0	42.5	31.4	17.0	17.1	43.1	n.a.	n.a.	n.a.	92.2
Nurseries, flowers and turf (f)	204.1	182.5	156.7	101.0	105.0	n.a.	287.5	342.0	297.0	327.8	293.9
Oilseeds	24.5	21.3	10.9	25.2	9.6	9.8	3.8	n.a.	n.a.	0.5	10.2
Pastures/grasses	57.5	69.1	106.0	129.7	95.4	n.a.	n.a.	n.a.	n.a.	n.a.	n.a.
Peanuts	26.4	18.5	21.0	28.5	20.3	15.6	13.8	n.a.	n.a.	n.a.	14.7
Tobacco	16.2	11.0	15.0	5.4	n.a.	0.2	n.a.	n.a.	n.a.	n.a.	n.a.
Other	92.4	179.6	93.0	131.2	n.a.	283.4	132.1	251.1	218.6	260.1	65.6
Total crops	**3391.2**	**3883.3**	**3466.7**	**3712.1**	**3703.6**	**4137.3**	**4751.8**	**4800.4**	**4883.5**	**4755.7**	**4901.2**

Source: ABARE 2012

The consumer and plant features

Features of a plant that are important to a consumer include:
- quality, for example lack of bruising
- variety
- freshness
- appearance, for example size of apples
- purity
- taste and texture, for example wine
- no contamination, for example lack of pests and diseases
- high nutritional value
- organic or chemical free
- availability, for example bananas in the winter
- ease of preparation and handling, for example pre-packaged lettuce leaves
- value-added products, for example fruit juice
- longevity, for example long storage life.

Practical 20

Creating a plant collection

common name
everyday name used to identify a plant, such as white clover

scientific name
universal Latin name used to identify a plant internationally, such as trifolium repens – the first word being the genus and the second the species

Aim
To collect, identify and display 20 important agricultural crops.

Equipment
- hand trowel
- newspaper
- bricks or other heavy weight
- display paper
- glue

Method
1. Collect 20 agricultural plants.
2. Store them between newspaper pages until they are dry. Replace newspaper if it becomes damp.
3. Place specimens on some display paper including portions of flowers, leaves, stems and roots.
4. Label with:
   - common name
   - scientific name
   - location
   - date
   - special features or characteristics
   - importance to agriculture.

AG FACT

Grain trade
Australia is a small producer of grain with the major cereals of wheat and barley each accounting for just 3 per cent of annual world production. However as about 80 per cent of this grain is exported, Australia accounts for between 8 and 15 per cent of total world trade in these grains. Only the United States, Canada and the European Union normally export more.

Activity 7.2

Use the following Internet sites to research your answers to the questions:
australia.gov.au/directories/australia/agriculture/web-resources-list
www.abs.gov.au   agnet.com.au
www.aglinks.com.au   www.daff.gov.au/abares
www.farmonline.com.au   www.daff.qld.gov.au/home.htm
www.dpi.vic.gov.au   www.dpi.nsw.gov.au
www.dpi.qld.gov.au   www.pir.sa.gov.au
www.dpiw.tas.gov.au

1   Find the most recent statistics on the volume of plant production in Australia.
2   What are the market requirements for five plant products? Wheat, for example has
    two important market requirements of protein content and purity as well as others.

Plant production areas

Many factors affect plant production as indicated in [7.6] below.

However climate is one of the most important. Australia is a dry continent
and 50 per cent of the land surface receives less than 300 mm of rain per year.
The volume and type of plant production depends on the amount of rain a
region receives, its seasonality and its reliability.

7.6 Factors affecting plant production

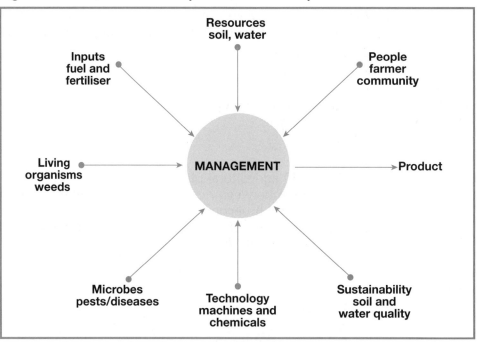

evaporative demand
amount of water vapour lost from the soil

The growing season is the number of consecutive months of effective
rainfall where rainfall exceeds one-third of the evaporative demand.

The shorter the growing season the greater are the restrictions on the type
of plants that can be grown in an area.

Seventy per cent of Australia has a growing season of less than five months
and these regions only support grazing systems based on drought-resistant
native pastures, trees and shrubs. Cropping regions have a growing season of
5–9 months and intensive agricultural production occurs in regions with a
growing season of 9–12 months.

7.7 Length of growing season

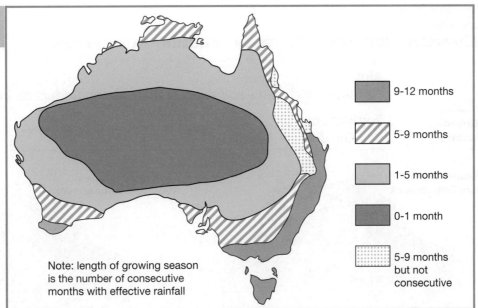

9-12 months

5-9 months

1-5 months

0-1 month

5-9 months but not consecutive

Note: length of growing season is the number of consecutive months with effective rainfall

Practical 21

Growing season in your region

Aim
To calculate the growing season of a local region from rainfall and evaporation rates.

Equipment
- rain gauge
- average monthly rainfall and evaporation levels for the local region.

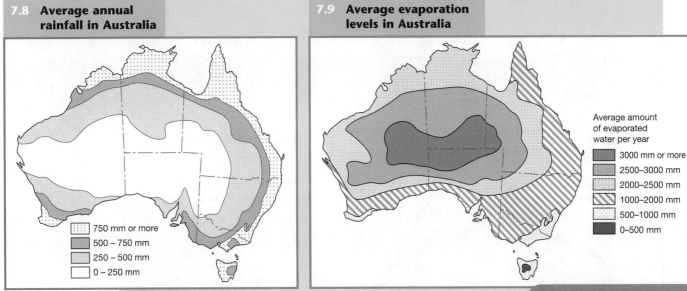

7.8 Average annual rainfall in Australia

750 mm or more

500 – 750 mm

250 – 500 mm

0 – 250 mm

7.9 Average evaporation levels in Australia

Average amount of evaporated water per year

3000 mm or more

2500–3000 mm

2000–2500 mm

1000–2000 mm

500–1000 mm

0–500 mm

Source: Bureau of Meteorology

Method
1 Record and graph daily rainfall levels.
2 Draw a bar graph of average rainfall levels and one-third of evaporation levels for each month.
3 Determine which months had effective rainfall as well as the growing season of your region.

Conclusion
State your conclusions from the results.

Practical 22

Climates and agricultural production in Australia

7.10 Climatic data for Australia

Aim
To study the climates and types of agricultural production in Australia.

Equipment
Climatic data for Australia.

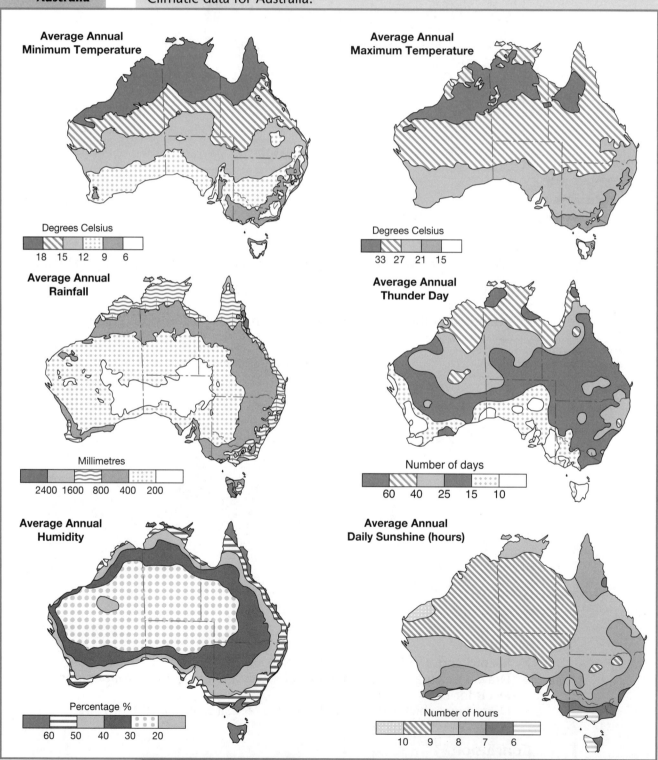

Average Annual Minimum Temperature

Degrees Celsius

18 15 12 9 6

Average Annual Maximum Temperature

Degrees Celsius

33 27 21 15

Average Annual Rainfall

Millimetres

2400 1600 800 400 200

Average Annual Thunder Day

Number of days

60 40 25 15 10

Average Annual Humidity

Percentage %

60 50 40 30 20

Average Annual Daily Sunshine (hours)

Number of hours

10 9 8 7 6

Method
1 Complete the table [7.11].

Max. and min. temp.	Median rainfall	Thunder No of days	Humidity %	Sunshine hours	Growing season	Clmate ie temperate, tropical
Sydney						
Melbourne						
Adelaide						
Perth						
Darwin						
Brisbane						
Alice Springs						

2 Draw a map of Australia and indicate the climatic zones.
3 Compare your diagram with the actual climates.

Results
1 What types of plants are found in each of the climatic regions?
2 What types of animals are found in each of the climatic regions?

Conclusion
State the conclusions that you can make from your results.

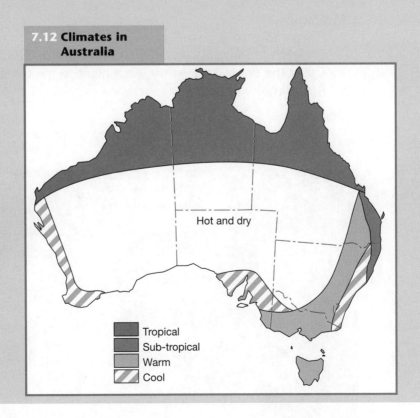

7.12 **Climates in Australia**

Hot and dry

Tropical
Sub-tropical
Warm
Cool

Practical 23

Temperature and germination

Aim
To see the effect of temperature on the germination of different plants such as wheat, barley, oats, sunflowers, lucerne and perennial ryegrass.

Background information
Plants and animals have evolved over millions of years to suit a particular climate and have their own cardinal temperature ranges [7.13].

petri dish
a flat plastic or glass dish with a lid used for scientific investigations such as seed germination trials

7.13 Temperature ranges of different plants

Plant	Min °C	Optimum °C	Max °C
Wheat	0–5	25–31	31–37
Barley	0–5	25–31	31–37
Oats	0–5	25–31	31–37
Sunflowers	4–11	31–37	36–44
Lucerne	9	24	27
Perennial ryegrass	10	20	26

Equipment
- 18 petri dishes
- cotton wool
- three temperature ranges, for example oven, refrigerator and room temperature
- 90 seeds of each of six plant types

Method
1. Place damp cotton wool in each dish.
2. For each of the six plants put 30 seeds in three petri dishes.
3. Cover the dishes and expose each plant to the three temperature ranges.
4. Record germination rates.

Results
What was the optimum temperature range for each plant?

7.14 Sunflower oil production

Plant structure

Most plants contain the following parts:
- flowers
- leaves
- buds
- seeds
- stems
- roots.

Flowering plants are divided into two main groups based on their structure. Monocotyledons (or simply monocots) have a single cotyledon or primary leaf and dicotyledons (or simply dicots) have two.

Other features used to differentiate the two classes include:

cotyledon
The first leaf or leaves developed by a germinating seed

vascular bundle
a strand of conducting tissue consisting of xylem and phloem that transports fluids between roots and stems

7.15 Characteristics of the two main plant groups

Feature	Monocotyledon	Dicotyledon
Number of cotyledons	One	Two
Shape of leaves	Narrow	Broad
Type of veins	Parallel	Reticulate
Structure of stem	No vascular bundles, no vascular cambium	Vascular bundles
Floral arrangement	Floral parts in multiples of 3	Floral parts in multiples of 4–5
Root system	Fibrous	Woody taproot
Examples	Cereals, for example wheat	Rose, peach and eucalypt

7.16 Flower production

Flowers

Flowers are the reproductive organs of a plant and consist of:
- a stem
- sepals
- petals
- stalk and anthers – the male reproductive organs
- ovary, style and stigma – the female reproductive organs.

Some flowers contain only one sex and are called imperfect flowers.

Grasses have modified flowers called florets, which have hard glumes, lemmas and paleas instead of sepals and petals.

7.17 Parts of a flower

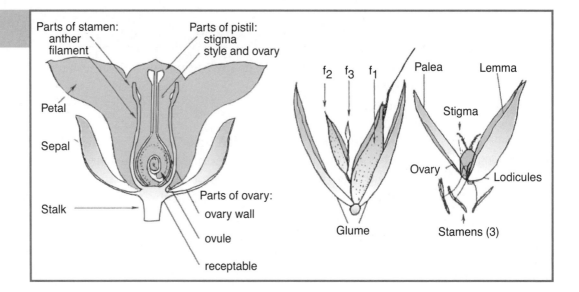

Parts of stamen:
 anther
 filament

Parts of pistil:
 stigma
 style and ovary

Petal

Sepal

Stalk

Parts of ovary:
 ovary wall
 ovule
 receptable

f2 f3 f1

Palea   Lemma

Stigma

Ovary

Lodicules

Glume

Stamens (3)

Activity 7.3

List the functions of each floral part in table form.

Part of flower	Functions
Stem	
Sepal	
Petals	
Stalk	
Anthers	
Stigma	
Style	

gametes
reproductive cells that unite to form a zygote

7.18 Stages of pollination

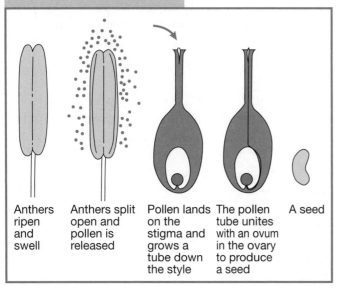

Anthers ripen and swell

Anthers split open and pollen is released

Pollen lands on the stigma and grows a tube down the style

The pollen tube unites with an ovum in the ovary to produce a seed

A seed

Pollination

Pollination is the union of male and female gametes to form a seed. Pollination occurs in the following stages:

1 the anthers rupture releasing pollen into the air
2 wind and insect vectors transport the pollen to the stigma
3 pollen germinates and grows down the style to the ovary
4 fertilisation occurs and a seed is formed
5 the ovary becomes the fruit and the ovule becomes the seed.

Activity 7.4

Explain why grasses such as wheat do not have colourful petals to assist pollination.

7.19 Structure of a wheat grain and a bean

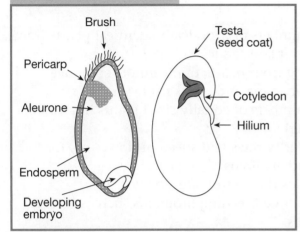

Seeds

Seeds consist of an outer coat, embryo and food reserves.

Seeds are important because they:
• produce the next generation of plants
• disperse and establish plants in new areas
• act as a survival mechanism by germinating when conditions are favourable.

Fruit

A fruit is the ripened ovary of the flower and encloses the seeds.

Practical 24

Anatomy of flowers

Aim
To collect and draw flowers of several important agricultural plants.

Equipment
• flowers of important agricultural crops

Method
Draw and label the reproductive organs.

Activity 7.5

List 20 flowers that are grown in Australia for commercial production, for example tulips and proteas.

Asexual reproduction in plants

Plants can be grown from segments without the union of male and female gametes. Organs commonly used include:
• rhizome – an underground stem such as iris
• tuber – swollen end of an underground stem such as dahlia
• corm – a swollen underground rounded base of a stem such as crocus and gladiolus
• bulb such as onion and tulip

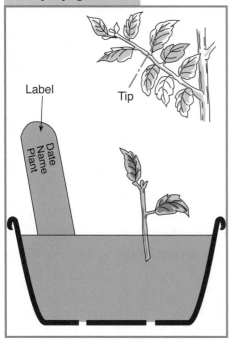

Label

Tip

Date
Name
Plant

- stolon – a stem growing horizontally on the surface such as strawberry
- suckers – an aerial shoot developing from an underground stem such as mint
- cuttings – a piece of branch, stem, root or leaf such as African violet leaves.

Asexual reproduction has many advantages because it:

- is quick
- is simple
- produces large numbers of genetically identical plants from a small amount of plant tissue
- produces offspring from plants that cannot reproduce sexually, such as banana and citrus fruit
- produces large numbers of equally sized plants in a small area and short period
- can increase maturity rates and speed of flowering, for example tulip and gladiolus
- is useful for species that germinate slowly
- is useful in specialised breeding programs such as disease-resistant programs.

Budding and grafting

Budding and grafting combines the best qualities of two or more plants. Budding is the placement of a bud from a high yielding plant onto another with a vigorous root system. Grafting is the placement of a stem from a high yielding plant onto another with a vigorous root system

Budding and grafting are commonly used on roses, citrus and stone fruits to:

- increase resistance to pests and pathogens
- produce large numbers of offspring from plants that are difficult to grow
- produce plants with vigorous root systems and high-yielding, good-quality fruit
- facilitate harvesting by reducing the size of the tree, for example cherry trees.

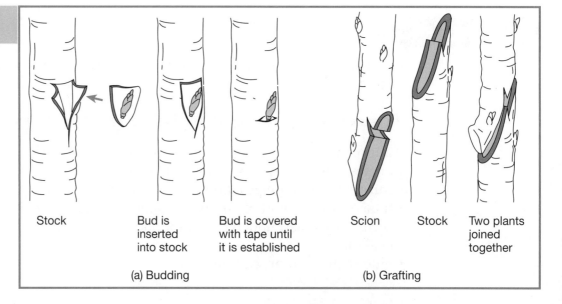

| Stock | Bud is inserted into stock | Bud is covered with tape until it is established | Scion | Stock | Two plants joined together |

(a) Budding   (b) Grafting

Leaves

A leaf is a green organ consisting of a base, stalk (or petiole) and blade (or lamina). Leaves are the site of photosynthesis, transpiration and gaseous exchange.

Leaves consist of:

- cuticle
- epidermis
- mesophyll
- stomata

- vascular bundles incorporating the xylem and phloem
- air spaces.

7.22 Function of a leaf

Part of leaf	Function
Cuticle	A waxy layer secreted by the epidermal layer that reduces transpiration and protects the plant from injury.
Epidermis	A series of interlocking cells that excrete cuticle and hold the contents of the leaf in position.
Mesophyll	Consists of palisade, parenchyma, collenchyma and sclerenchyma cells and chloroplasts. It is the site of photosynthesis and provides the leaf with support.
Xylem	Consists of tracheids, vessel fibres and parenchyma cells. It transports water and mineral salts from the roots to the rest of the plant and also provides the plant with support.
Phloem	Consists of elongated sieve tubes, sieve plates, companion cells and parenchyma cells. They transport proteins, sugars and ions around the plant.
Stomata	Small pores in the epidermis of leaves and stems. The site of transpiration and gaseous exchange.

Practical 25

Leaf structure

7.23 Spinach is a leaf crop

Aim
To study the anatomy of leaves.

Equipment
- samples of leaves, for example celery and wheat
- hand lens
- microscope
- slides of specific plant cells, for example spongy mesophyll, epidermis and dermal cells, vascular bundles and stomata.

Method
1. Cut thin vertical slices of the leaves.
2. Place a section on a slide and cover with a cover slip.
3. Look at the specimens under low power – 10×.
4. Draw and label your observations.
5. Look at the prepared slides of spongy mesophyll, epidermis, vascular bundles and stomata under low power.
6. Look at the prepared slides under high power and draw each cell type.

Research 7.6

7.24 Structure of a dicotyledon leaf

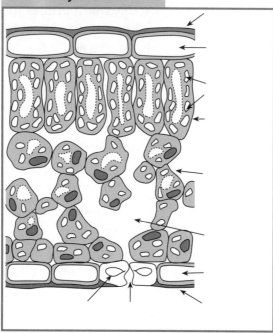

1 Label diagram [7.24] and describe the function of each structure: Parts to be labelled are air space, chloroplasts, guard cell, lower epidermis, palisade mesophyll cell, spongy mesophyll cell, stoma, upper epidermis, waxy cuticle (×2)

2 Label the diagrams in [7.25].
   a Parts to be labelled are chloroplast, guard cell, lower epidermis, nucleus, stoma open.
   b Parts to be labelled are epidermal cells, guard cell, stomata.

7.25 Structure of stomata

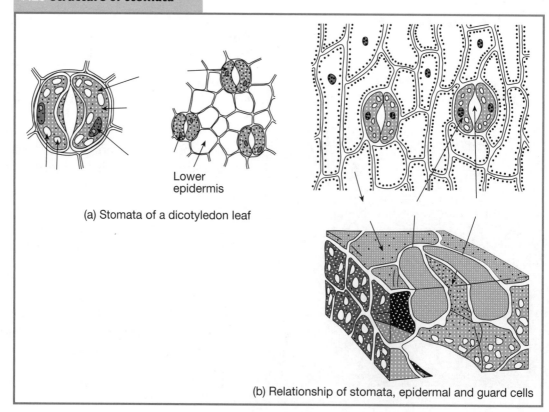

Lower epidermis

(a) Stomata of a dicotyledon leaf

(b) Relationship of stomata, epidermal and guard cells

Stems

A stem is the main axis of a vascular plant and has many functions, including:
- providing support
- holding the buds, leaves and flowers in position
- providing minimal photosynthesis
- moving water and nutrients around the plant
- acting as a storage organ such as in celery and cabbage.

Most stems have a similar structure consisting of:
- an epidermis
- cortex
- vascular tissue
- cambium.

7.26 Function of parts of a stem

Part of stem	Function
Epidermis	Single layer of uniform cells: forms tight skin around the stem; keeps cortex cells in position and reduces incidence of transpiration and microbial infection.
Cortex	Loosely packed cells with interconnecting air spaces. Provides the stem with its shape.
Phloem	Conducting tissue consisting of elongated sieve tubes, sieve plates, companion cells, fibres and parenchyma cells; transports proteins, sugars and ions around the plant.
Xylem	Conducting tissue consisting of tracheids, vessel fibres and parenchyma cells; provides leaves and stems with support and moves water and mineral salts from the roots to the rest of the plant.
Cambium layer	Layer of meristematic cells on the tips of stems and roots; divides to produce new phloem and xylem and increase the diameter of the plant.

Practical 26

Stem structure

Aim

To study the anatomy of stems.

Equipment
- celery and wheat stems
- eosin stain
- razor blade
- slides and cover slips
- hand lens
- microscope.

Method

1 Place the celery and wheat stalk in a beaker of eosin solution and allow to stand for several hours.
2 Cut a thin transverse section of the stems.
3 Place the section on a slide and examine under a microscope.
4 Draw and label your observations.
5 Complete the table [7.27].

7.27 Structure and function of parts of a stem

Structure	Function
Epidermis	
Cortex	
Phloem	
Xylem	
Cambium layer	

7.28 Structure of xylem and phloem in monocots and dicots

7.29 Structure of stems

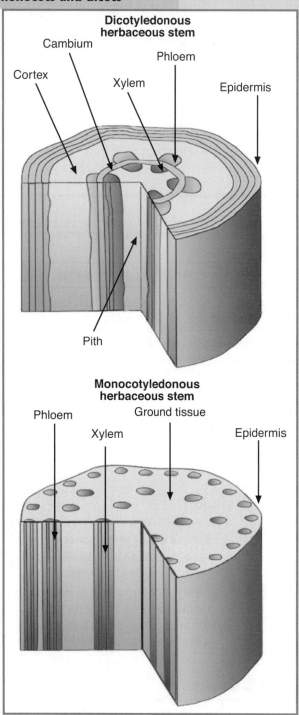

Dicotyledonous herbaceous stem

Cambium
Phloem
Cortex
Xylem
Epidermis

Pith

Monocotyledonous herbaceous stem

Phloem
Ground tissue
Xylem
Epidermis

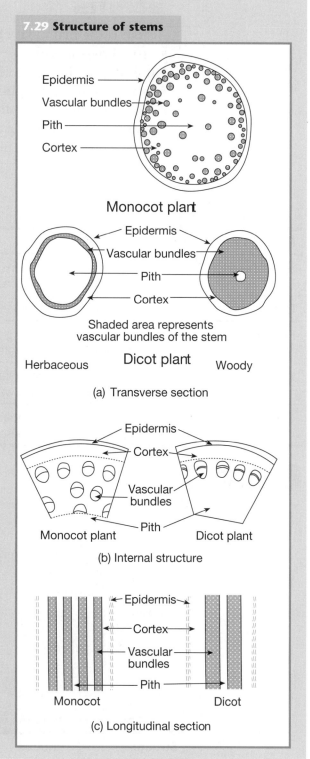

Epidermis
Vascular bundles
Pith
Cortex

Monocot plant

Epidermis
Vascular bundles
Pith
Cortex

Shaded area represents vascular bundles of the stem

Herbaceous   Dicot plant   Woody

(a) Transverse section

Epidermis
Cortex
Vascular bundles
Pith

Monocot plant   Dicot plant

(b) Internal structure

Epidermis
Cortex
Vascular bundles
Pith

Monocot   Dicot

(c) Longitudinal section

Activity | 7.7

Explain why hay quality declines when the percentage ratio of stems to leaves increases.

The root system

Roots absorb water and nutrients, store food material and hold the plant in position. Roots do not have chlorophyll or buds and have a different internal structure to stems.

The first root that a seedling produces is called the radicle and this can develop into a taproot or fibrous root system. Taproots have one main projection and fibrous roots have many small branches.

Roots grow from the actively dividing meristematic tissue at the top of the organ. Roots are covered in hairs, which increase their surface area and uptake of water and nutrients.

Rhizobium bacteria live on roots. They can live symbiotically with legumes and provide nitrogen to plants in a range of 50 to 400kg per hectare per year.

7.30 Rhizobium bacteria

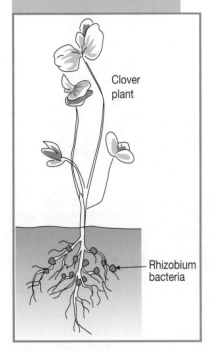

Clover plant

Rhizobium bacteria

symbiotically
a close relationship between two species that can be mutually beneficial

7.32 Root crop – potatoes

7.31 Root structure

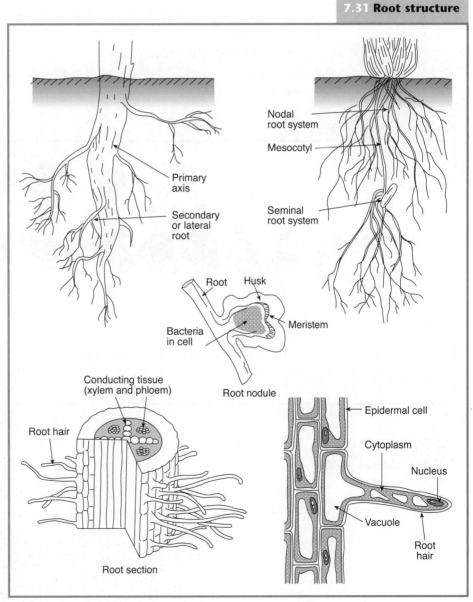

Primary axis

Secondary or lateral root

Nodal root system

Mesocotyl

Seminal root system

Root   Husk

Bacteria in cell

Meristem

Root nodule

Conducting tissue (xylem and phloem)

Root hair

Epidermal cell

Cytoplasm

Nucleus

Vacuole

Root hair

Root section

7.33 Rhizobium bacteria life cycle

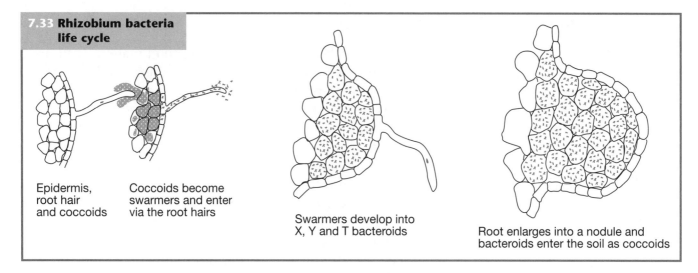

Epidermis, root hair and coccoids

Coccoids become swarmers and enter via the root hairs

Swarmers develop into X, Y and T bacteroids

Root enlarges into a nodule and bacteroids enter the soil as coccoids

Stages of growth of a plant

All plants undergo similar stages of growth and development:
• germination
• stem, bud and leaf production
• flowering
• seed production.

7.34 Sunflower growth stages

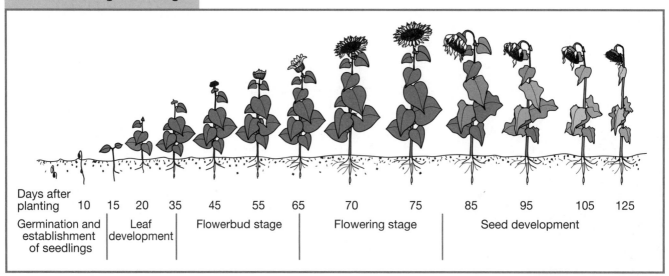

| Days after planting | 10 | 15 | 20 | 35 | 45 | 55 | 65 | 70 | 75 | 85 | 95 | 105 | 125 |

Germination and establishment of seedlings | Leaf development | Flowerbud stage | Flowering stage | Seed development

Activity 7.8

Explain why plants die when they are pulled out of the ground rather than dug out with a layer of soil.

Practical 27

Root systems

Aim

To study the anatomy of the root system.

Equipment

- root system of a carrot and wheat plant
- eosin solution
- razor blade
- slides and cover slips
- hand lens and microscope.

Method

1 Place the root system in eosin solution for half an hour.
2 Cut transverse and longitudinal sections of both roots.
3 Place the sections on a slide and draw and label your observations.
4 Complete table [7.35].

7.35 Structure and function of parts of a root

Structure	Function
Epidermis	
Root hair	
Cortex	
Endodermis	
Xylem and phloem	
Nodules	

Activity 7.9

1 Explain how microbes and root hairs play such an important part in root function.
2 List the major root crops grown in Australia.

Plant nutrient requirements

Plants require more than 16 elements to grow and most of these are derived from the soil. Plants absorb nutrients as soluble ions dissolved in the soil solution using energy, diffusion and osmosis.

Osmosis is the diffusion of a liquid through a semipermeable membrane from a weaker solution (with a lower level of solutes) to a concentrated solution (with a higher level of solutes).

Plants use energy if there is a lower concentration of nutrients in the soil than in the plant. In the plant, the water and nutrients move up the xylem to the leaves by suction forces created by:

• transpiration, or the loss of water from the leaves

• cohesive or attractive forces between water molecules

• capillary or adhesive forces between cell walls and water molecules.

7.36 Nutrient uptake by plants

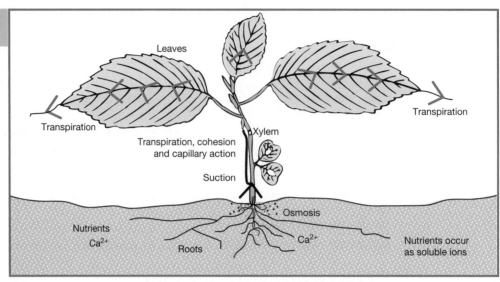

Leaves

Transpiration

Transpiration

Xylem

Transpiration, cohesion and capillary action

Suction

Osmosis

Nutrients
Ca²⁺

Roots

Ca²⁺

Nutrients occur as soluble ions

Activity 7.10

Tick which elements are present in the following fertilisers:

Elements
Ca = calcium
K = potassium
N = nitrogen
P = phosphorus
S = sulfur

Name	N	P	K	Ca	S
Rock phosphate					
Single superphosphate					
Double superphosphate					
Sodium nitrate					
DAP					
MAP					
Urea					
Ammonia					
Sulphate of ammonia					
Ammonium nitrate					
Blood and Bone					

Functions of plants

Photosynthesis, respiration and transpiration are three of the most important activities of a plant.

Photosynthesis

Photosynthesis is the conversion of carbon dioxide and water into glucose, oxygen and energy. The plant converts solar energy into chemical energy and

directly or indirectly supplies all forms of life with carbon and energy.
  Photosynthesis is affected by many factors, including:
* duration, intensity and wavelength of light
* carbon dioxide levels
* water availability
* temperature
* nutrient availability
* stage of development of the plant
* leaf area and canopy structure
* health of the plant
* radiation levels.

  Increasing day length and light intensity increases the photosynthetic rate until a maximum occurs at 20 000–40 000 lux. Chlorophyll can also only absorb red and violet light with a wavelength of 400–700 mμ.

canopy structure
layer of branches and leaves formed by plants above the ground

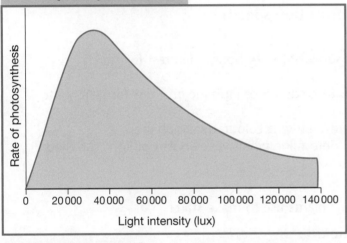

7.37 Effect of light intensity on photosynthetic rate

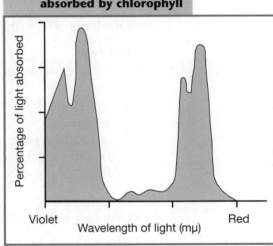

7.38 Wavelength of light absorbed by chlorophyll

Practical 28

Factors affecting photosynthesis

Aim
To determine what factors affect photosynthesis.

Equipment
* 150ml beaker
* aluminium foil
* bell jar
* glass plate
* three saucers
* mortar and pestle
* coloured cellophane paper, eg red, orange, green and blue
* microscope slides and cover slips
* 10–20ml stoppered flask

* needle
* forceps
* spectroscope
* three dishes
* stand
* lugol's iodine solution
* methylated spirits
* 80% acetone
* NaOH (sodium hydroxide) pellets
* vaseline
* wheat and maize grains
* 10 potted plants at the same stage of development
* plant with variegated leaves.

Testing for starch

Method

1 Place the leaf in boiling water for 2–3 minutes.
2 Place the leaf in warm methylated spirits to decolourise it and remove any chlorophyll.
3 Place the leaf in cold water for 2–4 minutes.
4 Place the leaf in a petri dish filled with iodine solution. The iodine turns blue if starch is present.

Importance of light

Method

1 Place two potted plants in direct sunlight for one day.
2 Remove a leaf from each plant and test for starch.
3 Leave one plant in direct sunlight and the other in a dark cupboard for 24 hours.
4 Test each plant for starch production.

Light wavelength the absorption spectrum

Method

1 Place two pots in direct sunlight for 24 hours then test for starch production.
2 Cover the light source with coloured cellophane and test for starch after 24 hours.
3 Repeat the procedure with different coloured cellophane.
4 Use the spectroscope to determine what wavelengths of light travelled through the cellophane.

Conclusion

Conclude which wavelengths plants use to make starch.

Importance of carbon dioxide

Method

1 Place a potted plant, for example bean, wheat or geranium, on a tray with a beaker of sodium hydroxide.
2 Cover the plant and tray with a jar and seal the bottom with vaseline.
3 Place another plant of the same type under a jar and seal.
4 Place both pots in direct sunlight and test their leaves for starch production.

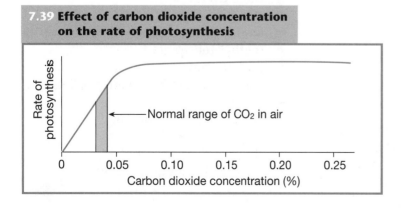

7.39 Effect of carbon dioxide concentration on the rate of photosynthesis

Rate of photosynthesis

Normal range of CO_2 in air

0   0.05   0.10   0.15   0.20   0.25

Carbon dioxide concentration (%)

Carbon dioxide

Carbon dioxide is essential for photosynthesis. Increasing carbon dioxide levels increases photosynthetic rate until maximum levels occurs.

Water availability

Water is essential for photosynthesis and drought or competition from other plants can severely reduce production. Photos [7.40} shows a healthy sunflower crop while [7.41] is already stressed for water as the planting is too dense.

7.40 Healthy sunflower crop

7.41 Water stressed sunflowers

Activity 7.11

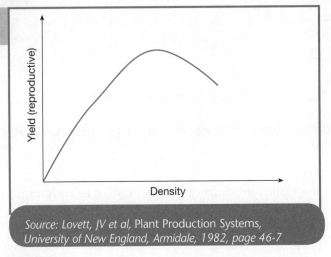

7.42 Effect of crop density on yield

Source: Lovett, JV et al, Plant Production Systems, University of New England, Armidale, 1982, page 46-7

Graph [7.42] shows the effect of crop density on yield.

1 Explain the shape of the graph.
2 What effect does very high or very low crop density have on yield?

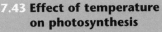

7.43 Effect of temperature on photosynthesis

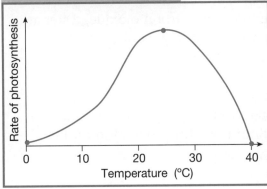

Temperature

Temperature affects the rate of all chemical reactions and increasing temperature directly increases photosynthetic rate. However very high temperatures increase evaporation and transpiration and can kill the plant.

Nutrient supply

Magnesium, nitrogen and iron are essential for chlorophyll function and deficiencies can reduce photosynthetic rates.

Age of plant

Young plants have lower rates of photosynthesis because they do not have a complete canopy of leaves. After maturity, levels decline because leaves shade one another and die.

Leaf area and canopy structure

Leaf size, shape and arrangement directly affects photosynthesis. Leaf area index is the leaf area relative to the ground covered by the plant and the larger the index the greater the photosynthetic rate. Leaves at the top and at right angles receive more light and have a higher photosynthetic rate than older, shaded leaves at the bottom of the plant.

Health of the plant

Disease and stress can reduce photosynthetic rates.

Interference and yield

Aim
To show the effect of seed density on interference and plant growth.

Equipment
- 25 pots
- quartz sand
- wheat grains

Method
1 Place 10, 15, 20, 25 and 30 grains in separate pots.
2 Have five replicates of each.
3 Record dry matter production and final yields once they have reached maturity.

Conclusions
What was the optimum density for dry matter production and yields? Explain why the optimum density for dry matter production is different to that for yield.

Respiration

Respiration is the breakdown of glucose to release carbon dioxide, water and energy. Respiration provides the plants with its energy requirements for maintenance.

Net assimilation rate

Net assimilation rate measures dry-matter production per unit of time and equals photosynthetic rate minus respiration rate (or production minus maintenance needs).

Crop growth rate

Crop growth rate measures the increase in dry-matter per unit area per unit time. Growth rate equals net assimilation rate times mean leaf-area index.

Practical 30
Yield estimation

Aim
To observe the stages of growth of wheat and estimate yield prior to harvesting.

Equipment
- 10 pots
- soil
- 100 wheat grains
- plot of wheat

Method to observe stages
1 Place 10 wheat grains in each pot.
2 At weekly or fortnightly intervals place a specimen in your plant collection.
3 Record changes in dry weight, height, number of tillers and ear development.

Method used to estimate yield
1 Place six, one-metre quadrants at random in a crop.
2 Record the following:
   A = average number of plants per square metre.
   B = average number of developed tillers per plant.
   C = average number of spikelets per head.
   D = average number of grains per spikelet.
   E = average weight of a grain.
   Yield = A $\times$ B $\times$ C $\times$ D $\times$ E per square metre.
Use this information to calculate the yield per hectare noting one hectare = 10 000 square metres.

quadrants
a measured area of vegetation selected for study

AG FACT

How much profit?
Yield estimation techniques can be used to calculate profits per hectare prior to harvesting.

Transpiration

Transpiration is the loss of water vapour from the surface of the plant. Transpiration keeps the plant cool and increases nutrient uptake by forcing water and nutrients up the plant.

Factors affecting transpiration include
- humidity
- temperature
- wind
- leaf adaptations.

Low humidity increases transpiration because it creates a concentration gradient for water to diffuse across. Wind removes the water vapour above the plant and increases transpiration levels. High temperatures increase transpiration by converting more water into vapour. Many plants have special adaptations such as sunken stomata, waxy cuticles and rolling leaves to reduce transpiration rates.

Activity 7.12

1 Explain how stomata control transpiration rates.
2 List examples of plants with adaptations to prevent water loss.
   Adaptations can include:
   - rolling leaves
   - waxy cuticles
   - hairy surfaces
   - leaves facing at an angle toward the sun
   - sunken stomata
   - reduced number of stomata
   - thick fleshy leaves.

Extension Activities

1 Discuss the effect of environmental factors such as light, temperature, available moisture, oxygen, carbon dioxide, wind and biotic factors on plant growth.

2 'Photosynthesis is one of the plant's most important functions supplying carbon and energy for all forms of life'. Discuss this statement.

3 Discuss the major constraints on a significant plant production system in your region.

4 What techniques have operators used to overcome these constraints?

Plant hormones

Plant hormones are chemicals that regulate growth.

7.44 Plant hormones and their effect

Plant hormone	Effect
Auxins	• Production of seedless fruit, eg tomatoes • Prevent fruit fall, eg apples • Weed killers (herbicides), eg broad-leaved weeds • Promote root growth in stem cuttings • Induction of flowering in pineapple • Control growth of stems, roots and flowers • In grafting, promotes callus tissue formation and joins the surfaces of the graft together • Stimulates root development in tissue culture • Causes bending in response to gravity and light • The auxin supply from the apical bud suppresses the growth of lateral buds • Delays fruit ripening • Promotes flowering in bromeliads
Cytokinins	• Delays aging • Stimulates cell division • Stimulates shoot initiation and bud formation in tissue culture • Stimulates the growth of lateral buds • Prolongs the storage life of green vegetables such as asparagus, broccoli and celery

Plant hormone	Effect
Gibberellins	• Promotes flowering, cellular division, and growth • Stimulates stem elongation • Breaks seed dormancy in plants which require stratification or light to induce germination • Seedless fruit development • Delays senescence in leaves and citrus fruits • Production of seedless grapes • Production of bigger, uniform bunches of larger grapes • Improved flower formation and fruit quality in cherries • Improvement of fruit setting in apples and pears • Production of hybrid cucumber seed
Ethylene	• Stimulates shoot and root growth • Stimulates leaf and fruit abscission • Used to ripen fruit, eg bananas • Promotes female flower production in cucumber, squash and melon • Promotes flower initiation and ripening in pineapples
Abscisic acid	• Causes seed and bud dormancy • Closes stomata in water stressed plants • Inhibits shoot growth

AG FACT

Australian rice

Nearly all the rice grown in Australia is grown in NSW, mainly in the Murrumbidgee Irrigation area, the Coleambally Irrigation area and in the Murray Valley. Although Australia produces only 0.2 per cent of world rice it accounts for about 3 per cent of rice exports. Major markets are Papua New Guinea, Japan, China, and the Middle East and Pacific countries.

Factors affecting plant productivity

Many factors affect productivity including:
• the environment, for example climate, soils, weeds, pests and diseases
• genetic potential of the plant
• social factors such as tastes and preferences of farmers and consumers
• goals of the farmer
• traditions
• economic factors, for example profitability of enterprises
• financial limitations on the farmer
• government intervention
• effect of overseas markets on supply and demand and prices
• level of technology
• skills and competence level of the farmer.

The environment

The environment is the surroundings in which the plant lives.

Rainfall determines the growing season of a region and insufficient rainfall can lower germination rates, slow growth, reduce yield or kill the plant. Excessive rain lodges crops, causes flooding and destruction and increases the incidence of shot and sprung, and mouldy grain.

Temperature affects germination rates, growth and development, and final yields. Very high temperatures increase evapotranspiration rates, damage delicate flowers and reduce yields. Very low temperatures and frosts can lower germination rates, damage delicate flowers, reduce yields or kill the plant.

Wind pollinates crops but also increases evapotranspiration rates, erosion, lodging and the incidence of weeds, pests and diseases.

evapo-transpiration
sum of evaporation from soils and evaporation from plant surfaces

7.45 Hail netting used to protect fruit trees

Soils

Soils provide plants with water, nutrients and support. Soils differ in fertility level, and physical and chemical properties, which can affect productivity.

Practical 31

Physical and chemical properties of the soil

Chapter 4 contains relevant practical exercises for soils.

Topography

The slope of the land has a major effect on the physical and chemical properties of the soil, and on agricultural production. Steep country is often eroded and has shallow, stony profiles and acidity problems. Soils at the bottom of slopes generally have deep, fertile profiles but are often water-logged and have drainage problems.

Microbes and invertebrates

fermentation
chemical decomposition of organic substances by microbial action

Microbes and invertebrates have a major effect on plant production through:
- mineral and energy cycling
- organic matter breakdown
- nitrogen fixation and nutrient absorption
- ruminant digestion
- diseases
- silage production
- fermentation, for example wine and beer production
- food production, for example bread and mushrooms
- food spoilage.

Mycorrhiza fungi (VAM) live on plant roots and increase their surface area and absorption of phosphorus and zinc. These fungi are of vital importance to field crops such as linseed, chickpea, sunflower, navy beans, pigeon peas and maize.

mycorrhiza fungi
fungi that live symbiotically with specific plants

Pests

Pests reduce productivity by:
- damaging or completely destroying the plant
- contaminating the product
- increasing production costs
- reducing yields.

Practical 32

Pest identification

1 Label the pests in [7.46] as rabbit, mouse, thrip, kangaroo, mite, weevil, aphid and bird.
2 List what damage they cause.

7.46 Common plant pests

Activity 7.13

7.47 Quarantine used to control the grape pest phylloxera

1 Select one pest and design an integrated control program for it.
2 Explain why integrated control methods are more effective than using only one control measure such as chemicals.
3 Give examples of biological control agents that are used to control weeds or pests and explain why the agents are effective.

7.48 Blackberry

Weeds

Weeds reduce productivity by:
- competing with the plant for water, light and nutrients
- reducing quality and yields
- contaminating the product
- harbouring diseases
- attracting insects and pests to the crop
- shading the crop and modifying its climate
- releasing toxic chemicals
- making harvesting difficult by blocking machinery
- increasing production costs in control methods.

Some common weeds affecting plant productivity include: saffron thistle, St Barnaby's thistle, thornapples, Paterson's curse, barnyard grass, lantana, horehound, prickly pear, blackberry, galvanised burr, variegated thistle and Scotch thistle.

Activity 7.14

Collect weed samples from your local area. Try and identify each weed that you have found.

Diseases

Diseases also reduce productivity by:
- inhibiting germination
- killing the plant
- increasing production costs in control methods.
- contaminating products
- reducing yields

7.49 Fungal diseases of plants

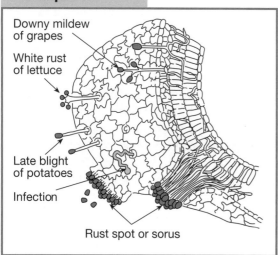

Downy mildew of grapes

White rust of lettuce

Late blight of potatoes

Infection

Rust spot or sorus

7.50 Common plant diseases	
Crop	**Disease**
Barley	Loose smut, powdery mildew, rusts, barley stripe mosaic
Cotton	Bacterial blight, leaf spot, boll rot
Lucerne	Fusarium wilt, downy mildew, black stem, seedling blight
Maize	Head smut, brown spot, stripe, black bundle
Oats	Loose smut, rusts, crown rot
Safflower	Damping off, rust, alternaria blight

Interaction between problem organism, host and the environment

Disease occurs because of an interaction between the disease-producing organism, the host plant and the environment. The severity of a disease depends on:

- the level of activity of the parasite or pathogen
- the level of resistance of a host
- the effect of environment on the disease.

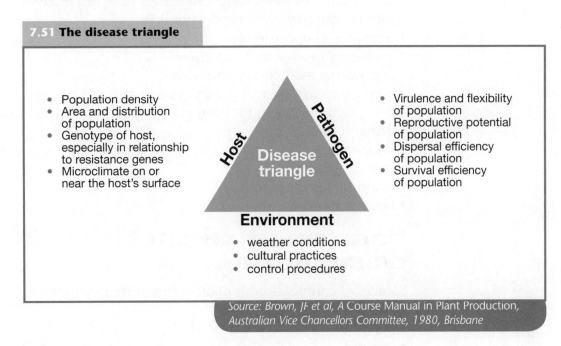

7.51 The disease triangle

- Population density
- Area and distribution of population
- Genotype of host, especially in relationship to resistance genes
- Microclimate on or near the host's surface

Host

Pathogen

Disease triangle

- Virulence and flexibility of population
- Reproductive potential of population
- Dispersal efficiency of population
- Survival efficiency of population

Environment

- weather conditions
- cultural practices
- control procedures

Source: Brown, JF et al, A Course Manual in Plant Production, Australian Vice Chancellors Committee, 1980, Brisbane

Genetic potential

The genetic potential of a plant sets an upper limit to its productivity. Humans have selectively bred plants for thousands of years to maximise this.

Social factors

The tastes and preferences of the farmer and community dictate what and how much is produced.

Goals such as profit, security and preservation of the land can influence the farmer's decisions. Other factors such as tradition, technology and the skills of the farmer also affect productivity.

Economic constraints

Economic factors have a major effect on production. Farmers normally avoid risky enterprises with huge capital outlays and prefer stable enterprises with guaranteed incomes. Financial restrictions can also limit the resources (such as technology, chemicals and fertilisers) available to the farmer and directly affect productivity.

Other factors such as overseas supply and demand, quotas and government restrictions also affect productivity.

Level of technology

Modern technology can significantly increase production. However some industries – such as cotton, rice and sugar cane – have become so specialised that only a few farmers have the knowledge and resources to undertake these enterprises.

Management

The capability of the manager directly affects productivity.

Farmers can maximise production by:

- planning all operations on the property
- budgeting income and expenses
- minimising inefficiency and waste
- keeping up to date with new advances and technology
- being well-informed, for example of world supply and demand
- being flexible
- preserving and improving their land, for example by crop rotation and soil conservation works
- planning for the future
- being sustainable.

Sources of competition in plant communities

Sources of competition in plant communities include:

- weeds
- pests
- diseases
- other plants.

microclimate
specific climate created within the canopy of the crop

Interference

Interference is when one organism affects another.

Weeds commonly interfere with crops by:

- competing with the crop for water, light and nutrients
- altering the crop's microclimate, for example by shading
- attracting insects and pests to the crop
- releasing toxic chemicals (allelopathy) that inhibit the crop
- making harvesting difficult
- reducing yields or quality of produce
- increasing production costs in control methods.

7.52 Field of corn

Practical 33
Allelopathic effects of weeds

Aim
To observe the allelopathic effect of a weed on a crop.

Equipment
- 200 wheat grains
- foliage from Paterson's curse
- 10 petri dishes
- cotton wool
- filter paper
- distilled water

Method
1. Place a moist filter paper and 20 wheat grains in each dish.
2. Crush some Paterson's curse in cold water. Use 10 ml of water per gram of plant material.
3. Filter the washings.
4. Place 5 ml of washing in half the petri dishes and 5 ml of distilled water in the other dishes as controls.
5. Record the following information:
   - germination rate
   - height of coleoptile
   - number of seminal roots

Conclusion
State your conclusions from your results.

> **coleoptile**
> a protective sheath that covers the shoot of a developing grass seed

Controlling weeds, pests and diseases

Many methods are used to control weeds, pests and diseases including:
- plant density
- chemical control
- biological control
- cultural practices
- ecological control
- integrated control.

Plant density

Plant density has a major effect on:
- ground cover levels
- the plants' competitive ability with weeds
- surface evaporation
- light interception
- lodging (crops falling over)
- plant yield.

Farmers should select a crop density which optimises yields and reduces competition. The optimum density will depend on the crop or variety (differences in vigour, height and branching), time of sowing and the season.

Chemical control

Chemicals have been used for many years because they were quick, simple and effective.

However many organisms became resistant to chemicals and more toxic chemicals were used which:
• were very expensive
• killed beneficial plants
• built up in food chains
• contaminated the environment.

7.53 Modern spray unit used in tomato production

Chemicals are still used but are now:
• more specific
• biodegradable and less toxic to the environment
• carefully and accurately used
• used in conjunction with other control methods

Care with chemicals

When using chemicals it is important to:
• Read and follow the label.
• Wear protective clothing such as gloves or safety glasses.
• Only use the chemical for what it is intended.
• Use the exact amount.
• Do not store in other containers.
• Apply when and where appropriate, for example not on windy days or near waterways.
• Note the withholding period and when plant material can be eaten after spraying.
• Never eat, drink or inhale chemicals.
• Wash well after use.
• Store in a chemical shed.
• Dispose of correctly.

withholding period
period of time product cannot be safely consumed as it is contaminated by the chemical

Practical 34

Interpreting chemical labels

Aim
To accurately read and interpret labels on chemical products.

Method
Study illustration [7.54] to complete the questions following:
1 Name the chemical?
2 What is its active ingredient?
3 What is the purpose of chemical?
4 What are the recommended application rates?
5 What procedure is to be followed in the event of poisoning?

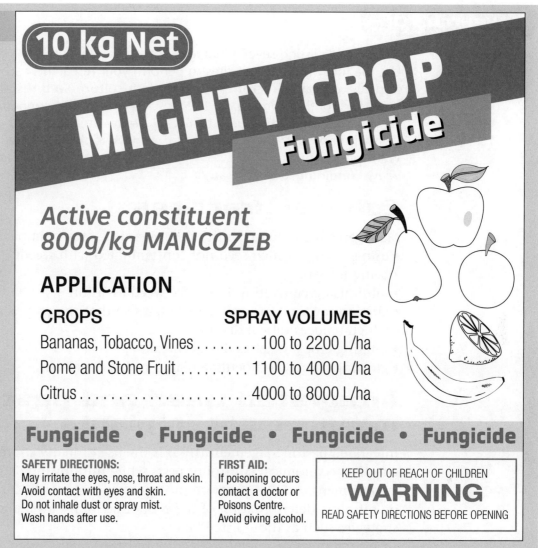

10 kg Net

MIGHTY CROP
Fungicide

Active constituent
800g/kg MANCOZEB

APPLICATION

CROPS	SPRAY VOLUMES
Bananas, Tobacco, Vines	100 to 2200 L/ha
Pome and Stone Fruit	1100 to 4000 L/ha
Citrus	4000 to 8000 L/ha

Fungicide • Fungicide • Fungicide • Fungicide

SAFETY DIRECTIONS:
May irritate the eyes, nose, throat and skin.
Avoid contact with eyes and skin.
Do not inhale dust or spray mist.
Wash hands after use.

FIRST AID:
If poisoning occurs
contact a doctor or
Poisons Centre.
Avoid giving alcohol.

KEEP OUT OF REACH OF CHILDREN
WARNING
READ SAFETY DIRECTIONS BEFORE OPENING

Biological control

Biological control is the use of natural predators and pathogens to control a weed. Biological control has many advantages because it:
• is selective
• has minimal resistance
• is self-perpetuating
• does not contaminate the environment
• actively seeks out the organism.
  Biological control has some limitations, including:
• a control agent is not available for every problem
• it is expensive in time, labour and money
• it can take years of research
• it does not always work
• it does not eradicate the organism only maintains it at a stable level.

Research 7.15

Draw a table listing several biological control agents used in plant production. Use the following Internet sites to perform your research:

australia.gov.au/directories/australia/agriculture/web-resources-list

www.farmonline.com.au/   www.aglinks.com.au

www.daff.qld.gov.au/home.htm   www.dpi.vic.gov.au

www.dpi.nsw.gov.au   www.dpi.qld.gov.au

www.pir.sa.gov.au   www.dpiw.tas.gov.au

www.kondiningroup.com.au

Cultural practices

Management can help control pest organisms, for example by:

- using clean, certified seed not contaminated with weeds, pests or diseases
- being hygienic
- minimising cultivation to reduce weed invasion
- altering sowing time and density rates so that the crop is more competitive, which reduces fungal disease
- rotating crops to act as disease breaks
- growing strong, competitive plants such as phalaris.

Integrated weed and pest management in plants

Integrated pest management (IPM) is the use of many strategies to provide effective, economical control of pests while minimising damage to the environment. An IPM program incorporates pest identification and monitoring, determination of the economic injury level and the use of strategies such as those listed below.

Cultural practices include selecting resistant plants, such as BT corn; maintaining plant health and vigour, such as watering and fertilising; pest and residue removal; and crop management, such as crop rotations to break disease cycles.

Biological control methods, including using natural enemies (predators), fly and insect trapping and the use of pheromone traps.

Chemical controls, such as using the most appropriate chemical after monitoring pest levels.

The tomato leaf miner fly

The tomato leaf miner fly destroyed up to 60 per cent of tomato yields in northern Australia. This was equivalent to a $10 million loss per season. Chemical control methods failed because the leaf miner developed resistance to the insecticides and the chemicals killed all of its natural enemies.

The fly is 2 to 2.5 mm long, greyish/black in colour and has yellow markings. The female lays eggs inside the leaf. The maggot undergoes three larval stages and then pupates on the surface of the leaf or in the soil. After approximately 15–20 days the fly emerges and completes its life cycle.

7.55 Methods used to control weeds and pests

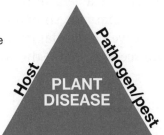

Resistant cultivars
- Genes for specific resistance
- Inter-regional deployment of resistant genes
- Intra-regional deployment of resistant genes
- Non-specific resistance
- Tolerance

Systemic biocides

Protectant biocides

Contact biocides

Host

Pathogen/pest

PLANT DISEASE

Environment

Improve growing conditions for plants and make conditions for pathogens unfavourable
- Soil drainage system
- Early maturing cultivars
- Time of sowing
- Early harvesting of crop
- Moving or grazing of forage crop
- Modification of greenhouse environments, etc

Exclusion
- Quarantine
- Certification
- Treatment

Elimination of inoculum
- Rotation
- Sanitation/hygiene
- Eliminate alternate hosts
- Decoy cropping
- Rogueing
- Soil disinfection
- Eradicant sprays
- Heat therapy
- Destroy insect vectors
- Meristem propagation

Source: Brown, JF et al, A Course Manual in Plant Production, Australian Vice Chancellors Committee, 1980, Brisbane

Effective control strategies include:
- farm hygiene
- removal of crop remains after harvest
- deep ploughing
- a crop rotation or break in the production cycle
- destruction of all tomato seedlings and alternate weed hosts.

Integrated pest management has been highly successful and in ten years leaf miner numbers have decreased by 90 per cent.

Pasture production

Pastures occupy more than 300 million hectares or one-quarter of the world's land area and play a significant role in agriculture by:
- providing cheap feed
- improving the fertility level of the soil
- stabilising temperature and moisture levels.
- reducing erosion
- diversifying income

7.56 Good quality pastures provide feed for the entire year

Types of pastures

Most pastures contain grasses and legumes.

Grasses

Grasses such as paspalum, cocksfoot and phalaris have an upright habit, long tapering leaves, a fibrous root system and provide animals with bulk feed, roughage and energy.

Ryegrasses are a very important component of many pastures. Four different types of rye grass are shown in [7.60] below. From 1 to 4 they are Rigid rye, Wimmera rye, Perennial rye and Italian rye. The flowering spikes are labelled as A, the seeds as B and the spikelets as C.

7.57 Paspalum

7.58 Cocksfoot

7.59 Phalaris

7.60 Characteristics of the ryegrasses

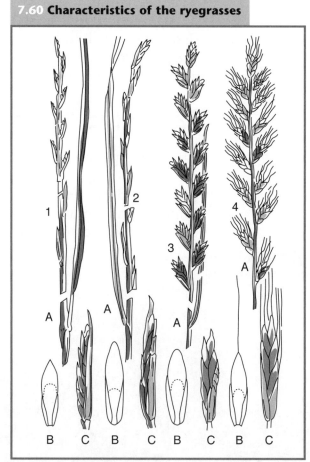

7.61 White clover

Legumes

Legumes such as peas, white clover and beans:
- have heart-shaped leaves
- have five-petalled flowers
- have seeds in pods
- have rhizobium bacteria on their roots that can fix nitrogen
- produce high-protein feed
- increase the fertility of the soil
- can cause bloat that kills animals.

7.63 Lucerne

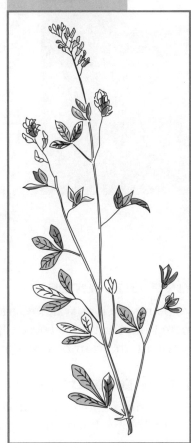

AG FACT

Pioneers

The planned use of legumes to enhance soil fertility was pioneered in Australia and is now practised widely around the world. Australian expertise in the use of leguminous forage plants and in tropical pasture technology is internationally recognised.

7.62 Subterranean clover

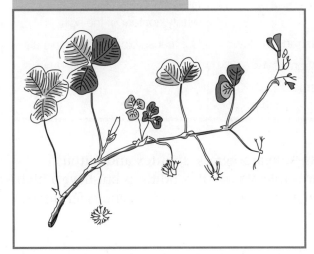

Practical 35

Legume growth

innoculant
dormant bacteria that is mixed as a fine dust over legume seed before sowing

1 Design your own practical experiment to show the effect of bacteria and lime on legume growth.
2 Treatments should include:
- control – legume seed without any treatment
- legume seed plus innoculant
- legume seed plus innoculant plus lime
- legume seed plus lime only
3 Draw conclusions from your results.

Native and introduced pasture species

Common native and introduced species and their roles in pastures are listed in the following table.

7.64 Improved pastures maintain high stocking rates

7.65 Native species	
Native species	**Role in pasture**
Native legumes	
Glycine genera	Withstand harsh conditions
Lotus genera	Put nitrogen in the soil
Cullen genera	Protein for stock
Introduced grasses	
Paspalum	Bulk roughage and energy
Cocksfoot	Good feed for livestock
Phalaris	Help prevent bloat
Ryegrass	
Introduced legumes	
Peas	High quality feed
White clover	Nitrogen fixation increases the fertility content of the soil
Subterranean clover	Can cause bloat and kill animals
Crimson clover	
Lucerne	
Common vetch	

Native pastures

Native plants such as wallaby grass, kangaroo grass, spinifex and saltbush originate from Australia. These plants tolerate harsh conditions but have a high fibre content and cannot withstand excessive grazing or nitrogenous fertilisers.

Natural pastures

Natural pastures consist of native plants and introduced species such as couch grass, which have been growing in a region for a long time.

Improved pastures

Improved pastures contain introduced species and have been fertilised to increase productivity.

Temporary pastures

Temporary pastures contain annual and biennial plants such as Italian ryegrass, red clover and subterranean clover and are maintained for up to five years.

Permanent pastures

Permanent pastures contain perennial species such as paspalum, phalaris, kikuyu, white clover and subterranean clover and are maintained for many years.

Practical 36
Pasture productivity

Aim
To determine the type of species in a pasture and its productivity.

Equipment
- measuring tape
- steel posts and meshing
- shears
- paper bags
- oven
- scales

Method
1 Stretch the measuring tape between two points in the pasture.
2 Calculate how many times a species appears on the line and the percentage of area it occupies.
   (A pasture should contain approximately 60 per cent grasses and 40 per cent legumes.)
3 Place four quadrants randomly on the pasture
4 Enclose the areas with steel posts and meshing.
5 Cut the pasture within the quadrants at monthly intervals.
6 Place the material in separate bags and determine their dry weight.

Results
Graph dry-matter production per hectare per month.

Conclusion
State your conclusions from the results.

Pastures in New South Wales

Climate and soil type determine the type of pastures in New South Wales. The southern regions have a Mediterranean climate and winter growing annuals predominate. In northern New South Wales, temperate and subtropical conditions prevail and summer growing perennials are more common.

Fodder and forage crops

Fodder crops such as oats, barley and cowpeas are cut and fed to animals during periods of shortage. Forage crops such as millet and sweet sorghum are grazed directly by the animal.

Activity 7.16

liveweight
the weight of a living animal

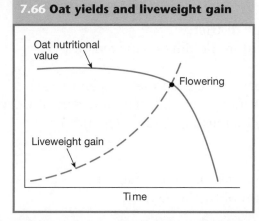

7.66 Oat yields and liveweight gain

Diagram [7.66] shows the effect of grazing on oat yields and liveweight gain of sheep.
a How does timing of grazing affect grain yields?
b How does timing of grazing affect sheep liveweight gain?
c What is more profitable: selling the oat crop as grain or using it for liveweight gain?
d What additional information do you require to make this decision?

Activity 7.17

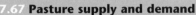

7.67 Pasture supply and demand

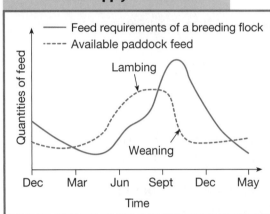

Graph [7.67] shows the amount of pasture available to stock throughout the year.
a Why is pasture growth seasonal?
b When do feed shortages occur?
c What could the operator do to compensate for this shortage?

Establishing a pasture

Establishing pastures is expensive in time, labour and money. When selecting pasture species, plants must:
• suit the local climate and soil type
• have the same growing period as the region
• provide feed all year round
• be palatable
• be digestible
• produce bulk, high-quality feed
• tolerate grazing and trampling
• produce no harmful side effects such as bloat from white clover
• be easy to establish
• be persistent
• be resistant to common diseases
• have vigorous seedlings
• produce abundant seed for survival and dispersal.

Time of sowing

Pastures can be sown at different times depending on:
• the local climate, for example rainfall and temperature patterns
• seasonal conditions
• growing period of the district
• soil type and its moisture-holding characteristics
• type of pasture.
    Winter and spring pastures are normally sown early in the season after opening rains and summer growing species are generally sown in late autumn.
    The method used to establish a pasture depends on:
• the topography
• pasture type
• skills and machinery available to the farmer
• the financial situation of the farmer.

Sowing methods

The most common sowing methods used are:
- traditional
- direct drill and minimum tillage
- aerial
- sowing in conjunction with a cereal crop.

Traditional methods

Traditionally the land was ploughed and seed was sown into a prepared seedbed.

Advantages of this method include:
- it provided a suitable seedbed
- seedlings did not compete with weeds for water, light and nutrients
- fallowing helped conserve water
- ploughing incorporated plant residues and the release of nutrients into the soil
- there was a 20–70 per cent germination rate.

However ploughing had disadvantages, including:
- it was expensive in time, labour and money
- machinery and skilled operators were required
- it damaged soil structure and made it more susceptible to erosion
- no feed was available while pastures were being established.

Direct drill and minimum tillage

Direct drilling is sowing seeds directly into existing pastures and controlling weeds with herbicides or intensive grazing.

Direct drilling has many advantages, including:
- it minimises cultivation and soil degradation
- it reduces erosion levels
- it is less expensive in time, labour and fuel
- pastures can be grazed while they are being established.

However this method also has limitations, including:
- it has lower germination rates of 10–20 per cent
- seedlings must compete with established plants for water, light and nutrients
- specialised machinery is required.

Aerial establishment

Pastures can be established by spreading seed and fertiliser from an aircraft. The method is quick and simple and is commonly used on inaccessible areas.

However it has some limitations, including:
- it is very expensive
- germination rates are low, often less than 5 per cent
- seed is washed away, dries out or is eaten by birds or ants
- only hardy species survive.

digestibility
proportion of feed used by the animal – if a feed is 80% digestible then 20% will be lost as waste and faeces

Pastures and cereal crops

Pastures can be sown with cereal crops to:
• grow a crop plus seed for the next year's pasture
• increase the fertility of the soil
• increase the digestibility and quality of the crop.

Activity 7.18

Design a crop rotation program for your region.

7.68 Stocking rate must be regulated to maintain pastures

Maintaining new pastures

New pastures must be given time to establish and should never be overgrazed. High stocking rates result in the loss of palatable plants and a build-up of weeds and coarse fibrous material.

Understocking results in weeds and grasses dominating the pastures and smothering the legumes.

The most common grazing systems used include:
• cell grazing
• continual grazing
• creep feeding
• rotational grazing.
• deferred grazing
• strip grazing
• zero grazing

Cell grazing

Cell grazing is when one herd is moved through a series of paddocks. Stock eat a paddock for 1–5 days and then are moved before they graze on new shoots.

Continual grazing

With continual grazing a set number of stock is left permanently on the pasture. This method is inexpensive in time and labour and keeps the grasses and legumes in balance. However:
• animals can develop campsites and dung and urine are lost from the rest of the paddock
• seed set is reduced
• seedlings are eaten before properly established
• less palatable species are undergrazed, and weeds seed spread
• animals form tracks and soil compaction occurs.

Creep feeding

Creep feeding is the progressive grazing of a pasture through a series of collapsible fences. This allows young stock first access to the best quality feed and minimises fouling and wastage. Young stock get first access as the fences allow small stock to walk underneath but block larger animals.

Rotational grazing

Rotational grazing involves moving stock in succession from one pasture to the next. This ensures that pastures are effectively grazed and urine and dung are distributed evenly around the pastures.

Rotational grazing allows plants time to regenerate and is commonly used on lucerne stands. However, it is expensive in time and labour and pasture quality can vary from time to time.

Deferred grazing

With deferred grazing, animals are only allowed to graze the pastures at certain times of the year. This maintains pasture composition because plants are only grazed when they are not at their most vulnerable stages, such as flowering.

Strip grazing

With strip grazing, pastures are divided by electric fencing into sections and intensively grazed. Pastures are effectively grazed and less digestible plants are eaten. Weeds are controlled and urine and dung are evenly distributed. However it is expensive in time and labour and is not suitable for weak plants.

Zero grazing

Zero grazing is the mowing and distributing of pastures via feeders. This method is used if pastures are too high or dense to be grazed effectively.

Pasture management

Animals have a significant effect on a pasture's:
• botanical composition
• growth rate
• leaf-area index
• maturity rate
• digestibility
• productivity.
Unregulated grazing can result in:
• loss of palatable species
• soil compaction
• trampling
• camp sites and loss of nutrients from the paddock
• reduction in ground cover.
Good managers can maintain pastures and maximise production by regulating the:
• stocking rate
• grazing system
• frequency or season of grazing
• erosion
• land degradation.

Grazing management for sustainable production

Sustainable grazing management includes:
- fencing and using the land according to its soil suitability classes
- matching stocking rate and grazing to feed availability
- using deep-rooted perennial species to give year-long groundcover and, in association with trees and shrubs, to reduce groundwater recharge and associated salinity
- using strategic combinations of fertilisers to maintain nutrient levels and herbicides to kill weeds
- rotational grazing to improve pasture composition and production
- not grazing eroded regions.

Sustainable grazing techniques

A well-grazed pasture is more productive, longer-lived and of better feed quality than a poorly grazed pasture. If stock are left in a paddock for too long they remove desirable species, and cause pasture degradation and soil erosion. Good management operations include:
- regulating timing, frequency and intensity of grazing
- matching stocking rates with pasture availability
- rotational grazing
- establishing critical pasture benchmarks for stocking rate
- developing a grazing plan to manage seasonal growth.

Riparian areas

These are the regions near creeks, rivers and wetlands. Well vegetated riparian areas are important because they filter sediment, nutrients and pathogens and reduce the amount of contaminants entering waterways. Riparian regions should:
- be fenced and planted with trees, shrubs and grasses to ensure 100 per cent groundcover
- be fenced to reduce erosion and runoff
- have off-stream watering points for livestock.

Drainage lines or regions should be fenced and revegetated to trap sediments, nutrients and pathogens before they enter waterways. Care must be taken to not fertilise too close to streams or drainage depressions where runoff is likely and not plough or use fertilisers or herbicides when rainfall and runoff is expected. It is also important to isolate lactating females and their young from drainage lines and streams because they can contaminate water with diseases that affect humans, such as cryptosporidium and giardia.

Other issues include locating new farm infrastructure away from streams, drainage lines and drainage depressions and installing runoff diversion structures for effluent drainage.

Effluent management

Effluent (urine and faeces) can:
• deplete oxygen levels in rivers
• reduce plant and fish populations
• transfer animal disease
• make streams unfit for drinking
• increase blue-green algal blooms.

Effluent contains valuable nutrients, organic matter and water and can be applied to pastures. However, it may contain excess amounts of nitrogen or potassium. Potassium can replace magnesium and calcium in the soil and animals can become deficient in these elements. This results in grass tetany (deficiency in magnesium) and milk fever (deficiency in calcium).

Effluent also contains a wide variety of bacteria, viruses and parasites such as Johne's disease. Stock should therefore be restricted from grazing pastures after they have been treated with effluent.

Research 7.19

1   What benefits does NSW Agriculture's Prograze program offer?
2   What computer programs are available to assist in pasture management?

7.69 Making rectangular bales

7.70 Round bales

Fodder conservation

Pasture growth is seasonal and quality often declines after flowering. Supplementary feed can include hay, silage and stored grain.

Hay

Hay is plant material that has been cut, dried and compressed into rectangular or round bales [7.69] and [7.70]. Quality varies, depending on:
• type and quality of pastures
• percentage of leaves to stems
• stage of maturity when cut
• moisture content of the hay
• climate
• soil fertility and fertiliser history
• skills of the operator in making the hay such as minimising losses from respiration, mechanical losses, fermentation, moulding and leaching.

Legumes and leafy plants have high protein and digestibility levels. Plants cut before flowering and seeding are more nutritious because protein, mineral and digestibility levels decline after maturity. Digestibility levels also decline with age because cellulose and lignin accumulate in the cell walls.

lignin
substances found in the thickened cell walls of plants that provide the plants with support

The soil's fertility level directly affects the botanical composition and protein content of the pasture. Soils with low nitrogen and high phosphorus and sulphur levels have a predominance of legumes and a higher protein content.

Hay should not be made during wet conditions because of leaching and microbial action. Hay should be dried quickly to minimise respiration but handled carefully to minimise leaf shattering.

7.71 Changing nutritional value of an annual grass

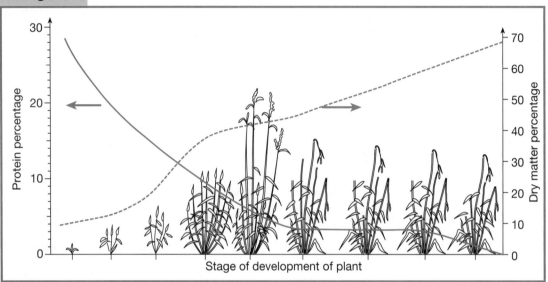

Activity 7.20

Table [7.72] shows the nutritional value of different types of hays.
a   Which is the best hay?
b   What factors affect the nutritional value of hay?
c   Why do hay sheds sometimes ignite?

7.72 Nutritional value of different hays

DM = dry matter
CP = crude protein
CF = crude fibre
EE = ether extract
Ash = ash
DCP = digestible crude protein
ME = metabolisable energy

Food	DM basis						
	DM g/kg	CP g/kg	CF g/kg	EE g/kg	Ash g/kg	DCP g/kg	ME MJ/kg
Hays							
Clover, red very good	850	184	266	39	84	128	9.6
Grass, very high digestibility	850	132	291	20	85	90	10.1
Grass, high digestibility	850	101	320	16	62	58	9.0
Grass, moderate digestibility	850	85	328	16	74	39	8.4
Grass, low digestibility	850	92	366	16	69	45	7.5
Grass, very low digestibility	850	88	340	16	78	38	7.0
Lucerne, half flower	850	225	302	13	95	166	8.2
Lucerne, full flower	850	171	353	31	96	116	7.7

<table>
<tr><td></td><td colspan="7">DM basis</td></tr>
</table>

Dried grass							
Grass, very leafy	900	161	217	28	123	113	10.8
Grass, leafy	900	187	213	38	102	136	10.6
Grass, early flower	900	154	258	28	107	97	9.7
Lucerne, bud	900	244	198	32	126	174	9.4
Straws							
Barley	860	38	394	21	53	9	7.3
Bean	860	52	501	9	53	26	7.4
Oat	860	34	394	22	57	11	6.7
Pea	860	105	410	19	77	50	6.5
Rye	860	37	429	19	30	7	6.2
Wheat	860	34	417	15	71	1	5.6

triticale
Hybrid of wheat and rye. It is grown primarily for animal feed as a grain or forage. Human consumption is currently low.

7.73 Dairy cattle require high-quality feed throughout the year to maintain milk quality and yields

Silage production

Silage consists of plant material that has been preserved by microbial action. The material is placed in pits, trenches, plastic containers or silos, and bacteria convert its sugars and carbohydrates into organic acids.

Silage can be made in most weather conditions and will last for many years but is heavy, unsaleable and has a sour taste.

Stored grain

Cereal grains such as wheat, oats, barley, triticale, and sorghum are commonly used as supplementary feed. Grains have a high food value and are easy to handle and transport.

They can be stored for long periods and sold if not required. However they can cause bloat if not slowly introduced to stock.

Activity 7.21

a   Design a grain ration to supplement wether sheep during a drought.
b   What information is required to design the ration?

Cropping in Australia

Crops are the cultivated produce of the ground. Some common crops in Australia are various grains, fruit, vegetables, and sugar-cane and cotton.

Using the following Internet sites:
a What were the five most important crops grown this year?
b Which states had the most crop production?
c Which crops are increasing in production levels?

www.daff.gov.au/abares   www.abs.gov.au
www.daff.qld.gov.au/home.htm   www.dpi.vic.gov.au
www.dpi.nsw.gov.au   www.dpi.qld.gov.au
www.pir.sa.gov.au   www.dpiw.tas.gov.au

Wheat production

Wheat is one of the oldest and most important crops grown in Australia.
   Wheat was grown because:
• it was easy to grow in a wide range of soils and climates
• it had a guaranteed minimum price
• an assured domestic and export market
• a well-organised transport, handling and marketing system developed to support its sale.

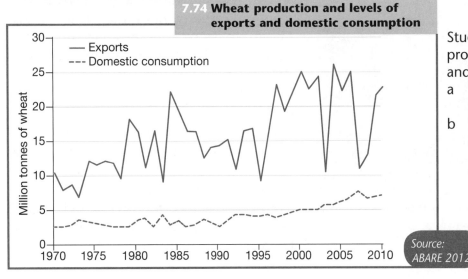

7.74 Wheat production and levels of exports and domestic consumption

Source: ABARE 2012

Study graph 7.74 showing wheat production and levels of exports and domestic consumption.
a What trends are apparent from the graph?
b What factors could have led to a sharp decline in exports?

Growing wheat

Wheat is an annual grass and is normally sown from May to June (except for late-maturing and short-season varieties that are sown in February and July–August respectively).

   Wheat has both a vegetative stage and a reproductive stage of growth and development.

   During the vegetative phase the plant germinates and establishes roots, leaves and stems. During the reproductive stage, ears develop, fertilisation occurs, grains mature and the plant dies.

7.75 Wheat

7.76 Harvesting wheat in the 1930s

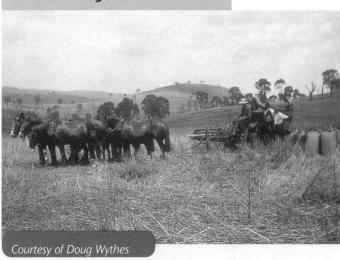

Courtesy of Doug Wythes

7.77 Calendar of operations

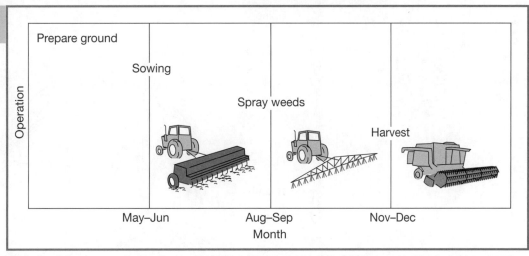

7.78 Wheat growth stages

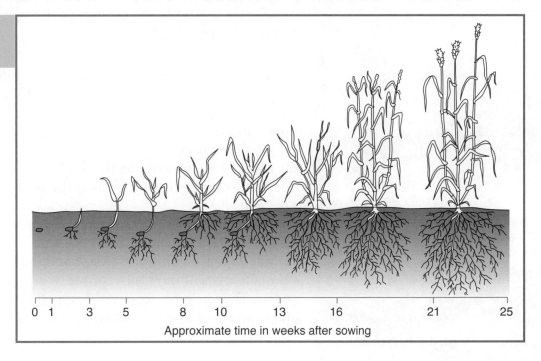

Approximate time in weeks after sowing

Flowers

A spike of wheat consists of groups of florets arranged along the main axis. Spikelets contain several florets, with hard glumes and paleas, and are pollinated by the wind.

7.79 Structure of a wheat plant

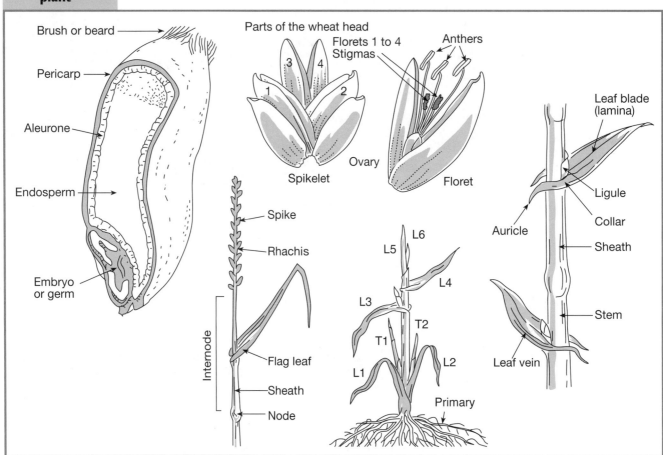

Brush or beard
Pericarp
Aleurone
Endosperm
Embryo or germ

Parts of the wheat head

Florets 1 to 4
Stigmas
Anthers

3 4
1 2

Spikelet
Ovary
Floret

Leaf blade (lamina)
Ligule
Collar
Auricle
Sheath
Stem
Leaf vein

Spike
Rhachis
Internode
Flag leaf
Sheath
Node

L6
L5
L4
L3
T2
T1
L1
L2
Primary

7.80 Disc ploughs

7.81 Traditional combine to sow wheat

Sowing wheat

Traditionally land was ploughed and left fallow for several months before sowing. This method was popular because:
• it prepared a suitable seedbed for germination
• it killed weeds that competed with the crop for water, light and nutrients
• it preserved water
• it killed many diseases in the soil
• decomposing residues increased the nutrient status of the soil.

However this method had many disadvantages, including:
• it compressed and compacted the soil
• it was expensive in time, labour and money
• it made the soil more susceptible to erosion.

Many farmers have replaced this method with minimum tillage practices and control weeds with herbicides and intensive grazing.

Activity 7.24

Look closely at the images of practical machinery in [7.82] to [7.88]. Name each machine and describe its function. Choose from air seeder, combine harvester, direct drill, disc harrow, disc plough, mouldboard plough, scarifier.

7.82

7.83

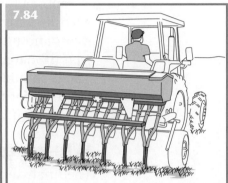

7.84

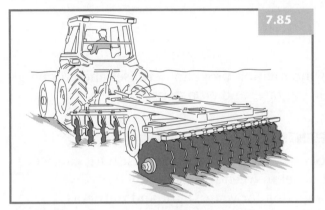

7.85

7.86

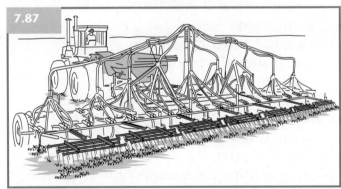

7.87

7.88

Varieties of wheat

The type of wheat a farmer uses depends on:
• the local climate, for example rainfall and temperature regimes
• growing period of the region
• soil type, for example fertility level and water-holding capacity
• demand for different varieties
• purpose of the crop, for example grazing or grain production
• its resistance to local pests and diseases such as rusts and smuts.

Time of sowing

Factors affecting time of sowing includes:
• variety used
• its growing season
• local soil types and their fertility level and water-holding capacity
• purpose of the crop, for example grazing for grain production.

Fertiliser requirements

The type and amount of fertiliser used will depend on:

- local soil types
- climate
- type of crop grown and its nutritional requirements
- cropping history of the paddock
- fertiliser history of the paddock
- cost and nutrient content of each fertiliser
- profit margin.

Soils should be tested and a fertiliser selected that supplies the desired elements for the least cost. Crop rotations including legume based plants can also be used to increase the nutrient status of the soil.

Wheat yields

The final yield depends on many factors including:

- climate
- soil type
- incidence of weeds, pests and diseases
- variety used
- management practices such as the rotation program, fertiliser and cropping history, irrigation practices, sowing rates and crop density.

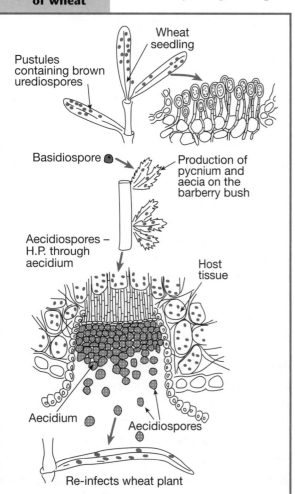

7.89 Stem rust of wheat

Wheat seedling

Pustules containing brown urediospores

Basidiospore

Production of pycnium and aecia on the barberry bush

Aecidiospores – H.P. through aecidium

Host tissue

Aecidium

Aecidiospores

Re-infects wheat plant

Weeds

Weeds such as wild oats, Bathurst burr, capeweed and skeleton weed reduce productivity by:

- competing for water, light and nutrients
- attracting pests and diseases
- reducing yields
- making harvesting difficult
- contaminating the product
- increasing production costs in control methods.

Weeds are controlled by several methods, including:

- chemical control
- biological control
- physical control, for example cultivating with ploughs and harrows
- integrated control.

Pests and diseases

Many pests and diseases affect wheat, including:

- insects, for example grasshoppers
- rusts
- take all
- root rot
- feral pigs.
- bunt
- birds
- kangaroos

Many of these pests and diseases can be controlled by:
- using resistant varieties
- good hygiene, for example destroying residues
- removing weeds that act as alternate hosts to pests and diseases
- using certified disease-free seed.
- crop rotations to break disease and pest cycles, for example yellow spot and take all
- timing of operations, for example warm humid conditions favour stem rust
- management practices, for example increased zinc levels in the soil reduces the incidence of rhizoctonia
- integrated pest management.

rhizoctonia commonly called black scurf can be a serious disease of potato

vertical integration control of marketing chain from growing to selling by one organisation

Other hazards

Wheat is also affected by natural disasters such as: droughts, rain, frosts, fire and hail.

The effect of these disasters can be minimised by:
- timing the sowing and harvesting to avoid frosts and hail
- adequate weather forecasting
- insurance
- irrigation
- diversifying income sources.

Marketing wheat

The majority of Australian wheat is sold overseas. Key export markets are in the Asian and Middle East regions and include Indonesia, Japan, South Korea, Malaysia, Vietnam and Sudan. Domestic and export markets are both deregulated.

Prices for wheat are based on:
- world supply and demand
- variety
- quality such as protein content and purity
- end use, for example livestock feed or bread production
- the marketing system.

Marketing tools used include:
- vertical integration where wheat is sold directly to its end user, for example feedlots, minimising costs and increasing efficiency
- value adding or altering wheat to increase its value, for example selling it as biscuits rather than flour
- using futures contracts so farmers receive a guaranteed price.

7.90 Modern grain storage silos

7.91 Modern wheat handling and storage facilities

7.92 Marketing wheat

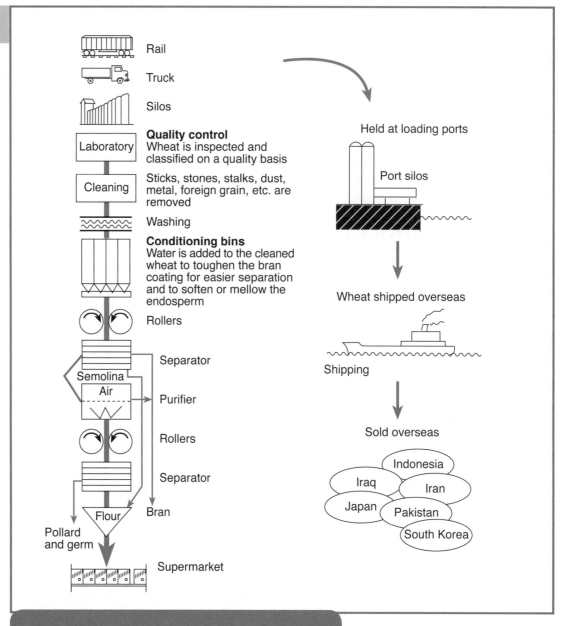

Rail

Truck

Silos

Quality control
Wheat is inspected and classified on a quality basis

Sticks, stones, stalks, dust, metal, foreign grain, etc. are removed

Washing

Conditioning bins
Water is added to the cleaned wheat to toughen the bran coating for easier separation and to soften or mellow the endosperm

Rollers

Separator

Purifier

Rollers

Separator

Bran

Flour

Pollard and germ

Supermarket

Held at loading ports

Port silos

Wheat shipped overseas

Shipping

Sold overseas

Indonesia
Iraq
Iran
Japan
Pakistan
South Korea

Source: Based on Australian Wheat Board occasional publication

Activity 7.25

1 Draw a systems diagram for wheat production (include inputs, outputs and processes, etc).
2 Draw a second systems diagram to show how a wheat enterprise interacts with other enterprises on a farm.

Research 7.26

1 Investigate the marketing system of another plant. Draw the marketing chain.
2 What are the market criteria for five plant products? For example protein content, size, purity.

Technology and plant production

7.93 Traditional haulage system

7.94 Modern haulage system

7.95 Modern harvesting equipment

7.96 Traditional water cart 1920s

Technology has had an enormous impact on plant production. Innovations include:

- new plant species, for example William Farrer developed rust-resistant wheat
- electricity, for example delivery to most rural areas from 1946 onwards
- machinery, for example tractors, headers and motor vehicles
- conservation tillage equipment
- fertilisers
- chemicals
- biological control agents, for example *cactoblastis cactorum* – a moth whose caterpillars feed on prickly pear
- irrigation systems
- hydroponics
- glasshouses
- refrigeration
- controlled atmosphere storage, for example carbon dioxide and nitrogen levels are controlled to prolong storage life
- transportation systems, for example road, rail and air systems
- processing and canning
- new packaging, for example cryovac vacuum seal packaging

7.97 Solar-powered pumping system

- new marketing techniques
- new sources of information and communication, for example computerised systems
- genetic engineering and new breeding techniques.

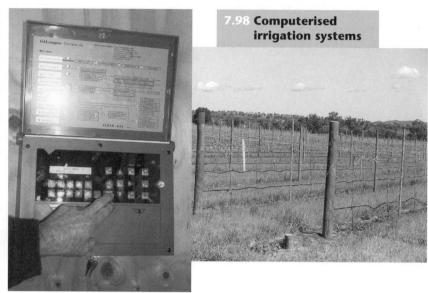

7.98 Computerised irrigation systems

7.99 Controlled atmosphere storage for fruit

Timeline

Developments have occurred rapidly as shown in this timeline:

broadcasting sowing of seed by hand

1600s

Small strips of land provide families' needs.
Ploughs are pulled by oxen and seed sown by broadcasting.
Crops are harvested with sickles.

1700s

Crop rotations introduced, for example wheat is grown in rotation with turnips, barley and clover.

1730 First cast iron plough developed.
1788 Cattle and other new livestock introduced into Australia.
Cotton and other new crops introduced into Australia.

1800s

1843 John Ridley developed stripper.
1858 Angus cattle imported.
1860s Branson Mullens developed scrub roller to clear mallee.
1876 Smith developed the stump-jump plough.
1884 Wolsey developed a machine to shear sheep.

AG FACT

Harvest time
In 1860 it took 50 hours of labour to harvest one acre or 0.4 hectare of grain. In 1960 it took only 3 hours to do the same job.

1900s

1900	William Farrer develops rust-resistant Federation wheat.
1903	First tractor arrives in Australia – a three-wheel, gasoline-powered Ivel. Horses still used up until 1940, as tractors were expensive.
1906	First radio broadcast.
1908	Alfred McDonald builds the first Australian tractor.
1909	Synthetic ammonia produced and used to make explosives and fertilisers.
1910	Superphosphate trialled on pastures.
1910	Headlee Taylor patents the first header harvester.
1914	Federal government introduces legislation to create a wheat board.
1915	Bunt disease controlled by using copper carbonate.
1916	Raimond Ash Squire develops the spring tyne drill, which is the forerunner of the combine.
1918	First silo for bulk handling of wheat built at Peak Hill, NSW.
1920	Cliff Howard develops the rotary hoe.
1920	Myxomas virus imported into Australia from South America.
1924	*Cactoblastis* moth released as a biological weapon against the prickly pear.
1924	Frozen food developed by adventurer Clarence Birdseye.
1926	David Shearer builds the first header.
1931	Rubber tyres made for tractors in the USA.
1933	Brahman cattle introduced into Australia.
1930–40	Motor trucks displace horse teams for transportation.
1936	Shopping trolley developed.
1937	Instant coffee developed.
1939	Precooked frozen food developed.
1945	DDT released.
1946	Rural electricity scheme established to connect country areas with state power grid.
1948	First supermarket in Britain.
1948	4WD Land Rover introduced into Australia.
1949	CSIRO established.
1947	Insects start becoming resistant to DDT.
1948	Ferguson TEA20 tractor with hydraulic three-point linkage released.
1950	First aerial application of superphosphate.
1951	Bill Hughes designs the grain auger.

1950–60s

- Discovery of DNA.
- Myxomatosis accidentally released.
- 1080 used as rabbit poison.
- Bulk handling of grain replaces bags at country silos.
- Diesel engines replace petrol and kerosene engines in trucks and tractors.
- Albert Fuss develops air seeder.
- Cane harvester developed.
- Polythene pipes introduced to transfer water.

DNA
deoxyribonucleic acid – a double helix molecule that acts as the genetic blueprint for many characteristics such as growth rate, and eye and hair colour

myxomatosis
highly contagious and fatal virus disease of rabbits used to control rabbit populations

- Dwarf wheat released.
- Liveweight selling of stock introduced.
- First commercial satellite launched.

1970–80

- Stubble retention pioneered by John Ronald.
- Knockdown herbicides – paraquat and glyphosate – developed.
- DNA is spliced.
- 300 companies marketed 8000 pesticides with market growing by 10–15 per cent per year.
- Global positioning system (GPS) developed.
- 4WD tractors introduced.
- Development of travelling irrigators.
- Bar code perfected.
- Estimated 60 per cent of wheat crops are sprayed with herbicide.
- First case of weed resistance is discovered, for example ryegrass to the chemical Hoegras.

1980–90

- Centre pivot irrigators developed.
- Personal computers used.
- Drip irrigation adopted in orchards and vineyards.
- CALM – computerised livestock selling – introduced.
- Genetech engineered life forms for industry and medicine.
- Plant variety rights introduced.
- Detection of organochlorine residues in beef exported.

1990–2000 onwards

- Landcare established.
- Last manual telephone becomes automatic.
- Mobile phones revolutionise telecommunications.
- Internet revolutionises information transfer.
- Genetic engineering.

Plant breeding

The genetic makeup of a plant sets an upper limit to its productivity. Maximum productivity is not always reached because environmental factors such as droughts, floods, weeds, pests and diseases affect production.

Methods used to promote genotype – environment interaction include:

genotype
the genetic makeup of an organism

- using plants and animals suited to a particular environment
- planning operations to coincide with the environment
- selectively breeding plants with the highest productivity
- modifying the climate, for example glasshouses, irrigation, windbreaks and mulches
- reducing the incidence of weeds, pests and diseases
- improving soils, for example using fertilisers and crop rotations.

The main objectives of a plant breeder include increasing:
- yields
- quality
- disease resistance
- tolerance of climatic extremes such as frosts and droughts
- defensive capabilities of plants against pests and diseases.

Breeding methods

Common methods used include:
- selective breeding
- cross breeding
- hybrid breeding
- vegetative propagation
- tissue culture
- genetic engineering.

Selective breeding

Selective breeding is the careful selection and breeding of plants with desired characteristics.

Cross breeding

Crossbreeding is the production of a new plant from two different parents. Crossbreeding is advantageous because it results in:
- a greater genetic pool
- superior offspring
- hybrid vigour.

Hybrid breeding

Hybrid breeding is the creation of plants from parents that have different genotypes and do not normally pollinate one another.

Chromosome doubling and embryo culture have been used to overcome the normal sterility barriers, and have helped create plants such as triticale, hybrid maize, sorghum and sunflowers.

Vegetative propagation

Plants can also be vegetatively propagated from segments such as leaves, stems and roots. This method has many advantages, including:
- producing large numbers of genetically identical plants from a single plant
- producing plants from seedless varieties such as citrus
- increasing maturation rates and speed of flowering
- allowing for specialised breeding programs such as disease resistance.

AG FACT

Selective breeding?

Humans have selectively bred plants unintentionally for thousands of years by keeping the best quality seed from the crop to sow the following year.

Aim
To study the chromosomes and genetic material of a plant.

Equipment
- beaker
- water
- microscope slides and cover slips
- razor blade
- 70% alcohol and 30% acetic acid mixture
- dilute hydrochloric acid
- aceto orcein stain
- microscope
- forceps.

Method

7.100 Onion experiment

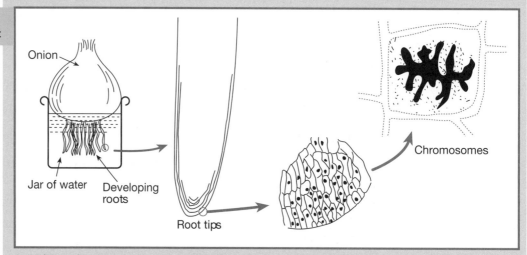

1. Place the onion in a jar of water.
2. Allow the roots to grow one centimetre in length and then remove the tips with forceps.
3. Place the tips in the 70% alcohol and 30% acetic acid solution.
4. Place the root tips in dilute hydrochloric acid at 60°C for five minutes.
5. Remove the last 3 mm from one tip.
6. Break this into smaller pieces and place it on a microscope slide with one drop of aceto-orcein stain and place a cover slip on the slide.

Results
Examine the specimen under the microscope and observe the chromosomes in the nucleus.

Conclusion
State your observations.

Tissue culture

Plants are propagated from tissues such as stem tips and axillary buds grown in artificial media. This method has the same advantages as vegetative propagation and is a very efficient method of plant propagation.

Biotechnology

Biotechnology uses the natural processes of microbes, and plant and animal cells for human benefit. Biotechnology has been used for thousands of years to make:

- bread
- beer and wine
- cheese
- yoghurt

- compost
- silage
- fuels
- medicines, for example penicillin.

7.101 Biotechnology and agriculture

The primary aim of modern biotechnology is to make a cell perform a specific task. Microbes have been altered to produce specific chemicals such as:

- insulin for diabetes
- growth hormone to treat dwarfism
- monoclonal antibodies which detect bacterial and viral infections.
- vaccine production, for example Hepatitis B.

7.102 DNA

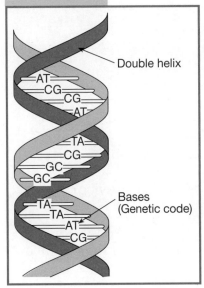

Double helix

Bases (Genetic code)

Genetic engineering

Genetic engineering is the manipulation of the plant's genetic material. DNA carries the genetic blueprint of an individual and is found in every cell.

Radiation and chemical substances such as ethyl methane sulfonate are commonly used to alter the genetic makeup of plants and produce new characteristics such as disease resistance and short-stemmed cereals.

The genetic makeup of plants has also been manipulated by other methods, including:

- reconstituting plants from single cells
- hybridising the cells of different species
- changing the genetic makeup of a plant by transferring genes from one species to another.

Scientists have used genetic engineering to produce:

- higher-yielding, better-quality crops
- improved pastures, for example CSIRO are developing sulfur-rich lucerne to improve wool quality
- drought-resistant plants that are tolerant to climatic extremes
- pest resistance, for example Ingard cotton contains bacillus thuringiensis (Bt) and is resistant to the heliothis caterpillar

7.103 Harvesting genetically engineered tomatoes

- disease resistance such as modified tomatoes that are resistant to the tobacco mosaic virus
- natural insecticides, for example the tomato plants in [7.103] contain an insecticidal protein that provides an in-built protection against insects
- selective herbicide resistance, for example crops contain genes resistant to the herbicide glyphosate and only weeds are affected if sprayed.

genetically modified (GM) food
food from plant sources modified by gene technology techniques such as food containing GM cotton, corn or potato

Many consumers are hesitant to accept genetically modified (GM) foods because of the fear of:

- threats to human health
- threats to the environment
- unknown consequences, for example weeds developing herbicide-resistant genes
- playing God and interfering with nature, for example Hitler wanted to create a master race in World War II
- companies owning living organisms
- companies having the power to control food chains if they own a key gene technology patent.

Research 7.27

Use the following web sites to perform the research:
www.foodstandards.gov.au
australia.gov.au/directories/australia/food-standards

a   Make a list of the genetically modified food that is available in the market place.
b   What are the advantages and disadvantages of genetic engineering?

Plant variety rights

Variety rights allow breeders exclusive access to plant material for a limited time. Advantages of this system include:

- encourages research and development
- encourages disclosure of new developments to the public
- protects the inventor
- encourages private enterprise into research and development.

However variety rights have some disadvantages, including:
• a person or company can own the rights to living things, which many consider improper
• limits access
• administration is expensive
• additional costs to consumers
• can delay further research due to restricted access.

Revision 7.28

1 Define the following words:
   • growing season
   • dicotyledon
   • pollination
   • grafting
   • phloem
   • respiration
   • technology
   • legume
   • minimum tillage
   • cell grazing
   • hybrid
   • biotechnology
   • monocotyledon
   • leaves
   • stem
   • stomata
   • photosynthesis
   • transpiration
   • native pastures
   • fodder crops
   • direct drill
   • strip grazing
   • tissue culture
   • flower
   • seed
   • budding
   • xylem
   • yield
   • weeds
   • grass
   • silage
   • hay
   • DNA
   • gene

2 Answer true or false to the following statements.
   a Wheat is the most important crop grown in Australia.
   b The growing season determines what plants can be grown in a region.
   c Temperature has no effect on germination.
   d Budding and grafting are types of asexual reproduction.
   e Phloem transports water and mineral salts around the plant.
   f Stomata control the transpiration rate.
   g Rhizobium bacteria increase the available nitrogen to plants.
   h Leaves are the main site of photosynthesis and transpiration.
   i Silage is made by microbial fermentation.
   j Pastures benefit from overgrazing.
   k Wheat marketing is deregulated.
   l Tissue culture is a form of cloning.
   m DNA is a genetic blueprint of our history.
   n Change is inevitable in agriculture.

Animal Production

In this chapter you will learn about:

- the commercial production of animals
- animal production systems
- plant, climate and resource interactions
- impact of microbes and pests on animal production
- use of technologies in producing and marketing animal products
- animal experimental design and research
- breeding systems
- ethics, welfare and legal issues and requirements.

Importance of animals

Animals provide us with food, fibre, raw materials and income.

8.1 Products derived from a steer

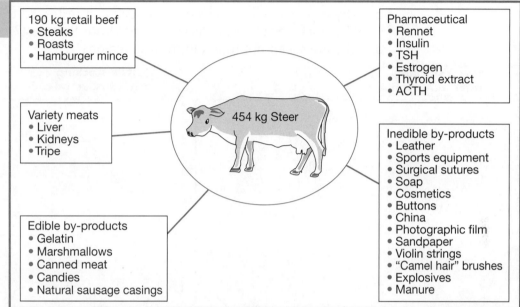

190 kg retail beef
- Steaks
- Roasts
- Hamburger mince

Variety meats
- Liver
- Kidneys
- Tripe

454 kg Steer

Edible by-products
- Gelatin
- Marshmallows
- Canned meat
- Candies
- Natural sausage casings

Pharmaceutical
- Rennet
- Insulin
- TSH
- Estrogen
- Thyroid extract
- ACTH

Inedible by-products
- Leather
- Sports equipment
- Surgical sutures
- Soap
- Cosmetics
- Buttons
- China
- Photographic film
- Sandpaper
- Violin strings
- "Camel hair" brushes
- Explosives
- Manure

Activity 8.1

8.2 Cattle

8.3 Angora goats

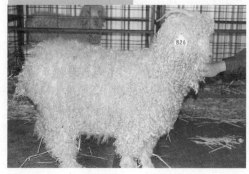

List the products derived from each animal.

Animal	Products
Cattle	
Sheep	
Chickens	
Pigs	
Alpacas	
Deer	
Rabbits	
Native species, for example crocodiles, emus	
Ostriches	
Other	

Activity 8.2

Maps [8.4] and [8.5] show the location and the stocking rates of sheep and cattle in Australia.
a Why are sheep more common and widespread than cattle?
b Why is prime lamb production and dairying restricted to specific locations?
c Why does stocking rate decline further from the coast?
d Why are sheep not found in tropical regions?

8.4 Sheep stocking rates in Australia

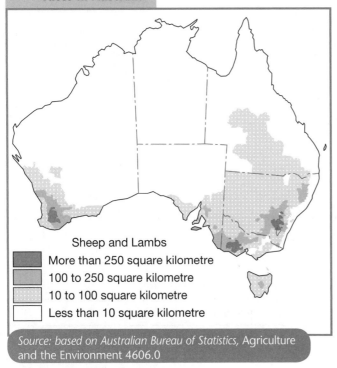

Sheep and Lambs
- More than 250 square kilometre
- 100 to 250 square kilometre
- 10 to 100 square kilometre
- Less than 10 square kilometre

Source: based on Australian Bureau of Statistics, Agriculture and the Environment 4606.0

8.5 Cattle stocking rates in Australia

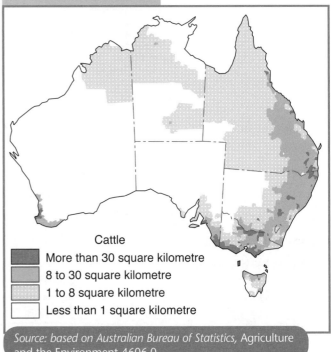

Cattle
- More than 30 square kilometre
- 8 to 30 square kilometre
- 1 to 8 square kilometre
- Less than 1 square kilometre

Source: based on Australian Bureau of Statistics, Agriculture and the Environment 4606.0

Activity 8.3

8.6 Sheep in Australia 1890–2010

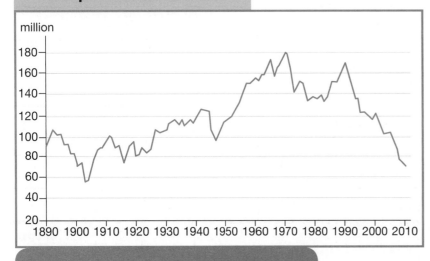

Source: Historical Selected Commodities by State (7124.0)

Graphs [8.6] and [8.7] show the change in sheep and chicken numbers with time.
1 What trends are apparent?
2 Why did sheep numbers decline in 1905 and 1945?
3 Chicken consumption is rapidly increasing. Why are consumers eating more chicken than lamb (for example convenience and health reasons)?

8.7 Chicken consumption 1950–2000

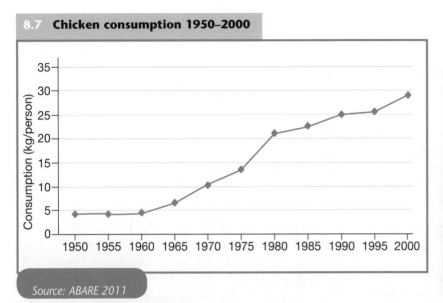

Source: ABARE 2011

8.8 Wool production

8.9 Alpacas

Use the following Internet sites to research what animal enterprises are in your region:
australia.gov.au/directories/australia/agriculture/web-resources-list
www.elders.com.au
www.wesfarmers.com.au
www.mla.com.au
www.farmonline.com.au/
www.aglinks.com.au
www.daff.qld.gov.au/home.htm
www.dpi.vic.gov.au
www.dpi.nsw.gov.au
www.dpi.qld.gov.au
www.pir.sa.gov.au
www.dpiw.tas.gov.au

Growth and development

Growth is the increase in weight and height of an animal over time.
  Growth has a marked effect on:
- time of selling
- feed requirements
- the type of carcase produced.
  Fast growth rates are desirable so that:
- animals reach slaughter weight as quickly as possible
- animals have high food conversion efficiencies
- there is faster turnover of livestock.
  Most animals have an S-shaped growth curve with rapid weight gain before maturity, and then their weight and height stabilises.

carcase
body of a slaughtered animal whose head, skin and internal organs have been removed

8.10 The growth curve

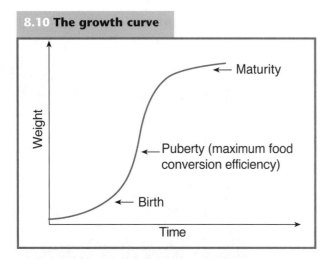

8.11 Maturity rates of different breeds

Early maturing	Angus	Southdown
↕	Hereford	Dorset
	Bo indicus	Suffolk
	Friesian	Border Leicester
Late maturing	Charolais	Merino

Growth rate is affected by many factors including:

- age
- breed
- number of offspring
- sex
- nutrition
- climate
- disease and parasites
- stress
- management.

Young animals rapidly increase in weight and height until they reach maturity. The breed of an animal sets a limit to the animal's rate of maturity and final size.

The number of offspring directly affects birth weight, with twins and triplets generally smaller than singles. The size and age of the dam affects birth weight with larger, older dams producing larger offspring.

Males are generally heavier and larger than females at birth and grow faster than castrates or females. However, at the same weight or age, heifers are fatter because they mature faster and lay down fat more quickly than males.

Insufficient, poor quality nutrition reduces growth rates and causes permanent stunting if not corrected. Compensatory growth is only possible if starvation occurs when the animal's tissues are not actively growing.

Climate can affect pasture quality and consumption rate. Stress caused by heat, fighting, diseases and parasites reduces food consumption and growth rates.

Manipulating growth and development using HGPs, feed additives and genetics

HGPs (hormonal growth promotants) are veterinary drugs that mimic growth hormones and increase muscle growth, mature size and lean yield. Approximately 40 per cent of Australia's beef is treated with them. HGPs increase growth rates by 10–30 per cent and feed conversion efficiency by 5–15 per cent. They enable cattle to meet market weights at an earlier age and increase production gains. The use of HGPs is strictly regulated and HGP products must be accredited by the APVMA (Australian Pesticides and Veterinary Medicines Authority), an Australian government agency. HGPs are used internationally but some countries, such as the European Union (EU), do not permit the use of HGPs in livestock.

castrates
male animals whose testicles have been removed to prevent unwanted matings and aggressive behaviour

compensatory growth
accelerated growth following a period of delay in growth caused by malnutrition, pests or disease

Practical 38

Liveweight gain

8.12 Twin lambs

Aim

To compare liveweight gains for single and twin lambs.

Equipment
- ewes and lambs of the same age, breed and condition
- scales
- identification tags.

Method
1 Ear-mark lambs for ease of identification.
2 Weigh lambs at weekly intervals.
3 Compare weight gains.

Results

Graph liveweight gain versus time.

Conclusion

State your conclusions from the results.

Activity 8.5

8.13 Weight of steers with age

Age of steers	Weight kg
Birth	20
7 months	200
12 months	300
16 months	450

Table [8.13] shows the weight of steers with time.
Graph the liveweight of the steers versus time.
  a What shape is the graph?
  b At what stage do the steers have the highest food conversion efficiency? It is the point where the line has the greatest slope.
  c What relevance is this graph to the producer?

Practical 39

Drenching and liveweight gain

Aim

To show the effect of drenching on the liveweight gain of lambs.

Equipment
- lambs of the same age, breed and sex
- drench
- sheep yards
- scales.

Method
1 Drench half the lambs. Leave the others untreated as the controls.
2 Weigh the lambs each week.
3 Record changes in liveweight with time.

Result

Graph your results.

Conclusion

State your conclusion from the results.

Development

Development is the change in shape and composition of an animal over time.

Essential tissues and organs such as the brain, lungs, heart and skeletal and muscular system are well developed at birth to ensure its survival.

Less essential organs and tissues – such as the reproductive system and fat – develop later.

8.14 Changes in body shape as an animal ages

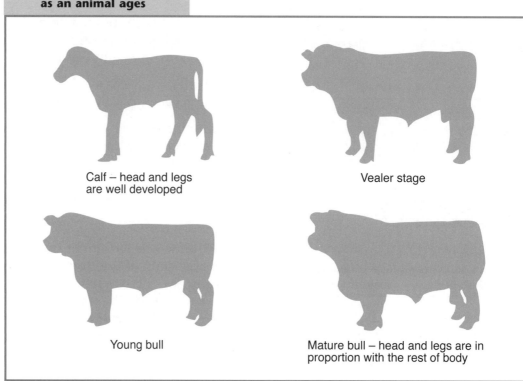

Calf – head and legs are well developed

Vealer stage

Young bull

Mature bull – head and legs are in proportion with the rest of body

8.15 The head and legs are well developed at birth to ensure survival

8.16 Tissues compete for the food supply

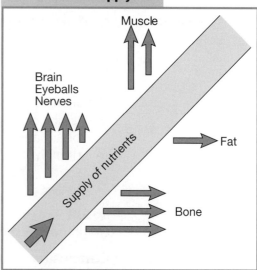

Muscle

Brain
Eyeballs
Nerves

Supply of nutrients

Fat

Bone

The ideal carcase

An ideal carcase has minimum bone, maximum muscle and optimum fat. Optimum fat levels depend on:
• consumer tastes and preferences
• dietary requirements
• the end use of the carcase.

Fat enhances flavour and stops the carcase drying out. However a kilogram of fat requires more production energy than a kilogram of muscle. Fatty carcases also require more handling and trimming before selling as retail cuts.

The percentage of muscle, bone and fat is determined by:
• weight
• age
• sex
• breed
• conformation.

Older animals have a higher percentage of fat to bone and muscle. They have a smaller proportion of retail cuts in the loin, ribs and forequarters, and have bigger flanks and briskets.

At the same weight or age, females are generally fatter because they mature faster. Early-maturing breeds at the same age have more fat than later-maturing animals. Animals with a blocky shape often appear meatier than leggy animals but they usually contain more fat and less muscle.

Muscle and fat scoring

Muscle and fat scoring is used to grade the quality of an animal. Muscle is scored from A (heavy muscle) to E (little muscle).

Fat scores are ranked from 1 with little fat to 5 or 6 with large amounts of fat.

An animal with a score of A 6 would have a lot of muscle and a lot of fat. An animal with a score of A 1 would have a lot of muscle and little fat.

Practical 40

Muscle and fat scoring cattle

Aim
To muscle and fat score cattle for market requirements.

Equipment
• At least five cattle of the same age, breed and sex.
• Cattle yards and crush.

Method
Use the charts for muscle and fat score in [8.17]–[8.20]:
1 Perform muscle and fat scores for five animals.
2 Work as a team to obtain consistent results.

8.17 Muscle scoring animals

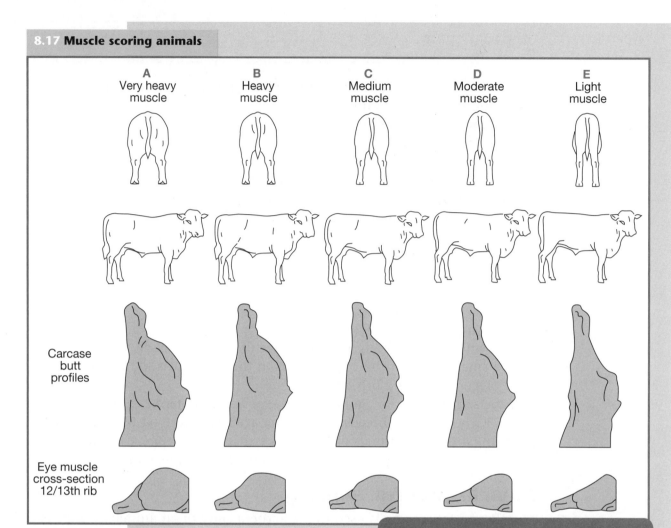

A	B	C	D	E
Very heavy muscle	Heavy muscle	Medium muscle	Moderate muscle	Light muscle

Carcase butt profiles

Eye muscle cross-section 12/13th rib

Source: NSW Agriculture, The Beef Business, *page 20*

8.18 Manual fat assessment at the loin area

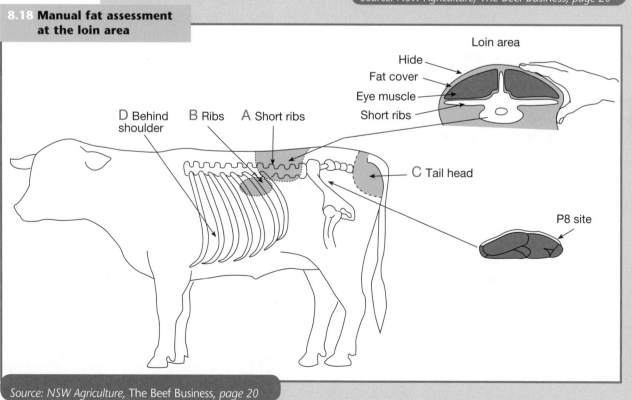

Loin area

Hide
Fat cover
Eye muscle
Short ribs

D Behind shoulder
B Ribs
A Short ribs

C Tail head

P8 site

Source: NSW Agriculture, The Beef Business, *page 20*

8.19 Sites to observe when fat scoring cattle

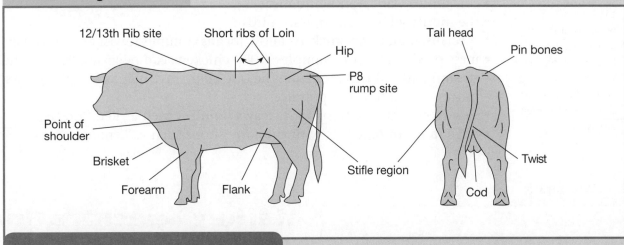

Source: NSW Agriculture, The Beef Business, *page 14*

8.20 Fat scores

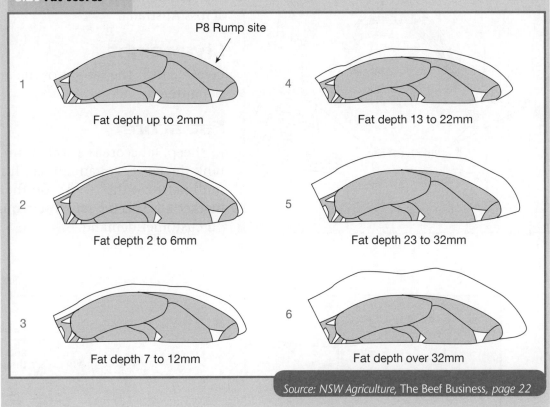

P8 Rump site

1 — Fat depth up to 2mm
2 — Fat depth 2 to 6mm
3 — Fat depth 7 to 12mm
4 — Fat depth 13 to 22mm
5 — Fat depth 23 to 32mm
6 — Fat depth over 32mm

Source: NSW Agriculture, The Beef Business, *page 22*

Consumer and market requirements

Consumers require meat that is:
- healthy
- versatile
- of consistent quality
- easy to cook and prepare
- inexpensive
- convenient.

Beef and chicken are the most popular meats. Chicken consumption has rapidly increased because:

- consumers want lean white meat
- the industry has bred superior birds
- specialised diets for chickens allow for maximum growth and turnover
- mass production, for example 50 000 chickens can be grown in one shed
- streamlined industry, for example one company such as Steggles grows, processes and sells the product
- easy to cut into portions for takeaway outlets such as Red Rooster
- huge range of products with specialty shops such as Lenards.

GR site
on lambs it is 110 millimetres from the backline along the second last long rib and is the standard site where fat levels are assessed

8.21 The GR site

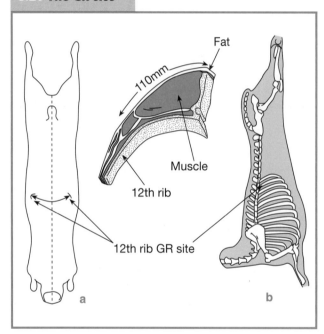

Fat
110mm
Muscle
12th rib
12th rib GR site
a
b

Market specifications

Market specifications are a description of the type of carcase that the buyer requires. AUS-MEAT is the standard language for market specifications across Australia.

Liveweight

Liveweight is the weight of the animal before it is slaughtered.

Fat score

In sheep, fat score is a scale from 1–5 used to rank the fatness of an animal. It is the depth in millimetres at the GR site on the twelfth rib. Each market has specific fat score requirements based on customer demand.

8.22 Fat scoring lambs

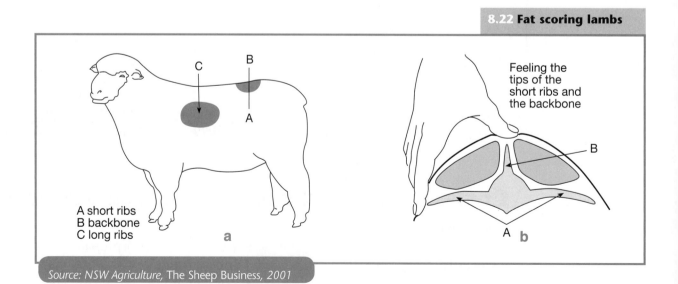

C
B
A
A short ribs
B backbone
C long ribs
a

Feeling the tips of the short ribs and the backbone
B
A
b

Source: NSW Agriculture, The Sheep Business, *2001*

	Fat score				
	1	2	3	4	5
GR tissue depth in mm	0–5	6–10	11–15	16–20	21 and over

Fat score

Source: NSW Agriculture, The Sheep Business, 2001

AG FACT

Too much fat?

Fat gives the carcase flavour and prevents it from drying out. However consumers do not want excessive fat as it is considered unhealthy and a waste of money. Lambs with a fat score of five are generally considered too fat and are worth less money because fat has to be trimmed from the carcase.

Hot carcase weight

Hot carcase weight (HSCW) is the weight of the animal after it has been killed and dressed.

Dressing percentage

Dressing percentage equals carcase weight divided by liveweight times 100. For example a 40 kg lamb with a carcase weight of 22 kg has a dressing percentage of 55 per cent.

Factors affecting dressing percentage include:
• time of the last feed before slaughter
• stress level
• liveweight and fatness level
• sex
• breed.

dressed
the removal from the carcase of inedible parts such as the head, legs, skin and internal organs

P8
standardised site on cattle where fat depth is measured on the carcase

dentition
the number of permanent teeth on the lower jaw of a beast which is used to determine the age of an animal

Practical 41

Carcase analysis

Aim
To match cattle with target market specifications.

Equipment
• table of carcase analysis [8.23]
• table of market specifications [8.24]

8.23 Carcase information

Ear	Body number	Sex	Dent	Fat depth	Butt	Bruising	Carcase weight
321	115	M	1	3	D	0	160
155	116	M	1	5	A	0	200
167	117	F	0	6	C	0	250
174	118	M	4	12	B	0	220
162	119	F	3	2	A	0	270
534	120	M	1	7	D	0	195
634	121	F	1	9	C	Present	205

8.24 Domestic supermarket specifications

Carcase weight	190–250 kg
P8 fat depth	6–10 mm
Meat colour	1a–2
Fat colour	0–2
Butt shape	A, B, C
Dentition	0–3 teeth
Price	250 c/kg

Method
1 Refer to the table of market requirements and carcase analysis.
2 Which animals reached market requirements?
3 What percentage of animals were not suitable for this market?
4 How much money did the producer receive for the smallest, average and largest animal?
5 One animal had an eye cancer and bruising. How does this affect the price received?

Eating quality

marbling
the amount of intramuscular fat which is influenced by breed, nutrition and age

Eating quality is influenced by the palatability and visual appearance of the meat. Palatability includes characteristics such as tenderness, juiciness and flavour. Visual appearance is influenced by meat and fat colour, degree of marbling, texture, portion size, thickness of cuts and the presence of fluid in meat trays.

Fine-textured meat is more appealing than coarse meat and is influenced by the animal's age and level of stress at slaughtering. Consumers prefer bright-coloured meat and this is influenced by age, sex and stress level.

If animals are stressed during slaughtering the pH does not drop to below 5.6 and the meat is dark purple in colour. (Meat must have a pH lower than 5.6 to be tender.) Stress can be minimised by:
- selecting animals with a quiet temperament
- regulating handling practices
- regulating nutrition
- the time without feed and water prior to slaughter.

Fat is white to yellow in colour and is influenced by breed, age and diet. Animals losing weight or fed grasses rich in Vitamin A often have more yellowish coloured fat.

Marbling refers to the degree of intramuscular fat and is considered to be an indicator of tenderness and flavour. Breed, nutrition, age and carcase weight can influence marbling levels.

Activity 8.6

Label the beef and sheep carcase and list the cuts derived from each section.

8.25 Cuts of meat from cattle and sheep

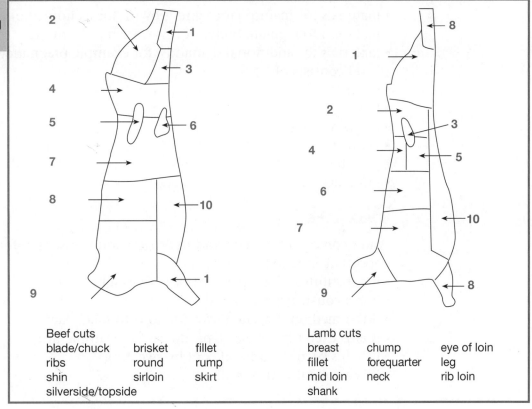

Beef cuts
blade/chuck	brisket	fillet
ribs	round	rump
shin	silverside/topside	skirt
silverside/topside		

Lamb cuts
breast	chump	eye of loin
fillet	forequarter	leg
mid loin	neck	rib loin
shank		

Practical 42

Eating quality of meat

Aim
To compare the eating quality of different cuts of meat.

Equipment
• five cuts of meat, for example blade, skirt, fillet, brisket and rump
• electric frying pan

Method
1 List the characteristics of the meat, for example texture, colour, fat colour, degree of marbling and pH.
2 Identify the most visually appealing sample.
3 Cook untouched samples of the meat and rate the samples from 1–10 for tenderness, flavour and juiciness.

Results
Record your results in tabular form.

Conclusion
State your conclusions from the results.

Food and nutrition

Food supplies animals with:
• energy for all life processes
• materials for maintenance and growth, for example bone, muscle and fat
• materials to regulate body processes such as hormones
• materials for additional demands, for example pregnancy.
  Food consists of:
• water
• fats
• carbohydrates
• vitamins
• proteins
• minerals.

Water

Water consists of oxygen and hydrogen and is essential for life. Some of the important functions of water are:
• it constitutes 75–95 per cent of bodyweight
• it is a constituent of blood
• it is a medium for chemical reactions to take place
• it aids excretion of waste products, for example urine
• it helps keep the animal cool by sweating
• it is a constituent of milk.

Energy

Carbohydrates, proteins and fats provide the animal with energy. Gross energy is the total amount of energy in a feedstuff. Net energy is the energy available after digestion for maintenance and production.

8.26 Metabolisable energy(ME) content of different feeds	
Type of feed ME	Dry matter (MJ/kg)
Wheat grain	13.0
Oat grain	12.5
Barley grain	13.0
Lucerne hay	8.5
Pasture hay	8.3
Grass and clover silage	8.2

8.27 Energy available from food

Food energy	Gross energy (GE)
	minus faecal energy
Absorbed energy	Digestible energy (DE)
	minus urinary energy (and methane energy in ruminants)
Available energy	Metabolisable energy (ME)
	minus heat energy
Energy for maintenance and production	Net energy (NE)

Activity 8.7

8.28 Metabolisable energy requirements of sheep and cattle	
Animal	Daily ME requirement (MJ)
40kg sheep	7.4
40kg pregnant ewe	8.2
40kg lactating ewe with one lamb	16.3
200kg beef steer	27.0
450kg steer	49.0
500kg pregnant beef cow	71.0
500kg beef cow lactating	156.0

Use table [8.28] to answer what are the energy requirements for the following animals:

a   500 kg beef cow lactating
b   200 kg beef steer – maintenance level
c   40 kg sheep – maintenance level
d   40 kg lactating ewe with one lamb

Carbohydrates

Carbohydrates such as cellulose and glucose consist of carbon, hydrogen and oxygen and provide the body with energy. All carbohydrates have the general formula: $C_n (H_2O)_n$ or $_{n-1}$

Proteins

Proteins contain carbon, hydrogen, nitrogen, oxygen and sometimes sulfur, and constitute almost half the animal's dry weight. Proteins consist of amino-acid chains and are found in muscles, nerves, enzymes, blood and connective tissue.

8.29 Protein content of feeds	
Food	**Protein content (%)**
Linseed meal	31
Lucerne hay	13
Poor lucerne hay	8
Wheat grain	10
Oaten hay	5
Grass pasture	5

8.30 Protein requirements of animals	
Animal	**Protein requirements in feed (%)**
Young chicken	22
Laying hen	15
Lean sheep	6
Cow lactating	15
Pregnant cow	10

Lipids

Lipids contain carbon, hydrogen and oxygen and are concentrated stores of energy. Lipids include fats, oils and waxes. Saturated fats such as lamb fat and butter do not have any double bonds in their structure. Unsaturated fats such as vegetable oil contain more than one double bond.

Vitamins and minerals

Vitamins are organic substances essential for normal body function. Vitamins are only required in small amounts but deficiencies can result in severe malfunctioning of the body.

Minerals are inorganic salts. Macrominerals are required in large amounts and include:

- calcium
- phosphorus
- potassium
- sodium
- chlorine
- sulphur.

Micronutrients are required in small amounts and include:

- iron
- zinc
- copper
- manganese
- iodine.

The types of vitamins and minerals, and their functions, are listed in tables [8.31] and [8.32] over.

8.31 Types of vitamins and their function

Vitamin	Function	Deficiency symptoms	Correction
A	Hydrogen transfer, growth, eye function	Retarded growth, scaly skin, night blindness and infertility	Green feed and fish oils
B (thiamine)	Carbohydrate metabolism, functioning of nerves and muscles	Reduced appetite, emaciation and polyneuritis in chicks	Synthetic vitamins and brewer's grain
B_2 (riboflavin)	Hydrogen transport and carbohydrate metabolism	Reduced appetite, eye abnormalities, reduced hatchability	Yeast, liver oils and green crops
Nicotinamide	Glycolysis and respiration	Digestive disorders and dermatitis	Legumes and liver extracts
B_6 (pyridoxine)	Protein metabolism and production of antibodies	Anaemia in pigs and poor growth in chicks	Normally adequate supply
Pantothenic acid	Carbohydrate metabolism	Slow growth and diarrhoea in pigs. Poor growth and dermatitis in chicks	Yeast, liver and milk
Biotin	Carbon dioxide fixation	Dermatitis and hair loss	Seldom occurs
Choline	Fat metabolism	Slow growth	Seldom occurs
Folic acid	Protein metabolism	Anaemia and poor growth in chicks	Green leaf feed and liver
C (ascorbic acid)	Oxidation/reduction reactions	Nil	Nil

8.32 Types of minerals and their function

Mineral	Function	Deficiency symptoms	Correction
Calcium	Essential for skeleton, teeth, nervous system, muscle contraction and blood coagulation	Rickets, enlarged joints, lameness, weak bones, thin eggshells and reduced egg production	Add legumes, ground limestone or dicalcium phosphate to diet
Phosphorus	Constituent of bone and necessary for metabolism of energy	Rickets, muscular weakness, reduced appetite and reduced growth rates	Add cereals. fish and meat products to diet
Sodium	Acid base balance and osmotic regulation	Poor appetite and growth rates, reduced milk and, for egg production	Add salt licks to diet
Magnesium	Carbohydrate metabolism	Hypomagnesaemia in dairy cattle and high death rates	Use magnesium fertilisers or add magnesium to diet
Copper	Part of enzymes and blood, pigmentation in fur and wool	Anaemia, poor growth rates, scouring. Light coloured wool, muscular incoordination (sway back) in lambs, steely wool	Use lick blocks or inject with copper glycinate

Mineral	Function	Deficiency symptoms	Correction
Iodine	Thyroid gland function and metabolic rate	Swollen thyroid gland, lower reproductive rates, lambs born dead	Iodine supplement
	metabolic rate rate of the processes or chemical reactions in an animal's body		
Cobalt	Microbes in rumen; use it to make vitamin B12	Reduced appetite and growth, muscular wasting, anaemia and death	Top dress with cobalt or administer pellets

Research 8.8

1 a Select five minerals and vitamins.
  b List their importance and deficiency symptoms in tabular form.
2 Determine the constituents of five feeds, for example wheat, hay and pastures.
3 Determine a ration for a lactating dairy cow.

Activity 8.9

Table [8.33] shows the effect of nutrition on ewes' reproductive performance.

8.33 Effect of nutrition on reproduction of Border-Leicester-Merino cross ewes

Treatment plane of nutrition	No. ewes	Mean body weight kg	Ewes mated in first 6 weeks %	Ewes mated at end of 9 weeks %	Ewes lambing %	Multiple births %	Lambs born %
High	67	40.2	83.6	89.6	38.8	57.7	61.2
Medium	67	29.3	54.5	72.7	31.3	33.3	42.4
Low	65	27.0	32.3	52.3	21.5	21.4	26.2

Source: The Livestock and Grain Producers Association of NSW, Sheep Production Guide, Macarthur Press, Parramatta

1 What effect does nutrition have on:
  a the number of ewes that lamb?
  b the percentage of multiple births?
  c the percentage of lambs born?
2 Discuss the effect of the ewes body weight on:
  a lambing problems
  b lactation potential
  c mothering abilities.
3 Of what practical use is this information to the farmer?

lactation
production of milk after the birth of offspring

Digestion

Digestion is the physical, chemical and sometimes microbial breakdown of food into a soluble form that the animal can absorb.

The two most common systems are the monogastric and ruminant digestive systems

monogastric
digestive system with a single stomach or gastric cavity such as humans

Ruminants

Ruminants such as sheep and cattle have four stomachs and use physical, chemical and microbial action to break down food.

The system consists of:

- mouth
- oesophagus
- rumen
- reticulum
- omasum
- abomasum
- small intestine
- large intestine
- rectum and anus.

Practical 43

Monogastrics and ruminants

Diagram [8.34] shows monogastric and ruminant digestive systems. Copy each diagram into your workbook. List their functions.

8.34 Comparison between monogastric and ruminant digestive systems

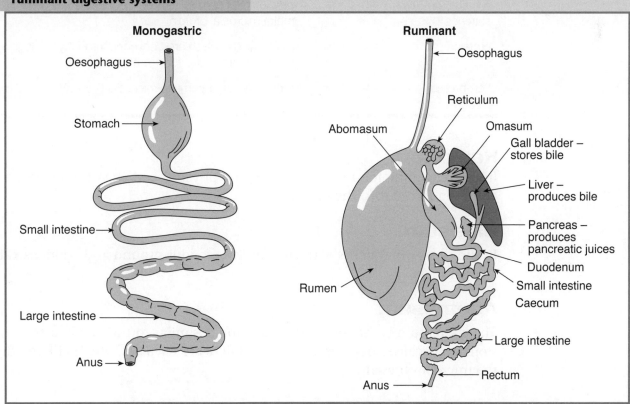

8.35 Microbes in the rumen and reticulum

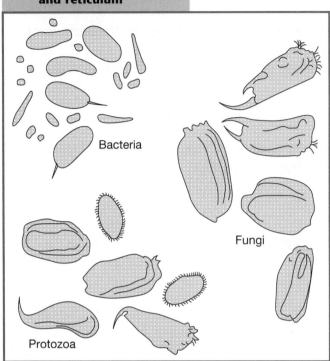

8.35 Microbes in the rumen and reticulum

Bacteria

Fungi

Protozoa

Mouth and rumen

Chewing, regurgitation and churning physically break down food. In the rumen, bacteria release enzymes that ferment the food. Microbes convert sugars, starches and cellulose into acetic, propionic and butyric acid that is absorbed into the blood stream or used to make microbial protein.

Microbes also convert proteins into amino-acids and nitrogen sources such as urea into ammonia, and use these to make microbial protein.

8.36 Breakdown of nutrients in the body

Food stuff		End product
cellulose sugars starches	→	volatile fatty acids, for example acetic, butyric, and propionic (absorbed into the bloodstream or used to make microbial protein)
proteins	→	amino acids, which are converted into fatty acids and ammonia (and used for microbial protein)
non-protein nitrogen	→	ammonia (used to make microbial protein)

Reticulum

In the reticulum, food is broken down by physical and chemical digestion and then forced into the omasum.

Omasum

In the omasum, water is extracted and the food is ground and condensed into a larger mass.

Abomasum

The abomasum is the fourth stomach and is similar to the monogastric stomach because enzymes and gastric juices are released, which kill and digest the microbes present.

Small intestine

In the small intestine, bile and pancreatic juices are released, which make the food alkaline and assist digestion and absorption. Simple sugars, amino-acids and minerals are absorbed through finger-like projections called villi, which increase the surface area of mucous membranes. Capillaries move the digested material to the liver where it is purified and stored until circulated to the rest of the body.

Large intestine

In the large intestine, waste material is condensed and stored until it is eliminated.

Organ	Function
8.37 Breakdown of nutrients in the body	
Mouth	Food is physically broken down into smaller particles. Saliva lubricates food and reduces acidity and alkaline problems
Oesophagus	Transports food to the rumen
Rumen and reticulum	Food is physically and chemically broken down by churning and microbial action
Omasum	Water is extracted and food is compacted into a larger mass
Abomasum	Enzymes are released, which kill the microbes and digest the materials present
Small intestine	Digestion and absorption (limited microbial digestion in the caecum of some animals)
Large intestine	Waste material concentrated and stored until expelled from the body

Advantages and disadvantages of the ruminant digestive system

Ruminants have many advantages. A ruminant can:
- digest cellulose
- upgrade low-quality feeds
- make protein from urea and other non-protein sources
- produce its own vitamin B by microbial action.
  However there are disadvantages, including:
- they are inefficient and energy is lost as heat, methane and carbon dioxide
- animals have to eat for many hours to meet nutritional requirements
- high-quality protein is depressed because energy is wasted converting it into microbial protein
- animals are susceptible to bloat.

Monogastrics

Monogastrics cannot digest cellulose, upgrade low-quality feeds or produce vitamins. However they spend less time eating and do not suffer from other dietary imbalances.

Some monogastrics such as poultry have developed gizzards and crops to aid digestion. The crop forms the lower part of the gullet and stores additional food. The gizzard is a tough muscular bag containing grit that helps grind food into smaller particles.

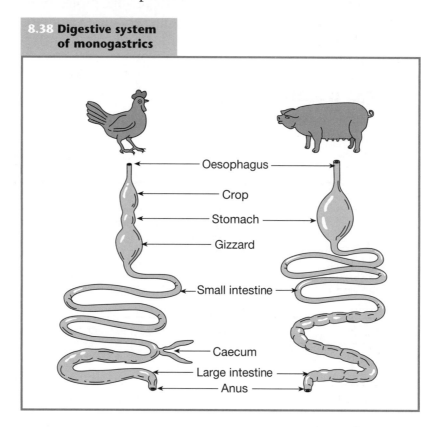

8.38 Digestive system of monogastrics

Activity 8.10

Table [8.39] shows a typical diet for feedlot cattle.

8.39 Diet feedlot for cattle

Constituent	Starter ration %	Middle ration %	Finishing diet %
Fibre	60 (hay)	40 (hay)	10 (forage sorghum)
Grain	31	50	75
Molafos	8	8	8
Lime	1	1	1
Ammonium sulfate		1	0.5
Protein meal			5
Bicarbonate soda			0.5

a   Why does the percentage of fibre and protein change in the rations?
b   Why do grain prices have a major impact on the profitability of feedlots?
c   Why is lime included in the ration?

Activity 8.11

8.40 Broiler chicken diets

Analysis ①

MIN %	Crude Protein	23
MIN %	Crude Fat	3
MAX %	Crude Fibre	4
Salt %	(Sodium chloride)	0.4
MAX %	Urea	0.
MAX %	Fluorine	0.03

INGREDIENTS

Wheat, Sorghum, Triticale, Barley, Oats, Corn, Meatmeal, Soybean meal, Safflower meal, Cottonseed meal, Fishmeal, Tallow, Salt, Molasses, Biotin, Calcium, Vit A, Vit B2, 6, 12 Zinc, Cobalt, Endox, Vit D3

Analysis ②

MIN %	Crude Protein	20
MIN %	Crude Fat	4
MAX %	Crude Fibre	4
Salt %	(Sodium chloride)	0.3
MAX %	Urea	0.
MAX %	Fluorine	0.03

INGREDIENTS

Wheat, Sorghum, Triticale, Barley, Oats, Corn, Meatmeal, Soybean meal, Safflower meal, Cottonseed meal, Fishmeal, Tallow, Salt, Molasses, Biotin, Calcium, Vit A, Vit B2, 6, 12 Zinc, Cobalt, Endox, Vit D3

Analysis ③

MIN %	Crude Protein	18
MIN %	Crude Fat	4
MAX %	Crude Fibre	4
Salt %	(Sodium chloride)	0.3
MAX %	Urea	0.
MAX %	Fluorine	0.03

INGREDIENTS

Wheat, Sorghum, Triticale, Barley, Oats, Corn, Meatmeal, Soybean meal, Safflower meal, Cottonseed meal, Fishmeal, Tallow, Salt, Molasses, Biotin, Calcium, Vit A, Vit B2, 6, 12 Zinc, Cobalt, Endox, Vit D3

8.41 Broiler chickens

1 A broiler chicken has three diets during its 8-month life. How do the diets differ?
2 Ingredients are listed in order of amount. What are the most important grains?
3 Explain why chickens often swallow grit or shells?
4 Broiler chickens have a feed conversion ratio of 2:1. What does this mean?
Hint Food Conversion Ratio (FCR) = Weight of food eaten divided by the weight gain of birds.

Extension Activities

1 Discuss how economic and energy-related factors determine the intensity with which resources are used in the animal production system.

2 Explain how metabolic disorders, nutrient deficiencies and toxicities can have significant effect on animal production.

Formulating a ration

ration
the amount and mix of food given to an animal

A ration must meet the nutritional requirements of the animal and be as inexpensive as possible. When designing a ration it is important to consider:
• the animal's nutritional requirements
• appetite and intake level
• maintenance or production level
• efficiency of food conversion
• cost and nutritional value of different feedstuffs
• palatability and digestibility of feedstuffs.

Animal requirements

The type and amount of food an animal requires depend on:
• age
• breed
• sex
• level of production, for example pregnancy or lactation
• climatic influences such as heat and cold stress
• incidence of disease
• stress level.

Young, actively growing animals have a huge nutritional demand for growth and development. Larger breeds of animals, and pregnant and lactating animals also have greater requirements. Climatic extremes, and disease and stress affect the animal's consumption rate and nutritional requirements.

8.42 Feed requirements of animals

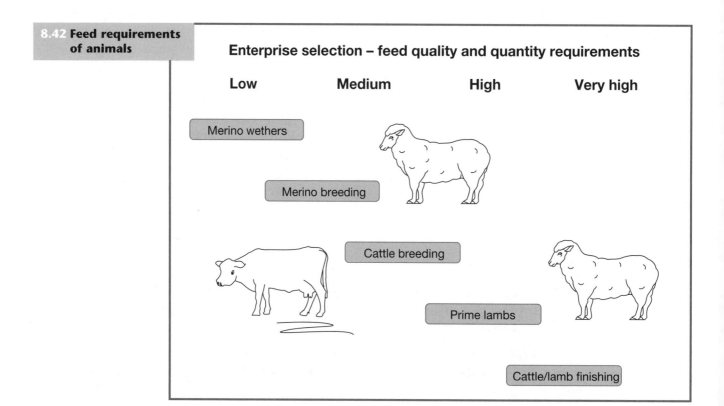

Enterprise selection – feed quality and quantity requirements

Low   Medium   High   Very high

Merino wethers

Merino breeding

Cattle breeding

Prime lambs

Cattle/lamb finishing

8.43 Feed standards for growing cattle

Weight kg	DM intake kg	Component		Daily liveweight gain kg						
				0.2	0.4	0.6	0.8	1.0	1.2	1.4
200	5	Emp	(MJ)	21.0	23.6	26.5	29.9	33.8	38.5	44.2
		APL		1.12	1.26	1.41	1.59	1.79	2.05	–
		DCP	(g)	250	330	380	425	480	535	590
		Ca	(g)	12	17	22	28	33	38	44
		P	(g)	6.6	8.7	11	13	15	17	20
		Mg	(g)	3.4	3.8	4.2	4.6	5.0	5.4	5.8
		Na	(g)	3.6	3.9	4.1	4.4	4.7	5.0	5.3
		Vit A	(i.u.)				13500			
		Vit D	(i.u.)				500			
		Vit E	(i.u.)				120			
250	6	Emp	(MJ)	24.4	27.2	30.4	34.1	38.4	43.6	49.8
		APL		1.11	1.24	1.38	1.55	1.74	1.97	–
		DCP	(g)	270	355	410	460	520	570	625
		Ca	(g)	13	19	24	29	34	40	45
		P	(g)	8.7	11	13	15	17	19	21
		Mg	(g)	4.1	4.5	4.9	5.3	5.7	6.1	6.5
		Na	(g)	4.5	4.8	5.0	5.3	5.6	5.9	6.2
		Vit A	(i.u.)				16700			
		Vit D	(i.u.)				625			
		Vit E	(i.u.)				150			
300	7	Emp	(MJ)	27.8	30.9	34.3	38.3	43.0	48.6	55.4
		APL		1.11	1.23	1.36	1.52	1.70	1.92	2.19
		DCP	(g)	295	385	435	490	545	595	650
		Ca	(g)	16	21	26	31	36	42	47
		P	(g)	12	14	16	18	20	22	24
		Mg	(g)	4.9	5.3	5.7	6.1	6.5	6.9	7.3
		Na	(g)	5.4	5.7	5.9	6.2	6.5	6.8	7.1
		Vit A	(i.u.)				20000			
		Vit D	(i.u.)				750			
		Vit E	(i.u.)				180			
350	8	Emp	(MJ)	31.2	34.5	38.3	42.6	47.7	53.7	61.0
		APL		1.10	1.21	1.34	1.49	1.67	1.88	2.13
		DCP	(g)	310	395	450	510	570	615	675
		Ca	(g)	18	23	28	34	39	44	49
		P	(g)	16	18	20	22	24	26	28
		Mg	(g)	5.6	6.0	6.4	6.8	7.2	7.6	8.0
		Na	(g)	6.2	6.5	6.7	7.0	7.3	7.6	7.9
		Vit A	(i.u.)				23500			
		Vit D	(i.u.)				875			
		Vit E	(i.u.)				210			

DM = dry matter
APL = animal production level

Emp = net energy allowed for maintenance
DCP = digestible crude protein

Source: Scottish Agricultural Colleges, Nutrient Allowances for Cattle and Sheep, Publication 29

8.44 Nutritional value of food

Food	DM g/kg	CP g/kg	CF g/kg	EE g/kg	Ash g/kg	DCP g/kg	ME g/kg
				DM basis			
Cereals and by-products							
Barley	860	108	53	17	26	82	13.0
Barley, brewer's grains, dried	900	204	159	71	43	145	10.3
Barley, malt culms	900	271	156	22	80	222	11.2
Brewer's yeast, dried	900	443	2	11	102	381	11.7
Maize	860	98	24	42	13	78	14.2
Maize, flaked	900	110	17	49	10	106	15.0
Maize, gluten feed	900	262	39	38	28	223	13.5
Millet	860	121	93	44	44	92	11.3
Oats	860	109	121	49	33	84	12.0
Oat husks	900	21	351	11	42	0	4.9
Rice, polished	860	77	17	5	9	67	15.0
Rye	860	124	26	19	21	105	14.0
Sorghum	860	108	21	43	27	87	13.4
Wheat	860	124	26	19	21	105	14.0
Wheat feeds, middlings	880	176	86	41	47	129	12.0
Wheat feeds, brans	880	170	114	45	67	126	10.8
Oilseed by-products							
Coconut cake meal	900	220	153	76	72	174	12.7
Cottonseed cake (undec.)	900	231	248	54	66	178	8.5
Cottonseed cake (dec.)	900	457	87	89	74	393	12.3
Groundnut meal (undec.)	900	343	273	21	47	316	9.2
Groundnut meal (dec.)	900	552	88	8	63	491	11.7
Linseed meal	900	404	102	36	73	348	11.9
Palm kernel meal	900	227	167	10	44	204	12.2
Soya bean meal	900	503	58	17	62	453	12.3
Sunflower seed cake (undec.)	900	206	323	80	80	185	9.5
Sunflower seed cake (dec.)	900	413	134	152	74	372	13.3
Leguminous seeds							
Field beans	860	314	80	15	40	248	13.5
Gram	860	263	57	13	57	173	12.4
Peas	860	262	63	19	33	225	13.4
Animal by-products							
Meatmeal	900	810	0	148	42	753	16.3
Meat and bone meal	900	597	0	50	62	465	9.7
Milk, cows, whole	128	266	0	305	55	250	20.2
Milk, skim	100	350	0	70	80	329	15.3
Milk, whey	66	106	0	30	106	91	14.5
White-fish meal	900	701	0	40	241	631	11.1

DM = dry matter   CP = crude protein   CF = crude fibre
EE = ether extract   Ash = remains after combustion   DCP = digestible crude protein
ME = metabolisable energy

Source: *Ministry of Agriculture and Fisheries of Scotland,* Technical Bulletin 33, *London*

8.45 Hay

8.46 Feed mixer

Types of feedstuffs

Feeds are classified into four main types:
- roughages have a high fibre content (20–40 per cent), low-digestibility and low-protein content, for example pastures
- succulents contain up to 80 per cent moisture and are very palatable and digestible, for example root crops, green crops, silage and immature pastures
- concentrates have a high protein content and contain only 10–14 per cent moisture or fibre, for example wheat, barley, triticale, lupins and sorghum
- animal products are rich in protein and highly digestible, for example meat meal, buttermilk and fishmeal.

A producer should choose feedstuffs that:
- provide the animal's nutritional requirements for the least cost
- are palatable
- are digestible
- are easy to transport.

Activity 8.12

1 Explain why the nutritional value of oats varies depending on if the animal is a monogastric or ruminant?
2 Why should animals not be fed contaminated animal by-products.
3 Why are ruminants slowly introduced to grain diets?

Activity 8.13

1 Explain how weeds can affect the nutritional value of feed.
2 How can weeds contaminate animal products?
For example, the effect of Paterson's curse on milk quality.

8.47 Pastures contaminated with Paterson's curse

Reproduction

An understanding of an animal's reproductive system is essential to maximise reproductive efficiency, turnover rate and profits.

8.48 Merino ram

Rams

The reproductive system of a ram consists of four main regions:

- testes
- epididymis
- vas deferens and urethra
- penis.

The testes are two oval organs suspended in the scrotum. The testes produce sperm and hormones such as testosterone, which give the rams its masculinity and behavioural characteristics.

The epididymis is a coiled tube connecting the testes to the vas deferens. The epididymis stores the sperm and keeps it in a favourable environment prior to mating.

The vas deferens and urethra are thin tubes connecting the epididymis to the penis. The tubes move sperm to the penis and mix it with secretions from the seminal vesicles, prostate and Cowper's gland. The secretions supply the sperm with nutrients and make them swim.

8.49 Reproductive organs of a ram

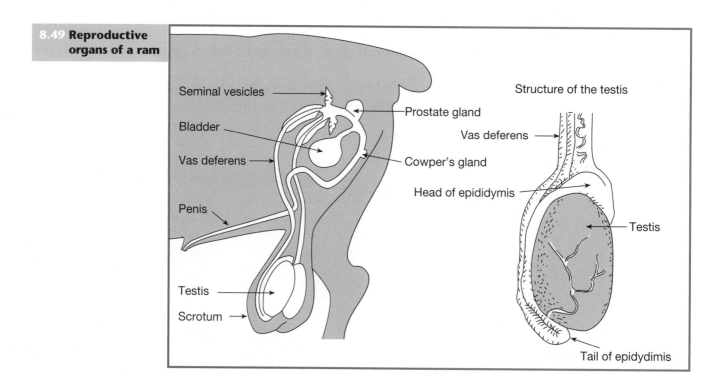

Seminal vesicles

Bladder

Vas deferens

Penis

Testis

Scrotum

Prostate gland

Cowper's gland

Structure of the testis

Vas deferens

Head of epididymis

Testis

Tail of epididymis

The penis contains erectile tissue and is used to eject sperm into the vagina. It contains spongy and muscular tissue and becomes erect when blood vessels distend following hormonal activation. The penis is also used to urinate.

Factors affecting the fertility of a male include:

- soundness of body
- serving capability
- nutrition
- climate and season
- inherited faults
- scrotal size
- semen quality
- sex drive or libido
- disease and stress
- management.

Management is a key factor affecting fertility and operators can maximise production by:

- not using rams which are too young or old
- annually culling poor and defective rams
- using sufficient rams, (the number of rams should be 2.5–3 per cent of the ewe population)
- minimising bullying and fighting by not mixing young and old stock
- drenching and vaccinating against disease and parasites
- providing animals with adequate food, water and shelter
- providing additional feed during periods of shortage
- planning operations such as crutching, shearing and dipping well before mating
- crutching ewes to assist mating.

culling
to remove inferior quality animals

8.50 Judging leg structure

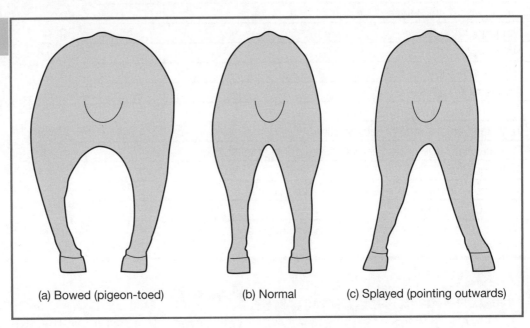

(a) Bowed (pigeon-toed)   (b) Normal   (c) Splayed (pointing outwards)

A ram that has sound, strong legs should be selected.
Animals that have pigeon-toes or splayed legs should be culled.

Practical 44

Best breeding ram

Aim
To select the best ram for breeding purposes.

Equipment
- five rams of the same age and breed
- sheep yards

Method
1. Place the rams in a line.
2. Score using each of the criteria listed below.
3. Use a scoring scheme of 1 for poor up to 10 for very good.
4. Choose the ram with the highest score as the best ram for mating.

Characteristic	Score
Age of ram – not too young or old	
Good teeth – not broken or worm	
Even jaw – not undershot or overshot	
Clear shiny eyes – no cancers or growths	
Horns not growing into eyes	
Strong back	
Strong legs – not bowed or straight	
Not pigeon toed	
No footrot	
Good temperament	
Two testicles present	
Testicles firm and springy	
Testicles free of lumps or inflammation	
Scrotum has large circumference, for example at least 28cm	
Good quality wool	
Absence of folded skin where flystrike can occur	
High muscle score	
High libido or sex drive (place in a pen with ewes and observe behaviour)	

Results
Do you think each criteria should be given the same weighting?

Conclusion
State your conclusions from the results.

8.51 Ewes

Ewes

The reproductive system of the ewe has four main areas:
- ovaries
- uterus
- fallopian tubes
- vagina.

The ewe has two ovaries, which produce ova and hormones. An ovum contains the genetic material of the ewe. The hormones control the oestrous cycle and sexual characteristics. The ovaries release one or more ova at regular intervals, after which the ewe goes on heat and mates with a ram.

The ovum travels down the fallopian tubes to the uterus where fertilisation and implantation occur.

8.52 Reproductive organs of a ewe

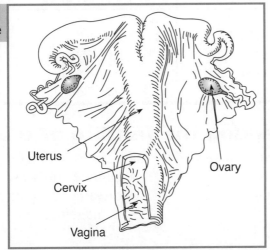

Uterus

Cervix

Vagina

Ovary

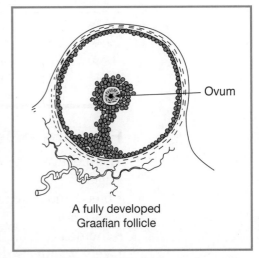

Ovum

A fully developed Graafian follicle

The uterus protects the foetus and supplies it with its nutritional requirements. At birth, the lamb is pushed through the vagina (or birth canal) to the outside.

Stages of reproduction in animals

Most animals undergo the following stages during reproduction:

- ovulation
- heat
- mating or copulation
- fertilisation
- pregnancy or gestation
- birth or parturition
- lactation or milk production.

8.53 Reproductive stages in sheep

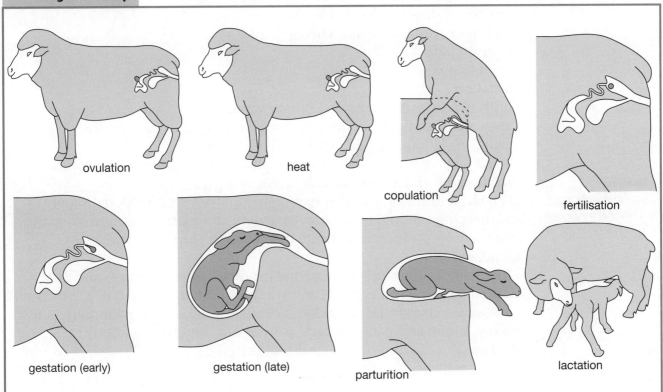

ovulation

heat

copulation

fertilisation

gestation (early)

gestation (late)

parturition

lactation

8.54 Breeding characteristics of animals			
Animal	**Length of cycle**	**Duration of oestrous**	**Gestation period**
Mare	21 days (18–24)	5 days (2–8)	338 days
Cow	21 days (18–23)	18 hours (13–27)	282 days
Ewe	17 days (15–19)	24 hours (12–36)	150 days
Goat	20 days (18–22)	48 hours (30–60)	150 days
Sow	21 days (19–23)	52 hours (36–72)	116 days

Factors affecting the fertility of a ewe

The fertility of a ewe is governed by many factors including:

- age
- breed and hereditary faults
- nutrition
- chemicals.
- climate and season
- diseases and parasites
- management

Very young ewes have lower lambing percentages because they have irregular oestrous cycles and a tendency to abandon their lambs. Ewes 4–5 years of age have the highest lambing percentages and then fertility declines after 8–9 years.

The breed of a sheep has a major effect on the ewe's:

- length of breeding season
- maturity rate
- pelvis size
- incidence of lambing problems
- mothering and milking capabilities.

British breeds such as the Border–Leicester have the greatest reproductive activity from March to May and are more fertile than breeds such as the merino.

Sheep can be born with hereditary faults such as cystic ovaries and fallopian tubes that reduce production levels.

Nutrition also has a major effect on the ewe's:

- maturity rate
- ovulation rate
- lactation
- birth weight and the survival rate of lambs

Ewes are often flushed prior to joining with rams to increase their body weight, ovulation rate and lambing percentages.

Some original varieties of subterranean clover contained oestrogenic chemicals which reduced fertility levels.

Climate and season can also have a major effect on nutritional supply and breeding season. Decreasing day length stimulates ovulation in many breeds of sheep which will ensure they lamb in the spring when there is abundant feed.

High temperatures can increase the incidence of miscarriages and malformed foetuses. Cold, wet and windy conditions can kill newborn lambs.

Diseases such as facial eczema and brucellosis increase the mortality rate of unborn lambs, and parasites such as liver fluke and worms affect the nutritional status and overall health of the ewe.

flushed
provided with additional feed

Producers can maximise production by:
- not using very young or old stock
- using sheep best suited to their region
- culling inferior and less productive ewes
- planning operations to coincide with the ewe's breeding season
- supplying ewes with adequate food, water and shelter
- drenching and vaccinating against diseases and parasites
- using sufficient rams
- restricting the mating period to 6–8 weeks so ewes will all lamb within a restricted time period
- planning operations such as shearing, dipping and vaccination before lambing to reduce damage and stress to ewes.

Practical 45

Effect of flushing

Aim

To see the effect of flushing on the number of lambs born and their survival rate.

Equipment
- ewes of the same age, breed, size and weight
- additional feed supply, for example grain or hay
- scales.

Method

1 Divide the ewes into four random groups.
2 Drench the ewes and place them under the same environmental conditions.
3 Group 1 and 2 will be the control and not receive any additional feed. Provide groups 3 and 4 with ad libitum (as much hay as they want).
4 Weigh ewes weekly.

Results

Record lamb number, weight and survival rate.

Conclusion

State your conclusions from the results.

Factors affecting survival rate of lambs

The survival rate of newborn lambs is determined by many factors including:
- age of ewe
- mothering ability
- milk supply
- number of offspring, as it effects birth weight and the milk supply available to each lamb
- nutritional supply
- climatic conditions
- incidence of predators such as crows and foxes
- incidence of diseases and parasites
- manager's skills and capabilities.

Activity 8.14

8.55 Effect of birth weight on lamb survival		
Mean birth weight (kg)	% survival	
	singles	twins
1.8	40	28
2.3	81	72
3.2	89	87
4.2	91	88
5.0	88	85
5.9	72	48
6.4	54	42

Table [8.55] shows the effect of birth weight on the survival rate of single and twin merino lambs.

a What effect did birth weight have on the survival rate.

b Discuss the effect of birth weight on the incidence of lambing difficulties such as mismothering and starvation, and also on the lamb's susceptibility to stresses from diseases and climatic extremes.

The reproductive system of the chicken

The reproductive system of the hen consists of a tube with six main parts. These are the:

- ovary
- magnum
- shell gland
- infundibulum
- isthmus
- vagina.

The chicken is born with two ovaries but only one matures and becomes functional. The ovary consists of two lobes and releases an ovum at regular intervals. The infundibulum connects the ovary to the magnum and is the site of fertilisation. Inside the magnum and isthmus, the albumen and membranes are added to the egg respectively before it passes to the shell gland, where it is coated with a shell. Once the egg is completed it passes through the vagina, where it is coated with a bloom to seal it and reduce infection. The egg is then laid.

8.56 Reproductive system of a rooster

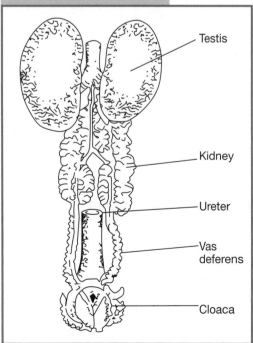

Testis

Kidney

Ureter

Vas deferens

Cloaca

8.57 Reproductive system of a hen

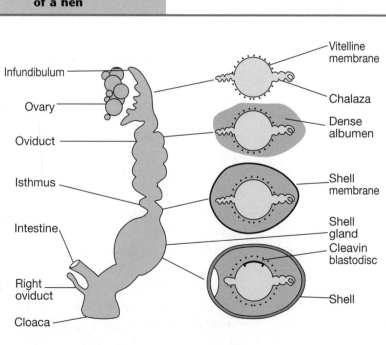

Infundibulum

Ovary

Oviduct

Isthmus

Intestine

Right oviduct

Cloaca

Vitelline membrane

Chalaza

Dense albumen

Shell membrane

Shell gland

Cleavin blastodisc

Shell

8.58 Reproductive system of a hen

Region	Average length (cm)	Time ovum spends in that region (hours and minutes)
Infundibulum	6	0:30
Magnum	33	2:45
Isthmus	10	1:05
Shell gland	10	20:45
Vagina	12	–
Total	71	25:05

Comparison of the reproductive systems of poultry and sheep

The reproductive systems of the sheep and chicken have many similarities and differences as indicated in the following table.

8.59 Reproductive systems of poultry and sheep

Feature	Poultry	Sheep
Female		
Ovaries	One	Two
Shape of ovaries	Lobed	Oval
Follicles	Project from ovary	Embedded in ovary tissue
Shape of reproductive organs	Long tube	T-shaped with two ovaries and a uterus and vagina
Fertilisation	Not necessary to produce egg	Necessary to produce offspring
Male		
Testicles	Two in abdomen	Two in scrotum
Mating season	Mate at any time	Only mate when ewe is on heat
Offspring		
Incubation	Outside mother	Inside mother
Birth	Still in egg	Born alive and fully functional
Protective devices	Protective shell	Little protection
Time to produce offspring	26 hours plus three weeks incubation	5 months

Activity 8.15

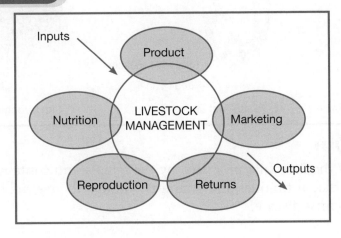

1 Discuss the interactions that occur in the systems diagram opposite.
2 How can a knowledge of systems help maximise production and profit?

Identify and discuss the constraints on a significant animal production system in your region. What management techniques have been used to combat these problems?

Milk production

8.60 Milking shed

Milk consists of water, butterfat, protein, lactose, minerals and vitamins and provides the offspring with nutrition and immunity against disease.

Milk is produced in the mammary glands. Progesterone and oestrogen stimulate the alveoli fatty tissues and the milk ducts to grow and develop after puberty and prolactin makes the alveoli cells multiply and produce milk in later pregnancy.

The release of milk is governed by the hormone oxytocin, which stimulates the muscles fibres to contract around the alveoli and force the milk down the teat.

8.61 Anatomy of the mammary glands

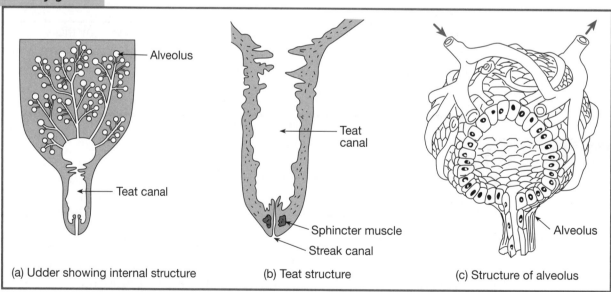

(a) Udder showing internal structure

(b) Teat structure

(c) Structure of alveolus

Colostrum

Colostrum is the first milk produced by the female and contains additional casein, butterfat, antibiotics and vitamins A and D to give the offspring immunity against disease.

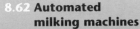
8.62 Automated milking machines

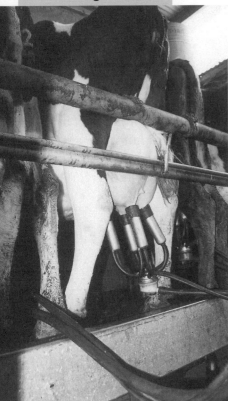

Milk composition and yield

Milk composition and yield is determined by:
- breed
- age
- nutrition
- climate and season
- disease and parasites
- stress
- incidence of heat (or oestrous)
- pregnancy
- number of offspring
- management.

Very old and young cows produce less milk and the percentage of solids-not-fat (SNF) decreases 0.2% per lactation.

Dairy breeds such as the Friesian produce more milk than beef breeds and the composition of the milk also varies between breeds.

Nutrition affects the development of alveoli cells and the milk composition and yields. Poor nutrition reduces yields and shortens lactation. The amount of fibre and energy in the diet affects the percentage of fat and SNF respectively in the milk.

Climate directly affects feed quality, consumption rates and yields.

Diseases (such as mastitis and brucellosis) and parasites (such as ticks and worms) significantly reduce milk quality and yields.

Stress caused by starvation, bullying and fighting, rough handling and change of routine can significantly affect milk quality and yields.

8.63 Refrigerated storage vats

Animals on heat are often excited and have lower yields because they do not let their milk down. Pregnant animals produce less milk and have a shorter lactation period as the glands prepare for the next pregnancy.

Managers can maximise production by:
- using animals suited to their region
- culling inferior animals
- providing adequate food, water and shelter
- drenching and vaccinating against diseases and parasites
- minimising stress, for example cold stress, rough handling and sudden changes in routine
- milking twice per day to ensure that the cows do not dry up
- milking efficiently to maximise yields and fat content.

Activity 8.16

1. Explain why Friesians are the most popular dairy breed?
2. Why do dairy farms sometimes have several Jerseys or Guernseys in their herd?
3. What are the product specifications for marketing milk?

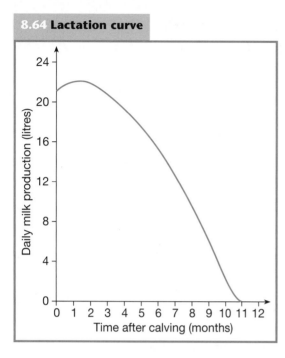

8.64 Lactation curve

Daily milk production (litres) vs Time after calving (months)

Length of lactation

The amount of time an animal produces milk depends on:

- age
- breed
- nutrition
- climate
- incidence of diseases and parasites
- pregnancy
- management.

Very young and old cows have a shorter lactation period. Dairy cows such as the Friesian have a longer lactation than beef breeds. Poor-quality nutrition, climatic extremes, diseases, parasites and pregnancy can also reduce lactation length.

Managers can maximise productivity by:

- selectively breeding better-performing animals
- providing animals with sufficient food, water and shelter
- minimising stresses, for example vaccinating and drenching against diseases and parasites
- providing additional feed in periods of shortage
- handling animals carefully and quietly
- establishing a regular milking routine and milking at least twice per day to maintain lactation.

Activity 8.17

Draw a systems diagram to show the main factors that affect milk production.

Activity 8.18

8.65 Lactation production

Months	Daily milk production
0	20
1	22
2	23
3	22
4	20
5	18
6	14
7	11.5
8	8
9	5
10	1
11	0

Table [8.65] shows milk production over time for a Friesian cow.

a Graph these figures.
b What conclusions can you draw from the graph?
c How does this affect the dairy producer?

The endocrine system

The endocrine system consists of a group of glands that control other organs by sending chemical messengers or hormones in the blood stream to the target area.

The endocrine system controls many processes including the animal's:
- shape
- growth and development
- behaviour
- metabolic rate
- blood pressure
- digestion
- reproduction, for example the oestrous cycle, pregnancy and mating behaviour
- milk production.

Hormones, reproduction and behaviour

Hormones regulate the internal environment of the animal as well as allowing it to respond to changes in its external environment.

8.66 Glands in the human body	Where the hormone is produced	Hormone(s) secreted	Hormone function
	Adrenal glands	Adrenalin Cortisol	Prepares the body for emergency responses (eg fight or flight); anti stress
	Pituitary gland	FSH LH ADH Growth hormone Oxytocin Prolactin	Menstrual cycle Menstrual cycle Water homeostasis Stimulates cell division Birth contractions Milk production
	Pancreas	Insulin Glucagon	Lowers blood sugar levels; stimulates metabolism of glucose, protein and fat
	Hypothalamus	Growth hormone releasing factor	Stimulates growth hormone production
	Ovaries	Progesterone Oestrogen	Menstrual cycle Menstrual cycle
	Pineal gland	Melatonin	Controls body rhythms
	Parathyroid glands	Parathyroid hormone	Affects bone formation and excretion of calcium and phosphorus
	Testes	Testosterone	Male characteristics
	Thyroid	Thyroxine	Controls metabolism and metabolic rate
	Thymus	Thymosin	Matures white blood cells

Pineal gland
Pituitary gland
Thyroid gland
Adrenal gland
Pancreas
Ovaries
Testes

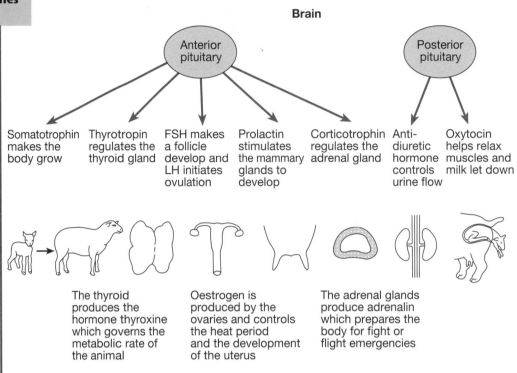

Brain

Anterior pituitary

Posterior pituitary

Somatotrophin makes the body grow

Thyrotropin regulates the thyroid gland

FSH makes a follicle develop and LH initiates ovulation

Prolactin stimulates the mammary glands to develop

Corticotrophin regulates the adrenal gland

Anti-diuretic hormone controls urine flow

Oxytocin helps relax muscles and milk let down

The thyroid produces the hormone thyroxine which governs the metabolic rate of the animal

Oestrogen is produced by the ovaries and controls the heat period and the development of the uterus

The adrenal glands produce adrenalin which prepares the body for fight or flight emergencies

FSH

follicle stimulating hormone is secreted by the pituitary gland and stimulates the growth of the graafian follicles in the ovary

lutenising hormone

chemical secreted by the pituitary gland that causes the growth of the corpus luteum in the ovary

Hormones and the oestrous cycle

The oestrous cycle and pregnancy are controlled by several hormones, as indicated in the steps below:

1 FSH (follicle stimulating hormones) is released from the pituitary gland and stimulates a follicle to develop in the ovary.

2 Once the follicle has developed, the ovary releases the hormone oestrogen to stop FSH production.

3 FSH production stops and the pituitary gland releases the hormone LH (lutenising hormone) to make ovulation occur.

4 Following ovulation the follicle degenerates into the corpus luteum which releases the hormones progesterone. This hormone stops the oestrous cycle and prepares the body for pregnancy.

5 If pregnancy occurs, progesterone levels are maintained and the reproductive organs prepare for the developing offspring.

6 If pregnancy does not occur, progesterone levels decline and this stimulates the pituitary gland to release FSH and start the cycle again.

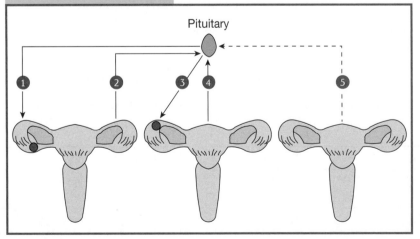

Pituitary

1 2 3 4 5

Activity 8.19

1 Research the function of the following hormones:
   a oestrogen   d testosterone   g growth hormone
   b FSH   e adrenaline   h thyroxin
   c progesterone   f oxytocin   i insulin

2 Complete the following sentences with the correct word.
   hormones
   oestrogen
   FSH
   lutenising hormone
   progesterone

   The oestrous cycle and pregnancy are controlled by _____.
   _____ is released from the pituitary gland and stimulates a follicle to develop in the ovary. Once the follicle has developed the ovary releases the hormone _____ to stop _____ production.
   _____ production stops and the pituitary gland releases the hormone _____ to make ovulation occur.
   Following ovulation the follicle degenerates into the corpus luteum, which releases the hormone _____. This hormone stops the oestrous cycle and prepares the body for pregnancy.
   If pregnancy occurs, _____ levels are maintained and the reproductive organs prepare for the developing offspring.
   If pregnancy does not occur, _____ levels decline and this stimulates the pituitary gland to release _____ and start the cycle again.

Animal welfare

8.69 Rough handling can stress animals

In the past some animals have been neglected, cruelly treated and abused.
   Concern is held for animals kept in:
• the community such as in homes and pet shops
• by agriculturalists, for example graziers
• research institutions
• schools
• processing and handling facilities, for example abattoirs and transport operators
• veterinary clinics.
   The community feels there is a moral duty to respect all living things and minimise harm to animals.

Acts have been established to protect animals and include:
- *NSW Prevention of Cruelty to Animals Act 1979*, which prohibits neglect and cruelty to all animals
- *NSW Animals Research Act 1985*, which governs the use of animals in schools and research facilities
- *NSW National Parks and Wildlife Act 1974*, which prohibits the taking of native fauna except under licence
- *Companion Animal Act 1988* for the management of cats and dogs
- *Queensland Meat Industry Act 1997*, which controls the slaughter of stock for human consumption
- *NSW Poisons and Therapeutic Goods Act 1966*, which controls the drugs used by veterinarians for the treatment of animals
- *NSW Rural Land Protection Act 1998*, which regulates the control of noxious and feral animals.

Model codes have been developed that describe the minimum standards for the keeping, handling, and transportation of animals.

8.70 Animals can be stressed during transportation

These acts are enforced by many authorities including:
- NSW Agriculture
- National Parks and Wildlife Service
- NSW Police
- RSPCA
- Animal Welfare League
- School Animals Care and Ethics Committee.

Animal welfare encompasses all aspects of animal health and well-being. Australia's animal welfare strategies involve:
- government and non-government organisations
- veterinary and community groups
- animal industries
- animal welfare groups
- individual animal owners and handlers.

All states and territories regulate animal welfare in their jurisdiction to prevent animal cruelty, such as the *Animal Care and Protection Act 2001* (Queensland) and the *Animal Welfare Act 2002* (Western Australia). The Australian Government is responsible for trade and international agreements relating to animal welfare and works with exporters to maintain international export standards.

Physical and behavioural characteristics that can assist in the management of animals

Both physical and behavioural characteristics can assist in animal management. Physical features include:

- polled animals are less dangerous to handle than horned animals
- Hereford cattle with brown hair around their eyes are less susceptible to skin cancers than those with white hair
- animals with ruminant digestive systems can upgrade low-quality feed and produce their own vitamins
- Brahman breeds of cattle are heat and tick resistant because they have short hair and more sweat glands
- breeds of sheep without wrinkles are less susceptible to flystrike
- increasing nutrition levels of ewes before joining increases ovulation rate and lambing percentages.
  Behavioural features include:
- male animals are castrated to reduce aggressive behaviour
- chickens are de-beaked to prevent pecking
- old bulls are separated from young bulls to prevent fighting
- dim light is used in chicken sheds to reduce activity levels and food consumption
- increasing day length stimulates ewes to ovulate.

Husbandry operations that minimise animal welfare issues

Good management can ensure the welfare of animals via:

- using appropriate equipment, for example cattle crushes to de-horn cattle
- improving the skill of the operator, for example training courses for shearing
- timing operations to reduce stress, for example castration of livestock when young
- providing food, water and shelter to stock after weaning and marking
- the use of chemicals, for example analgesics during surgical operations.

Ethical issues and animal production

Ethical issues relating to animal production include:

- mulesing
- live export
- battery egg production
- the use of farrowing crates
- genetic engineering and genetically modified organisms
- testing on animals, for example in the production of beauty products.

Mulesing

Mulesing is the removal of strips of skin from around the breech of a sheep to prevent flystrike. Animal rights activists consider un-anesthetised mulesing to be inhumane and unnecessary. Retailers including John Lewis have banned Australian wool in opposition to mulesing. The Australian Wool Innovation (AWI) has pledged to phase out the practice. Alternatives suggested to replace mulesing include:

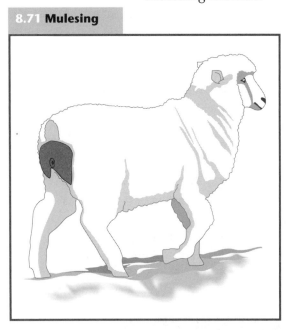

8.71 **Mulesing**

- breeding programs that select animals with fewer wrinkles
- using topical protein-based treatments, which kill wool follicles and tighten skin in the breach area
- the use of plastic clips, which act like castration bands on the skin of the animal
- use of tea tree oil, which has a strong repellent effect against adult flies.

Live exports

The live export of sheep and cattle is considered cruel by many animal welfare activists. The government, industry and trading partners are working to improve the transportation, handling and slaughter of livestock in overseas markets. Australia is the only country that requires specific animal welfare outcomes for livestock exports.

Government legislation (Australian Standards for the Export of Livestock) regulates the industry. Under the *Australian Meat and Livestock Industry Act 1997*, animal mortalities on sea voyages to ports outside of Australia must be tabled in each House of Parliament every six months. The Australian Quarantine and Inspection Service (AQIS) investigates all consignments which record a reportable mortality event. Australia has signed a Memoranda of Understanding (MOU) with ten countries in the Middle East and African regions to improve post arrival, handling and slaughtering procedures.

Battery egg production

Battery cages are used primarily for egg production. Welfare issues associated with cages include:
- lack of space
- inability of chickens to stand on the ground
- de-beaking of chickens to stop vent pecking
- killing of rooster chicks, as only females are required for egg production
- dimming lights to reduce activity and food consumption
- abnormal behaviours including feather pecking, cannibalism and vent pecking, which occur when chickens are placed in confined spaces
- osteoporosis caused by high calcium demands for egg production and a lack of exercise
- starving chickens for 7–14 days to force moulting and increase egg production.

8.72 Battery hens

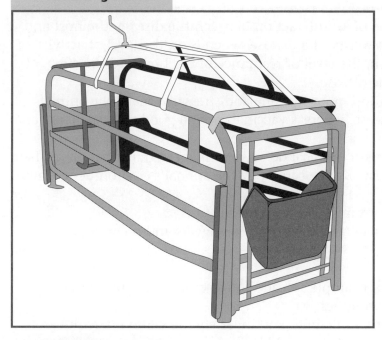

8.73 Farrowing crate

Farrowing crates

Breeding sows may be confined to stalls or farrowing crates for most of their adult lives. A stall is a metal-barred crate that houses the sow during pregnancy. It is two metres long and 60 cm wide and has a concrete floor with a slat-covered trench for manure at the rear. Sows cannot turn around or walk in the stall. A farrowing crate is a metal pen of similar size to a sow stall. The sow gives birth in the crate and is kept there until the piglets are weaned at 3–4 weeks of age.

Stalls allow the individual monitoring of sows, reduce feeding competition and bullying, and enable higher stocking rates. Farrowing crates prevent crushing and maximise the survival rate of piglets. However, pigs are intelligent, social animals and have a complex range of behaviours and needs.

Pigs in stalls and farrowing crates cannot forage nor interact socially with other pigs. This leads to behavioural problems, including biting the bars of the stall, swaying their heads and unresolved aggression. Their muscles and bones also deteriorate due to lack of exercise and they may have difficulty in standing up or lying down.

Activity 8.20

1 What animal welfare issues may be apparent in the following situations:
  a mulesing sheep
  b intensive poultry production
  c cattle feedlots
  d debeaking chickens
  e castrating male animals with a knife
  f shooting wild horses and feral animals
  g animal experimentation

Disease

Disease is the abnormal functioning of the body and is mainly caused by living organisms, environmental effects and hereditary faults.

8.74 Diseases caused by living organisms

Viruses	Bacteria	Protozoa	Parasitic invertebrates
Influenza	Brucellosis	Malaria	Liverflukes [8.75]
Rabies	Anthrax	Coccidiosis	Lice [8.76]
Smallpox	Food poisoning	Tick fever	Ticks
Mumps	Salmonellosis	African sleeping sickness	Mites
Scabby mouth	Pulpy kidney	Toxoplasmosis	Leeches
Distemper			Tapeworms
Fowl pox			Hydatids
Foot and mouth			Roundworms [8.77]
Blue tongue			Blowflies

pathogen
disease-producing organism

Disease occurs because of an interaction between the disease, the host and the environment. The severity of a disease depends on the level of activity of the parasite or pathogen, the level of resistance of the host and the effect of the environment on the disease.

Factors such as starvation, poor hygiene and stress can make the animal more susceptible to disease, whereas vaccination and good management can reduce its incidence.

Animals can be born with physical defects or inherited traits that affect their performance. Diseases can also be caused by the animal's environment. Causes include:
- climatic extremes, for example heat and cold stress
- nutritional disorders such as bloat, phalaris staggers and pregnancy toxaemia
- bullying and fighting
- poor management, for example spread of mad-cow disease by eating contaminated animal residues.

Living organisms such as microbes and invertebrates cause many diseases such as flystrike, foot rot, anthrax and blackleg.

AG FACT

Anthrax

Bacteria called Bacillus anthracis cause anthrax. Anthrax is a disease normally associated with plant-eating animals (sheep, goats, cattle, and to a lesser extent pigs). In Australia it occurs infrequently due to effective compulsory control measures. An anthrax outbreak is most likely to be first recognised in animals. Immediate control measures involve quarantine and notifying health authorities to look for symptoms in humans.

Anthrax spores survive for long periods of time in certain soils, in animal products such as hair, hides and wool, and in feeds and fertilisers prepared from animals that died of anthrax. When an animal eats viable spores, the spores germinate and reproduce rapidly inside the animal. The resulting bacteria produce toxins that normally cause a quick death.

8.75 Lifecycle of a liverfluke

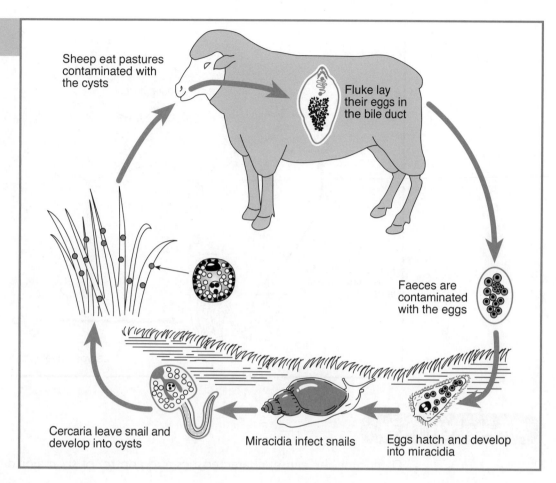

Sheep eat pastures contaminated with the cysts

Fluke lay their eggs in the bile duct

Faeces are contaminated with the eggs

Eggs hatch and develop into miracidia

Miracidia infect snails

Cercaria leave snail and develop into cysts

8.76 Lifecycle of lice

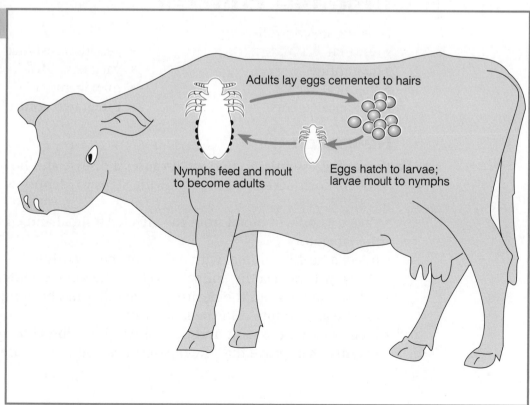

Adults lay eggs cemented to hairs

Nymphs feed and moult to become adults

Eggs hatch to larvae; larvae moult to nymphs

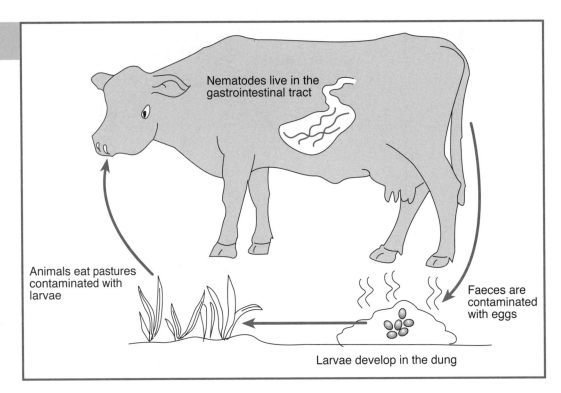

Nematodes live in the gastrointestinal tract

Animals eat pastures contaminated with larvae

Faeces are contaminated with eggs

Larvae develop in the dung

Research 8.21

Determine the cause, characteristics and control of six major diseases.

Disease control

Diseases are controlled by:
- research
- quarantine
- chemical agents
- biological agents
- genetic resistance
- vaccines
- management
- integrated control.

Research

Research is essential to find what causes a disease and how to control it.

Robert Koch developed the following steps to identify what caused a disease [8.78]:

- Take a sample of blood from the affected animal and culture it in the laboratory.
- Inject a healthy animal with a dose of the organism.
- Observe if the healthy animal develops the same symptoms.
- Take a sample from the healthy animal that has been injected with the disease and culture it in the laboratory.
- If cultures are the same and the animals have the same symptoms then scientists can prove that the organism caused the disease.

8.78 Koch's postulates

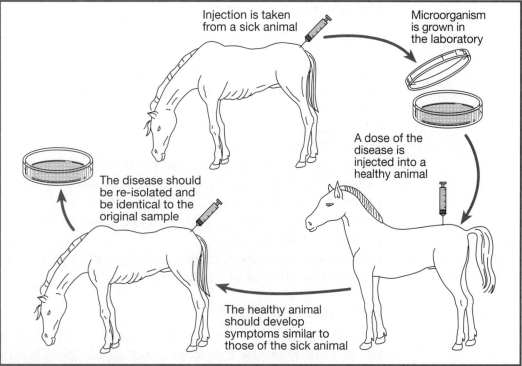

Injection is taken from a sick animal

Microorganism is grown in the laboratory

A dose of the disease is injected into a healthy animal

The disease should be re-isolated and be identical to the original sample

The healthy animal should develop symptoms similar to those of the sick animal

8.79 Saleyard restrictions to prevent OJD

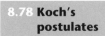

OJD INFECTED
SHEEP & LAMBS ONLY THIS GATE

OJD
Ovine Johnes Disease – a bacterial disease of sheep that lives in the soil and is controlled by isolating affected areas and restricting stock movement

Quarantine

Quarantine is the isolation of an animal or region to stop the movement of a disease.

Animals are quarantined before they enter Australia.

Natural barriers such as oceans, mountains and deserts also prevent the movement of diseases.

Chemical control

Insecticides and drenches have long been used to control many diseases. Chemicals were quick, simple, inexpensive and effective.

However chemicals have some disadvantages, including:

- organisms have developed resistance to many chemicals and so more and more toxic chemicals have had to be used, which has resulted in the killing of beneficial organisms and contamination of the environment
- they became less effective
- they became more expensive
- some chemicals have disrupted the natural balance and created secondary pests.

Chemical control methods are still used and are more effective if the chemicals are:

- selective
- biodegradable
- used in conjunction with other methods.

Biological control

Biological control is the use of natural predators and pathogens to control a disease.

Biological control has many advantages, including:
• it is selective and actively seeks out the disease
• it is self-perpetuating
• it is non-toxic
• it has fewer resistance problems
• it does not contaminate or disrupt the environment.
However it has some disadvantages, including:
• there is not a control method for every known disease
• research can take many years and is expensive in time, labour and money
• it does not always work
• it does not eradicate the disease, only maintains it at a constant level
• it is a slow method of controlling diseases.

Genetic control

Animals can be bred to make them resistant to a disease. Brahmans are resistant to cattle ticks because they have short coats. Sheep with fewer folds of skin have a lower incidence of flystrike.

8.80 Life cycle of the cattle tick

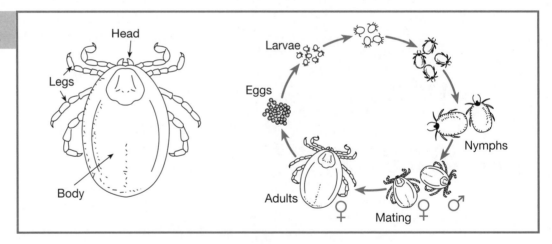

8.81 Resistance of animals to diseases

Animal	Disease	Action
Cattle	Ticks and tick fever	Using Brahmans because they have a short coat and ticks cannot hold on
Cattle	Eye cancers	Using breeds such as Angus, which has a dark pigment around its eyes
Pigs	Sunburn	Using breeds with dark-coloured skin
Poultry	Leucosis or cancer	Using resistant stock

phagocytes
part of the immune system of an animal that ingest foreign particles by engulfing them into their own cytoplasm

Vaccines

A vaccine is a dead or attenuated form of a disease-producing organism. Vaccines stimulate animals to produce antibodies that give the animals active immunity against the disease. The antibodies inactivate the organism or combine with it so phagocytes can destroy it.

Vaccines have been developed to control many diseases such as rabies, typhus, tetanus, typhoid, smallpox, yellow fever and tuberculosis.

Practical 46

Reading a chemical label

Study label [8.82] to answer the questions following.
a   What is the name of chemical?
b   What is the active ingredient?
c   What is the concentration of the active ingredient?
d   Which organisms are controlled by this chemical?
e   What is the dose rate for a 30kg ewe?
f   What is the withholding period?

8.82 Chemical label

CAUTION
USE STRICTLY AS DIRECTED
KEEP OUT OF REACH OF CHILDREN
READ SAFETY DIRECTIONS BEFORE OPENING
FOR ANIMAL TREATMENT ONLY

Kilparas

Liquid for Sheep
Broad Spectrum Oral
Antiparasitic Solution
Active constituent: Ivermectin 0.8g/l
For the treatment and control of ivermectin sensitive strains of internal parasites (including benzimidasole, levamisole, and morantel resistant strains), nasal bot and itchimite of sheep

2.5 Litres

DOSAGE AND ADMINISTRATION
Kilpara's Liquid is administered orally using any standard drenching equipment
Use the following dosage schedule:

Weight range (kg)	Dose Volume (mL)	Doses per 2.5 litre pack
11-20	5.0	500
21-30	7.5	333
31-40	10.0	250
41-50	12.5	200
51-60	15.0	166
61-70	17.5	142
71-80	20.0	125

WITHHOLDING PERIODS:
DO NOT ADMINISTER LATER THAN 21 DAYS BEFORE SLAUGHTER FOR HUMAN CONSUMPTION. WHEN MILK OR MILK BYPRODUCTS ARE TO BE USED FOR HUMAN CONSUMPTION. DO NOT ADMINISTER TO DAIRY SHEEP WITHIN 28 DAYS PRIOR TO LAMBING OR DURING LACTATION.

STORAGE
STORE BELOW 30°C AWAY FROM DIRECT SUNLIGHT.

Management

Good managers can minimise the incidence of disease by:
- using disease-free stock
- isolating animals from sources of infection, for example restricting the movement of livestock
- minimising stress, for example by providing adequate food, water and shelter
- removing disease-producing poisons, for example arsenic compounds
- culling deformed and inferior animals
- drenching and vaccinating against diseases and parasites
- being hygienic and conducting all operations such as castration and mulesing under sterile conditions.

Integrated control

Integrated control is the use of many control practices together and it is the most effective control method.

Advantages include that it:
- is specific
- is more effective
- simulates nature
- has fewer resistance problems
- does not create secondary pests
- does not contaminate the environment.

IPM of blowflies and lice

An IPM program includes consideration of animal welfare as well as environmental, economic and occupational health and safety concerns. IPM includes identifying and monitoring pests, setting action thresholds and controlling the pest. Integrated methods used to control blowflies include:
- monitoring climatic conditions to predict blowfly activity, for example wet, humid conditions
- monitoring populations, for example trapping
- reducing blowfly numbers, for example trapping
- catching, clipping and treating affected sheep
- jetting or backlining susceptible sheep, for example weaners and hoggets
- breeding and selection programs, for example rams should be purchased from a stud that has blowfly resistance
- culling struck sheep and sheep that have fleece rot
- providing good nutrition, disease control (vaccination), worm control and an environment with minimal stress
- having complete musters and shearing all sheep at once.

Significant resistance has been detected in blowflies and lice to the organophosphate (OP) and synthetic pyrethroid (SP) chemical groups.

Activity 8.22

Diagram [8.83] shows the lifecycle of the blowfly.
a   At what stage would control methods be most effective and why?
b   State an integrated program that could be used to control flystrike.

8.83 Lifecycle of a blowfly

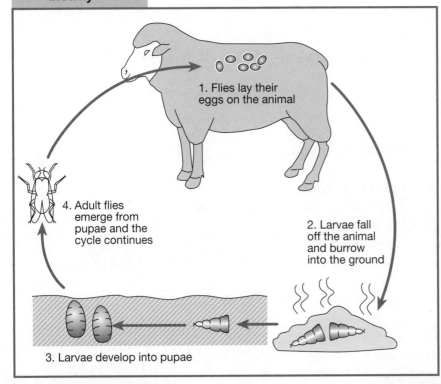

1. Flies lay their eggs on the animal

2. Larvae fall off the animal and burrow into the ground

3. Larvae develop into pupae

4. Adult flies emerge from pupae and the cycle continues

8.84 Crutching sheep to prevent flystrike

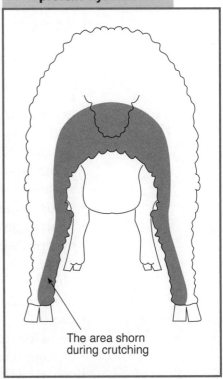

The area shorn during crutching

8.85 Crutching shears

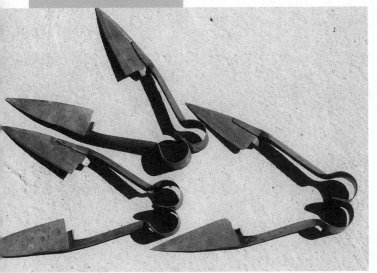

8.86 Shearing to prevent flystrike

Extension Activities

1 'Understanding the lifecycle of a pest is the first step in controlling it.' Discuss this statement with reference to five major pests in your region.

2 Discuss the general management practices used by farmers to reduce the constraints that disease agents, parasites and pests place on agricultural production systems.

Technology, production and marketing

Technology and innovation has had a profound effect on animal production. Developments include:

- new breeds of animals, for example the Murray Grey
- new pasture species
- fertilisers
- electricity and other forms of energy
- refrigeration
- synthetic fibres, for example nylon
- modern transportation systems by land, air and sea
- modern processing facilities
- new packaging, for example cryovac
- modern communication systems such as satellites, Internet and mobile phone
- modern marketing systems, for example AuctionsPlus
- vaccines
- pesticides and drenches
- biological control agents
- genetic engineering.

Timeline of developments

- **1600s** Oxen and horses pulled ploughs.
- **1796** Cowpox vaccine developed.
- **1826** First Hereford imported.
- **1854** Pasteurisation developed to stop food spoilage.
- **1858** First Angus imported to Australia.
- **1884** Rayon developed.
- **1890** Birth of rabbit from embryo implanted in surrogate rabbit.

1900–10s

- Wolseley shearing machines developed.
- Wire netting developed to control rabbits.
- Motor lorry used to cart wool.
- Hamburger developed.

1920–30

- Nylon developed.
- Carbon tetrachloride used to control fluke in sheep.
- Live merinos exported from Australia to Europe.

8.87 Modern transport systems

8.88 Modern dairy processing plant

8.89 Solar powered electric fencing

clostridial
oval or spindle shaped anaerobic bacterium that are pathogenic to humans and animals

1930–40

- Motored transport displaces horse teams.
- CSIRO develop vaccines for protection of sheep against clostridial diseases.
- Mulesing operation developed to prevent flystrike.
- Controlled atmosphere storage enables shipment of chilled beef from Australia to Britain.
- Brahmans imported to Australia.
- Polythene developed.

1940–50

- Broad-spectrum sheep drench developed.
- Rural electricity connected to state power grid.
- Bovine sperm frozen and stored.

1950–60s

- Chlorinated hydrocarbons used to control sheep and cattle parasites.
- Japanese agricultural motorbikes introduced.
- Liveweight cattle selling introduced.
- Hydraulic wool presses developed.
- Santa Gertrudis cattle introduced.
- Implantation of embryo in cow's uterus.
- Birth of calf by artificial insemination.
- Cloning of frog embryo cells.
- Discovery of DNA.
- Unravelling of genetic code.

1970–80

- Sale of wool using objective measurement.
- Pour on chemical for cattle lice control-Tiguvon
- Mouse born from stored frozen embryo.
- Split DNA.
- First test-tube baby born.

1980–90

- Pour-on sheep dip – Clout developed.
- Computers affordable for farm use.
- Wide shearing combs introduced.
- Computerised livestock marketing launched.
- Detection of organo-chlorine residues in beef to United States results in meat-testing procedures.
- Birth of baby from stored frozen embryo.
- Genetic fingerprinting developed.
- Cloning of embryo cells from sheep.

1990–2000 onwards
• Human-made strains of mice used in cancer research.
• On farm QA CATTLE CARE scheme launched.
• Satellites, mobile phones and Internet revolutionise communication.
• Transplantation of heart from genetically altered pigs into baboons.
• Birth of Dolly, the first cloned lamb.
• Genetically modified plants and animals.

Research 8.23

Diagram [8.90] shows the marketing chains for beef. Explain how innovation and technology have impacted on the enterprises.

8.90 Marketing beef

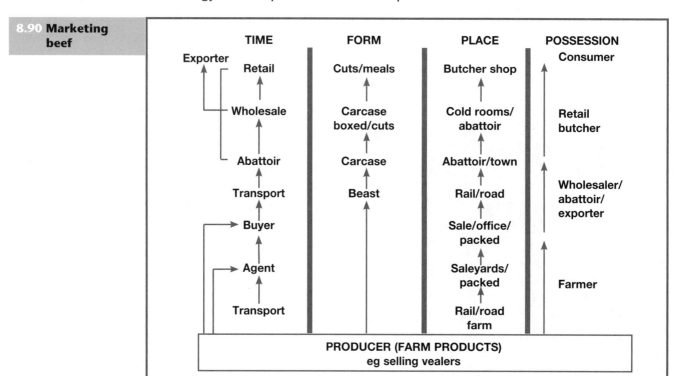

Breeding and genetics

Genes control the characteristics of an animal and are found on the chromosomes in the cell nucleus. Chromosomes are strand-like structures and consist of DNA. DNA consists of nucleotide units consisting of an organic base, deoxyribose sugar and phosphate.

When an ovum is fertilised by a sperm the offspring receives half its total chromosomes from each parent. However genes can be linked, reshuffled and mutated so great variation occurs.

Genotype refers to the genetic makeup of an animal.

Phenotype is the outward appearance of an animal and is the result of its genes and the environment.

Heritability

Heritability measures how strongly a characteristic is passed on from one generation to the next. Heritability is expressed by a scale from 0–100 and can be used to measure how strongly phenotype is influenced by the genotype and what progress can be achieved in breeding programs.

In general, characteristics governed by one or several genes are easier to breed for, than those governed by multiple numbers of genes.

8.91 Heritability of different characteristics			
Characteristic	**Heritability %**	**Characteristic**	**Heritability %**
Sheep production		**Poultry**	
Fleece weight	35–45	Egg production	20–25
Fibre diameter	20–45	Egg size	12
Staple length	35	Body weight	45
Beef cattle		**Pigs**	
Efficiency of weight gain	40	Litter size	10–24
Weaning weight	35	Litter weight	30
Post-weaning weight gains	35	Post-weaning weight gain	14–58
Dairy cattle			
Milk production	25–30		
Butterfat production	25–30		
Butterfat %	50		
Persistence of lactation	30		

8.92 Structure of DNA

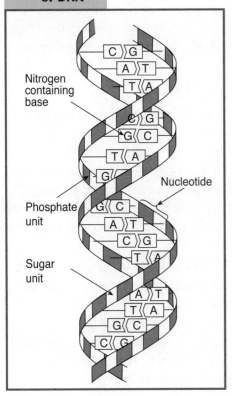

Nitrogen containing base

Phosphate unit

Sugar unit

Nucleotide

Breeding systems

Some of the most common methods used include:
- random breeding
- selective breeding
- pure breeding
- in breeding
- line breeding
- crossbreeding
- artificial insemination
- embryo transfer.

Random breeding

With random breeding animals are allowed to mate at will.
Advantages include:
- there is a large genetic pool
- natural pecking orders are established and only the best males mate with the females
- great variation occurs.

However results can be unpredictable and undesirable traits can occur.

Selective breeding

Selective breeding is the careful selection and breeding of animals with specific characteristics.

Advantages include:
• there is a limited genetic pool of preferred characteristics
• results are predictable
• significant improvement can be made in a relatively short time.

The rate of improvement is governed by:
• the number of characteristics selected; for example the fewer selected the faster the improvement can be achieved
• the heritability of the characteristic, for example the greater the heritability the faster the improvement
• the selection differential
• the number of stock selected
• the accuracy of selection.

Some methods commonly used in selective breeding include:
• visual assessment
• progeny testing
• performance testing
• herd records.

Visual assessment

Animals can be chosen on their appearance [8.93] and specific traits such as:
• conformation
• size
• degree of muscling
• masculinity and sex drive
• presence of physical defects such as undershot and overshot jaw
• temperament.

As examples, animals are culled if small, have deformed limbs, eye cancers or poor wool.

8.93 Selecting animals on appearance

Progeny testing

Dams and sires can be selected based on the performance of their offspring. Progeny are placed under the same conditions and the parents of the highest-performing animals are used for breeding. However progeny testing is expensive in time, labour and money and it can take many years before results become apparent.

Performance testing

With performance testing, animals are placed under the same conditions and the best performers are selected for breeding.

Herd recording is common in studs, breeding farms and dairy producers. They often keep records of characteristics such as:

- lambing or calving percentages
- milking volume
- fat content
- fleece weight
- fibre diameter
- greasy wool content.

  This information can be used to cull inferior animals and choose the best animals for breeding.

BREEDPLAN and LAMBPLAN

There are national genetic evaluation programs that give an animal's estimated breeding values (EBV) for characteristics such as meat quality and feed-conversion efficiency.

Activity 8.24

Table [8.94] shows the EBV for rams at a stud sale. Select the ram with the best characteristics.

8.94 EBV values of four stud rams

Ram	EBV for ywt kg	EBV for y fat mm GR	Yemd mm	Index
A	0.6	1.1	-0.4	94.0
B	2.6	-0.4	0.3	116.2
C	-1.1	-1.3	0.3	105.0
D	-2.0	-1.4	0.4	102.0

EBV for ywt = extra liveweight at 12 months
EBV for yfat = a negative value means that it is leaner than the average animal
Yemd = Eye muscle level
Index score = 100 is average.
so select the ram with highest value for fast growth, leanness and superior muscling

Activity 8.25

With reference to the Internet site:
www.breedobject.com
a obtain a listing of bulls and semen for sale that has been evaluated by the BREEDPLAN program
b select the best animals from the information provided.

Pure breeding

Pure breeding is mating animals of the same breed. Advantages include:
- animals are of similar size, shape and appearance
- there is a limited genetic pool
- results are predictable
- animals can be registered with the breeders association.

Inbreeding

Inbreeding is mating closely related animals such as father and daughter and mother and son. Advantages include:

- there is a limited genetic pool
- good traits quickly appear because there is a greater incidence of homozygous gene pairs
- results are predictable
- a uniform collection of animals is produced.

However because there is a limited genetic pool, recessive genes and undesirable characteristics such as deformities and sterility problems often occur.

Line breeding

Line breeding is a form of inbreeding in which one dam or sire is mated over successive generations.

Advantages include:

- the genes of a valuable sire or dam are used over several generations
- there is a limited genetic pool
- offspring have similar characteristics
- results are predictable.

However line breeding has the same problems as inbreeding and undesirable traits can appear.

8.95 Hybrid vigour

Crossbreeding

Crossbreeding is the mating of two different breeds. Advantages include:

- there is a large genetic pool
- offspring often inherit the best qualities of both breeds
- offspring sometimes show additional vigour – called hybrid vigour – and are more productive than either parent.

Examples of crossbreeding systems include:

- terminal over first-cross (F_1) cows [8.96]
- topcross [8.97]
- criss cross [8.98].

8.96 Terminal over F_1 cows

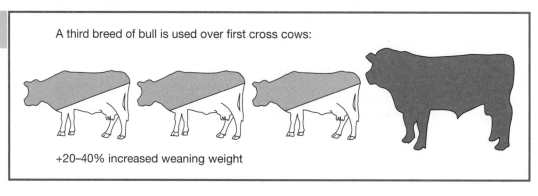

A third breed of bull is used over first cross cows:

+20–40% increased weaning weight

8.97 Topcross

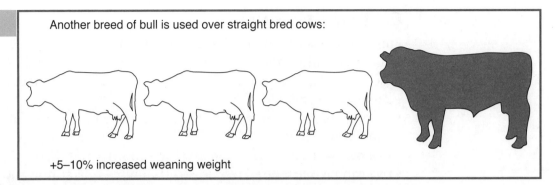

Another breed of bull is used over straight bred cows:

+5–10% increased weaning weight

8.98 Criss cross

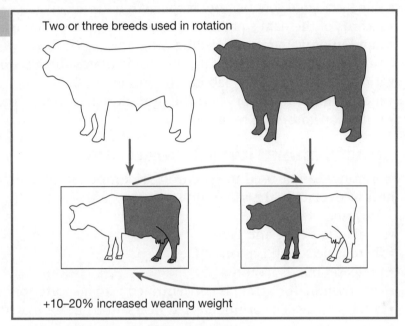

Two or three breeds used in rotation

+10–20% increased weaning weight

Artificial insemination

Artificial insemination is the collection of sperm from a male donor and its injection into the female's vagina using a straw or pipette.

Advantages include:

- there is a huge selection of sperm
- sperm can be stored for many years and used after the donor has died
- sperm can be diluted and used to fertilise more females than possible with normal matings
- sperm can be transported overseas with minimal quarantine and disease problems
- comprehensive records are available of the male's pedigree and genetic makeup
- bulls are not necessary in small herds
- rapid improvement in breeding programs is possible.

However artificial insemination also has some disadvantages, including:

- animals can be injected only when they are on heat and this is sometimes difficult to detect
- it does not always work and the procedure has to be repeated
- it is expensive in time, labour and money
- skilled technicians are required to inseminate the animal.

Embryo transfer

Embryo transfer is the removal of an ovum from its mother and its implantation in another female. With embryo transfer the second female raises the offspring but has no effect on the genetic makeup of its young.

Advantages include:

- a large number of offspring can be produced from a valuable mother in a short time
- ova can be frozen and used after the mother has died
- ova can be transported overseas with limited quarantine and disease problems
- there is a large genetic pool for selection
- records of the dam's pedigree and genetic makeup are readily available
- rapid improvement in breeding programs is possible.

However embryo transfer also has some disadvantages, including:

- it is expensive in time, labour and money
- it does not always work and the procedure has to be repeated
- skilled operators are required.

Synchronisation of oestrous

Hormones can be used to synchronise oestrous so that all animals come on heat or ovulate at the same time.

Advantages include:

- it takes less time and labour
- there is better utilisation of feed
- no teaser bull is required
- the inseminator's time is concentrated into a shorter period
- cows with a silent or undetected heat can be inseminated
- more animals can be included in an AI program
- calving index is 365 days.

Disadvantages include:

- the need to use drugs
- veterinarian supervision is required
- there is increased semen usage.

calving index
the time between one pregnancy and the next and ensuring that a cow has a calf each year

Progesterone treatment

Progesterone is a hormone that establishes or maintains pregnancy and can be used to synchronise oestrous.

PRID is a progesterone releasing intravaginal device. It is placed in the cow's vagina and removed after 12 days. Cows are then inseminated once at 56 hours or twice at 48 hours and 72 hours.

Progesterone can also be used in ear plants such as Crestar. These are removed after nine to ten days and the animals are then inseminated.

Prostaglandin injection

Prostaglandins are hormones that make the corpus luteum degenerate and induce ovulation.

Two injections are given at 11 days apart followed by two inseminations at 72 and 96 hours after the second injection.

Increasing ovulation rate

Ovulation rate can be increased by:
- selecting breeds with multiple births, for example Border–Leicester sheep
- selecting animals within a flock that produce more offspring
- flushing animals with high quality nutrition prior to mating to increase ovulation rate
- injecting animals with drugs that stimulate follicle stimulating hormone (FSH) production such as pregnant mare serum.

Genetic engineering

The cloning, altering and transferring of genes has resulted in huge changes to animal production. However there are many moral and ethical questions that must be addressed with genetic engineering.

Activity 8.26

Conduct a survey on consumer attitudes to genetically engineered agricultural products.

Extension Activity

Explain how agriculturalists have manipulated the environment or the genetic makeup of animals to increase production levels.

Revision 8.27

1 Define the following words:
   - growth
   - hot carcase weight
   - dressing percentage
   - animal welfare
   - carbohydrates
   - muscle scoring
   - embryo transfer
   - development
   - liveweight
   - disease
   - minerals
   - colostrum
   - quarantine
   - EBV
   - carcase
   - energy
   - proteins
   - digestion
   - lactation
   - vaccine
   - DNA
   - fat scoring
   - vitamins
   - lipids
   - ruminant
   - ration
   - AI

2 Answer true or false to the following questions
   a DNA stands for deoxyribonucleic acid.
   b The surrogate mother in embryo transfer affects the genetic makeup of the offspring.
   c Common breeding systems include selective breeding, cross breeding and random breeding.
   d Inbreeding can result in the appearance of recessive genes and deformities.
   e EBV means estimated breeding verification.
   f Heritability levels are usually greater than 50%.
   g A vaccine is a dose of the disease producing organism.
   h Disease refers to any abnormal functioning of the body.
   I Oxytocin is a hormone responsible for milk let down.
   j Concentrate feeds contain little moisture and high levels of protein.
   k Ruminants have one stomach.
   l Sheep and cattle are the main anmals found in Australia.

3 See page 388 for the find-a-word activity.

Product Study

chapter 9

In this chapter you will learn about:

- farming as a business operation
- the effect of supply and demand on pricing
- the importance of marketing to agriculture
- the production and marketing of Australia's main farming produce
- decision-making and management strategies of farmers
- the impact of technology on agricultural production and marketing.

The farm as a business

Farming is a business. It consumes resources and services, and produces raw materials for other industries [9.1].

Many businesses are involved in the production and marketing of agricultural products [9.2].

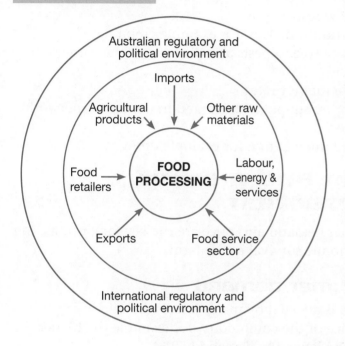

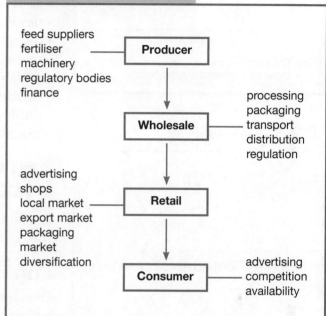

Business structures of farms

Traditionally, most farms were family owned and operated. Business structures now used include:

- sole trader – where a single person controls and manages a business
- partnership – where individuals or entities that control the business are partners and jointly receive income
- family trust – where a trustee holds property and earns and distributes income to the beneficiary
- company – a legal entity that is separate from its shareholders or owners; directors are elected by the shareholders and are responsible for making all the decisions for the company.

The type of structure chosen depends on:

- the purpose, nature and objectives of the business
- credit and capital requirements for the business
- limiting liability for business debts
- ease of operating the business
- management and control of the business
- simplicity
- minimising taxation liability
- ease with which the interest in the business may be transferred to others.

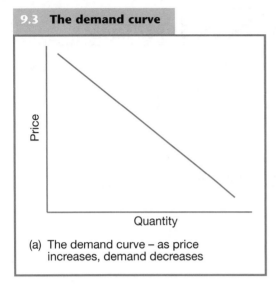

(a) The demand curve – as price increases, demand decreases

Value

Variety • **CONSUMERS** • Health

Taste interest   Convenience

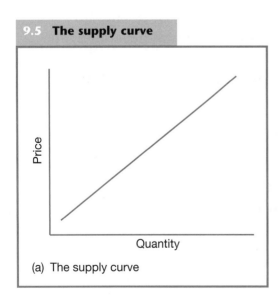

(a) The supply curve

Financial pressures that impact on farmers

Financial pressures that impact on a farmer include:
• fluctuating prices
• high input costs, for example machinery and herbicides
• changing exchange rates, for example as the Australian dollar increases in value our exports become more expensive for other countries to buy
• cash flow restrictions
• production time lags, for example cropping
• impact of weeds, pests and diseases on the value of the product
• variable interest rates
• fluctuating supply and demand in domestic and world markets
• risk and uncertainty, for example drought.

Farm and market interaction

Consumer demand and price are the key factors affecting the economic survival of the farm.

Consumer demand

Demand is affected by many factors including:
• the price of the commodity, for example the higher the price the lower the demand [9.3]
• the price of similar products, for example consumers will buy cheaper alternatives if available
• tastes and preferences of consumers
• perception of the product, for example whether it is fresh, healthy, convenient and easy-to-prepare
• income of consumers and how much they have to spend
• the size of the population.

Supply

A supply curve is a graph showing the relationship between the price and supply of a product.
  Normally there is a direct relationship: as price increases so too does the quantity for sale.
  Many factors affect supply including:
• price of the product
• cost of inputs
• profitability of other enterprises
• number of producers supplying the market
• skills of the operator
• level of technology available

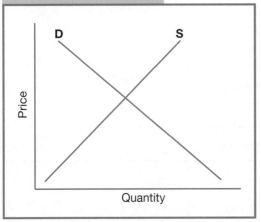

9.6 Equilibrium market price

- technical efficiency of the producer
- climatic effects, for example droughts
- effects of weeds, pests and diseases, for example mad cow disease
- seasonality of production, for example fruit and vegetables
- perishability and storage life of product, for example flowers
- world supply and its effect on demand and price
- government restrictions or incentives such as quotas or tariffs.

Equilibrium market price

The equilibrium market price is determined where supply equals demand and the supply curve intercepts the demand curve.

Activity 9.1

9.7 More farmers will sell their steers at a higher price

Use the data below to draw a graph showing the effect of price on producers supplying steers to the market.

Price of steers $	Quantity of steers supplied
200	100
250	200
300	300
350	400
400	500

Marketing agricultural products

Marketing includes all operations in moving products from the farm to the consumer, such as:
- buying
- transporting
- storing
- grading
- packaging
- distribution, for example to wholesalers, independent dealers then retailers and consumers
- selling and promotion, for example advertising catalogues, in-store displays
- research, for example new products, development and new-end uses
- financing.

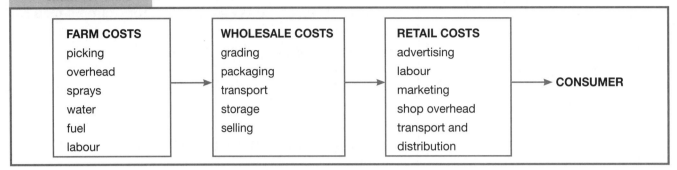

9.8 The marketing chain for fruit

FARM COSTS	WHOLESALE COSTS	RETAIL COSTS	
picking	grading	advertising	
overhead	packaging	labour	
sprays	transport	marketing	→ CONSUMER
water	storage	shop overhead	
fuel	selling	transport and	
labour		distribution	

Marketing strategies

Marketing strategies commonly used include:

- vertical integration, such as in the broiler industry where one company controls the whole marketing chain
- horizontal integration, such as selling meat, fruit and vegetables in a supermarket to increase turnover and make advertising more effective
- cooperatives under the democratic control of members, for example fruit growers
- contract selling, for example a contractual agreement for a set amount of produce to be delivered
- direct marketing, such as peas from the farm to the cannery
- future selling, for example selling cotton at a set price for a future date
- Commonwealth statutory marketing boards such as:
  - the Australian Wheat Board, which used to control all wheat exports. The board controlled quality, research and promotion. It also increased bargaining power and provided an orderly export system.
  - the Australian Meat and Livestock Corporation
- the computerised auctioning system, known as AuctionsPlus, used in Australia
- agricultural shows and field days
- a free-market system where producers selects the system of their choice.

> **horizontal integration**
> firms link together at the same level of marketing to reduce production and distribution costs and to increase control over the market

Research 9.2

Research how the following products are marketed.

Product	Marketing strategies
Flowers	
Aquaculture	
Sugar cane	
Eggs	
Canola	
Alpacas	
Hay	

> ## AG FACT
> **Effective marketing system**
> All marketing systems have advantages and disadvantages. Vertical integration where one company owns the entire chain from the producer to the consumer (such as from a feedlot to the abattoir and supermarket) is one of the most effective methods because costs are minimised.

Government intervention

Agricultural prices have traditionally undergone huge fluctuations. Because of this, the Australian Government has used intervention as a method of price control. It has introduced many policies to stabilise prices and improve efficiency of production.

Research 9.3

With reference to articles [9.9] and [9.10] and Internet site **www.nntt.gov.au** (National Native Title Tribunal) answer the following questions:
a   What was the Mabo decision and why was it introduced by the government?
b   Why did many agriculturalists fear the Mabo outcome?
c   Since 1992 what changes have occurred to our views of Aboriginal land rights?

9.9

Religious leaders join in Mabo call

Australia's Jewish, Christian and Muslim religious leaders including Cardinal Edward Clancy have joined with former Royal Commissioners into Aboriginal Deaths in Custody to call attention to the basic issues of justice and morality reflected in the High Court's Mabo decision.

In letters to major secular and religious newspapers, they express concern that confusion caused by lack of information, extravagant claims and counterclaims, and a preoccupation with finance may jeopardise the reconciliation process: The full text reads:

We are concerned, as non-Aboriginal Australians, that in the confusion caused by lack of information, extravagant claims and counterclaims, and financial preoccupation, the message of the Mabo case may be obscured, and the opportunity to advance reconciliation in Australia may be lost.

The message is simple. This continent once belonged to many Aboriginal peoples. Over two centuries most of it was taken from them piece by piece

without compensation. Where this has happened, it cannot now be undone; a new nation has been built and is here to stay.

But some groups of Aboriginal people, mostly in remote areas, still have their traditional land. Simple justice requires that we respect their rights, no less than we respect the rights of other Australians who have inherited land. Indeed, because land often has sacred significance to Aboriginal people, we should avoid their displacement wherever possible, even for money compensation. If we wish to use their land, we should seek to negotiate terms acceptable to them as has often been successfully done in the past.

The Racial Discrimination Act, which protects Aboriginal title from discriminatory treatment, was passed in 1975 to fulfil an international agreement that signatory countries would not deny the human rights of any race or ethnic group amongst their citizens. It would be a denial of those human rights if we did not protect their title to the lands Aboriginal people still own. Australia,

which speaks for human rights in other countries, can not reject them at home.

Mabo presents the opportunity to start negotiating a sensible and realistic basis for reconciliation with all Aboriginal and Torres Strait Islander people, not only those who can still claim traditional land. Its challenge is to accept the fact that the building of modern Australia has involved Aboriginal dispossession, and to accept responsibility for dealing justly with the consequences.

What justice requires can only be worked out over time with careful thought and patient negotiation on a basis of equality and mutual respect. But we believe it should be built on recognition, national responsibility, and the largest measure of self-determination for Aboriginal people that Australia can accommodate.

We call on all Australians to speak out for the principles of recognition of surviving Aboriginal rights to land, negotiation wherever possible, support for the Racial Discrimination Act, and patient progress towards reconciliation.

Source: Catholic Observer, 25 July 1993

Mabo's sea change ten years on

In recent weeks, Talking Native Title has spoken to many people including native title claimants, pastoralists, local councillors, executives from mining companies and the heads of peak bodies about what they think of native title – 10 years on from the High Court's Mabo decision.

Many of them remarked on the profound shift in attitude towards native title that has come about since 1992. With that shift had come a more positive environment for making agreements and building relationships between parties.

Most people acknowledged that native title was now a fact of life in Australia for everyone from Indigenous communities to big business. For some, this has led to agreements that deliver jobs, training and partnerships. For others it has meant years of lengthy discussion, meetings and negotiation.

For Leeanne and John Williams, whose pastoral property was the first in South Australia to be covered by a native title claim, the concept was initially alarming but as their understanding of it grew, so did their acceptance.

'I felt very sick, very angry and very scared, not knowing what might happen,' Mrs Williams said.

'I rang the Farmers Federation. We started to have meetings with claimants, which were heavy to start with, but once we learnt what the claimants wanted, we went into mediation leading towards an agreement.

'At the first meeting we seemed like the enemies – they were on one side of the room, we were on the other, eyeballing each other. With every meeting it got better.' The Williamses now say they don't have the concerns they had in 1992.

According to the chairman of Western Australia's Pastoralists and Graziers Association, Mr John Clapin, there is a lot of goodwill between pastoralists and Aboriginal claimants, however overlapping claims can make it difficult to reach mediated outcomes …

People now realise what native title is. Not everything good came out of it due to overlapping claims. However, once people were explained the reasons for overlapping claims – adoption, inter-marriages etc. – people realised they occurred for a reason.

It is that recognition that the Indjilandji people of north-west Queensland also regard as the most important benefit of native title. After almost four years of negotiation with the Queensland Department of Transport, an agreement was reached for the construction of a new bridge that crosses through Indjilandji country – the subject of a native title claim.

Now, 50 per cent of the bridge construction workforce is Indjilandji and the non-Indigenous workers are participating in an education program about the traditional culture of the area.

'Cultural perceptions are being broken down,' said Mr Colin Saltmere, a traditional owner and Indjilandji man who was key to the negotiations. 'We're seeing respect – racial tolerance is starting to increase in the (workers') camp.'

Mining and exploration companies, which were among the most vocal detractors after the Mabo decision, now say native title is just a part of doing business.

Tribunal President Mr Graeme Neate said that through mediation, relationships were built and communities often strengthened as a result.

Source: Talking Native Title, *National Native Title Tribunal, 2002*

Government policies and social issues

Government policies include:
- controlling supply, for example through quotas
- establishing marketing boards, for example the Australian Wheat Board
- creating new markets, for example through new overseas trading agreements
- providing grants, for research and development and establishing new agribusinesses
- subsidies, for example transporting livestock and water during periods of drought at subsidised rates
- tax concessions, for example the diesel fuel rebate
- special financial assistance such as drought or flood relief
- advertising and promotion such as promoting Australian produce to overseas markets
- research and development, for example through the CSIRO (Commonwealth Scientific and Industrial Research Organisation)
- public works, for example roads, transport and dams for irrigation
- traditionally provided specialist insurance and banking for rural activities.

Supporting prices and income

The government helps support prices and incomes by manipulating supply and demand or providing monetary payments or adjustments.

The government also manipulates supply by:
- controlling inputs
- limiting production
- destroying excess produce
- diverting excess to other markets
- selling excess produce at a later time as with the buffer stock scheme.

Quotas and incentive payments have been used in the past to control wheat, sugar, rice and dairy production.

Marketing authorities have also restricted the size and quality of produce accepted and have banned overseas supplies or imposed large tariffs to help support domestic prices.

Countries such as Brazil in the past have destroyed excess coffee to help stabilise income. Products, such as wool, have been diverted to other markets or sold at a later date to stabilise income.

Buffer-stock scheme

Many industries stabilise income by withholding excess produce and selling it when prices improve. The Australian Wool Corporation, for example, established a minimum-price scheme and bought all the wool that did not reach this price and sold it later when demand improved.

Multiple-price schemes

Different prices can be charged for a product when:
- there are separate markets such as the domestic and export market
- a product has different brand names
- a product has different end uses such as milk which can be made into butter, yoghurt, cheese or dried milk etc.

Stimulating demand

The government has helped stimulate demand by:
- forcing manufacturers to use local products, for example tobacco manufacturers pay lower tariffs on imported leaf if they used a prescribed amount of Australian leaf in their product
- restricting production or importation of substitutes
- branding regulations, that force manufacturers to specify the contents of their products, such as the amount of wool in a garment
- expanding and safeguarding markets by negotiating with other governments and making them buy Australian produce, for example bilateral agreements with Japan, New Zealand, USA and Malaysia.

Financial methods of stabilising income

The government can stabilise agricultural income through financial means such as:
- subsidies
- use of deficiency payments
- adjusting exchange rates and export taxes.

incentive payment
financial reward given to encourage producers to grow a particular crop or to limit production

bilateral
trade agreement between two countries such as Australia and Japan

deficiency payment
payment given to producers if the value of their produce falls below a guaranteed price

exchange rate
value of the Australian dollar relative to other currencies

In the past the government has used income tax concessions to subsidise the wheat industry and the use of superphosphate. It has also paid deficiency payments as in 1952 during the 15-year meat agreement with the United Kingdom (when prices fell below the guaranteed price). The government has also controlled prices by depreciating the exchange rate and stimulating demand overseas.

Stabilisation funds

Some industries such as wheat and dried fruits have also controlled income by establishing stabilisation funds to set aside excess profits that can be used when necessary.

Research and development (R&D)

The government provides funding for research and development such as that undertaken by CSIRO, universities and research centres.

> ### AG FACT
>
> **El Niño**
> Climate research has given farmers new tools to better understand and adapt to the extremes of Australia's climate. The unfolding story of El Niño Southern Oscillation (ENSO) has been one of the great recent scientific developments.

Marketing of specific farm products

9.11 Clearly labelled organic carrots

Traditionally producers have grown their products with little understanding of consumer demand and requirements. Understanding quality and product specifications is essential to ensure the success of any operation.

Product quality criteria

Many consumers – both domestic and overseas – demand produce of the highest quality with attributes such as:
• consistent and reliable quality
• standardised labelling and information, for example the 'AUS MEAT' label
• freshness
• hygienically prepared
• pure ingredients
• minimal bruising and damage
• free of contaminants such as chemical residues.

Activity 9.4

Complete this table on the criteria used to assess the quality of the products:

Product	Quality criteria
Wheat	protein level, purity, not shot or sprung
Beef and lamb	age, meat and fat colour, pH, tenderness, degree of marbling
Grapes	sugar level, acid content, acid strength
Wool	fibre diameter, staple length and strength, purity
Vegetables	
Milk	
Fruit	

Activity 9.5

9.12 Wool symbols used on garments and fabrics

The Woolmark® and Woolmark Blend® symbols guarantee that a product consists of either 100 per cent pure new wool or wool blended with another thread, and meets performance specifications. Give examples of other symbols used to ensure quality of agricultural products.

Product specifications

Market specifications are the quality standards required by the buyers (consumers) of a product.

Activity 9.6

9.13 Australian lamb for sale

Table [9.14] shows the market specifications for different lamb markets. What is the hot standard carcase weight and fat score for the following markets:
a   Australian range lamb
c   Middle East
b   United Kingdom
d   Europe?

9.14 Lamb market specifications for the export trade

Market	HSCW (kg)	Fat score	Use
Fresh Australian range lamb	18–26	2–4	chilled primal cuts or 8-way cut
Middle East	8–18	1–2	frozen carcases
Europe	8–12	2–3	chilled carcases
United Kingdom	18–20	2–3	chilled carcases

Activity 9.7

9.15 Wheat product requirements

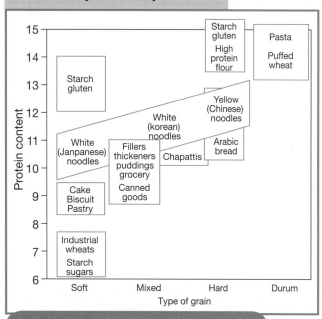

Source: Adapted from Schroder W, Australian Food, Agrifood Media, 1995

Use diagram [9.15] to determine the protein and grain requirements for the different wheat products:

a   pasta
b   cake and biscuit pastry
c   Arabic bread
d   Japanese noodles
e   canned foods.

9.16 Harvesting wheat

Processing agricultural commodities

Processes are the alterations involved in turning the raw agricultural commodity into various forms to satisfy consumer demand, for example various fish are caught, cleaned, cooked and turned into ready-made frozen meals sold at the supermarket.

Research 9.8

9.17 Sunflowers are the main raw material of sunflower oil

Research the processes involved in making the final product then complete this table.

Product	Raw material	Processes
Wine		
Yoghurt		
Flour		
Fruit juice		
Sunflower oil		
Woollen jumper		
Lamb kebabs		

Advertising and promotion

Advertising and promotion are essential to increase demand. Some popular ways to promote agricultural produce are to depict it as:
- healthy, for example iron in meat or dairy products to stop osteoporosis
- convenient, for example frozen meals
- a lifestyle choice, for example wine and leisure
- a luxury item, for example expensive chocolates
- fresh, for example fresh fruit and vegetables
- disease-free, for example free of mad-cow disease
- environmentally friendly, for example tuna caught without drag nets
- chemical-free, for example organic vegetables
- available in a large variety, for example jams
- having an interesting taste
- being good value for money
- being of the highest quality.

Promotion methods used include:
- labelling and packaging
- media, for example TV, newspaper and radio
- mail-out catalogues
- displays
- taste-testing sites
- field days.

9.18 Labelling and packaging promotes the product

Practical 47

Advertising and promotion

Aim

To evaluate the effectiveness of advertising campaigns

Method

1 Select several campaigns using different mediums such as radio, TV, newspapers or field days.

Results

1 How effective was
- the message
- the targeting of consumers
- the communication of the message
2 How effective was the use of the chosen media?
3 Which advertising medium was the most effective?

Conclusions

State your conclusions from your analysis.

Value adding

Value adding is the process of changing or transforming a product from its original state to a more valuable state. Examples include:
• converting wheat into flour
• producing organic or chemical free produce
• creating regionally-branded products that increase consumer appeal and willingness to pay a premium over similar but undifferentiated products
• free-range eggs
• hormone-free beef
• biofuel production.

Scheduling the timing of operations to meet market specifications

Producers can maximise profits by scheduling the timing of operations to meet market specifications, including:
• cold storage of apples so they can be sold in winter
• air freighting produce overseas to maximise international demand and price, for example cherries
• selling livestock at optimum fat levels to meet market specification
• freezing and preserving produce to extend its storage life, for example cryovac.

Activity 9.9

Give five examples of value adding that are different to the examples above.

Product case studies

9.19 Wheat has been one of Australia's main agricultural products for nearly 200 years

The following case studies of some of Australia's main agricultural products highlight the various aspects of production and marketing discussed earlier in this chapter.

Wheat production and marketing

Australia produces approximately 22.5 million tonnes of wheat annually of which 5.5 million tonnes is consumed domestically and approximately 17 million tonnes is exported.

9.20 Steps in marketing wheat

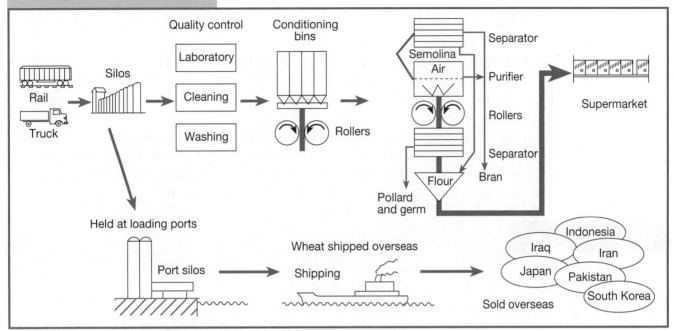

Wheat is one of the most important plants produced in Australia because historically it:
• was profitable
• was easy to grow
• suited most soil types
• had an assured domestic and export market.

9.21 Wheat types grown in Australia

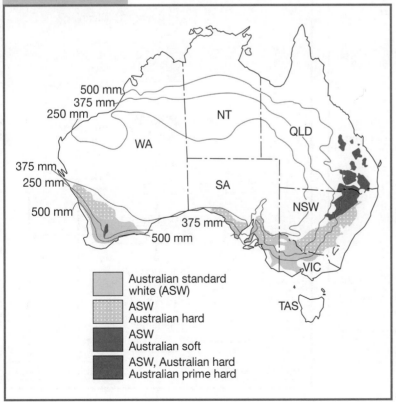

Australian standard white (ASW)

ASW Australian hard

ASW Australian soft

ASW, Australian hard Australian prime hard

The Australian Wheat Board was traditionally the sole marketing authority for wheat but the domestic and export markets are both now deregulated. In the domestic market, open market-growers now have the choice of using any grain traders to sell their product.

Farmers transport their wheat to silos, bunkers and sub-terminals operated by the grain handling authority. These are linked by rail to the seaboard terminal elevators at Sydney and Newcastle [9.20].

Wheat is analysed and categorised according to its:
• grain type
• protein content
• milling quality
• darkness
• purity
• dough properties
• moisture content.

The four major classes of Australian wheat are:
• Australian prime hard, which has the highest protein level and price
• Australian hard
• Australian standard white (ASW)
• Australian soft, with the lowest protein level and price.

The main growing areas for the different varieties are shown in [9.21].

The price of wheat is based on quality and the demand for the different varieties.

High-protein wheat is used to make bread because it has better volume and water absorption, and makes more loaves per unit weight of flour. Biscuit manufacturers prefer low-protein wheat because it does not absorb as much water and biscuits do not shrink or crack during baking.

Activity 9.10

Research the Internet to answer the following questions:
a   How are wheat prices calculated?
b   Who are the major buyers of Australian wheat?
c   Draw a flow diagram showing the conversion of wheat to a loaf of bread in a supermarket. See diagram [9.23].
d   With reference to illustration [9.22] what factors determine the protein level of wheat and whether it is soft or hard? Some factors to consider are varieties, climate and soil fertility levels.

9.22 Structure of a wheat grain

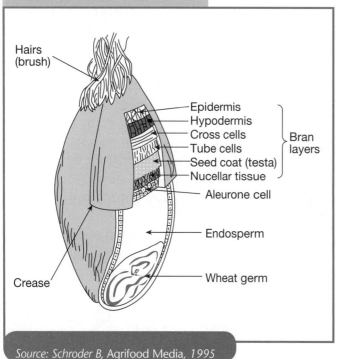

Source: Schroder B, Agrifood Media, 1995

9.23 Conversion of wheat into flour

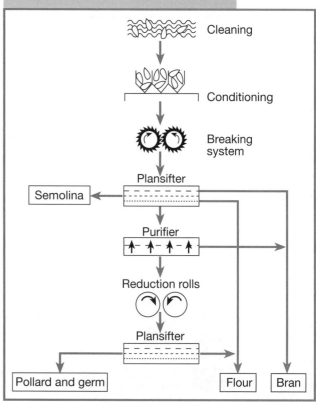

AG FACT

Cotton

The Australian cotton industry exports about 95% of production to the main markets of Indonesia, Japan and the Republic of Korea. About 80% of production is in New South Wales with the rest coming from Queensland. Most cotton is grown under flood irrigation on farms owned and operated by family farmers. Raw cotton is marketed under a free market system so there is no government intervention.

Viticulture

Viticulture is the production of grapes. It involves growing grapes for various products including wine, dried fruit, and table grapes. Grapes are grown in all states of Australia. The major production areas are in New South Wales, South Australia and Victoria.

Research 9.11

a   Draw a map to show where grapes are grown in Australia.
b   Explain why grapes are grown in these regions.
c   What are some common varieties of wine grapes?

Activity 9.12

9.24 Grape production over time

Year	Wine grapes	Dried grapes	Table grapes
1900–01	30 285	10	13 500
1910–11	33 750	35	13
1920–21	63 380	65	9
1930–31	72 250	180	13 500
1940–41	92 055	280	16
1950–51	149 825	160	18
1960–61	194 285	240	19 600
1970–71	316 815	170	25 330
1980–81	473 760	200	22 240
1995–96	575	147 400	44 500
1999–2000	1 125 840	117	78

Source: ABARE, 2000

Table [9.24] shows the changes in grape production in Australia over time.
a   Graph the figures.
b   What trends are apparent?
c   Explain why demand is increasing.
d   Find the current level of grape production in Australia.

Wine production and marketing

Grapes are converted into wine by the process of fermentation [9.27].

Australia produces more than 800 million litres of wine per year and the number of producers is increasing by 10 per cent per annum.

Seventy per cent of production is consumed on the domestic market, with Australians drinking an average of 20 litres of wine per person per year.

The quality criteria for wine production include:

• sugar content
• acid content
• berry size, grape colour and skin texture.
• flavour
• pH

9.25 Cask for ageing wine

Table [9.26] shows the quality criteria of wine grapes compared to table grapes and grapes used for drying.

9.26 Quality criteria for grapes

Grape use	Sugar level of Brix	Acid content grams/ litre	pH
Wine	14-30	6-10	3.2-3.6
Table grapes	15-18	3-6	3.5-4.0
Dried vine fruit	22-24	n/a	n/a

Options available to market wine include:
- at the farm through cellar doors
- retail liquor outlets
- displays at agricultural shows or specialised wine exhibitions.
- Internet sales
- mail-order

Large companies produce the bulk of Australia's wine and vertically integrate their system from production to sales.

Independent growers can grow grapes for the larger companies and have contractual agreements or are paid on current price. They can use large companies to process their grapes and then label and sell their product at the cellar door.

Larger companies and some independent growers have created boutique wines and incorporate restaurants and tourist attractions to promote marketing.

9.27 Steps in making wine

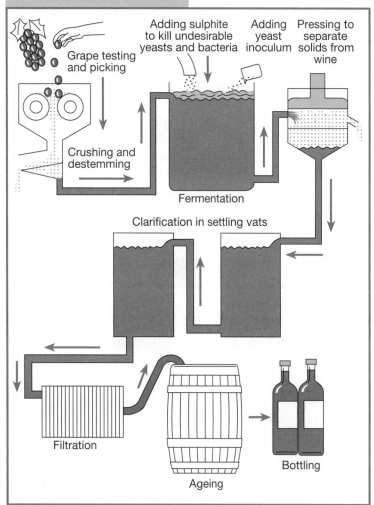

9.28 Wine bottling line

Wool production and marketing

Traditionally wool-broking companies, on behalf of the producer, sold wool at public auction. The entire wool clip was analysed by the testing authority for type and quality, and then offered for sample by auction in conjunction with a certificate indicating the wool's yield, fibre diameter and vegetable-matter content.

Producers received a guaranteed minimum floor price for their wool, which was fixed by the Australian Government in association with the Australian Wool Corporation (AWC). The corporation bought all the wool that did not reach the reserve price and sold it later when demand increased. This led to an oversupply of wool.

The producer financed the reserve-price scheme and any research and promotion by paying a wool tax on the gross value of all first-hand wool.

The floor price was established in 1974 to stabilise income and maintain a constant supply of wool to the trade.

This system is no longer used because of the huge accumulation of debt and wool that occurred. Most Australian wool is now sold at auction under a free-market system and has no reserve-price support.

reserve price
the AWC bought all wool that did not meet this minimum floor price at auction

Auction system

In Australia, 80 per cent of the wool clip is sold through the public auction system.

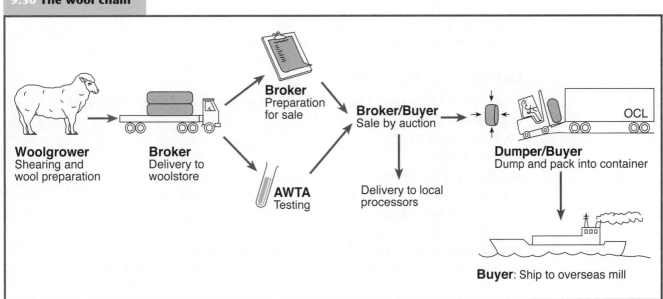

Woolgrower
Shearing and wool preparation

Broker
Delivery to woolstore

Broker
Preparation for sale

AWTA
Testing

Broker/Buyer
Sale by auction

Delivery to local processors

Dumper/Buyer
Dump and pack into container

OCL

Buyer: Ship to overseas mill

Advantages of public auction include:
- world-wide competition
- the value is determined on test results
- test information feedback is available to the producer.
  Disadvantages include:
- 3–5 weeks wait after shearing for payment
- the high costs of transport, handling and selling.

Sale by public tender

Bidding for described lines of wool can be undertaken through a linked computer system. Buyers submit prices by tender on lots and the highest price is accepted.

Stains and dags are commonly sold using this method and unsold wool can be re-offered or placed in the auction system.

Advantages include:
- quicker than the public auction system
- continuous sales can be made on any day
- costs are reduced, for example there is no testing.
  Disadvantages include:
- less competition
- prices can be lower.

stain
wool with a discolouration commonly caused by urine and faeces

dags
faeces attached to the wool

Sale by private treaty

Wool buyers can visit a property, test the wool and offer a price on the property.

Advantages include:
- immediate payment
- cartage costs are paid by the buyer
- the seller incurs no transport, handling or selling costs.
  However disadvantages include:
- buyers reduce prices to allow for fluctuations in the market
- less competition
- little feedback information
- payment is not guaranteed as with a broker.

Direct to the mill

Wool can be consigned to a mill after shearing and a price is offered based on test results.

Advantages include:
- quick payment
- regular producers receive a premium for reliability
- the producer can cater to the mill's requirements.
  Disadvantages include
- there is little competition
- higher prices may have been achieved elsewhere
- supply is expected even in periods of shortage such as drought.

Sale by specification

Sale by specification uses a bidding system based on electronic sales and sale by description without samples. The characteristics of the wool must be carefully analysed, and buyer and vendor confidence must be developed for this system to work.

Group marketing

Marketing alliances may be formed by producers who combine their wool for business purposes.

marketing alliances
formalised business and trading relationships along a marketing chain that may result in increased prices due to larger supply and control of the market

Forward selling

Wool can also be sold up to 18 months prior to shearing through a wool broker or by direct sales to mills.

Quality assurance

Quality assurance guidelines are used in the production and handling of wool. Examples include:
• dark-coloured animals are culled
• shearing sheds are cleaned prior to shearing, with separate eating areas and no smoking allowed
• classing is performed by a registered wool classer
• bales are identified with standard labelling.

Activity 9.13

1 The AWEX ID system is a standard system used to describe wool. Complete the following table by referring to these Internet sites:
australia.gov.au/directories/australia/agriculture/web-resources-list
www.farmonline.com.au/   **www.aglinks.com.au**
www.daff.qld.gov.au/home.htm   **www.dpi.vic.gov.au**
www.dpi.nsw.gov.au   **www.dpi.qld.gov.au**
www.pir.sa.gov.au   **www.dpiw.tas.gov.au**
www.wool.com.au

Description	Contents
AAAM	
AAM	
PCS	
BLS	
LKS	
STN	

2 Explain how the following factors influence wool quality?
  a fibre diameter   b length
  c strength   d colour
  e wool base   f yield

3 With reference to the wool sale data results in [9.31] below, complete the following:

a number of bales
b net weight per bale
c average micron
d cut per head
e gross value of wool per head
f net wool proceeds.

9.31 Wool sale data

WESTERN WOOL MARKETING
PO BOX 130 PARKES NSW 2870
PH: 02 68621344 FAX: 02 68624288
ABN 51 076 320 182
** WOOL CLIP STATISTICS AND ANALYSIS – SALE S20 **   31/01/12

NAME: ADRET PASTORAL P'SHIP   ACCOUNT: ADRET

CLIP ANALYSIS				CLIP PERFORMANCE		
	BALES	CLIP%	TESTED%		AV MIC	AV VM	AV SCH DRY YLD
FLEECE	9	100.0	100.0	FLEECE	20.8	.4	79.4
PIECES	0	.0	.0	FLC, PCS, BLS	20.8	.4	79.4
BELLIES	0	.0	.0	LAMBS	.0	.0	.0
ODDMENTS	0	.0	.0				
BINNING	0	.0					
TOTAL	9	100.0	100.0	(INTERLOTS EXLUDED FROM CLIP STATISTICS)			
LAMBS	0						

SHEEP SHORN (FROM CLASSERS SPECIFICATIONS & EXCLUDING LAMBS): 200/9 BALES
CUT PER HEAD: 5.69 KILOS   GROSS WOOL VALUE PER HEAD $45.82
CLIP VALUES (EXCL GST)

	BALES	NET KG	NET KG/ BALE	GROSS PRICE /NET KG	GROSS VALUE /BALE	AV CLEAN PRICE (TESTED LOTS)
FLEECE	9	1132	126	808.3	1016.67	1018.0
FLC, PCS, BLS	9	1132	126	808.3	1016.67	1018.0
WHOLE CLIP	9	1138	126	805.3	1018.29	

SALE DAY QUOTATIONS
CLEAN PRICES BASED ON WEIGHTED AVERAGE OF TYPES

MICRON	THIS SALE	LAST SALE	SAME WEEK LAST YEAR	% CHANGE +/-
18.0	1686	1616	2153	-21.70
19.0	1232	1192	1326	-7.09
21.0	990	920	651	52.07
22.0	985	918	629	56.59
23.0	974	895	580	67.93
24.0	923	883	554	66.60
28.0	636	612	444	43.24

NORTHERN REGION MI 962+36 THE MARKET JUMPED SHARPLY THIS WEEK ON THE BACK OF RENEWED CHINESE BUSINESS & SHORT SUPPLY. 21-24 WERE THE BEST PERFORMERS RISING TO 60% ABOVE THE SAME SALE LAST YEAR WHILE FINEWOOLS ALSO JUMPED 40-70C/KG. MAJOR BUYERS: BWK ELDERS, ITOCHU, GH MICHELL, CIL, AS GEDGE, LEMPRIERE. NEXT WEEKS SALES SYDNEY 35,000 BALES TO BE OFFERED.

Broiler production and marketing

Today more than 500 million broilers are grown, compared to four million in 1960. Retail sales return more than $2 billion annually.

Each Australian person consumes an average 38 kilograms of chicken per year.

9.32 Meat consumption

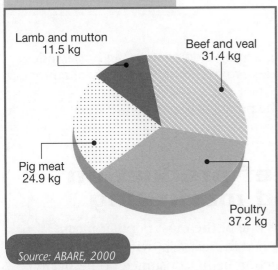

Lamb and mutton
11.5 kg

Beef and veal
31.4 kg

Pig meat
24.9 kg

Poultry
37.2 kg

Source: ABARE, 2000

Production

Broiler production has been successful because of:
- selective breeding and superior birds
- highly formulated, nutritional diets
- intensive, housed production
- vertical integration and a streamlined industry
- the proliferation of take-away outlets, such as Red Rooster and KFC
- the huge range of different end products
- specialty shops, such as Lenards
- consumer demand for healthy, lean, white meat.

Activity 9.14

9.33 Stages in broiler production

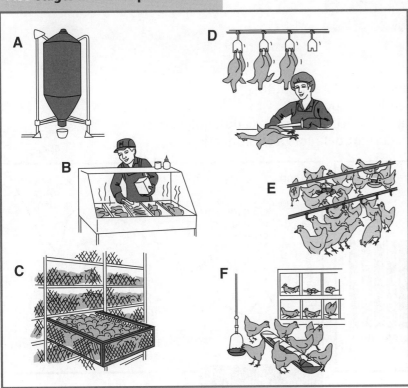

A

D

B

E

C

F

1 Place each of the diagrams in [9.33] into the correct sequence of breeding, hatching, feed formulation, growing, processing and marketing.

2 Draw a diagram to show vertical integration in the broiler industry.

3 What are the advantages and disadvantages of vertical integration?

Marketing

Seventy-five per cent of chicken production is sold to supermarkets and retail outlets, and 25 per cent is used by service industries, such as take-away outlets, restaurants and hotels/motels.

Of all the chicken sold, 85 per cent is sold as fresh meat and 15 per cent as frozen or precooked meat.

Activity 9.15

1 Discuss the effects of scientific research and development on the broiler industry.
2 Describe the actions a producer may take to maximise the quality of a product before it leaves the farm.
3 Explain how product quality affects the profitability of an agricultural production system.

9.34 **Marketing meat**

Beef production and marketing

Beef is one of the most popular meats consumed in Australia, with 40 per cent of production being consumed domestically. The remaining 60 per cent is exported and the major markets are USA and Japan.

Activity 9.16

Refer to diagrams [9.35 and [9.36]:
a What trends are apparent?
b What caused a decline in prices and numbers?
c Research current data for beef production.

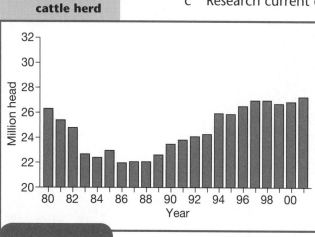

9.35 **Australian cattle herd**

Source: ABS, 2001

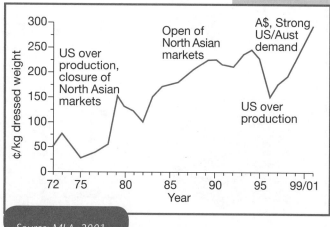

9.36 **Cattle prices**

Source: MLA, 2001

Buyers

The main buyers of beef are:

- **Store markets** where producers purchase stock from farms or saleyards to increase their liveweight and resell.
- **Backgrounders** produce stock under contract of a standard weight for feedlotters.
- **Feedlotters** buy cattle of a set weight and feed them under intensive conditions until they reach market specifications. Japanese and Asian markets pay premium prices for marbled beef. Angus and Murray Grey cattle are preferred because of their marbling characteristics.
- **Wholesalers** purchase, slaughter and distribute meat to retail outlets such as butchers and restaurants.
- **Processors** purchase cattle and use them to make products such as frozen meals, meat pies and canned goods.
- **Live cattle exporters** ship cattle live to areas such as Southeast Asia as feeder or stud stock.

Methods used to sell cattle include:
- saleyards
- over-the-hook
- market alliances.
- paddock sales
- AuctionsPlus

9.37 **Beef cattle in saleyards**

9.38 **Scales used to weigh livestock**

Saleyard sales

At saleyards animals are auctioned on a dollars per head or cent per kilogram (c/kg) liveweight.

Advantages include:
- competition
- it is simple for the producer
- small lots can be sold
- the buyer assumes the risk after purchasing
- agents attend to stock, paperwork and buyer default
- no knowledge is required about markets
- it supports local employment.

Disadvantages include:
- high costs, for example of yard dues, weighing fee, freight to saleyards, transit insurance, agents commission and transaction levy (6–7 per cent of the gross price)
- no feedback is given regarding carcase specifications and market requirements
- additional handling
- greater stress and inferior meat quality
- buyers pay on estimated average dressing percentages and meat quality
- price is not known until the sale day
- the costs involved for many buyers who have to travel to the sales.

Paddock sales

Cattle can be sold in the paddock on a dollars per head or cent per kilogram liveweight.

Advantages include:
- lower costs and stress
- no agents' fees
- the producer can build a relationship with the buyer and understand their requirements.

Disadvantages include:
- little competition
- the producer must be aware of current stock values
- it can be difficult to negotiate with an experienced buyer
- there is no cover if the buyer does not pay.

dressed weight
weight of a carcase after removal of head, limbs, hide and offal

Over-the-hook sales

Animals can be sold directly to the abattoir in over-the-hook sales. Payment is on a cent per kilogram dressed weight or a grid price according to carcase measurements.

Advantages include:
- less stress and bruising to the animal
- clear feedback information
- a premium is paid for quality stock
- the close relationship between producer and buyer.

Disadvantages include:
- no competition
- it can be hard to negotiate with a professional buyer
- the producer pays for bruising and condemned animals
- there are penalties for stock that do not meet specifications
- payment is not guaranteed.

Activity 9.17

Explain how the quality of a product is assessed
a on the farm
b and by the processor.

AuctionsPlus

AuctionsPlus is a computerised selling system based on sale by description. Stock is assessed on the farm by assessors and auctioned as:
- dollars per head,
- cents per kilogram liveweight or dressed weight
- a grid system.

Advantages include:
- greater competition than saleyards
- buyers do not have to inspect stock before purchasing
- stock move directly to abattoirs
- a reserve price can be set.

grid system
table of prices paid for livestock of different weights and lower prices are paid if the animal is not within the required grid weight range

Disadvantages include:
- stock must be mustered twice for assessment and delivery
- the difficulty of small lots
- the assessment cost
- more planning is required
- there is a listing fee
- there is not enough awareness of the system.

Market alliances

Market alliances are formalised business and trading relationships along a marketing chain. Such alliances are less expensive than vertical integration where one company owns the whole system.

Other schemes include Elders' integrated genetic management (IGM) and Certified Australian Angus Beef (CAAB).

Market descriptions

AUS-MEAT is the authority for the uniform specification of meat and livestock. It has developed a set of objective descriptions for use by producers, abattoirs, wholesalers, retailers and the food service industry.

The most important characteristics are:
- sex
- dentition
- P8 fat depth
- hot-carcase weight
- bruising.

Research 9.18

With reference to the following Internet sites find:
a   the market specifications for different beef
b   the current prices paid for different types of beef
c   our main export markets.
    www.mla.com.au
    www.ausmeat.com.au
    www.elders.com.au

Meat quality

Meat quality can be influenced by many factors including:
- genetics
- nutrition
- handling
- pre-slaughter and post-slaughter operations
- chilling, storing and packaging systems.

The age, sex and stress level of the animal influences texture, firmness, and meat colour.

pH has a marked effect on the colour and shelf life of the meat and is influenced by the temperament of the animal, handling practices, nutrition and time of feed prior to slaughter.

Breed, diet and age affect fat colour. Pasture-fed animals have more yellowish-coloured fat than grain-fed animals.

Breed selection, nutrition, age and carcase weight influence marbling levels. It is associated with tenderness and flavour.

The eye muscle area is the size of the rib muscle in square centimetres at the 10/11 rib site of quartered beef [9.39].

9.39 Eye muscle area

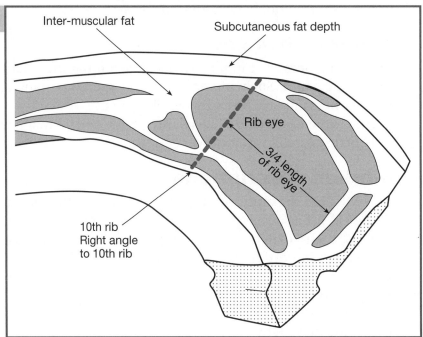

Inter-muscular fat

Subcutaneous fat depth

Rib eye

3/4 length of rib eye

10th rib
Right angle to 10th rib

Meat quality is reflected in factors including:
• visual appearance, for example texture, meat and fat colour, marbling, thickness and size of cuts
• palatability, for example tenderness, juiciness and flavour
• consumer safety, for example clean, hygienic and chemical-free.

Market specifications

Activity 9.19

1 With reference to diagram [9.40], which cuts of beef are the most valuable? Give reasons for this.
2 Diagram [9.41] shows the market specifications for different beef consumers. What are the liveweight, carcase weight and fat scores for the following markets:
   a supermarket
   b Japan
   c European Union
   d hotel and restaurants
   e Korea?
3 a Perform a survey at your local butcher and supermarket on current retail prices for different cuts of beef.
   b Display your results in tabular form.

9.40 **Cuts of beef**

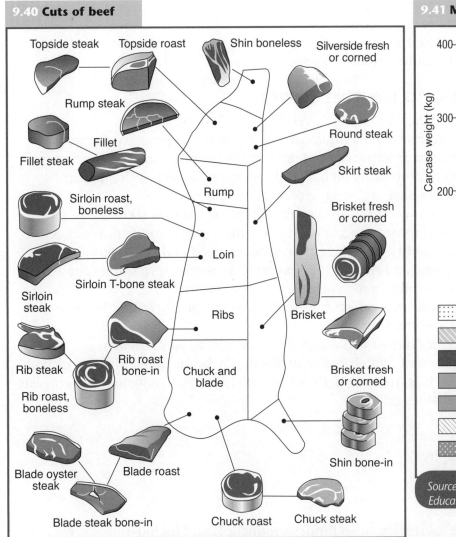

9.40 **Cuts of beef**

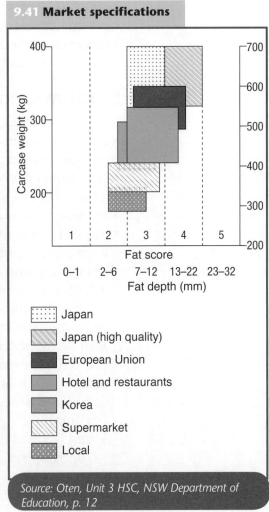

9.41 **Market specifications**

Source: Oten, Unit 3 HSC, NSW Department of Education, p. 12

Farm management

Agriculture is a business and managers must be skilled and efficient operators to maximise productivity. Farm management involves planning, organising, running and controlling a property and the people who work on it.

Some of the decisions the farm manager must make include:
• what to produce
• how much to produce
• how to produce it
• how to sell the product/s.

The decision-making process

A good decision can only be made with accurate information and planning.

To make the right decision managers should take the following steps:
• realise that a decision must be made
• collect all relevant information
• look at the alternatives

- choose one course of action
- put the choice into action
- determine whether the results are satisfactory
- take responsibility for the decision.

Limitations on the farmer

Many factors affect a manager's decisions, including:

- goals, for example to maximise profit, improve the property, increase annual income or improve the family standard of living
- aspirations or ambitions such as to have the best stud in the district
- attitude to risk such as being conservative or a risk taker
- attitude to change, for example willingness to use new technology
- degree of flexibility as specialists, for example grape and fruit producers have less flexibility to change than wheat, sheep and cattle producers
- level of income and finance, for example high debt levels limit choices
- information available such as access to the Internet
- individual skills and capabilities such as age of producer and level of education and training
  Many external factors can also affect production, in particular:
- The environment, which is one of the major factors affecting agricultural production. It is the surroundings in which the farm operates and consists of such variables as:
  – climate
  – soil
  – topography
  – weeds
  – pests
  – diseases.
- Limited resources can also hinder production and include:
  – money
  – land
  – labour
  – technology
  – skills.
- Change and uncertainty such as that caused by:
  – changing consumer demand
  – new technology
  – changing world markets.
- Financial pressures that impact on the farmer, including:
  – fluctuating supply and demand
  – world competition
  – competing with subsidised producers, for example US or European Union (EU) farmers
  – a cost–price squeeze, for example where costs are rising at a faster rate than prices
  – production lag and cash flow shortages
  – the cost of new technology.

production lag
period of time from when a crop is grown to when it is harvested and sold

Timing of operations in production

Agricultural production, such as cropping, is cyclical and is based on:
- the growing period of the crop
- the growing season of the region
- decisions made by the producer.

Activity 9.20

a   Draw and label a production cycle for one farming enterprise.
b   Explain how the decisions made by the producer can affect the performance
    of the system and quality and quantity of production, for example use of
    herbicides, fertilisers and pesticides.

Risk and uncertainty

Agriculture – more than any other industry – must contend with risk and
uncertainty caused by:
- climate and weather, for example droughts and floods
- weeds, pests and diseases
- varying supply and demand
- changing consumer tastes and preferences
- uncertain markets, both domestic and overseas
- fluctuating income, which hinders long-term planning and investment
- government intervention, for example quotas, tariffs and restrictions
- changing technology.
  Managers can reduce the level of risk and uncertainty by:
- diversification, for example producing more than one enterprise to reduce
  fluctuations in income
- deriving other forms of income such as a part-time job, share farming on
  other properties or investing money in real estate and other ventures
- share farming, for example where farmers reduce costs by allowing other
  people to grow crops on their land in exchange for a share of their profits
- future contracts for produce with a guaranteed price
- insurance, for example insuring people, livestock, buildings, machinery or
  crops against damage
- maintaining reserves for periods of shortage, for example storing hay, grain
  and silage or building more dams for periods of shortage
- reducing the debt load on the property
- being flexible, for example conducting enterprises that can be changed to
  suit supply and demand such as wool and prime-lamb production
- being well-informed, for example being aware of changes in supply and
  demand, world markets, consumer tastes and preferences, and technology
- avoiding risky enterprises
- maximising performance and the quality and quantity of farm produce.

Farm records and budgets

The basis of good farm management is good records and budgets. Records have many uses including:

- planning operations on the property
- monitoring progress of the property
- monitoring quality, quantity and performance
- pinpointing areas of inefficiency and waste
- planning for the future
- helping with taxation returns
- preparing applications for monetary loans.

Records must be useful, simple and concise. The two most common types are physical and financial records:

- **Physical records** commonly used include:
  - diaries showing daily events
  - rainfall records
  - paddock records, for example types of crops grown and fertiliser used
  - inventories, for example fertilisers, seed, machinery, herbicides, pesticides, drenches, vaccines and other stocks.

[See Chapter 5 Farm Case Study for additional information.]

- **Financial records** can monitor the flow of money and assess the farm's performance. Types of financial records include:
  - statement of assets and liabilities
  - equity or net worth
  - cash-flow budgets
  - gross margins
  - partial budgets
  - parametric budgets
  - development budgets
  - whole-farm budgets.

Activity 9.21

Decide if the following factors are assets or liabilities:

a farm	b tractor
c debt on farm	d rates
e wages	f stored hay
g livestock	h telephone bill
i ute	j credit card bill
k account at local supermarket	l machinery and implements
m insurance bill	

Impact of research and technology

Scientific research and new technology has had a profound effect on production and marketing.

Research 9.22

For each enterprise give examples of the effect of research and technology on production and marketing. An example for beef is provided.

Enterprise	Research and technology examples
Beef	<ul><li>New breeds of cattle</li><li>AI embryo transfer and genetic engineering</li><li>Improved pastures</li><li>Fertiliser, vaccines and drenches</li><li>Ultrasound scanner for fat testing</li><li>Computerised selling systems such as AuctionsPlus</li><li>Modern transportation, for example refrigerated</li><li>Modern abattoirs</li><li>Cryovac packaging [9.42] and [9.43]</li><li>Modified atmosphere packaging (MAP)</li></ul>
Crops	
Fruit	
Wine	
Wool	
Lamb	
Dairy	
Aquaculture	

9.42 Cryovac packaging (vacuum sealed)

9.43 Machine used for cryovac packaging

9.44 Refrigerated storage

Revision 9.23

1 Define the following words in relation to agricultural production:
- supply
- demand
- marketing chain
- bufferstock scheme
- subsidies
- research
- quality criteria
- specifications
- value adding
- viticulture
- auction
- group marketing
- wholesalers
- retailers
- AuctionsPlus

2 Answer true or false to the following statements:
a Agriculture is a consumer and a producer.
b With vertical integration one company usually controls the whole marketing chain.
c The Australian Wheat Board controls the sale of all export wheat.
d The auction system is the best selling system for agricultural production.
e If the rate of exchange falls, Australian exports are cheaper for other countries to buy.
f An example of a multiple-price scheme is the export and domestic market.
g Value adding increases processing costs and reduces profits.
h Liabilities includes loans, debts and money owing.
i The broiler industry is an integrated system.
j Viticulture is an example of intensive production.
k A drench inventory is an example of a physical record.
l Whole-farm budgets show the profit made by an enterprise.

A B B B C C C

B C B A C B C

Experimentation and Research

10

chapter

In this chapter you will learn about:

- observing, collecting and recording information
- designing and conducting simple trials using appropriate methodology
- measuring and monitoring plant and animal production systems
- analysing and interpreting agricultural data
- calculating a measure of variability
- making recommendations based on the interpretation of results.

Impact of research on agricultural production systems

Research has many impacts on agricultural production, including:
- reducing costs per unit of production
- increasing supplies of food and fibre
- increasing productivity and a farmer's ability to remain competitive in world markets
- generating jobs and incomes in the non-farm sector
- improvements in food quality, food safety, and nutrition
- greater variety of products
- improved standards of living as people spend less on food
- economic growth
- reduced spoilage and contamination due to food processing, packaging and preparation
- solutions to improve environmental quality, for example minimum tillage farming and integrated pest management
- increasing the productive life of farmers because machines, equipment and chemicals have replaced laborious jobs.

Biometry

Biometry is the statistical study of living organisms. Biometry uses statistical approaches to solve or better understand biological problems.

Populations

Populations vary in features such as eye colour, growth rate or reproductive capacity.

Most populations have a bell-shaped or normal curve distribution for any characteristic.

The centre of the curve shows the mean and the spread shows the variability that occurs around the mean.

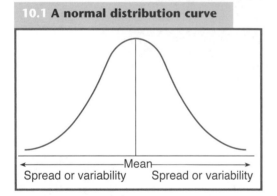

10.1 A normal distribution curve

Mean

Spread or variability   Spread or variability

10.2 A population

10.3 Variation in a population

Samples

Scientists cannot study a whole population because it is too expensive in time, labour and money. Samples are studied and used to make assumptions about the whole population.

A sample has a mean ($\bar{x}$) and a standard deviation (s) and is used to make assumptions about a population with a mean (μ) and a deviation (σ), as shown in table [10.4].

10.4 Comparison of some symbols used to represent populations and samples		
Value	**Population**	**Sample**
Mean	μ	$\bar{x}$
Variance	σ^2	s^2
Size	N	n

sample
small group tested and used to make assumptions about the whole population

randomised
to select a sample without preference or bias with each member having an equal chance of being selected as in pulling numbers out of a hat

control
an untreated sample used to compare before and after treatments

Designing an experiment

A good experiment should have the following characteristics:
• a hypothesis
• large number of samples or replicates
• a control
• a randomised design
• be carried out under similar conditions
• be carefully and accurately undertaken
• follow animal welfare, occupational health and safety and legal guidelines
• comply with legal, moral and ethical issues.

A hypothesis is an idea or belief that the experiment proves or disproves.

As many samples as possible should be used to represent the population and all experiments should have a control or untreated sample to compare before and after treatments. Samples should be chosen without bias or preference so that every member of the population has an equal chance of being selected.

A random sample can be obtained by allocating a number to every member of the population and drawing them out of a hat or by choosing the numbers through a computer program.

When designing an experiment, all external influences such as climate, soil type, breed, age and sex should be identical to minimise their effects on the results.

All procedures should also be carefully and accurately undertaken to prevent inaccurate and misleading results.

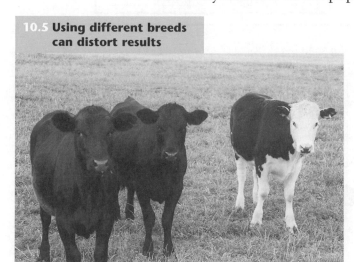

10.5 Using different breeds can distort results

Activity 10.1

10.6 Cattle in a feed trial

10.7 Effect of trees on an experiment

1 Photo [10.6] shows the conditions livestock were kept in during a nutrition trial. What animal welfare issues are apparent in this photo?

2 Seventy cabbage plants are growing in a row and 15 plants are required for an experiment. Explain how you could obtain a random sample of plants.

3 A research scientist wanted to compare the yields of two varieties of rice. Twenty plots are available and these are divided in half by a line running north to south. Which would be the best method of setting up the experiment?

4 A canola trial was conducted in paddocks lined with trees. How could the trees influence the results?

5 Diagram [10.8] shows the block design for a cotton variety trial. Which trial has a random design?

6 An experiment was conducted in a pig shed as shown in illustration [10.9]. What faults are present in this experimental design?

10.8 Random plot design

1	A	A	A	B	B	B	C	C	C
2	A	A	B	C	B	A	C	B	C
3	A	B	C	A	B	C	A	B	C
4	A	A	A	C	C	C	B	B	B

10.9 Pig shed

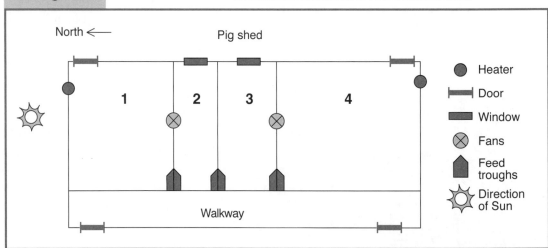

North ← Pig shed

1 2 3 4

Walkway

Heater
Door
Window
Fans
Feed troughs
Direction of Sun

Presenting results

Results can be presented in many different forms including:
- tables
- pie graphs
- histograms
- continuous line graphs.

10.10 **Statistical data presentation**

Level of fertiliser	Yield t/ha
0	0.2
1	0.6
2	1.5
3	2.2
4	2.7
5	3.1

Table

Air 30%
Mineral 48%
Water 20%
Organic 2%

Pie graph

Wheat yield (kg/ha)
Old variety
New variety

Histogram

Average weight of steers
Time (months)

Line graph

Tables

Tables are clear and concise, but are not as easy to understand or interpret as visual forms such as pie charts, histograms and line graphs.

Pie charts

Pie charts often present qualitative or categorical data (such as percentage distributions) and are simple to construct and understand.

Histograms

Histograms often present data summarised as frequency distributions (such as monthly rainfall) and are similar to bar charts.

Line graphs

Line graphs show the relationship between two factors, such as rainfall over time, and are simple to construct and understand.

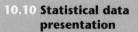

Activity 10.2

10.11 **Residual amounts of malathion in stored wheat**

X	0	4	8	12	16	20	24
Y	168	154	140	127	121	116	112

where X = time in weeks and
Y = Residual malathion (µg) in 25 gram samples of stored wheat

A report in the Journal of Food and Agriculture volume 15 (1964) recorded the residual amounts of malathion in stored wheat.
Graph the results on two separate pieces of paper.

a On the first graph on the Y-axis have a range of 100–170µg for malathion levels and on the second graph change the Y-axis so it shows a range from 0–170µg for malathion levels.

b Does the rate of breakdown of malathion look the same on both graphs?

c How does this demonstrate the importance of accuracy and integrity in agricultural research?

Measuring the sample data

There are a range of measurements that can be used to analyse the data.

The sample mean

The sample mean is the average of all the scores. As an example for the scores 1, 2, 3, 4, 5, the sample mean $= \dfrac{1+2+3+4+5}{5} = \dfrac{15}{5} = 3$

The sample mean is easy to calculate but can be distorted by extreme numbers.

The median

The sample median is the middle score that occurs when scores are arranged in order from the smallest to the largest number. For example, for the scores 1, 2, 3, 4, 5 the sample median is 3. In samples with an odd number of scores, it is simply the middle score. Otherwise it is the arithmetic average of the two middle scores.

The median is simple to calculate and is not distorted by unusual scores.

The mode

The sample mode is the score that occurs with the highest frequency.
For example, for the scores 1, 2, 3, 4, 4, 4, 4, 5 the mode is 4.

The mode is simple to calculate and is also not distorted by unusual scores.

Sample range

The sample range measures the spread that occurs within the sample and equals the highest score minus the lowest score. For example, for the scores 1, 2, 3, 4, 5 the sample range equals 5 – 1 = 4.

Sample variance

The sample variance measures the degree of spread around the mean. Each score is subtracted from the mean and then squared to counteract the positive and negative signs on either side of the normal curve.

variates
number of individuals in the sample

The variance is then summed and is equal to:

$$s^2 = \frac{\sum (x_i - \bar{x})^2}{n}$$

where
- s^2 = the total variance in the sample
- $\sum$ = the sum of
- x = the individual variate
- $\bar{x}$ = the mean
- n = total number of variates in the sample.

The greater the variance, the less accurate is the mean in making assumptions about the whole population.

For example, for the set of scores 1, 2, 3, 4, 5 the variance is shown in table [10.12].

10.12 Variance calculation

	$X_i - \bar{x}$	$(X_i - \bar{x})^2$
1	1 – 3 = -2	4
2	2 – 3 = -1	1
3	3 – 3 = 0	0
4	4 – 3 = 1	1
5	5 – 3 = 2	4
		10

$$s^2 = \frac{10}{5} = 2$$

Sample standard deviation

The sample standard deviation measures the variance around the mean, but unlike the sample variance its units are the same as the original variates.

The sample standard deviation equals the square root of the sample variance and is the preferred measure of variance.

$$s = \sqrt{\text{sample variance}}$$

$$s = \sqrt{\frac{\sum(x_i - \bar{x})^2}{n}}$$

where s = sample standard deviation.
The population standard deviation is

$$\sigma = \sqrt{\frac{\sum(x_i - \mu)^2}{N}}$$

where σ = population standard deviation
x_i = the individual variate
μ = the mean
N = the total number in the population

Once the mean and standard deviation of the sample are determined they are used to make assumptions about the mean and standard deviation of the population. As many samples as possible should therefore be used so that the results are representative of the population.

Using the standard deviation

The standard deviation measures the spread of scores around the mean.

For all distributions, approximately:
- 68 per cent of scores lie within one standard deviation on either side of the mean
- 95 per cent lie within two standard deviations of the mean
- 99.7 per cent lie within three standard deviations on either side of the mean.

For example, if the average height of Australian men is 170 cm and the standard deviation is 8 cm then:
- 68 per cent, or about two-thirds of the men, are in the range 170 ± 8cm or 162–178 cm in height
- 95 per cent are in the range 170 ± 16 cm or 154–186 cm in height
- 99.7 per cent are in the range 170 ± 24cm or 146–194 cm in height.

10.13 Using the standard deviation

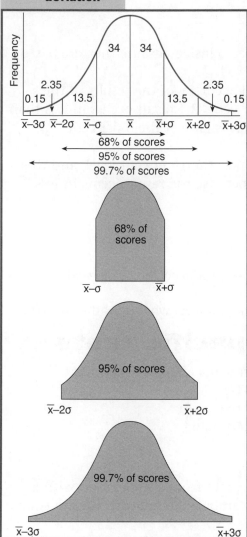

Activity 10.3

Find the mean, median, mode, range, variance and standard deviation of the following scores: 1, 1, 2, 2, 3, 3, 3, 3, 4, 5, 6, 7, 8, 9, 10.

Statistical analysis

Experiments must be analysed to see if the results are significant.

Common symbols used in statistical analysis include:

$N(\mu, \sigma)$ = normal distribution with mean μ and variance σ

n = sample size

N = population or total sample size

s = standard deviation of this sample

s^2 = variance of the sample

σ = standard deviation of population

σ^2 = variance of population

One-sided and two-sided tests

One-sided tests are used when a prediction is made as to which variance estimate will be the larger.

Two-sided tests do not predict which variance estimate will be larger and use evidence from both ends of the curve.

Both tests have similar calculations but two-sided tests have double the significance level.

Significance levels

Experimental results are not 100 per cent conclusive because they are based on samples rather than populations.

Significance levels help show the level of accuracy of the results. If the probability of a result (p) is less than 5 per cent, the result occurs in less than 5 per cent of all samples and the hypothesis is false at the 5 per cent probability level.

If $p < 1$ per cent the results are significant at the 1 per cent level, and there is strong evidence against the hypothesis because the result occurs in less than 1 per cent of the samples.

Activity 10.4

Two oat varieties were compared to see if they produced the same yields. That is, the hypothesis is that $\mu_1 = \mu_2$

If the results were not significant at the 5 per cent level what does this mean?

These tests are, however, only for reference and are not part of the syllabus.

Analysis of data-specific tests

The following tests are included to help students analyse experiments.

- chi- square test
- binomial test
- variance ratio test
- t-Test
- F test, and
- AOV table.

Testing for one variable

Some experiments test whether a sample comes from a population with a specified distribution. These experiments can be analysed with the chi-square test, or the binomial distribution test.

The chi-square test (χ^2)

The chi-square test is used when there is only one sample and the variance of the population is known

$$\chi^2 = \sum_{i=1}^{k} \frac{(O_i - E_i)^2}{E_i}$$

or

$$\chi^2 = \sum_{i=1}^{k} \frac{O_i^2}{E_i} - n$$

where O_i = the observed frequencies or the number of scores in the sample which belong to a given category

E_i = are expected frequencies or the number of scores in the sample that are expected to belong to each given category

n = the total number of scores in the sample

k = the number of categories

χ^2 has $k-1$ degrees of freedom.

Example

A dice is rolled 300 times and we want to know if the dice is fair and shows heads or tails an equal number of times.

Solution

Step 1 State the hypothesis.

Hypothesis: the dice is fair.

Alternative: the dice is not fair.

Step 2 Record observed results.

Number showing on dice	1	2	3	4	5	6
Frequency or number of times occurred	60	100	40	47	10	43

Step 3 Calculate expected results.

Number showing on dice	1	2	3	4	5	6
Frequency or number of times occurred	50	50	50	50	50	50

Step 4 Calculate chi square.

$$\chi^2 = \frac{60^2}{50} + \frac{100^2}{50} + \frac{40^2}{50} + \frac{47^2}{50} + \frac{10^2}{50}$$

Step 5 Determine whether the result is significant by looking at the critical values in a chi-square table.

10.14	Critical values of the χ^2 distribution			
Significance level (1 – tail)	5%	2.5%	1%	0.1%
df = 1	$\chi^2 \geq 3.9$	5.0	6.6	10.8
2	6.0	7.4	9.2	13.8
3	7.8	9.3	11.3	16.3
4	9.5	11.1	13.3	18.5
5	11.1	12.8	15.1	20.5
6	12.6	14.5	16.8	22.5
7	14.1	16.0	18.5	24.3
8	15.5	17.5	20.1	26.1
9	16.9	19.0	21.7	27.9
10	18.3	20.5	23.2	29.6
11	19.7	21.9	24.7	31.3
12	21.0	23.3	26.2	32.9
13	22.4	24.7	27.7	34.5
14	23.7	26.1	29.1	36.1
15	25.0	27.5	30.6	37.7
16	26.3	28.8	32.0	39.3
17	27.6	30.2	33.4	40.8
18	28.9	31.5	34.8	42.3
19	30.1	32.9	36.2	43.8
20	31.4	34.2	37.6	45.3
25	37.7	40.6	44.3	42.6
30	43.8	47.0	50.9	59.7
40	55.8	59.3	63.7	73.4
50	67.5	71.4	76.2	86.7
60	79.1	83.3	88.4	99.6

Step 6 Select the significance level (say) 0.1%.
Compute the degrees of freedom, df = k – l = 6 – 1 = 5
and read the value from table [10.14] = 20.5.
87.16 is greater than 20.05, so there is a significant difference between the results and the dice is not fair.

Binomial experiments

A binomial experiment is used when:
• there are only two possible outcomes
• there is a constant probability for one outcome.
   Binomial experiments are analysed using the following equation:

$$Z = \frac{A - B}{\sqrt{A + B}}$$

where   A is the number of scores in the first category
        B is the number of scores in the second category
Z is assessed using a table of critical values, for example:

2-tail 1-tail	10% 5%	5% 2.5%	2% 1%	0.2% 0.1%
Z	> 1.64	> 1.96	2.33	3.10

10.15 Critical values of A (or B) in a binomial test

2-tail 1-tail	10% 5%	5% 2.5%	2% 1%	0.2% 0.1%
N				
5 A or B ≤	0			
6	0	0		
7	0	0	0	
8	1	0	0	
9	1	1	0	
10	1	1	0	0
11	2	1	1	0
12	2	2	1	0
13	3	2	1	0
14	3	2	2	1
15	3	3	2	1
16	4	3	2	1
17	4	4	3	1
18	5	4	3	2
19	5	4	4	2
20	5	5	4	2
21	6	5	4	3
22	6	5	5	3
23	7	6	5	3
24	7	6	5	4
25	7	7	6	4
26	8	7	6	4
27	8	7	7	5
28	9	8	7	5
29	9	8	7	5
30	10	9	8	6
31	10	9	8	6
32	10	9	8	6
33	11	10	9	7
34	11	10	9	7
35	12	11	10	8
36	12	11	10	8
37	13	12	10	8
38	13	12	11	9
39	13	12	11	9
40	14	13	12	9
41	14	13	12	10
42	15	14	13	10
43	15	14	13	11
44	16	15	13	11
45	16	15	14	11
46	16	15	14	12
47	17	16	15	12
48	17	16	15	12
49	18	17	15	13
50	18	17	16	13

Example

Some agricultural students were given a reasoning test and analysed to see if they were above or below the expected score of 50.

Step 1 List the two categories
A = above average
B = below average

Step 2 Write down the results of the test

Categories		
A (above average)	B (below average)	A + B
4	14	18

Step 3 Refer to the table of values [10.15].
N = 18 and category A is less than the critical value of 5 for the 10% significance level.

The results are not significant and so there is no evidence to suggest that the students' results are not similar to expected results.

Testing for two variables –
variance ratio test

The variance ratio test determines whether two samples come from the same population by comparing their standard deviations.

$$\text{Variance ratio } F = \frac{\text{larger variance}}{\text{smaller variance}}$$

10.16 Critical values of the F distribution

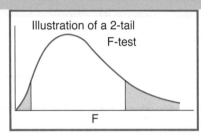

Illustration of a 2-tail F-test

df₁	df₂	2-tail 10% 1-tail 5%	5% 2.5%	2% 1%	0.2% 0.1%
1	2	$F \geq 18.5$	38.5	98.5	998.5
1	3	10.1	17.4	34.1	176.0
1	4	7.7	12.2	21.2	74.1
1	5	6.6	10.0	16.3	47.2
1	6	6.0	8.8	13.7	35.5
1	7	6.0	8.1	12.2	29.2
1	8	5.3	7.6	11.3	25.4
1	9	5.1	7.2	10.6	22.9
1	10	5.0	6.9	10.0	21.0
1	12	4.7	6.5	9.3	18.6
1	14	4.6	6.3	8.7	17.1
1	16	4.5	6.1	8.5	16.1
1	18	4.4	6.0	8.3	15.4
1	20	4.3	5.9	8.1	14.8
1	25	4.2	5.7	7.8	13.9
1	30	4.2	5.6	7.6	13.3
1	40	4.1	5.4	7.3	12.6
1	50	4.0	5.3	7.2	12.2
1	100	3.9	5.2	6.9	11.5
1	200	3.9	5.1	6.8	11.2
2	3	9.5	16.0	30.8	148.5
2	4	6.9	10.6	18.0	61.2
2	5	5.8	8.4	13.3	37.1
2	6	5.1	7.3	10.9	27.0
2	7	4.7	6.5	9.5	21.7
2	8	4.7	6.1	8.6	18.5
2	9	4.3	5.7	8.0	16.4
2	10	4.1	5.5	7.6	14.9
2	12	3.9	5.1	6.9	13.0
2	14	3.7	4.9	6.5	11.8
2	16	3.6	4.7	6.2	11.0
2	18	3.5	4.6	6.0	10.4
2	20	3.5	4.5	5.8	9.9
2	25	3.4	4.3	5.6	9.2
2	30	3.3	4.2	5.4	8.8
2	40	3.2	4.0	5.2	8.2

If samples are from the same population, they should have similar deviations and the variance ratio should be close to one.

Example

An experiment was carried out to see if exam results of male students were more variable than females.

Step 1 Write down the results.

Women's scores: 39,45,49,53,57,60,60,61, 55, 71, 78, 82

Men's scores: 24, 28, 31, 37, 53, 59, 64, 70, 75, 75, 83, 90, 91

Step 2 Calculate the variance of each sample.

Variance for women's scores:

$$\sigma^2 = \frac{\sum x^2 - (\sum x)^2 / N}{N - 1}$$

$$= \frac{45\,000 - 720^2 / 12}{11} = 163.6 \ (11 \ df)$$

Variance for the men's scores:

$$\sigma^2 = \frac{53\,496 - 780^2 / 13}{13} = 558 \ (12 \ df)$$

Step 3 Calculate the variance ratio

The variance ratio $F(12,11) = \dfrac{558}{163.6} = 3.4$

Step 4 Compare the result with table figures.

The results are significant at the 5% level. The men's results are more variable than those of the women.

df$_1$	df$_2$	2-tail 10% / 1-tail 5%	5% / 2.5%	2% / 1%	0.2% / 0.1%
2	50	3.2	4.0	5.1	8.0
2	1000	3.1	3.8	4.8	7.4
2	200	3.0	3.8	4.7	7.2
8	25	F > 2.3	2.8	3.3	4.9
8	30	2.3	2.7	3.2	4.6
8	40	2.2	2.5	3.0	4.2
8	50	2.1	2.5	2.9	4.0
8	100	2.0	2.3	2.7	3.6
8	200	2.0	2.3	2.6	3.4
9	9	3.2	4.0	5.4	10.1
9	10	3.0	3.8	4.9	9.0
9	12	2.8	3.4	4.4	7.5
9	14	2.6	3.2	4.0	6.6
9	16	2.5	3.0	3.8	6.0
9	18	2.5	2.9	3.6	5.6
9	20	2.4	2.8	3.5	5.2
9	25	2.3	2.7	3.2	4.7
9	30	2.2	2.6	3.1	4.4
9	40	2.1	2.5	2.9	4.0
9	50	2.1	2.4	2.8	3.8
9	100	2.0	2.2	2.6	3.4
9	200	1.9	2.2	2.5	3.3
10	10	3.0	3.7	4.9	8.8
10	12	2.8	3.4	4.3	7.3
10	14	2.6	3.1	3.9	6.4
10	16	2.5	3.0	3.7	5.8
10	18	2.4	2.9	3.5	5.4
10	20	2.3	2.8	3.4	5.1
10	25	2.2	2.6	3.1	4.6
10	30	2.2	2.5	3.0	4.2
10	40	2.1	2.4	2.8	3.9
10	50	2.0	2.3	2.7	3.7
10	100	1.9	2.2	2.5	3.3
10	200	1.9	2.1	2.4	3.1
12	12	2.7	3.3	4.2	7.0
12	14	2.5	3.1	3.8	6.1
12	16	2.4	2.9	3.6	5.5
12	18	2.3	2.8	3.4	5.1
12	20	2.3	2.7	3.2	4.8
12	25	2.2	2.5	3.0	4.3
12	30	2.1	2.4	2.8	4.0
12	40	2.0	2.3	2.7	3.6
12	50	2.0	2.2	2.6	3.4
12	100	1.8	2.1	2.4	3.1
12	200	1.8	2.0	2.3	2.9

10.17 Critical values of t for students t distribution

df	2-tail 10% / 1-tail 5%	2-tail 5% / 1-tail 2.5%	2-tail 1% / 1-tail 0.5%
2	t >= 2.92	4.30	9.92
3	2.35	3.18	5.84
4	2.13	2.78	4.60
5	2.02	2.57	4.03
6	1.94	2.45	3.71
7	1.89	2.36	3.50
8	1.86	2.31	3.36
9	1.83	2.26	3.25
10	1.81	2.23	3.17
11	1.80	2.20	3.11
12	1.78	2.18	3.05
13	1.77	2.16	3.01
14	1.76	2.14	2.98
15	1.75	2.13	2.95
16	1.75	2.12	2.92
17	1.74	2.11	2.90
18	1.73	2.10	2.88
19	1.73	2.09	2.86
25	1.71	2.06	2.79
30	1.70	2.04	2.75
40	1.68	2.02	2.70
50	1.68	2.01	2.68
60	1.67	2.00	2.66

t-test

The t-test is used to test the significance of different mean values. Unlike the variance ratio test the t-test takes into account the number of observations in a sample and acknowledges the x̄ and s are only estimates of the values of the population.

t is calculated with the following equation:

$$t = \frac{\bar{x}_1 - \bar{x}_2 - (\mu_1 - \mu_2)}{\sqrt{s^2p\,(1/n_1 + 1/n_2)}}$$

where $s^2p = \dfrac{SS_1 + SS_2}{df_1 + df_2}$

It is a pooled estimate of variance. An example is provided on the next page.

Example

An experiment was carried out to see if sheep and cattle had the same volume of blood cells (as a percentage of whole blood volume) and the following results were observed:

Sheep data: 42.7, 50.5, 40.2, 47.2, 46.8, 48.2, 45.9, 46.5, 43.6, 41.5

Cattle data: 44.4, 44.7, 43.9, 44.5, 38.7, 40.8, 36.3, 42.0

Using students t-Test examine the hypothesis the $\mu_{sheep} = \mu_{cattle}$

Step 1 State equation for t-test

$$t = \frac{\bar{x}_1 - \bar{x}_2 - \mu_1 - \mu_2}{\sqrt{s^2p \, (1/n_1 + 1/n_2)}}$$

$\bar{x}_1 = 45.32$ $\bar{x}_2 = 41.91$

$$s^2p = \frac{SS_1 + SS_2}{df_1 + df_2}$$

$$SS = \sum x_1^2 - n\,\bar{x}^2$$

For cattle:

$$SS = 14\,120.93 - 8 \left(\frac{335.3}{8}\right)^2$$

$$= 67.6$$

For sheep:

$$SS = 20\,623.17 - 20\,529.96 = 93.209$$

$$s^2p = \frac{SS_1 + SS_2}{df_1 + df_2} = \frac{67.6 + 93.209}{9 + 7} = 10.05$$

$$\text{Student's } t = \frac{45.32 - 41.91}{\sqrt{10.05 \times (1/8 + 1/10)}}$$

$$= \frac{3.4}{5} = 2.26$$

$$df = (10 - 1) + (8 - 1) = 9 + 7 = 16$$

Using t distribution tables (see [10.17])

F 5% 16df (97.5) = 2.12

1% = 2.92

The results are not significant at the 5% level.

This suggests that there is no evidence against the hypothesis and both means are equal and sheep and cattle have similar volumes of blood cells.

For more than two samples

The F test is used when there are more than two samples

$$F = \frac{\text{between group variance estimate}}{\text{within group variance estimate}}$$

$$\text{Variance estimate (or mean squate)} = \frac{\sum x^2 - \frac{(\sum x)^2}{N}}{N-1}$$

The variance estimate also equals the mean square or the sum of squares divided by the degrees of freedom that is

$$\text{the variance estimate} = MS = \frac{SS}{df}$$

The variance estimate can also

$$= \frac{\text{between group variance estimate}}{\text{within group variance estimate}}$$

For simplicity these calculations are presented in a table called an AOV table (analysis of variance table) [10.18].

10.18 AOV table

Source of variation	df	SS	MS	F
Between samples	k–1	between SS	between MS	$\frac{\text{between MS}}{\text{within MS}}$
Within samples	k(n–1)	within SS	within MS	
Total				

When F is significant the samples do not come from populations with the same means.

$$\text{Total SS} = \sum x_{ij}^2 - N\bar{x}^2$$

$$\text{Between SS} = n\sum \bar{x}_i^2 - N\bar{x}^2$$

$$\text{Between MS} = \frac{\text{between SS}}{k-1}$$

Example

Test the hypothesis that the following samples have the same means and are from the same populations.

Hypothesis: $\mu_A = \mu_B = \mu_C = \mu_D = \mu_E = \mu_F$

10.19 Samples data

	Samples					
	A	**B**	**C**	**D**	**E**	**F**
	36	32	30	31	36	42
	47	38	37	43	31	39
	44	41	34	27	36	36
	43	31	37	27	29	43
	33	23	24	31	34	39
Total	203	165	162	159	166	199
Mean	40.6	33.0	32.4	31.8	33.2	39.8
SS	137.2	194.0	121.2	172.8	38.8	30.8

10.20 Suggested AOV table

Source	**df**	**SS**	**MS**	**F**
Between	5	392.55	78.51	2.71
Within	24	694.95	28.95	
Total	29	1087.5		

Within SS $= $ Total SS $-$ Between SS

$$\text{Total SS} = \sum x_{ij}^2 - N\bar{x}^2$$

$$= 38.118 \ \frac{-N\ (40.6 + 33 + 32.4 + 31.8 + 33.2 + 39.8)^2}{6}$$

$$= 38\,118 - 37\,030.5$$

$$= 1087.5$$

$$\text{Between SS} = n \sum x_i^2 - N\bar{x}^2$$

$$= 5(40.6^2 + 33^2 + 32.4^2 + 31.8^2 + 33.2^2 + 39.8^2) - 37\,030.5$$

$$= 392.55$$

F = 2.71 df = 5,24   5% = 2.62
                        1% = 3.90

The results are significant at the 5% level which suggests that the hypothesis is wrong and that A to F do not produce an equal mean response.

Electives

In this chapter you will learn about:

- Agri-food, fibre and fuel technologies
- Climate challenge
- Farming for the 21st century.

Electives outline

Students should investigate one of the following electives:
• Agri-food, fibre and fuel technologies
• Climate challenge
• Farming for the 21st century.

1 Agri-food, fibre and fuel technologies

Biotechnology

DNA

DNA is found in the chromosomes of cells. It has a double helix shape and consists of two strands of simple units called nucleotides. These contain an organic base, deoxyribose sugar and a phosphate group. The sequence of four bases – guanine, adenine, thymine and cytosine – determines the genetic code of an organism.

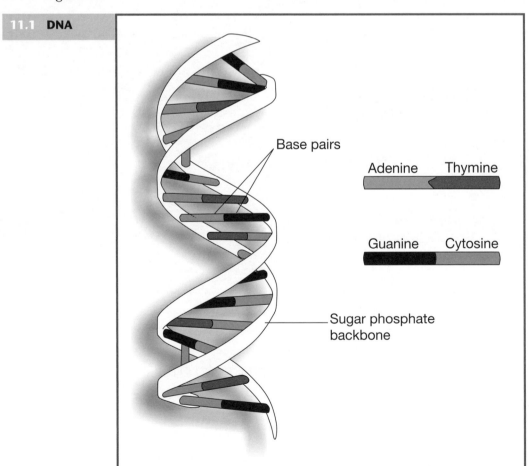

11.1 DNA

Base pairs

Adenine   Thymine

Guanine   Cytosine

Sugar phosphate backbone

Gene

A gene is the basic unit of inheritance and consists of a segment of DNA. Genes contain the information to build and maintain an organism's cells and pass on genetic traits to offspring.

11.2 Gene

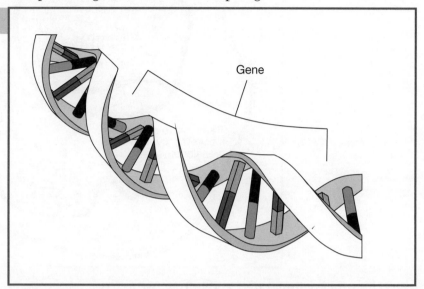

Genetically-modified organisms (GMOs)

A genetically-modified organism (GMO) is one whose genetic material has been altered by genetic engineering, for example bacteria, mice, plants, fish and mammals.

Genetic markers

A genetic marker is a gene or DNA sequence having a known location on a chromosome. Genetic markers can be used:
• in animal breeding and selection, for example to select animals with the required genes for a particular trait
• to study the relationship between inherited diseases and their genetic cause
• to remove a faulty section of DNA and replace it with a functioning gene sequence from another source (used in genetic engineering)
• to determine if an individual is at risk of developing an inherited disease
• for genealogical DNA testing to see if individuals or populations are closely related
• for assessing paternal lineages, for example genes on the Y chromosome
• for autosomal markers to study ancestry.

Genetic engineering

Genetic engineering is the alteration of the genetic material of an organism.

Protein synthesis

Protein synthesis refers to the processes in which cells produce new proteins.

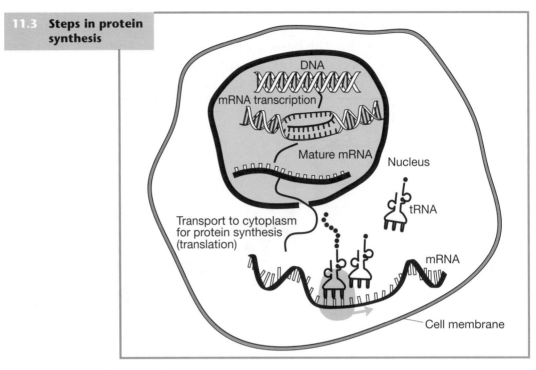

11.3	Steps in protein synthesis

The process illustrated above has two parts:

1. Transcription – one strand of the DNA double helix is used as a template by the RNA polymerase to synthesise a messenger RNA. This migrates from the nucleus to the cytoplasm. The coding mRNA sequence is a unit of three nucleotides, called a codon.

2. Translation – the ribosome binds to the mRNA at the start codon (AUG) which is recognised by the initiator tRNA. Complexes, composed of an amino acid linked to tRNA, bind to the codon in mRNA by forming complementary base pairs with the tRNA anticodon. The ribosome moves from codon to codon along the mRNA. Amino acids are added and translated into polypeptidic sequences dictated by the DNA and mRNA. At the end, a release factor binds to the stop codon. This finishes translation and releases the completed polypeptide from the ribosome.

Biotechnology in the agri-foods, fibre and fuel industries

Biotechnology is the use of living systems and organisms to develop or make useful products. It is used in the medical, agricultural, industrial and environmental industries.

Agriculture

Agricultural uses of biotechnology include:
• yoghurt, cheese and beer production
• the ruminant digestive system
• cloning, for example Dolly the sheep
• decomposition by microbes in the soil
• silage production
• biological control agents of pests

- vaccine production
- genetic engineering
- plant and animal breeding programs
- fibre production, for example bacterial cellulose and polyester, genetically-engineered silkworms that produce superior silk, biological wool shearing and breeds of sheep that are resistant to flystrike and produce better quality wool. Plant geneticists are developing plants with the following characteristics:
- increased growth and development
- increased yields
- improved nutritional qualities
- improved taste, texture or appearance, for example sweeter peas
- tolerance of salinity, drought, frost and heat, for example frost-tolerant sugar cane
- reduced dependence on fertilisers, pesticides and other agrochemicals
- pesticide control, for example Bt corn expresses a Bt toxin which kills the corn borer insect
- herbicide tolerance in soybean, corn and cotton
- delayed ripening in fruit to prolong shelf life, for example slow-ripening pineapples and tomatoes
- salad vegetables that do not 'brown'
- fruit and vegetables that contain extra vitamins
- long-lasting flowers
- multi-coloured flowers, for example blue roses.
   Animal geneticists are using biotechnology to:
- clone animals, for example Dolly the sheep
- increase growth and development
- increase yields, for example wool
- produce blowfly-resistant sheep
- increase tolerance of animals to heat stress, for example cattle
- disease resistance, for example the cattle tick.

Medicine

Biotechnology has been used in medicine to produce:
- vaccines and medicines, for example penicillin and insulin
- detecting and treating genetic disorders and diseases, for example cystic fibrosis, sickle cell anaemia and Huntington's disease
- in-vitro fertilisation and sex determination of embryos
- prenatal diagnostic screening
- forensic science
- the Human Genome project
- paternity tests.

Environment

Biotechnology has been used to:
- protect and preserve endangered species by storing their DNA for future use
- remove oil spills
- leach metals out of the soil during mining
- remove arsenic and heavy metal contamination
- recycle, treat waste, and clean sites that have been contaminated by industrial activities.

Concerns regarding biotechnology

Many believe that GM technology is the key to feeding a growing world population.

They view it as a continuation of the selective plant and animal breeding that has been conducted in agriculture for centuries. However, many people do not like biotechnology because of:

- the industrialisation of agriculture, for example where companies own patents on plants and animals and research is driven by profit and greed
- the control of the world's food supply by single companies
- no international rules and regulations
- concerns that potential risks to health and the environment have not yet been adequately investigated
- the fact that independent research is blocked by the GM corporations which own the GM seeds and reference materials
- unknown potential long-term effects
- horizontal gene transfer – the unknown movement of genetic material to normal crops or species in the wild
- contamination of the non-GM food supply, for example traces of genetically altered maize which was only approved for feed use appeared in maize products for human consumption in the USA
- the cost of research and development
- animal welfare issues
- reducing biodiversity, for example uniform crops with the same gene pool
- ethical concerns, for example playing 'God' and tampering with nature
- reproductive issues, for example creating designer babies, human cloning and errors in genetic engineering passed on to future generations
- privacy and anti-discrimination, for example protection for people with inherited deformities who may be discriminated against when applying for a job or health insurance
- public fear, for example of the speed of change, the unknown side effects, having no knowledge of what they are eating and a desire for more information.

Food safety and labelling

Individual governments assess and manage the risks associated with the release of genetically-modified organisms and food. America and Europe have individual regulations. Some countries do not have any regulations or their legislation is evolving. Supporters of GM food believe it is safe but it is inferred that it is dangerous. They trust that regulators and the regulatory process are objective and rigorous.

Regulation in Australia

The development and use of genetically-modified organisms in Australia is regulated by the *Gene Technology Act 2000* and corresponding state and territory legislation. The Act aims to protect the safety of people and the environment. The individual states and industries regulate economic and marketing considerations, such as coexistence and segregation in agricultural supply chains.

GM products are also regulated by agencies such as the Therapeutic Goods Administration (TGA), Food Standards Australia New Zealand (FSANZ) and the Australian Pesticides and Veterinary Medicines Authority (APVMA).

GM crops in Australia

GM crops such as carnations, cotton and canola have been approved for commercial release in Australia by the Office of the Gene Technology Regulator. GM carnations produce different coloured flowers while GM cotton varieties are resistant to certain pests and/or herbicides and GM canola varieties are resistant to herbicides. GM cotton has been grown in Australia since 1996 and constitutes 95 per cent of Australia's cotton. Tasmania has a moratorium on the release of GMOs until 2014 while South Australia's moratorium on GM food crops continues until 2019.

The role of biosecurity

Biosecurity refers to the control of:
- the introduction and release of genetically-modified organisms and their products
- plants, animals and food entering Australia, for example weeds, pests and diseases
- infectious and non-infectious agents entering Australia
- disease outbreaks
- the theft of biological materials from research laboratories
- biological weapons and bioterrorism
- food import protocols
- storage and stockpiling of vaccines
- the introduction and management of invasive alien species and genotypes.

The Department of Agriculture, Fisheries and Forestry (DAFF) has primary responsibility for managing Australia's biosecurity system.

Current developments in biotechnology

Biofuels

The term 'biofuel' (short for biorganic fuel) refers to any plant or animal substance that is burnt to provide energy. First generation biofuel is produced by fermenting plant-derived sugars into ethanol, using a similar process to that used in beer and wine-making, or by converting plant-oils into biodiesel. Feedstock such as sugar cane, corn, wheat, oil seeds or sugar beet is used. Research and development has been promoted by:
- rising oil prices
- global warming
- climate change
- interest in rural development
- the instability of the fuel supply from the Middle East.

Biofuels such as ethanol are widely used in America, Europe and Asia for transportation, cooking and heating. However, in Indonesia the clearing of land for biofuel production has resulted in deforestation, loss of biodiversity, the displacement of Indigenous peoples, contamination of water supplies with pesticides, and erosion. The clearing of land has also contributed to global warming.

Biofuel production, world food demands and sustainable and efficient use of carbon

In 2010 worldwide biofuel production reached 105 billion litres and biofuels provided 2.7 per cent of the world's fuels for road transport. The world's largest biodiesel producer was the European Union, accounting for 53 per cent of all biodiesel production.

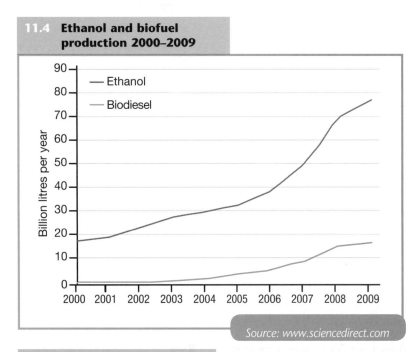

11.4 Ethanol and biofuel production 2000–2009

Source: www.sciencedirect.com

11.5 US grain feeding/cars

Source: Earth Earth Policy Institute, USDA, UN

Social, economic, environmental and technical issues relating to biofuel production include:
- the effect of moderating oil prices, for example biofuels are not profitable to make if oil prices fall
- the 'food vs fuel' debate, for example good agricultural land is being used to grow fuel rather than food and food prices have increased as a result of shortages
- poverty reduction potential, for example biofuels provide poor farmers with a profitable enterprise
- carbon emissions levels, for example biofuel production can result in higher carbon emissions if rainforests are cleared to grow biofuels
- deforestation, soil erosion and loss of biodiversity caused by clearing land
- impact on water resources
- energy balance and efficiency, for example scientists are trying to develop biofuel crops that require less land and water resources, such as algae.

The graphs on this and the following page [11.4–11.8] illustrate some of the issues related to biofuel production.

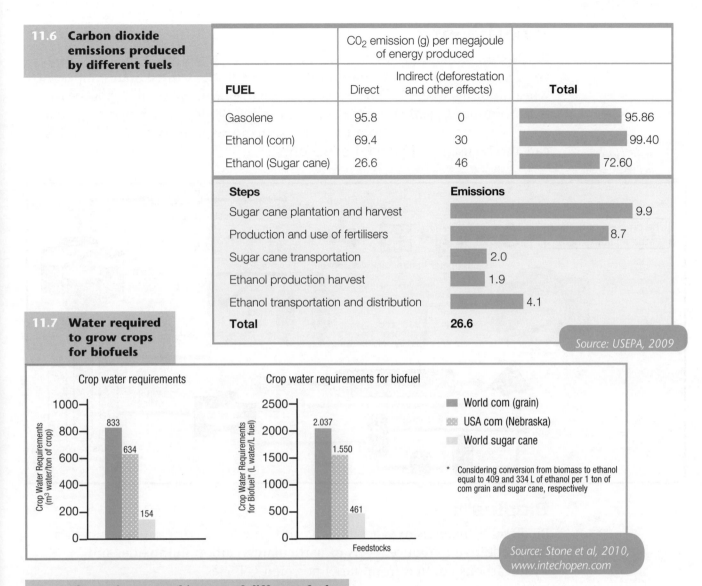

11.6 Carbon dioxide emissions produced by different fuels

| FUEL | CO_2 emission (g) per megajoule of energy produced | | Total |
	Direct	Indirect (deforestation and other effects)	
Gasolene	95.8	0	95.86
Ethanol (corn)	69.4	30	99.40
Ethanol (Sugar cane)	26.6	46	72.60

Steps	Emissions
Sugar cane plantation and harvest	9.9
Production and use of fertilisers	8.7
Sugar cane transportation	2.0
Ethanol production harvest	1.9
Ethanol transportation and distribution	4.1
Total	**26.6**

Source: USEPA, 2009

11.7 Water required to grow crops for biofuels

Crop water requirements

Crop water requirements for biofuel

* Considering conversion from biomass to ethanol equal to 409 and 334 L of ethanol per 1 ton of corn grain and sugar cane, respectively

Source: Stone et al, 2010, www.intechopen.com

11.8 The environmental impact of different fuels

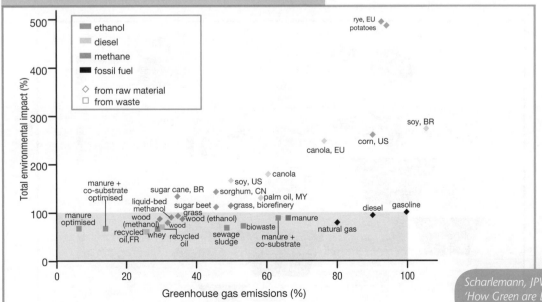

Scharlemann, JPW and Laurence, WF, 'How Green are Biofuels?', Science, January 2008: Vol. 319, no. 5859, pp. 43–44

Bioethanol

Bioethanol (ethanol) is an alcohol made by fermenting sugar or starch from crops such as corn, switch grass, and soybeans in the United States; rapeseed, wheat and sugar beet in Europe; sugar cane in Brazil; palm oil in Southeast Asia; sorghum in China; and jatropha in India. Biodegradable waste, such as straw, sewage and food, from industry, agriculture, forestry and households can also be used for biofuel production.

11.9 Production of fuel from corn

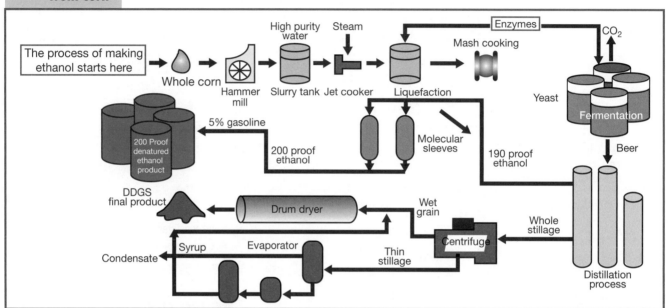

Biodiesel

Biodiesel is made from vegetable oils and animal fats. It used as a fuel or a diesel additive to reduce levels of particulates, carbon monoxide, and hydrocarbons emitted from diesel-powered vehicles.

11.10 The biodiesel production process

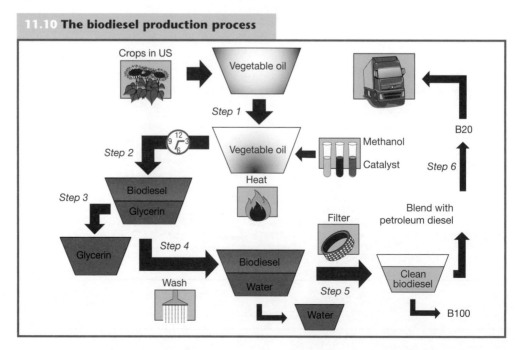

Algae and biofuel production

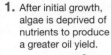

11.11 Biodiesel from algae

1. After initial growth, algae is deprived of nutrients to produce a greater oil yield.

3. Solvents used to separate sugar from oil; solvents then evaporate.

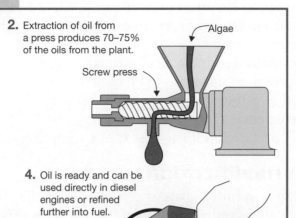

2. Extraction of oil from a press produces 70–75% of the oils from the plant.

Algae

Screw press

4. Oil is ready and can be used directly in diesel engines or refined further into fuel.

Solvents
Solvents

Source: www.oilgae.com

Algae can use unproductive land and wastewater from industries to generate biofuel. This production does not use valuable land needed for food production.

Biomass

Biomass is derived from living things such as plants and animals. Two billion people use wood to cook and heat their homes. Coal is also a form of biomass that is non-renewable and polluting. Landfill gas (LFG) can be burned to generate heat or electricity. It contains approximately 50 per cent methane, which is found in natural gas.

Industry and uses of biofuels

Uses of biofuel include:
• fuel source
• power source for vehicles, for example cars
• heating homes
• cooking
• power and electricity production.

Biopesticides

Biopesticides (biological pesticides) are derived from natural products or living organisms and are used to control pests. Types of biopesticides include:
• biochemical pesticides, which are naturally occurring substances that control pests, for example garlic, canola oil and pheromones
• microbial pesticides, which contain bacteria, fungi, viruses or nematodes and control pests
• plant-incorporated protectants or PIPs which have been genetically altered and are resistant to pests
• organisms that have genetic material from other species incorporated into their DNA, for example BT corn.

Biopesticides have been used to control downy mildew, damping-off, root-rot and seedling blights. Advantages of biopesticides include they:
• have no harmful residues
• are cheaper than chemical pesticides if produced locally
• can be more effective than chemical pesticides in the long term.
   Disadvantages include:
• the pest or pathogen must be identified
• multiple products may have to be used
• slow speed of action
• variable efficiency
• resistance can develop if the pest is not completely exterminated.

Rumen modification

Ruminants such as cattle, goats, sheep, camels, giraffes, buffalos and deer produce methane which is contributing to global warming. The rumen contains bacteria, protists, fungi and viruses which ferment the food. Recombinant DNA technology is being used to introduce genetically-altered microorganisms into the rumen to increase the efficiency of fermentation. This will result in less methane production and increased meat, milk or wool production.

Gene markers

Gene markers identify the genes responsible for particular traits. Researchers are attempting to identify the genes that determine production traits, carcase quality, environmental adaptation and growth. The Beef Cooperative Research Centre (BeefCRC) and CSIRO are researching gene markers for beef marbling and tenderness. Animals containing the desired markers can then be used for breeding purposes.

Vaccine production

Vaccines were derived from weakened or killed forms of the microbe, its toxins or one of its surface proteins. These stimulate the body's immune system to recognise and destroy it as well as prepare for future attacks. Biotechnology is now used to produce vaccines.

Embryo and sperm testing

Pre-implantation genetic diagnosis (PGD or PIGD) and Pre-implantation genetic screening (PGS) are used to screen embryos for genetic diseases such as cystic fibrosis, Huntington's disease, Fragile X syndrome and myotonic dystrophy. Scientists can determine the genetic source of any additional or missing chromosomes, for example the sperm or the egg, and whether these abnormalities occurred before or after fertilisation.

Embryo splitting

Embryos can split spontaneously in nature to form identical twins. Scientists use embryo splitting to clone and produce large numbers of identical organisms with the desired characteristics, for example tissue culture and orchid production.

Developments and concerns in biotechnology

Developments in biotechnology

Developments in biotechnology related to agriculture include creating:
- genetically-modified crops with resistance to pests and diseases, for example transgenic cotton
- herbicide-tolerant crops, for example Roundup Ready soybean
- a terminator gene to produce sterile male fruit flies
- hormonal treatment to slow the ripening of fruit
- differing light regimes to alter the time and length of flowering, for example to have chrysanthemums for Mother's Day.

Production and ethical concerns of biotechnology

Ethical concerns include:
- experimentation is driven by profit and private corporations
- animal rights, for example testing on animals
- consumer choice, for example many consumers want to know if they are eating genetically-modified foods
- production of biofuels in developing countries at the expense of food production
- use of hybrid seed in developing countries and the resulting dependence on international seed companies for supplies
- loss of biodiversity
- lack of regulations.

Analysis of agricultural research in biotechnology

Research has had a significant effect on agricultural production. However, it must be conducted properly to ensure that it is valid. Factors that should be considered include:
- design of the study (how the experiment is set up)
- aim (what the scientist is trying to prove or find)
- hypothesis (what the scientist believes will be the result)
- methodology (how the experiment is conducted or performed)
- use of controls (untreated samples used for comparison)
- randomisation (experiment set up without bias or preference)
- replication (use of many samples to increase accuracy)
- standardisation (removing variation in the experiment, for example using the same age, sex and breed of sheep)
- collection of data, for example the number of samples and the size of the population studied
- time-frame, for example the longer the experiment and the more times it is repeated, the greater the accuracy
- depth of information, for example time-frame, number of samples and the size of the population

- use of second-hand data, for example is the data from an accurate source such as scientific research or from a newspaper article
- accuracy of collection, including accuracy of equipment and measurement
- use of qualitative (without measurement) and quantitative methods (including measurement)
- presentation of data, for example forms of presentation such as graphs and tables
- analysis of the data, for example statistical analysis
- validity, for example was the research conducted by a company that makes profits from the chemical being tested
- appropriateness, for example is the experiment relevant
- ethics, for example animal welfare issues
- conclusion, recommendations and the need for further research.

2 Climate challenge

Australia's variable climate

Australia is the one of the driest continents in the world and has a highly variable and unreliable climate. Agricultural production is directly affected by the amount of rainfall a region receives and its seasonality and reliability. Coastal regions receive the highest rainfall and reliability decreases and variability increases with distance from the coast.

Fifty per cent of the land surface receives less than 300 mm of rainfall per year. Seventy-five per cent of Australia has a growing season of less than five months and only supports grazing systems based on drought-resistant native pastures, trees and shrubs.

Northern regions receive the bulk of their rainfall during the summer while southern regions have a predominantly winter rainfall. Most cropping regions have a growing season of 5–9 months and intensive agricultural production occurs in regions with a growing season of 9–12 months. Australia has many climates including:

- tropical
- subtropical
- temperate
- alpine
- Mediterranean
- arid regions.

Mean and standard deviation of rainfall and maximum and minimum temperatures in local and contrasting regions

The average rainfall and temperature directly affect the type of production that can be conducted in a region.

The mean or average

The mean is the average of all scores. For example, for the score 1, 2, 3, 4, 5

The mean $= \dfrac{1+2+3+4+5}{5}$

The sample standard deviation measures the variance or spread around the mean and equals the square root of the sample variance (refer to Chapter 10 for additional information).

Table 11.12	Temperature and rainfall of different regions of Australia		
City	**Min. Temp**	**Max. Temp**	**Rainfall**
New South Wales			
Coffs Harbour	14°C	23°C	1679 mm
Sydney	14°C	22°C	1213 mm
Armidale	7°C	20°C	791 mm
Penrith	14°C	22°C	696 mm
Wagga Wagga	9°C	22°C	566 mm
Broken Hill	12°C	24°C	245 mm
Queensland			
Brisbane	14°C	26°C	1061 mm
Mackay	18°C	27°C	1667 mm
Cairns	20°C	29°C	2223 mm
Townsville	18°C	29°C	1144 mm
Tasmania			
Hobart	8.3°C	16.9°C	616 mm
Launceston	7.2°C	18.4°C	666 mm
Devonport	8.1°C	16.8°C	778 mm
Strahan	7.9°C	16.5°C	1458 mm

Source: Bureau of Meteorology

11.13 Average rainfall of different regions

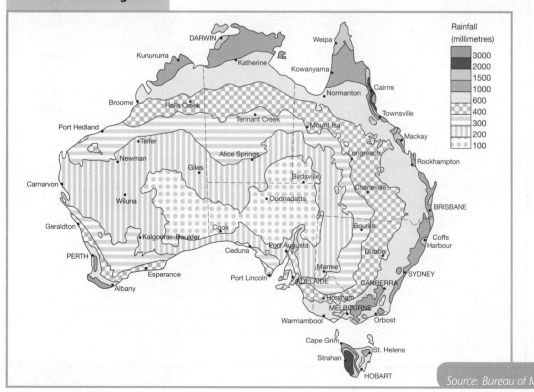

Source: Bureau of Meteorology

11.14 Maximum temperatures of different regions

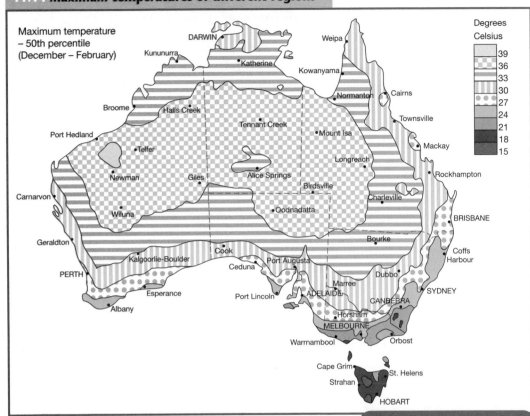

Maximum temperature
– 50th percentile
(December – February)

Degrees Celsius

39
36
33
30
27
24
21
18
15

Source: Bureau of Meteorology

11.15 Minimum temperatures of different regions

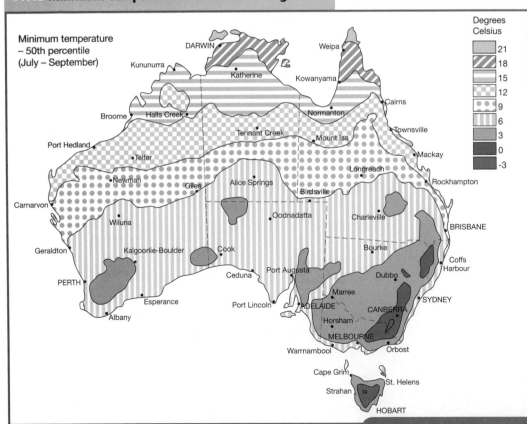

Minimum temperature
– 50th percentile
(July – September)

Degrees Celsius

21
18
15
12
9
6
3
0
-3

Source: Bureau of Meteorology

Frequency of wet, normal and dry years in the local area and a contrasting region

Extreme rainfall events have become more common in Australia during the twentieth century. The figure below illustrates the percentage of Australia experiencing extreme wet conditions [11.16] (———— – above 90th percentile of annual total) and extreme dry conditions (———— – below 10th percentile) in each year from 1900–2000.

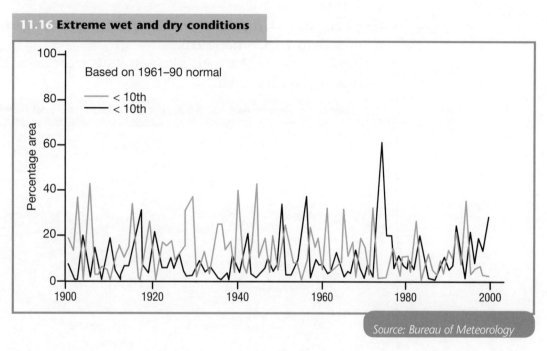

11.16 Extreme wet and dry conditions

Source: Bureau of Meteorology

The figure below [11.17] shows the percentage change in extreme daily rainfall from 1910–1995, as defined by the 99th percentile or the top one per cent.

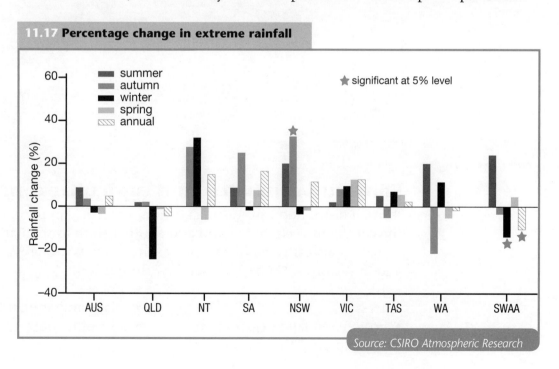

11.17 Percentage change in extreme rainfall

Source: CSIRO Atmospheric Research

Frequency of hot, normal and cool years in the local area and a contrasting region

A few statistics related to temperature frequency are listed below.

• Each decade has been warmer than the previous decade since the 1950s.
• Australian annual average daily maximum temperatures have increased by 0.75°C since 1910.
• Australian annual average daily mean temperatures have increased by 0.9°C since 1910.
• Australian annual average overnight minimum temperatures have warmed by more than 1.1°C since 1910.
• 2010 and 2011 were Australia's coolest years recorded since 2001 due to two consecutive La Niña events.

11.18 **Climatic zones in Australia based on temperature and humidity**

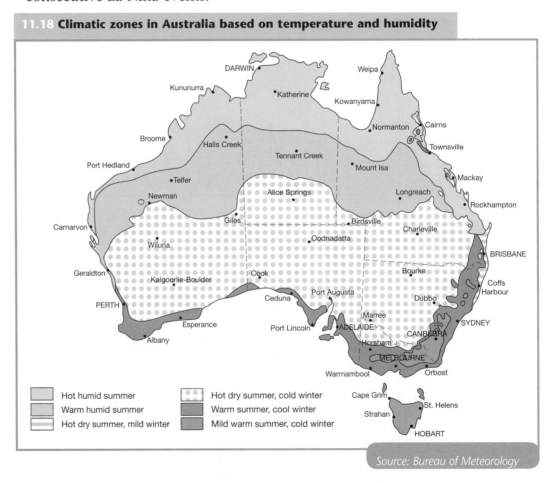

Hot humid summer
Warm humid summer
Hot dry summer, mild winter
Hot dry summer, cold winter
Warm summer, cool winter
Mild warm summer, cold winter

Source: Bureau of Meteorology

Climate variability and agriculture production

Rainfall distribution in Australia is non-uniform. Approximately one third of the continent is classed as arid and another third as semi-arid. Australia's climate is also affected by extreme events such as droughts, floods, fires, frosts and dust storms. Climatic variability can result in:

• risk
• stress
• erosion and land degradation
• bankruptcy of the farmer.

• uncertainty
• plant and animal death
• loss of income

Variability of climate in different geographical regions of Australia

Variability of rainfall is lowest on the coastal regions and highest in the arid inland desert regions of Australia.

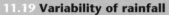

11.19 Variability of rainfall

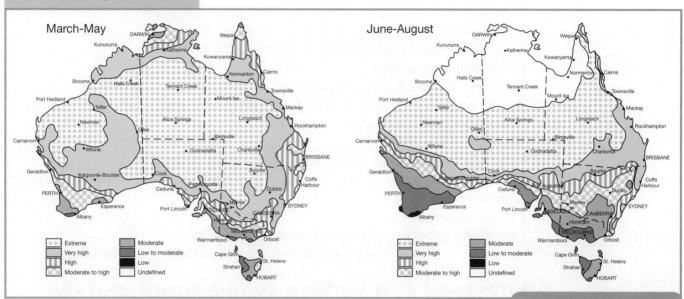

Source: Bureau of Meteorology

Effects of climate change on production

Research evidence of long-term climate change

Evidence that supports the belief that our climate is changing includes:
- global records of surface temperatures from the mid-late nineteenth century
- climatic changes inferred from indicators that are affected by climate, including vegetation, ice cores and sea levels
- changes in settlement and agricultural patterns, for example archaeological evidence, historical documents and the collapse of civilizations
- changes in the size of glaciers
- changes in the type, distribution and coverage of vegetation, for example 300 million years ago rainforests covered the equatorial region of Europe and America
- pollen analysis, for example the type of pollen found in the sediment of lakes or river deltas show changes in plant communities caused by climate change
- analysis of tree ring growth patterns, for example thick rings indicate a fertile, well-watered growing period, while thin, narrow rings indicate a time of lower rainfall
- ice cores, for example ice drilled from the Antarctic ice sheet show a link between temperature and global sea level variations
- analysing beetles and fish remains specific to a climate for evidence of past environments.

Changes in rainfall

The southwest of Western Australia has experienced long-term reductions in rainfall during winter. There has been also been a trend towards increased spring and summer monsoonal rainfall across Australia's north, higher than normal rainfall across the centre, and decreased late autumn and winter rainfall across the south.

Our climate is changing and projections suggest that there will be:
• decreases in rainfall for southern and eastern mainland Australia
• a rise in average temperatures from 0.6 to 1.5°C by 2030
• increased evaporation
• changes in rainfall and temperature patterns throughout the year
• an increase in the number of hot days and warm nights, and a decline in cool days and cold nights
• below average runoff
• increase in frequency of extremely hot and dry years
• increased frequency of extreme weather events, for example floods, droughts and severe storms
• rising sea levels
• increased incidence of tropical diseases and pests
• changes in agricultural production to allow for changes in the climate.

Effects of sea surface temperature and the SOI on Australia's climate

The Southern Oscillation Index (or SOI) indicates the development of El Niño or La Niña events in the Pacific Ocean. The South American El Niño current is caused by interactions between the ocean and the atmosphere and alters weather patterns across the world. SOI is calculated using the mean sea level pressure differences between Tahiti and Darwin.

11.20 Areas affected by El Niño

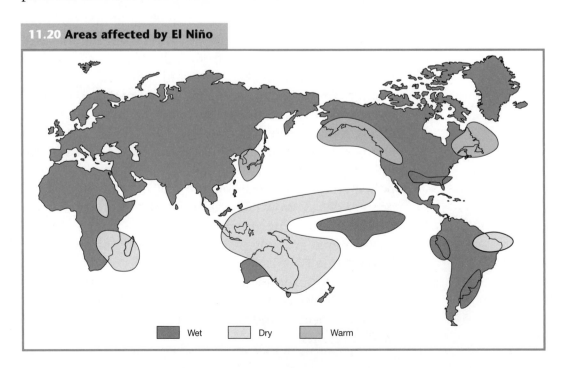

Wet   Dry   Warm

Negative values indicate an El Niño event and this results in:
- the warming of the central and eastern tropical Pacific Ocean
- decrease in the strength of the Pacific trade winds
- less winter and spring rainfall over eastern Australia and the Top End.
  Positive values of the SOI are typical of a La Niña episode. This results in:
- stronger Pacific trade winds
- warmer sea temperatures to the north of Australia
- waters in the central and eastern tropical Pacific Ocean become cooler
- eastern and northern Australia are wetter than normal.

Crop yields and the SOI

Crop yields have been directly correlated to the SOI as indicated in the following figure [11.21].

11.21 SOI and wheat yields

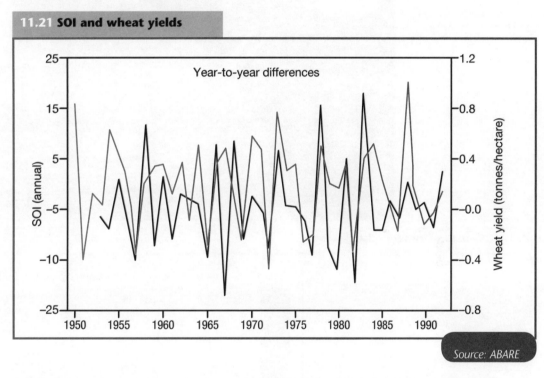

Source: ABARE

Peanut producers have found that when the November–December SOI phase is positive there is an 80 per cent chance of exceeding average yields. This has allowed the industry to adjust strategically for the increased volume of production. In drier years producers use management practices to conserve moisture by using summer weed control, minimum tillage and sowing early with long season varieties.

The greenhouse gases: carbon dioxide, methane and nitrous oxides

Greenhouse gases absorb and emit radiation. The primary greenhouse gases in the Earth's atmosphere are water vapour, carbon dioxide, methane, nitrous oxide and ozone. The burning of fossil fuels and land use changes such as clearing have promoted the releases of these gases and the warming of the Earth.

Effects of the greenhouse gases include:
- changing weather patterns, for example higher temperatures and shifting climate patterns
- warming of the oceans
- glaciers melting
- an increase in sea levels
- a change in the incidence and intensity of storms.

11.22 The greenhouse effect

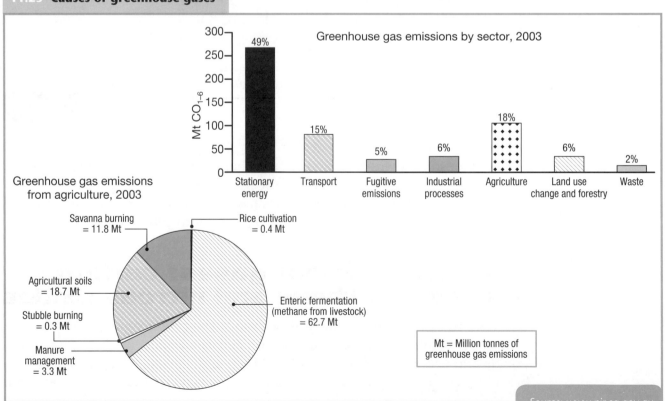

11.23 Causes of greenhouse gases

Greenhouse gas emissions by sector, 2003

Sector	Percentage
Stationary energy	49%
Transport	15%
Fugitive emissions	5%
Industrial processes	6%
Agriculture	18%
Land use change and forestry	6%
Waste	2%

Greenhouse gas emissions from agriculture, 2003

- Savanna burning = 11.8 Mt
- Rice cultivation = 0.4 Mt
- Agricultural soils = 18.7 Mt
- Stubble burning = 0.3 Mt
- Manure management = 3.3 Mt
- Enteric fermentation (methane from livestock) = 62.7 Mt

Mt = Million tonnes of greenhouse gas emissions

Source: www.pir.sa.gov.au

Carbon dioxide

Carbon dioxide is a colourless gas derived from:
• volcanic eruptions
• ocean–atmosphere exchange
• animal and plant respiration
• the burning of fossil fuels
• deforestation.

The burning of fossil fuels has resulted in a 40 per cent increase in the concentration of carbon dioxide in the atmosphere. Fossil fuels such as wood, coal, oil and natural gas are used for industrial, residential and commercial uses, and transportation. The concentration of CO_2 in the atmosphere in 2011 was 390 parts per million – higher than at any time for the past 800 000 years.

11.24 Carbon emissions

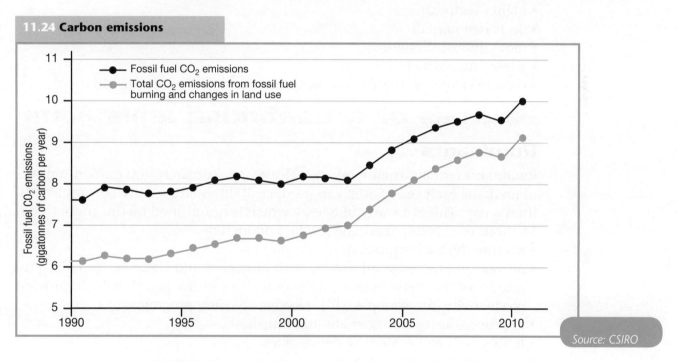

Source: CSIRO

Nitrous oxide

Nitrous oxide naturally occurs in the atmosphere. Human activities such as agriculture, fossil fuel combustion, wastewater management and industrial processes are increasing N_2O levels. Nitrous oxide is released by:
• the use of synthetic fertilisers
• the breakdown of livestock manure and urine
• burning fuels, for example motor vehicles
• industry, for example nitrous oxide is a by-product of nitric acid production (which is used to make synthetic fertilisers and fibres).

Methane CH_4

Natural sources of methane include:
• livestock
• geological emissions
• termites
• fires
• bodies of water
• wetlands.

Methane is produced when organic material decomposes. Humans have increased methane levels by:

- extracting it from coal
- livestock production, for example ruminant animals release methane
- bacteria in rice paddies which break down organic matter
- decomposition of garbage in landfills.

Vegetation changes, land clearing and its effect on climate

Land clearing describes the removal of native vegetation in Australia. This can result in:

- greenhouse gas emissions
- higher temperatures
- decreased rainfall
- more intense droughts
- altered humidity levels
- climate change as there is no vegetation to absorb carbon dioxide.

Sources of greenhouse emissions

Ruminants

Ruminants ferment their food and release approximately 100 million tonnes of methane each year. Sheep can produce 30 litres and a dairy cow up to 200 litres a day. This is a waste of energy which is not utilised by the animal. Methods of reducing methane production include:

- altering the feed composition
- introducing methane inhibitors, both biological and chemical, to reduce the activity of the methanogenic microorganisms in the gut, thereby improving productivity, for example with selective breeding programs
- improve grazing management and nutrition
- testing soils and correcting deficiencies
- providing nutrient supplements
- controlling pests and diseases of stock
- providing good quality water
- improving genetics and reproductive efficiency.

Nitrogen fertiliser

Artificial and manure-based fertilisers add nitrogen to the soil. This can be broken down by bacteria to release nitrous oxide.

Climate change and water

Storing water resources

Agriculture consumes 65 per cent of water in Australia. Of the states, NSW and Queensland use the most water. Twenty-nine per cent of Australia's agricultural water comes from irrigation channels; 27 per cent from rivers, creeks and lakes; 21 per cent from groundwater; and 18 per cent from farm dams and tanks.

Traditionally, many irrigation systems were:
- developed in inappropriate regions
- had problems of water logging, land or river salinisation
- had low returns
- had small unviable farm sizes
- had inefficient irrigation systems
- were allocated water at the expense of rivers and waterways.

In 1994 Australia's National Water Commission separated land from water rights to increase the efficiency of water distribution. Water access entitlements, allocations and trading were key elements to water reforms in Australia.

Water trading

Water trading is the process of buying, selling, leasing or exchanging water access entitlements (permanent trade) or water allocations (temporary trade).

A water access entitlement, such as a water licence, allows farmers a share of water. A water allocation indicates the volume of water that is allocated in a given season. High prices encourage users to allocate resources to the most profitable activities.

11.25 Water consumption in agriculture, by activity

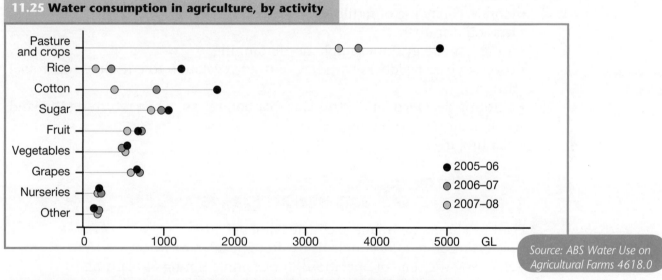

Source: ABS Water Use on Agricultural Farms 4618.0

11.26 Sources of agricultural water, Murray-Darling Basin 2005–2007

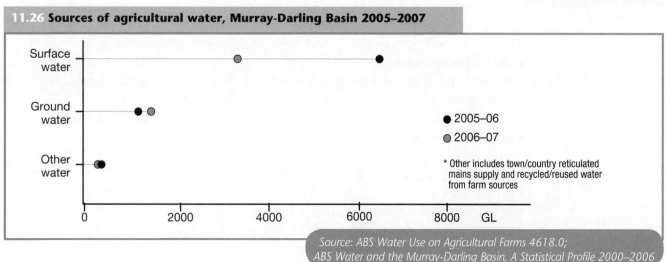

Source: ABS Water Use on Agricultural Farms 4618.0;
ABS Water and the Murray-Darling Basin, A Statistical Profile 2000–2006

Reducing greenhouse gas emissions

Methods which could be used include:
- not burning fossil fuels
- using alternative sources of energy, for example solar energy
- reducing methane emissions by livestock
- sequestering carbon in soils
- replanting trees
- pollution controls
- education and sustainable development
- reducing wastage and increasing efficiency of production.

Sequestering carbon in soils

Carbon sequestration is the process of removing carbon from the atmosphere and depositing it in the soil. This would reduce the levels of greenhouse gases and climate change as the soil is an effective carbon sink. Other methods farmers could use to reduce energy wastage and carbon emissions include:
- increasing the efficiency of farm operations, for example use plants and animals suited to the environment
- more accurate use of fertilisers
- less soil disturbance
- using less energy, for example no-till farming
- covering bare paddocks with hay or dead vegetation to encourage microbial action
- restoring degraded land – this slows carbon release while returning the land to agriculture or other uses
- planting trees.

Managing climate variability in plant and animal production

Plant producers can manage climate variability by:
- plant breeding, for example using drought-tolerant wheat
- changing the time of operations, for example timing of planting
- using irrigation, for example drip irrigation
- conserving moisture, for example using mulches
- monitoring moisture levels and planning operations accordingly
- altering crop density
- diversifying their enterprises, for example both plants and animals.
  Animal producers can manage a variable climate by:
- breed selection, for example drought-tolerant breeds such as Brahman
- grazing strategies, for example cell grazing
- altering stocking rates
- conserving fodder, for example hay
- providing shelter or shade areas
- new enterprises, for example Boer goats
- diversification, for example native animals and plants
- financial analysis and whole farm planning.

Analysis of research on climate variability and its management

Research has had a significant effect on agricultural production. However, it must be conducted properly to ensure that it is valid. Factors that should be considered include:

- design of the study (how the experiment is set up)
- aim (what the scientist is trying to prove or find)
- hypothesis (what the scientist believes will be the result)
- methodology (how the experiment is conducted or performed)
- use of controls (untreated samples used for comparison)
- randomisation (experiment set up without bias or preference)
- replication (use of many samples to increase accuracy)
- standardisation (removing variation in the experiment, for example using the same age, sex and breed of sheep)
- collection of data, for example the number of samples and the size of the population studied
- time-frame, for example the longer the experiment and the more times it is repeated, the greater the accuracy
- depth of information, for example time-frame, number of samples and size of population
- use of second-hand data, for example is the data from an accurate source such as scientific research or from a newspaper article
- accuracy of collection, including accuracy of equipment and measurement
- use of qualitative (without measurement) and quantitative methods (including measurement)
- presentation of data, for example forms of presentation such as graphs and tables
- analysis of the data, for example statistical analysis
- validity, for example was the research conducted by a company that makes profits from the chemical being tested
- appropriateness, for example is the experiment relevant
- ethics, for example animal welfare issues
- conclusion, recommendations and the need for further research.

3 Farming for the 21st century

Issues relating to the development of technology

Research and development was initially funded by governments across the world. International research centres developed global food crops such as rice, wheat, corn, cassava, potatoes, millet and beans. National centres provided advice and counselling to farmers, and this diffused knowledge into each country.

Advances in science and biotechnology, economic globalisation and trade liberalisation encouraged multinational corporations to market products such as seeds, agrochemicals and agricultural machinery. This motivated private investment in agricultural research and technology, particularly by international corporations who had access to world markets.

Factors affecting the development of technologies include:

- sources of funding
- legislation governing research
- animal welfare issues
- plant breeding rights and patents
- cost of research
- profitability
- consumer demand
- price.

Agriculture and new technology

Technology that is used in agriculture includes:

- satellites, for example satellite imaging and global positioning systems used in cultivation, tracking and fertiliser use
- mobile phones
- computers, for example the Internet, weather forecasting and monitoring, Spatial Information Exchange website (to observe the local area and its vegetation), and marketing systems, for example AuctionsPlus Livestock website
- lasers for levelling and land preparation
- biotechnology, for example transgenic cotton, soybean and canola
- electronic identification systems, for example NLIS (National Livestock Identification System)
- robotics, for example milking and shearing machinery.

Some of these uses of technology are illustrated below [11.27–11.30].

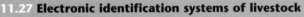

11.27 Electronic identification systems of livestock

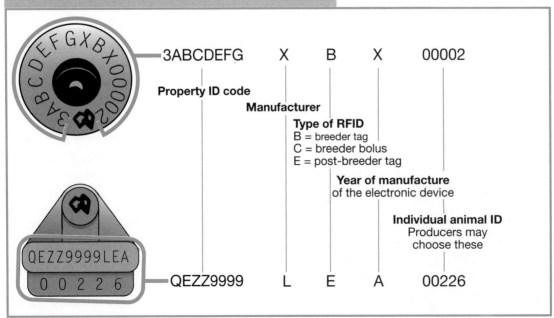

3ABCDEFG   X   B   X   00002

Property ID code

Manufacturer

Type of RFID
B = breeder tag
C = breeder bolus
E = post-breeder tag

Year of manufacture
of the electronic device

Individual animal ID
Producers may
choose these

QEZZ9999   L   E   A   00226

11.28 The use of GPS systems in cropping

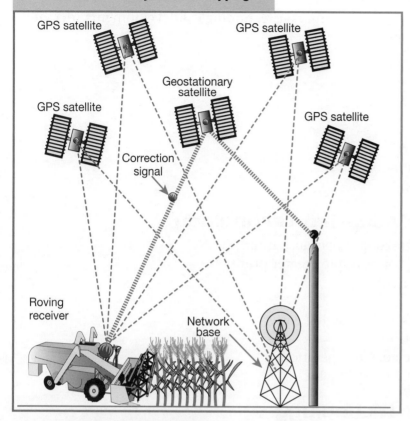

11.29 Robotic sheep shearer

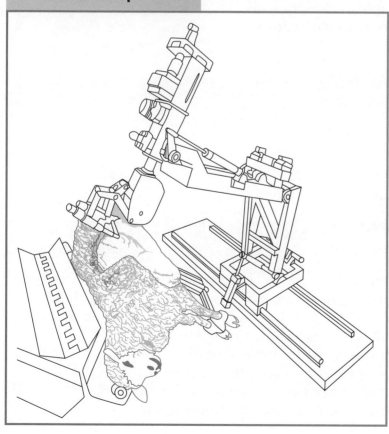

11.30 Genetic engineering of crops

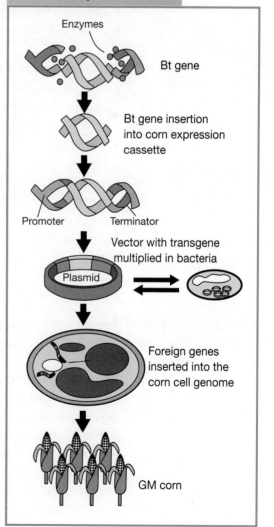

Marketing technology

Methods that companies use to market technological developments include:
- advertising and promotion
- newspapers
- radio
- the Internet
- field days
- trial sites
- samples for farmers
- agricultural consultants
- agricultural shows.

Reasons for adopting technology

Technology has been adopted because it has:
- economic benefit, for example greater profits
- environmental benefit
- social benefit
- reduced workloads and made life easier
- provided information
- improved the efficiency of operations
- increased productivity and yields.

Examples of technology

Technology used in Australia includes:
- machinery, for example tractors, headers and motorbikes
- irrigation systems, for example hydroponics
- herbicides
- pesticides
- fertilisers
- breeding of plants and animals
- genetic engineering
- computers
- synthetic fibres
- satellites
- refrigeration and transportation systems.

Importance and analysis of research

Research has had a significant effect on agricultural production. However, it must be conducted properly to ensure that it is valid. Factors that should be considered include:
- design of the study (how the experiment is set up)
- aim (what the scientist is trying to prove or find)
- hypothesis (what the scientist believes will be the result)
- methodology (how the experiment is conducted or performed)
- use of controls (untreated samples used for comparison)

- randomisation (experiment set up without bias or preference)
- replication (use of many samples to increase accuracy)
- standardisation (removing variation in the experiment, for example using the same age, sex and breed of sheep)
- collection of data, for example the number of samples and the size of the population studied
- time-frame, for example the longer the experiment and the more times it is repeated, the greater the accuracy
- depth of information, for example time-frame, number of samples and size of population
- use of second-hand data, for example is the data from an accurate source such as scientific research or from a newspaper article
- accuracy of collection, including accuracy of equipment and measurement
- use of qualitative (without measurement) and quantitative methods (including measurement)
- presentation of data, for example forms of presentation such as graphs and tables
- analysis of the data, for example statistical analysis
- validity, for example was the research conducted by a company that makes profits from the chemical being tested
- appropriateness, for example is the experiment relevant
- ethics, for example animal welfare issues
- conclusion, recommendations and the need for further research.

Useful Internet sites

australia.gov.au/directories/australia/agriculture/web-resources-list
www.aglinks.com.au
www.agriculture.gov.au
www.csiro.au
www.daff.gov.au/abares
www.dpi.nsw.gov.au
www.dpi.qld.gov.au
www.dpi.vic.gov.au
www.dpiw.tas.gov.au
www.elders.com.au
www.farmonline.com.au
www.hsc.csu.edu.au
www.kondiningroup.com.au
www.pir.sa.gov.au
www.wesfarmers.com.au

Essay and Examination Techniques

12

chapter

In this chapter you will learn:

- how to write an essay
- how to study for examinations
- about study techniques
- how to prepare for an examination

Writing an essay

Preparation

Before attempting any question do the following:
• Read the questions thoroughly before selecting an essay.
• Spend the same amount of time on equally valued questions.
• Do not spend more time on one essay at the expense of another. It is easier to get 50 per cent each for two essays than 100 per cent for one essay.
• Always try to finish an essay.
• Before time runs out quickly list the relevant points if you will not finish.

Selecting an essay

• Do not select an essay because it is short and simple to understand. It may be too specific and difficult to write about for 30 minutes.
• Never ignore an essay question because it is long. These essays are often quite simple and have many areas where marks can be easily obtained.
• Underline or highlight the key words in each essay.
• Choose an essay question carefully and make sure you know enough about the topic area.

Planning the essay

• Underline or highlight the key words in the question.
• Divide the essay into its individual questions or sections.
• Give equal weighting to each part of the essay.
• Plan your essay.

• Put your plan on the first page of your answer sheet because if your do not complete your essay you will be given marks for your plan.
• Make sure your essay has three main sections:
  – **Introduction**
  – **Body**
  – **Conclusion**

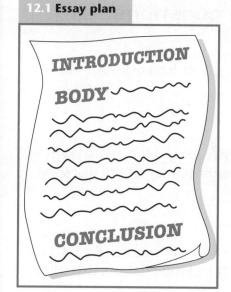

12.1 Essay plan

INTRODUCTION
BODY
CONCLUSION

Introduction

Introduce the topic area and outline in one or two paragraphs what you are going to write.

Body

Give a detailed explanation of the points you have in your plan and include examples and diagrams.

Conclusion

The conclusion should be one to two paragraphs in length and it should summarise your essay. It must be interesting and should not include new information.

Sample essay 1

Discuss the factors involved in the genesis of soil. Describe the composition and properties of a major soil type in your region and comment on its probable genesis.

Underline key words

Discuss the <u>factors</u> involved in the <u>genesis of soil</u>. Describe the <u>composition</u> and <u>properties</u> of a <u>major soil type</u> in <u>your region</u> and comment on its probable <u>genesis</u>.

Rewrite the essay as simple questions

1 How are soils formed?
2 What factors affect soil formation?
3 What is the composition and properties of a major soil type?
4 How was that soil formed?

Sample essay 2

'Agriculturists tend to exploit soils, changing their physical and chemical nature. Soil management practices which conserve the soil and improve its fertility should be developed.' Discuss this statement.

Highlight key words

Agriculturists tend to <mark>exploit soils</mark>, changing their <mark>physical</mark> and <mark>chemical nature</mark>. Soil <mark>management practices</mark> which <mark>conserve</mark> the soil and <mark>improve</mark> its <mark>fertility</mark> should be developed.

Rewrite the essay as simple questions

1 How has agriculture damaged soils?
2 How has their physical and chemical nature been changed?
3 How can the farmer conserve the soil and increase its fertility level?

Sample essay 3

Discuss the significant structural differences between the alimentary tracts of monogastrics and ruminants and explain the terms fermentation, digestion and absorption.

Underline key words

Discuss the significant <u>structural differences</u> between the <u>alimentary tracts</u> of <u>monogastrics</u> and <u>ruminants</u> and explain the terms <u>fermentation</u>, <u>digestion</u> and <u>absorption</u>.

Rewrite the essay as simple questions

1 What are monogastrics and ruminants, giving examples of both?
2 How are their digestive systems structurally different?
3 Define fermentation, digestion and absorption.

Dos and don'ts in essay writing

Do
- make a draft essay
- give equal weighting to every part of the essay question
- write clearly and concisely
- ensure material is relevant
- use point form
- use paragraphs and headings
- underline headings and key words
- use diagrams and graphs
- label diagrams and indicate what they show
- give many examples and list the most important ones first
- make sure the conclusion is interesting and has impact because this is the last thing read by the marker before marks are allocated
- type your essays
- ensure you have back up files and a hard copy if using a computer
- attend essay writing workshops at TAFE, Universities or Colleges. Always proofread your essay and look for the following mistakes:
- lack of clarity
- incorrect sentences
- vagueness
- poor sentence structure
- omitted words
- illegibility
- punctuation errors
- spelling errors
- lack of examples
- unnecessary repetition.

Don't
- use slang or abbreviations in an essay
- write 'I think' in an essay
- write 'it is obvious' or 'I have shown or proven' in an essay
- waffle
- waste time writing long-winded, boring sentences
- use humour as markers might not appreciate your particular sense of humour
- make broad sweeping generalisations, such as, 'all farmers are poor'
- introduce new information in the conclusion – it should be a summary of your essay.

Studying for examinations

Amount of study

The number of hours a student should study depends on interest in the subject and the difficulty of the work. It is recommended, however, that students study for at least three hours per night across all their subjects.

When to study

• Draw up a study schedule based on your own commitments and when you can study most efficiently. An example is provided in [12.2]

12.2 Study timetable

Mon	Tue	Wed	Thu	Fri	Sat	Sun
English		Work	Sport	Maths		History
	Biology		Business Studies	Sport	Ag	

• Divide your time equally between all your subjects.
• Give difficult subjects additional time if possible.
• Break up large blocks of study time to offset fatigue and allow yourself time to absorb the work.
• Alternate between difficult and simpler subjects.

Physical setting for study

12.3 Study area

Good light

Good desk

Good chair

• Use a specific area for study that is well ventilated.
• Use a good desk and comfortable chair.
• Use good lighting.
• Keep physically active to help you concentrate on the work, for example take notes, underscore revision notes or talk aloud.
• Keep away from distractions such as television or friends.

Study methods

The most common study methods are:
• talking
• reading
• skimming
• summarising.

Talking

Asking questions and discussing work can help clarify difficult concepts.

Reading

Reading notes, set texts or library references can reinforce work.

Skimming work

Glancing at contents, indexes, illustrations, tables and charts can help in revising work.

Summarising

Making a master outline from notes, textbooks and supplementary information can aid revision and reinforce memory.

Boost to study

Studying can sometimes be more effective by using one of the study methods:
• SQ3R method
• PQRST method

The SQ3R method

Survey – look over the material.
Question – pose questions about the work.
Read – read the material several times.
Recite – recall what you have read.
Revise – constantly revise the work.

The PQRST method

Preview – read over the study material.
Question – ask yourself questions about the material and determine your weak spots.
Read – read the material several times.
State – state the material in your own words.
Test – test yourself on the work.

Preparing for an examination

- Make your own study notes.
- Revise previous examination papers.
- Record the date, time and location of the examination.
- Familiarise yourself with the layout, time and type of questions usually asked in the examination.
- Reduce your recreation time.
- Get plenty of sleep.
- Do not use pills to keep yourself awake.
- Check that all your equipment, such as your calculator, is working properly.
- Arrive early before the start of the examination.
- Keep away from nervous people.
- Do not guess examination questions. It is better to prepare each topic as a whole than risk losing all your marks.
- Have a positive attitude towards the examination.

During the examination

- Read the instructions carefully, that is:
  - duration of the examination
  - number of questions to be answered
  - compulsory questions
  - allocation of marks
  - instructions for filling in answer books.
- Read the whole examination before starting.
- Mark the questions you are going to attempt.
- Allocate your time.
- Answer the easiest questions to boost your confidence.
- Plan your answer before you attempt it.
- Make sure you answer all compulsory questions.
- Check that papers are in the right order and are well-secured.
- Make sure your name or identification number appears on all answer sheets.
- Never leave an examination early.
- Always revise your work and look for mistakes or ways of improving your answer.

Find-a-word

Chapter 2

Find-a-word

Y	T	N	I	A	T	R	E	C	N	U	S	T	U	P	T	U	O	O	G
L	S	D	E	E	W	N	L	P	T	U	O	S	E	S	A	E	S	I	D
R	B	P	R	O	C	E	S	L	B	N	I	A	H	C	D	O	O	F	S
U	O	T	N	E	M	N	O	R	I	V	N	E	O	R	P	E	M	M	O
T	S	I	N	F	O	R	L	D	G	M	R	P	K	Y	S	D	A	A	C
A	E	L	A	R	U	T	A	N	E	S	A	S	S	O	Y	S	T	N	E
N	R	M	P	S	M	W	E	T	L	S	I	R	P	R	R	N	O	N	E
Y	U	A	R	U	T	E	S	E	R	R	N	M	A	E	E	I	R	T	L
G	T	N	O	B	I	Y	T	E	R	I	O	D	C	M	T	W	S	N	B
O	L	A	E	S	S	A	M	P	O	C	N	U	N	A	O	S	E	E	A
L	U	D	D	O	M	U	E	S	E	U	D	R	M	O	U	E	S	M	N
O	C	G	C	I	S	S	C	D	O	O	E	R	F	B	O	P	S	E	I
N	O	E	L	N	T	L	N	B	R	V	O	L	I	O	S	B	E	G	A
H	N	C	O	U	T	C	A	P	O	F	N	H	C	E	T	K	C	A	T
C	O	C	P	O	S	U	L	G	N	L	Y	E	N	O	M	R	O	N	S
E	M	N	P	U	Y	S	A	I	S	M	E	T	S	Y	S	A	R	A	U
T	I	S	T	S	E	P	B	S	O	S	T	E	K	R	A	M	P	M	S

SYSTEMS	RISK
WEEDS	INPUTS
UNCERTAINTY	DISEASES
OUTPUTS	CLIMATE
MANAGEMENT	PROCESSES
SOIL	GOVERNMENT
BOUNDARY	INFORMATION
MONEY	NATURAL
PESTS	ECOSYSTEM
SUSTAINABLE	TECHNOLOGY
PRODUCERS	FOODCHAIN
ENVIRONMENT	CONSUMERS
BALANCE	MARKETS
DECOMPOSE	MONOCULTURES
DEBT	

Chapter 3

Find-a-word

F	R	O	D	O	I	R	E	P	G	N	I	W	O	R	G	C	S	S	G
R	E	N	O	I	T	A	G	I	R	R	I	M	D	T	S	L	R	L	L
N	A	E	N	A	R	R	E	T	I	D	E	M	A	N	R	S	E	L	A
D	I	R	A	E	D	P	W	I	D	D	M	U	O	T	K	H	L	A	S
L	A	C	I	P	O	R	T	B	U	S	E	S	S	A	T	I	K	F	E
M	V	H	N	O	I	T	A	R	O	P	A	V	E	G	A	M	N	N	S
U	A	U	L	V	T	A	W	R	A	E	I	R	N	T	E	G	I	I	U
L	P	M	I	R	A	E	I	R	S	S	B	E	T	N	I	Y	R	A	O
C	O	I	E	A	T	R	N	I	Y	D	L	L	I	T	T	R	P	R	H
H	R	S	M	A	Y	U	D	G	N	Y	T	H	O	I	N	O	S	E	S
A	E	F	M	P	L	T	B	I	A	U	S	C	D	E	L	W	L	V	S
D	H	I	F	O	A	A	W	D	L	N	E	I	R	A	F	L	D	I	A
I	L	X	Z	R	R	R	T	C	U	S	M	H	C	M	A	D	A	T	L
C	T	O	D	A	O	E	S	S	E	U	R	I	A	F	L	S	Y	C	G
R	S	S	N	S	T	P	E	L	H	H	P	S	N	P	M	E	L	E	L
A	O	E	I	E	S	M	R	I	N	O	R	I	L	A	L	S	E	F	I
I	R	V	W	A	A	E	O	M	R	I	A	P	D	E	H	E	N	F	A
N	F	A	T	S	P	T	F	T	G	R	N	R	I	W	O	N	S	E	H

TEMPERATURE
DAMS
DESERT
ARID
MEDITERRANEAN
TROPICAL
SUBTROPICAL
PASTORAL
FOREST
IRRIGATION
GLASSHOUSE
WINDBREAKS
MULCH
SPRINKLER

EFFECTIVE RAINFALL
RAINFALL
FROST
HUMIDITY
EVAPORATION
WIND
HAIL
SNOW
SUNSHINE
DAYLENGTH
SEASONS
CLIMATE
GROWING PERIOD

Chapter 5

Find-a-word

S	E	R	I	F	E	L	E	C	O	T	P	F	I	S	P	O	R	I	F
A	C	S	L	A	C	I	M	E	H	C	L	Z	G	E	T	A	W	E	B
N	H	D	S	S	E	N	F	A	E	D	S	N	O	S	I	O	P	T	U
I	A	E	T	E	E	S	P	M	E	K	I	B	R	O	T	O	M	U	R
M	I	A	R	K	D	L	O	O	R	R	S	H	E	A	L	M	C	C	L
S	L	B	A	E	R	L	W	T	E	G	D	Z	N	W	O	R	D	O	S
L	B	N	T	N	O	U	E	D	N	I	E	L	E	W	T	S	T	R	E
O	S	S	R	R	W	B	N	I	S	F	S	L	A	N	Y	L	S	T	N
O	R	L	E	U	G	I	C	L	S	G	B	S	X	A	F	O	I	C	I
T	O	A	L	B	R	N	E	E	B	A	N	L	W	A	L	A	R	E	L
R	T	M	F	G	E	U	S	M	M	I	G	R	E	I	H	S	X	L	R
E	C	I	I	F	F	R	I	M	A	F	E	D	S	C	T	G	B	E	E
W	A	N	R	F	O	N	A	H	I	T	G	N	I	R	A	E	H	S	W
O	R	A	S	H	A	L	C	R	A	M	O	T	O	R	B	G	C	S	O
P	T	T	I	I	F	P	O	W	T	O	R	E	G	U	A	L	A	M	P

TRACTOR
ELECTROCUTE
MOTORBIKE
CHAINSAW
FLAMMABLE
SILOS
GRINDER
CHEMICALS
POWER TOOLS
AUGER
SNAKE
FENCING
WATERWAYS

POWERLINES
ROPS
DROWN
ANIMALS
DEAFNESS
FUELS
FIRE
PTO
POISONS
BULLS
SHEARING
HORSES
RIFLE

Chapter 8

Find-a-word

G	S	E	B	N	I	A	R	G	E	V	A	L	T	O	L	D	E	E	E
E	L	W	E	G	A	R	O	F	R	E	F	I	E	H	S	K	C	I	T
B	A	E	R	M	E	T	A	N	I	C	C	A	V	D	R	W	F	D	E
L	E	R	E	E	T	A	R	T	N	E	C	N	O	C	O	V	O	L	E
A	V	E	T	E	T	A	R	T	S	A	C	S	S	C	C	E	L	O	F
R	D	D	S	E	S	A	E	S	I	D	T	F	I	F	O	A	L	E	R
B	H	D	U	P	M	D	C	L	S	E	H	H	G	I	E	W	U	G	E
N	C	O	M	A	N	C	L	C	K	E	E	O	L	E	B	L	C	A	E
O	N	F	S	A	M	U	A	R	S	G	I	E	A	S	C	M	G	L	T
I	E	H	R	S	B	A	A	A	E	E	R	D	G	E	E	J	A	I	S
T	R	B	T	T	S	M	H	Y	M	O	P	T	A	R	N	O	L	S	F
A	D	U	E	K	T	C	E	F	C	S	A	A	T	U	T	I	I	D	E
T	R	G	R	U	R	K	S	S	A	N	S	O	R	T	F	N	S	R	V
S	E	A	E	U	N	S	T	A	A	W	T	L	A	S	S	A	Y	A	L
E	M	H	P	I	E	A	T	E	R	E	U	B	E	A	R	T	A	Y	A
G	B	E	P	R	F	T	W	T	K	L	L	E	S	P	D	E	H	S	C

PURCHASE	DRENCH
SILAGE	SELL
MUSTER	PASTURES
JOIN	YARD
FODDER	GESTATION
DRAFT	FORAGE
CALVE	MARKETS
BLOAT	WEAN
VEAL	DISEASE
MARK	STEER
PINKEYE	BRAND
HEIFER	TICKS
WEIGH	COW
CASTRATE	BULL
EARTAG	FEEDLOT
VACCINATE	GRAIN
FATSCORE	CONCENTRATE
CULL	HAY

Glossary

adsorptive – attraction of ions or compounds to the surface of a solid

advection – horizontal transfer of energy or heat in the atmosphere

agronomists – consultant that specialises in plant production, such as a cotton agronomist

allelopathic – chemical process where some plants release toxic chemicals to inhibit the growth of other plants

altitude – height above sea level of a point or place

ammonisation – conversion of organic compounds in decaying plant material into ammonia by soil bacteria

anaerobic – chemical reaction that occurs in the absence of oxygen.

aspect – direction in which land faces, for example, land with a northerly aspect faces north

bearing strength – amount of force a soil can withstand without compaction – sandy soils have a higher bearing strength than clay textured soils

bilateral – trade agreement between two countries, such as Australia and Japan

biological control – strategy for the control of pests or disease-causing organisms that uses other living organisms rather than chemical pesticides

broadcasting – sowing of seed by hand

calving index – time between one pregnancy and the next and ensuring that a cow has a calf each year

canopy structure – layer of branches and leaves formed by plants above the ground

capillary – movement of water through a soil due to a potential gradient and surface tension

carcase – body of a slaughtered animal whose head, skin and internal organs have been removed

carcase equivalent weight – weight of an animal after slaughter and dressing

cast for age – checking animal's teeth and selling those which are old and have broken teeth

castrates – male animals whose testicles have been removed to prevent unwanted matings and aggressive behaviour

cations – positive charged ions dissolved in the soil solution

cloning – asexual reproduction that results in an identical individual

clostridial – oval or spindle shaped anaerobic bacterium that are pathogenic to humans and animals

coleoptile – protective sheath that covers the shoot of a developing grass seed

colloids – organic and inorganic matter with small particle size and large surface area

common name – everyday name used to identify a plant such as white clover

compensatory growth – accelerated growth following a period of delay in growth caused by malnutrition, pests or disease

concentration gradient – number of molecules or ions in a given volume. Gradients result in water moving from a high concentration in the roots to a low concentration in the leaves

consumer demand – quantity of goods buyers will buy at a particular price

consumers – organisms which cannot create their own energy supplies and derive it from other sources eg sheep eat grass

control – untreated sample used to compare before and after treatments

cotyledon – first leaf or leaves developed by a germinating seed

crutched – removal of wool from the breech of a sheep to prevent the accumulation of urine and faeces and flystrike

culling – to remove inferior quality animals

dags – faeces attached to the wool

decomposers – organisms such as fungi and earthworms which break down plant and animal remains to derive their energy requirements

deficiency payment – payment given to producers if the value of their produce falls below a guaranteed price

degradation – deterioration in the quality of the environment such as air, water and soil pollution, deforestation and extinction of flora and fauna

denitrifying – organisms such as bacteria which reduce nitrates to nitrites, nitrous oxide or nitrogen under anaerobic conditions to provide energy

dentition – number of permanent teeth on the lower jaw of a beast which is used to determine the age of an animal

deregulation – free trade of produce with minimal restrictions

digestibility – proportion of feed used by the animal. If a feed is 80% digestible then 20% will be lost as waste and faeces.

direct drilling – placing seed and fertiliser directly into the ground without cultivation

diversify – have a variety of enterprises

DNA – Deoxyribonucleic acid – a double helix molecule which acts as the genetic blueprint for many characteristics such as growth rate and eye and hair colour

docked – removal of the tail of an animal using a knife or ring – helps prevent flystrike by preventing the build up of urine and faeces

dormancy – period of reduced metabolic activity as in seeds and dormant buds

dressed – removal from the carcase of inedible parts such as the head, legs, skin and internal organs

dressed weight – weight of a carcase after removal of head, limbs, hide and offal

dry sheep equivalent – 1 DSE equals one dry sheep or wether per hectare – so it is a measure of the stocking rate of the land

effective rainfall – where rainfall exceeds one-third of evaporative demand

enzymes – proteins that catalyse chemical reactions and are commonly found in the digestive system of animals

evaporation – loss of water vapour from soil or water surfaces through heat and wind

evaporative demand – amount of water vapour lost from the soil

evapotranspiration – sum of evaporation from soils and evaporation from plant surfaces

exchange rate – value of the Australian dollar relative to other currencies

fallowing – leaving part of a farm free of cultivation for a period

fermentation – chemical decomposition of organic substances by microbial action

flushed – provided with additional feed

fraction – portion of the soil

FSH – follicle stimulating hormone is secreted by the pituitary gland and stimulates the growth of the graafian follicles in the ovary

gametes – reproductive cells that unite to form a zygote

gaseous exchange – refers to the movement of gas particles such as carbon dioxide and oxygen within the soil

genetic engineering – alteration of the chromosome structure of cells to control the characteristics of offspring

genetically modified food – food from plant sources modified by gene technology techniques such as food containing GM cotton, corn or potato

genotype – genetic makeup of an organism

GR site – standard site where fat levels are assessed and on lambs is 110 millimetres from the backline along the second last long rib

grid system – table of prices paid for livestock of different weights and lower prices are paid if animal is not within the required grid weight range

gross value – total worth of products

homozygous gene pairs – pair of identical genes, written as PP if they are dominant and suppress the expression of other genes or pp if they are recessive

horizons – layer of soil parallel to the surface such as topsoil and subsoil, each with their own individual characteristics

horizontal integration – farms link together at the same level of marketing to reduce production and distribution costs and to increase control over the market

immunoglobulins – group of proteins in milk that act as antibodies helping to provide the newborn with resistance to disease

incentive payment – financial reward given to encourage producers to grow a particular crop or to limit production

infiltration – downward movement of water into the soil

inoculant – dormant bacteria that is mixed as a fine dust over legume seed before sowing

inverse relationship – two factors directly affect the level of each other such as increasing oxygen levels decreases carbon dioxide levels

lactation – production of milk after the birth of offspring

latitude – angular distance north or south (on the meridian) of a location

leaching – loss of nutrients from the soil by water moving through the soil profile

legumes – plants of the leguminosae family, often used for feed, food or as a soil improving crop

leguminous – plants of the leguminosae family such as clover, peas and beans; root nodules contain rhizobium bacteria which can fix nitrogen

ley farming – use of pastures in production to maintain the fertility level of the soil

lignin – substances found in the thickened cell walls of plants that provide the plants with support

liveweight – weight of a living animal

lodge – to blow over as in the wind lodges cereal crops

lutenising hormone – chemical secreted by the pituitary gland which causes the growth of the corpus luteum in the ovary

lux – unit of measurement equal to one lumen per square metre that measures the amount of light which falls on a unit area

marbling – amount of intramuscular fat which is influenced by breed, nutrition and age

marginal cost – additional expense incurred in producing one more unit of output, such as one more hectare of wheat

marginal revenue – additional income received from producing one more unit of output

marketing alliances – formalised business and trading relationships along a marketing chain that may result in increased prices due to larger supply and control of the market

mean – arithmetic average of the scores and is the sum of all the members in the sample divided by the total number in the sample

metabolic rate – rate of the processes or chemical reactions in an animal's body

microbial – organisms which can only be seen with the aid of a microscope such as bacteria, fungi and protozoa

microclimate – specific climate created within the canopy of the crop

mineralogy – types of naturally occurring substances of set chemical composition and physical properties such as olivine, micas and feldspars present in a rock

monogastric – digestive system with a single stomach or gastric cavity such as humans

mulesing – removal of skin from the breech of a sheep – helps prevent flystrike by removing wrinkles, and preventing the accumulation of dung and urine

mycorrhiza fungi – fungi that live symbiotically with specific plants

myxomatosis – highly contagious and fatal virus disease of rabbits used to control rabbit populations

net value – monetary value of production after costs have been deducted

nitrate ions – chemical consisting of nitrogen and oxygen; salts or esters of nitric acid; used in explosives and fertilisers

nitrification – conversion of organic nitrogen compounds into nitrates by nitrifying bacteria.

normal – bell shaped curve with the majority of results in the middle and fewer results at either end of the curve

oestrous – period when ova are released from the females ovary, the animal comes on heat and mating occurs

OJD – Ovine Johnes Disease is a bacterial disease of sheep which lives in the soil and is controlled by isolating affected areas and restricting stock movement

P8 – standardised site on cattle where fat depth is measured on the carcase

pathogens – organisms that cause a disease such as viruses, bacteria and protozoa

persistent – chemical that takes many years to break down in the environment eg DDT can persist for up to 50 years in the soil.

petri dish – flat plastic or glass dish with a lid used for scientific investigations such as seed germination trials

phagocytes – part of the immune system of an animal that ingest foreign particles by engulfing them into their own cytoplasm

photosynthesis – conversion by plants of carbon dioxide and water into oxygen and energy rich glucose that provides the plant with its energy requirements

plasticity – ability to mould soils like plasticine – very plastic soils can compact and form clay pans if cultivated when wet

porosity – relative percentage of air spaces in the soil so the greater the porosity the greater the aeration, water storage and drainage in the soil

primary industry – sector of the economy related to farming, fishing, forestry and mining activities

producers – organisms that make their own energy supplies; plants during photosynthesis make complex organic molecules from simple compounds

production lag – period of time from when a crop is grown to when it is harvested and sold

profile – vertical section of the soil showing its horizons and characteristics

protected – buying and selling of goods is restricted to benefit some industries in a country

protozoa – subkingdom of animals that are unicellular, reproduce by fission or conjunction and move by cilia or flagella

quadrants – measured area of vegetation selected for study

radiometric sensing – using devices which can measure acoustic or electromagnetic radiant energy

radiation – electromagnetic waves produced by the sun

randomised – to select a sample without preference or bias with each member having an equal chance of being selected as in pulling numbers out of a hat

reproductive yield – yield per hectare of saleable product

reserve price – minimum floor price at auction. The AWC bought all wool that did not meet this price

respiration – metabolic process of living organisms in which organic compounds are broken down to release energy as ATP

rhizoctonia – commonly called black scurf can be a serious disease of potato

runoff – removal of soil by running water

rust – fungal disease of plants where leaves and stems become spotted and turn reddish brown in colour

sample – small group tested and used to make assumptions about the whole population

scientific name – universal Latin name used to identify a plant internationally such as *Trifolium repens* – the first word being the genus and the second the species

secondary industries – those that make up the manufacturing sector

selection differential – measure of how much better selected animals perform relative to the original group from which they were chosen

SEPP46 – government legislation which restricted the clearing of land

specific – target and kill one particular pest

stain – wool with a discolouration commonly caused by urine and faeces

standardised – conducted under identical conditions to minimise discrepancies caused by outside factors, for example using same soil types or age and breed of livestock

stud – properties specialising in the breeding and improving of a particular type of animal

subsystem – smaller individual units which make up the whole system eg animal subsystem and soil subsystem.

topography – refers to the slope, terrain or undulations of the land

transpiration – loss of water vapour from the surface of a plant

triticale – hybrid of wheat and rye. It is grown primarily for animal feed as a grain or forage. Human consumption is currently low

value add – modifying a product to increase its value

variates – number of individuals in the sample

vascular bundle – strand of conducting tissue consisting of xylem and phloem that transports fluids between roots and stems

vertical integration – control of marketing chain from growing to selling by one organisation

withholding period – period of time product cannot be safely consumed as it is contaminated by the chemical

zoonosis – disease that is communicable to humans from animals such as rabies

Index

NOTES

NOTES

NOTES